THE FREEST SPEECH IN RUSSIA

The Freest Speech in Russia

POETRY UNBOUND, 1989–2022

STEPHANIE SANDLER

PRINCETON UNIVERSITY PRESS

PRINCETON & OXFORD

Published by Princeton University Press
41 William Street, Princeton, New Jersey 08540
99 Banbury Road, Oxford OX2 6JX

press.princeton.edu

Library of Congress Cataloging-in-Publication Data

Names: Sandler, Stephanie, 1953– author.
Title: The freest speech in Russia : poetry unbound, 1989–2022 / Stephanie Sandler.
Description: Princeton : Princeton University Press, 2024. | Includes bibliographical references and index.
Identifiers: LCCN 2024012585 (print) | LCCN 2024012586 (ebook) | ISBN 9780691169965 (paperback) | ISBN 9780691261904 (hardback) | ISBN 9780691261898 (ebook)
Subjects: LCSH: Russian poetry—21st century—History and criticism. | Russian poetry—Foreign countries—21st century—History and criticism. | Russian poetry—20th century—History and criticism. | Russian poetry—Foreign countries—20th century—History and criticism. | Liberty in literature. | Freedom of speech—Russia (Federation)
Classification: LCC PG3057 .S26 2024 (print) | LCC PG3057 (ebook) | DDC 891.71/509—dc23/eng/202450401
LC record available at https://lccn.loc.gov/2024012585
LC ebook record available at https://lccn.loc.gov/2024012586

British Library Cataloging-in-Publication Data is available

Editorial: Anne Savarese and James Collier
Production Editorial: Kathleen Cioffi
Cover Design: Haley Chung
Production: Lauren Reese
Publicity: William Pagdatoon
Copyeditor: Melanie Mallon

Jacket image: Srikanth Varma / Unsplash

This book has been composed in Arno

10 9 8 7 6 5 4 3 2 1

In memory of my mother, who taught me to read

CONTENTS

ILLUSTRATIONS

PREFACE

Poetry today is without question a luxury, just as much a luxury as a free mind and free speech.

—ALEXANDRA TSIBULYA, 2016

THREE ENCOUNTERS with poets made me the person who could write this book, and I retell them here because they are emblematic of this book's aims and approach. Joseph Brodsky taught in the Five College area during my first fifteen years of teaching at Amherst College. I barely knew his work then, so much did I live my scholarly life in Russia's Golden Age. I audited his poetry classes and was lucky enough to have had any number of conversations with Brodsky. He kept telling me that I was missing out on the greatness of contemporary poetry in English, and he put poems by Paul Muldoon, Seamus Heaney, Derek Walcott, and Les Murray in front of me. This was his pantheon, and I could soon begin to create my own as I set about reeducating myself in the poetry of my lifetime, in English and in Russian.

Then, on one of my research trips to Russia in the 1980s, when I was still writing about Pushkin and Pushkin myths, I went to see Arkady Dragomoshchenko on the recommendation of Andrew Wachtel. Here was another poet whose work I had barely read. He, too, pressed on me some poetry in English that I did not know, starting with Lyn Hejinian. This was a canon quite different from Brodsky's. Dragomoshchenko had translated Hejinian, as well as John Ashbery, Susan Howe, Charles Olson, and others. Through him, I met Lyn Hejinian, and through her, Marjorie Perloff, and there opened a whole new approach to English-language poetry, different from the Eliot-Stevens-Frost-Auden modernism in which I had been educated as an undergraduate. It was a shift in my view of American literary culture, and of Russia's recent poetry as well.

The third encounter began with a text, not a person. During the heady years of glasnost and perestroika, I was following every month's fresh journals (in paper copies in our college and university libraries, it's worth remembering). Like everyone else, I was keen to read daring new work as well as long-suppressed masterpieces. The October 1988 issue of *Druzhba narodov* included a small selection of poems by someone named Olga Sedakova. The preface by the legendary scholar Vyacheslav Ivanov got my attention, too. The poetry was otherworldly, potent, with a Pushkinian lucidity that intensified the sense of mystery. How could someone be writing this poetry in the Soviet Union? Sedakova's work, and the very different poems of Arkady Dragomoshchenko, signaled to me that beyond Brodsky, who the previous year had won the Nobel Prize in Literature, there was a flourishing and tremendously variegated poetic culture in Russia. That culture and its evolution over the next twenty-five years is the subject of this book.

I tell these three encounters not just to rehearse my many stages of ignorance, but also because the stark differences among these three figures—Brodsky, Dragomoshchenko, Sedakova—define me as a chronicler of these years and as a reader of poetry. Just as American poetry has accommodated voices so different as to seem to be speaking multiple languages—including in multilingual poetry—in Russian poetry, advocates of strict form have flourished alongside those whose poems are spread out on the page like fireworks; stridently political prose-like poems have come from the pen of a poet who also writes tenderly of a loved child, a dead father, or a provincial town where factory whistles toot; and poets who have taken subtly different positions on social issues have argued about all of this on Facebook, at symposia and public readings, and on the print or web pages of Russian-language journals published in Latvia, Israel, New York, and Moscow. Inspiring criticism is addressing specific strands of aesthetic and philosophical argument within this multiplicity. My project is to offer a wide-angle if still partial view of this rich body of work, contextualizing unfamiliar poets, offering fresh views of the better known, and finding for all the poets, I hope, new readers and new critics.

One thing that Brodsky, Dragomoshchenko, and Sedakova have in common is their status within the tradition of unofficial literature of the late Soviet period. All the poets treated in this study are the heirs of that tradition of unofficial literature, and this lineage has defined my own take on contemporary poetry and my choice of poets to study.[1] Ilya Kukulin has argued that the defining feature of unofficial poetry was not political but aesthetic, even though the crucial trait is its not having been subject to censorship: "Uncensored art is art that is aesthetically free."[2] By making freedom a key element of unofficial art and, as he goes on to show, of unofficial poetry in particular, Kukulin sets up the lineage that I pursue here. I am following trends initiated by unofficial poets—their themes, their formal innovations, and their intonations. Of the last, there are several, from spiritually urgent to comically ironic to ostentatiously lazy. The freedom to choose a tone, a form, a crucial image defines their work. It is a reason I have emphasized freedom throughout: this poetry has been considering its own potential to create the grounds for political freedoms; and these poems exude a freedom to roam among ideas, poetic forms, affiliations, and instances of self-fashioning.

Kukulin's sentence has one more important clause. Here it is in full: "Uncensored art is art that is aesthetically free and thereby responsible." The word with which he ends that sentence, *otvetstvennyi*, holds a richer set of connotations than the English word *responsible*, because the Russian suggests a kind of ethical responsiveness, a capacity to respond to many kinds of stimuli and an awareness that one is responsible for one's reactions. The word played its own role in official Soviet public discourse, where it could be a coded signal of what the theory of socialist realism called the "social command" (sotsial'nyi zakaz). A writer was meant to be responsible to uphold certain standards, to tell the stories of a society building socialism, and so forth. But Kukulin is not trying to sneak in some hidden criticism of underground writers with this word. He is rescuing this term for its ethical potential and listening for its presence even in unlikely texts.[3] I share his conviction that the term is valuable. That conviction is felt when I choose, for example, to write of poets who have spoken out about sexual violence and about Russia's war on Ukraine, or of poets who have sought a language of faith and spiritual quest that does not replicate the harms of institutional power.

The story of this book's origins is expected content for a preface, but I need to conclude with a note about how my writing ended. The world of Russian poetry faced radical changes just as I was finishing the book. The war Russia unleashed on Ukraine in February 2022 and the radical curtailing of freedom of expression on Russia's territory and in internet sites reach far beyond the world of poetry, but poems and poets have also been powerfully affected by this horror. The leadup to this more aggressive and destructive phase of the war had long been a part of this book, and texts about the Russia-Ukraine war are treated in chapters 1 and 2, as well as in the afterword. But nearly the whole book was drafted before February 2022, written in a spirit of openness and optimism that could sound grotesque in a time when Russian forces are targeting civilians in Ukraine and when thousands of Russians who oppose the war have fled to a safety that Ukrainian citizens cannot find anywhere in their home- land. At the least, the dream that poetry's free speech would inspire greater freedoms was rudely interrupted on February 24, 2022. It could be a painfully long time before the sense of community, online and in public, which is this book's subject, is once again fully flourishing, although I hasten to add that it has persisted in crucial ways. Or it could be a very short time indeed before we see it thriving in all its vibrancy: the precipitous demise of the USSR proved that Russians' supposed penchant for endless endurance of the state's deprivations and horrors can turn on a dime.

Either way, the story I tell here no longer has the open-ended quality I had celebrated as I was drafting this book. I used to joke that it took me so long to write it because more and more remarkable poems were turning up, because new journals and websites were opening, and because poets themselves were regrouping and reconnecting in ways that made me change my mind. Joking comes less easy now, but the spirit of expecting fresh new work persists. The war will end, Ukraine will be free, and Russians will begin the hard work of rebuilding their own national identity. Russian poetry will be there through it all, and the poems of the near future and perhaps for a longer term will be haunted by the violence and terror that the state is exporting, on a scale exceed- ing even what it did in Syria or Chechnya. Poems are already being written about the guilt and chaos this cannot but wreak on language itself. I occasionally will note some of this very new, raw work, and I speak to it directly in the after- word. Still, the material for this book largely predates the current war.

Especially since February 2022, but beginning before then, the term *Russian* has become highly charged. I want to explain why and how I use it. When I refer to Russian poetry, I do not mean poetry by ethnic Russians, or even necessarily poems written by Russian citizens. This book includes poets who have renounced Russian citizenship and who live outside Russia's borders. It does not include Russian nationalist poets, known since 2022 as Z poets; it focuses instead on a community of poets who view critically the imperial am- bitions of the Russian state, and who, wherever they live and whatever their citizenship, value the project of investigating Russia's past and present, and even its possible futures. I define the contours of this community further in the introduction, particularly its inheritance of the tradition of unofficial Russian poetry from the Soviet period.

Some critics are using the term *Russophone* to denote this broader com- munity. The analogy is to Francophone writing, an established term that marks writing by those living outside France, most often in former French colonies. The analogy is imperfect, both because of the imprecise match of Russia's and France's colonialist legacies, and because some poets included here are not, or while they were alive were not, living outside Russia at all. These poets have many and quite varied identities and affiliations, and I situate each of them as they are discussed. Overall, and with some reluctance, I have stayed with *Russian* as an umbrella term, for all its imperfection. The poets themselves have reckoned with the term, and with the legacy of Russia's violence, and they have used the term *Russian* in that reckoning. It remains the best recognizable term in English. The poets have not given up on the project of creating a version of the culture that is not imperial, dishonest, and violent, and part of my project is to chart their labor in probing a relentlessly disturbing past and present.

I am finishing this book at a moment unimaginably unlike the hopeful mood of its inception. I feel enduring respect for what the poets have done in the thirty years since the fall of the USSR, and I believe that we all stand to learn from their exhilarating, complicated, and bold work. It is a foundation on which the culture will rebuild when the Russia-Ukraine war ends.

ACKNOWLEDGMENTS

MY RESEARCH for this book was made possible by fellowships from the American Council of Learned Societies, the National Endowment for the Humanities, and sabbatical leaves from Harvard University. The Davis Center for Russian and Eurasian Studies through the Abby and George O'Neill research fellowship program supported multiple trips to Russia and elsewhere, as did generous funding from then Dean of Arts and Humanities Diana Sorensen in years when my research funds ran out. Until the pandemic and the Russia-Ukraine war made such travel first difficult, then unthinkable, this support made it possible for me to meet poets and scholars, collect material, and attend events where I could see firsthand the communities in which these poems find readers. Harvard's research funding let me hire research assistants, who provided invaluable help, and I appreciate the superb work of James Browning, Nathan Goldstone, Anna Ivanov, and Maria Vassileva, and the proofreading by Lizzie Place.

The poets treated here have inspired me with their work, and I have had the good fortune to know several of them. I want to single out Polina Barskova, Elena Fanailova, Mara Malanova, Alexandra Petrova, Olga Sedakova, Alexander Skidan, and Lida Yusupova, as well as the late Joseph Brodsky, Arkady Dragomoshchenko, Inna Lisnianskaia, Elizaveta Mnatsakanova, Dmitry Aleksandrovich Prigov, Lev Rubinstein, Elena Shvarts, and Aleksei Tsvetkov for their generosity and readiness to let me learn from them. The American poet Susan Howe has had a larger effect on me than she can know, and she has taught me by the example of her writing about Emily Dickinson what it is to read a poet across the boundaries of genre, time, and space. In a class by himself is Dmitry Kuz'min. In addition to his poems, translations, and critical writings, he has created journals, anthologies, websites, festivals, events, and spaces for intrepid conversation, all of which make it possible for poems and poets to find their way to ever wider audiences.

In the United States, I learned about new Russian poets and new ways of reading from colleagues in a workshop founded in 2000 at Amherst College and then sustained annually for more than a decade. Workshop members included Polina Barskova, Catherine Ciepiela, Susanne Fusso, Katherine O'Conner, Sarah Pratt, Gerald Smith, Michael Wachtel, Boris Wolfson, and the professors, poets, and graduate students at Harvard, Princeton, and the University of Southern California. These gatherings were made possible by the generous deans and institutional funds at the various campuses where we met, and it is a special pleasure to note that Princeton hosted us several times through its Institute for International Research Studies. Having learned my Russian as an undergraduate at Princeton, I loved going back for a chance to read poetry in such good company. In recent years, Kevin Platt has also organized invaluable workshops for poets and translators at the University of Pennsylvania, "Your Language, My Ear." Readers of this book will see their effect as early as the introduction, where I begin with "The Battle," a poem by Polina Barskova that we translated and performed at Penn.

Bits and pieces from some of these chapters, and a great deal more that was shed along the way, were offered as talks at symposia and professional meetings, or appeared in earlier versions as articles and book chapters. Countless suggestions, questions, and criticisms from those who read or heard these presentations have changed my thinking. I am grateful to all who have listened to me develop these ideas. I want as well to thank others who taught me through their own work and through our conversations about poetry, or who had a way of answering my questions on the spot that changed my view of a text or a poet: Jacob Edmond, Caryl Emerson, Michael Flier, Amelia Glaser, Ksenia Golubovich, Gerald Janecek, Andrew Kahn, Martha Kelly, Daria Khitrova, Maria Khotimsky, Eugene Ostashevsky, and Henrieke Stahl. Two readers for Princeton University Press provided wonderfully detailed reports, and Ilya Kukulin and Mark Lipovetsky, in addition to being splendid interlocutors over the years about so many poets, read some near-final chapters. Several others named above also read earlier versions or portions of chapters. I so appreciate the corrections and suggested changes they sent my way, and the readiness to put aside their own work to help me improve mine.

At Princeton University Press, Anne Savarese has been an attentive and generous editor. The assistance of James Collier and Kathleen Cioffi as well as the splendid copyediting of Melanie Mallon and the careful index by Steven Moore have helped turn a book manuscript into a printed book.

I am extremely lucky to share my life with an incomparable scholar, thinker, and teacher, Austin Sarat. His books on rhetoric, violence, and the law inspired me to think about how poems and poets might in their own ways create new possibilities of free thought. Benjamin Sarat, Emily Sarat, and my father, Bob Sandler, cheered me on in this work and cheered me up at every turn. My debt to my mother, Adele Sandler (1930–2018), is reflected in the dedication, but Austin knows that everything I write is also always for him.

A NOTE ON TRANSLITERATION
AND SOURCES

FOR TRANSLITERATION from Cyrillic, the modified Library of Congress system is used, but the names of poets and critics are anglicized according to well-established conventions, thus Svarovsky not Svarovskii, Alexandra not Aleksandra, and Olga not Ol'ga, as well as spellings commonly used in English publication (Arseniev, Aygi). Final soft signs in names are dropped (Lyubov, Gogol) but in the middle of names, the soft sign is retained (Kuz'min, Zav'ialov). The exceptions are spellings that poets or photographers have told me they strongly prefer (thus Yusupova rather than Iusupova; Singer rather than Zinger; Vikenti rather than Vikenty). For all names, bibliographic references revert to the modified LC system.

Where possible, I cite print sources, which are more stable if not always as convenient. For many critical sources, like the journals I most relied on, *Vozdukh* and *Novoe literaturnoe obozrenie* (always abbreviated as *NLO*), online points of access are easily findable through search engines. I provide the bibliographic data that should make it possible to find both print and digitized versions; thus, for *NLO*, where online archives do not use the sequential numbering found in the print version, I include the issue number for a given year within the parentheses for the year; for *Vozdukh*, I provide sequential numbering once the journal cover started featuring it. For quoted poems, I cite print sources whenever possible, but searching databases like *Vavilon* and *Novaia karta russkoi literatury* (*Litkarta*) may turn up digitized versions as well.

Another important resource for studying contemporary Russian poetry are social media sites, particularly Facebook and before it, LiveJournal; when I quote any post by an individual, I do so with their permission whether the post was open or closed. For social media posts, I indicate the source and date but omit web addresses. Following current recommended practices, I do not give dates of access; links were verified in August and September 2023.

All poems discussed here are presented in English and Russian. Unless I say otherwise, these are my translations. Sometimes I quote published translations, and I often include information about other versions in the notes, even when I provide my own, to call attention to excellent work by translators. I am grateful to the publishers, many of them small independent presses, who granted permission to cite this work. Permission was sought for all quotations of poetry in English or Russian; in a few cases, no response was received after several requests. I will be grateful if, on seeing this book, rightsholders would reach out to me so that permission requests can be completed.

Excerpt from Keats, "Ode on a Grecian Urn," from *The Poems of John Keats*, edited by Jack Stillinger, Cambridge, Mass.: The Belknap Press of Harvard University Press, Copyright © 1978 by the President and Fellows of Harvard College. Used by permission. All rights reserved.

Excerpt from Lida Yusupova, "Dead Dad" from *Dead Dad*, courtesy by Kolonna Publications, 2016.

Excerpts from Olga Sedakova, "Old Songs," *In Praise of Poetry*. Printed with permission from Open Letter Books at the University of Rochester. *In Praise of Poetry* first published in full by Open Letter in 2014.

"And it's not like I can run off somewhere" from *Endarkenment: Selected Poems* © 2014 by Arkadii Dragomoshchenko. Published by Wesleyan University Press and reprinted with permission.

Excerpt from "They're off for their Afghanistan" © Elena Fanailova, from *The Russian Version* (Ugly Duckling Presse, 2nd Edition, 2019). Translation Copyright © Genya Turovskaya, Stephanie Sandler, from *The Russian Version* (Ugly Duckling Presse, 2nd Edition, 2019), digital version https://uglyducklingpresse.org/publications/the-russian-version-2nd-edition/.

"freedom is" ©Vsevolod Nekrasov, from *I Live I see: Selected Poems* (Ugly Duckling Presse, 2013). Translation Copyright © Ainsley Morse, Bela Shayevich, from *I Live I See: Selected Poems* (Ugly Duckling Presse, 2013), digital version https://uglyducklingpresse.org/publications/i-live-i-see-selected-poems/.

Excerpts or full texts from the following works copyright © Novoe Literaturnoe Obozrenie and used by permission: "Prazdnik" by Galina Rymbu in *Zhizn' v prostranstve* (2018); "Tikhii chas" by Grigorii Dashevskii in *Duma Ivan-chaia: Stikhi 1983–1999* (2001); phrase beginning "{[vse]" from untitled poem by Nika Skandiaka in

[12/4/2007] (2007); "Glubokii starik" by Leonid Shvab in *Duma Ivan-chaia: Stikhi 1983–1999* (2015); "splelos' iz ostatkov strun" and "iz peregnoia rozhdaetsia kislyi dykhatel'nyi vozdukh" by Anna Glazova in *Dlia zemleroiki* (2001); "My tak izognuli stenu" by Anna Glazova in *Petlia, nevpolovinu* (2008); "Uekhavshie, vyslannye, kanuvshie i pogib-shie" and "Nedavno uznala, chto v domashnei pyli" by Ekaterina Simonova in *Dva ee edinstvennykh plat'ia* (2020); "Andrei Ivanovich ne vozvrashchaetsia domoi" by Faina Grimberg in *Chetyrekhlistnik dlia moego ottsa* (2012); "Agora" and "A mne i ne ubezhat'" by Arkadii Dragomoshchenko in *Tavtologiia* (2011); "Puteshestvie" and "Smert' Perakisa" by Fedor Svarovskii in *Slava geroiam* (2015); "chast' no. 0" by Fedor Svarovskii in *Puteshestvenniki vo vremeni* (2009); "Prirodnye vozzreniia slavian na poeziiu" by Sergei Kruglov in *Sniatie Zmiia so kresta* (2003); "Natan i vybory pravitelia" by Sergei Kruglov in *Perepishchik* (2008); "Molitva," "Molitva," and "Auktsion Iudaiki / Lot 6" by Boris Khersonskii in *Semeinyi arkhiv* (2006); "ne veter a prosto vse glukhie govoriat na odnom iazyke" by Kira Freger in *Novoe Literaturnoe Obozrenie 162* (2020).

THE FREEST SPEECH IN RUSSIA

Thirty Years of Free Poetic Speech

THIS IS A BOOK that began with a falling wall, a wall that came down literally in Berlin in 1989 and then figuratively within and around poetic expression. My working title was *Breaking Down the Walls*, and I knew that the book I wanted to write would chart the ways in which contemporary Russian-language poetry was being built on the ruins of walls that no longer cordoned off generations, genres, aesthetic movements, geographic entities, and individual persons. I had the hypothesis that the lowering of barriers both physical and psychological was the source of explosive energy in the new poetry, and a reason for its flourishing against considerable odds.

That metaphor of the breached wall remains, and it will help make sense of the impulses and reactions that give such an emotional charge to poetry written in the last thirty years. The wall, though, has become to my mind less an architectural structure meant to keep populations separate, but instead more like a membrane, like the wall that keeps a cell intact. I came to see that it wasn't a matter of a wall that was knocked down, but rather of a permeable barrier, one that increasingly permitted the exchange of persons and materials, or—and this metaphor emerged as more significant, the more I worked—the circulation of air.

A further change in my argument occurred as I tried to account for the emotional intensity, the sense of a life force that this poetry exuded. I wanted to understand the fierce allegiances, the surging anguish, the joyous praise, and the shifting metaphysical moods of these new poems. The only word that felt able to accommodate that expansive surge of possibilities was freedom, a term I approached with some wariness. As an American, I had seen it co-opted by right-wing radicals for whom the right to bear arms, for example, was the epitome of US values. But I resisted the idea that a value like freedom could be contaminated by its most perverse uses. In fact, I was increasingly finding in the poets I was reading an idea of freedom that was quite different. It was captured well by the poet Elena Fanailova in the announcement that regularly introduced her podcast *Babylon-Moscow* (*Vavilon Moskva*), as she adjusted it in 2022: she would be featuring cultural figures who loved their own freedom and that of others ("oni liubiat svobodu—svoiu i chuzhuiu").[1]

This belief that someone else's freedom is as much to be prized as one's own has a history in Russia. Fanailova's wording recalls the slogan that poet Natalia Gorbanevskaya unfurled on Red Square in 1968 to protest the deployment of Soviet tanks against Czechoslovakia: "For your freedom and for ours!" (Za vashu i nashu svobody). Gorbanevskaya was herself reprising a famous phrase by nineteenth-century writer Alexander Herzen, meant to support Poles fighting for independence from imperial Russia.[2] Fanailova, a fierce supporter of Ukrainian independence, surely intended the parallel.

Shared freedom, and the idea that poetry is responsible for spreading that freedom, is a value explored here from multiple angles. In writing this book, I started from a curiosity about what had set poems and poets free (what walls had come down), but what sustained my work was a desire to explain how that sense of freedom might spread, and how the poems generate intense emotional and affective charges that make them so compelling.

Let one signal example stand at the outset for many others, to show concretely where the sense of freedom starts and then how it reverberates. It occurs at the end of Polina Barskova's poem "The Battle" ("Bitva," 2011), where the speaker, who has unflinchingly described the Siege of Leningrad in the winter of 1941, ends with the claim that, at that moment, she "was happy" (byla schastliva). This revelation comes after lines that juxtapose the blockade's starvation and privation with the clatter of music and of bombardment. Here is the poem's conclusion:

She listened to Tchaikovsky on the radio yesterday she was happy
Soyez hardiz en joye mis!

It was lovely to hear:
Loud music
Loud music
and she was happy

Слушала вчера по радио Чайковского была счастлива
Soyez hardiz en joye mis!

Было красиво на слух:
Громкую музыку
Громкую музыку
и была счастлива[3]

Barskova is not just a poet but also a scholar of the Siege of Leningrad.[4] Here she imagines the blockaded city, where the barricades are keeping out food, where people are freezing and starving. Within that horror is someone radiant with improbable happiness amid the alarming sounds, smells, and sights of war. Where does that freakish joy come from? And where did Barskova, originally from the city that suffered the blockade, find the inner freedom to rewrite that most iconic of historical moments not as a scene of deprivation, but as one of plenitude?[5]

One answer to that question has shaped many modern studies of Russian poetry: the poet found her freedom by reading other poets. The poets, the argument has it, imbibe an inner experience of independence and liberation from the tradition even amid the worst experiences of war, repression, censorship, or terror. Barskova flaunts the possibility that poets may yet gain inspiration from their predecessors, quoting intermittently from a French Renaissance poem by Clément Janequin, "La Guerre" (1528), as in the passage just cited. She uses Janequin's title to inspire her own, "The Battle," and she borrows his theme of music. But her turn to Janequin is also a marked turn to a foreign source. Barskova's radically liberating gesture is to connect the Siege of Leningrad, a defining Soviet historical event, to the struggles of another country and another time. She opens a space where the music of the Siege can be imagined outside national mythologies.

Barskova enacted a further form of freedom in her first public performance of the poem, using the text as a kind of script on which she freestyled. She said, by way of preface, that the poem was inspired by another and notably non-Russian source, the poet Ernesto Estrella, who was in the Philadelphia audience where she read.[6] The poem sounds like nothing Estrella (or Janequin, for that matter) had written, and in many ways it does not even sound like what Barskova had written to that point. It represented a radical gesture of one poet's freedom, a form of free speech.

Polina Barskova's pathway to that freedom is telling. Some of that freedom surely came to her as a result of her years in the United States; her intense contact with poets writing in English, Spanish, and other languages; her years of graduate study and teaching in an American context; her peregrinations from place to place to recite her poems, share her scholarship, meet her peers. After 1989, that free movement was the rule, not the exception, for poets writing in Russian. Many began to move easily among the institutions of higher education, journalism, publishing, and performance art, and, like Barskova, they could travel widely. Those who emigrated were no longer cut off by cultural or political boundaries. The end to restrictions on travel, the end to censorship, and the advent of the internet, with its boundless access to others' writings—these are all definitive aspects of the last thirty years of poetry, as definitive as changes in government or economic structure. The fact that the Russia-Ukraine war has increased the numbers of those leaving and that travel back and forth is (one hopes, temporarily) curtailed makes the years of freer movement until 2022 all the more significant.

It is hard to overstate how powerfully these forms of openness changed Russian poetry. What exploded, because of travel across actual boundaries and the mental travel afforded by the internet, with its information overload and ease of sharing ideas across multiple platforms, is the very notion of daily experience in the present. An intensified sense of the present moment, of the felt experience of the body in space and of the sensory impact of sights, sounds, smells, and the movement of the air itself—these are defining traits of the poetry as studied here. And they were amplified by the wish to let that intensity saturate one's creative output, to hang on to it long enough to let it make a poem. A focus on the present had important political implications, too: as the artist Vitaly Komar pointed out, totalitarian regimes live in a temporality of the past (often glorified and distorted) or the future (a promised utopia).[7] To focus on the present was to insist on an alternative temporality, one in which life could be experienced in the moment, one that was potentially liberating. Freedom came to poets from the experience of the present, wherever they found themselves, and their reaction, in turn, was to register the experience of presence in new forms of poetry.[8] They defined that experience in political, philosophical, psychological, and spiritual ways, all tracked in the pages to follow.

Freedom may be a surprising metaphor for writing and thinking about Russia, especially given all it has done to try to curtail the autonomy of Ukraine. The limits on freedom are more repressive as of 2022, but they are not new. In 2018, Timothy Snyder published a widely reviewed book, *The Road to Unfreedom: Russia, Europe, America*.[9] His approach is comparative, but he tells a brutal story about Russia.[10] The rise of intolerance, the ruthlessness of the country's leader, the incursion into Ukraine, the meddling in foreign elections, and the inability to hold free and open elections internally all mark the current regime as the opposite of liberal democracy. One can challenge some of Snyder's conclusions, perhaps especially his seeing little opening for individual acts of resistance.[11] But there can be no doubt that the Russia he describes suppresses many of the freedoms its citizens might hope to enjoy.

I take a different approach to Russia's cultural life since 1989, without for a moment diminishing the depravity of the current regime. The difference is less in the assessment of just how authoritarian Russia's government is and more in how citizens—and poets—behave under such a regime. As Orwell might have said, it isn't a question whether the state grants freedom of speech, it's a question whether people use it, and the time may be ripe for reconsidering the idea of free speech in Russia's story of itself. It is not a straightforward tale. Even in periods of relative tolerance, the spirit of individualism inherent in ideals of free speech was often missing. If we cast a backward glance, from post-Soviet Russia to the USSR, and still further back to imperial Russia and the earlier cultural formations known as Rus', authoritarian rulers insistent on demonstrative loyalty seem more emblematic than free-speaking citizens. And yet there were free-speaking writers and public figures, some famous, like Alexander Radishchev, some fictionalized, like Nikolai Leskov's hero in "Single-mind" ("Odnodum," 1879) or Tolstoy's Pierre Bezukhov in *War and Peace*.

Still, the idea of governmental rule did not depend on conversation and debate among citizens. One had duties to the state, and by long tradition, any lack of authentic deference could be concealed behind the common performances that, as Sheila Fitzpatrick has shown, had no small share of imposture. The communal social patterns that enabled the creation of a Communist state after 1917 deemphasized individual speech acts, preferring instead public gestures of patriotism and ardent commitment to building the new state. Diaries from the Communist period have shown individuals building a self from the familiar slogans of public life.[12] Despite a whole host of differences in the circumstances of the post-Soviet period, many of the shared values and rhetorical patterns persisted. Fitzpatrick rightly called the 1990s a period of "anxious individual reinvention."[13]

Of course, a tradition of unofficial literature also appears throughout Soviet history, a tradition on which all the poets I treat here in some ways rely. Among the many singular traits of that tradition was an attempt to recover some measure of authenticity in personal identity formation and in public (if restricted to a small counter-public) utterance. Unofficial culture particularly flourished in and after the 1960s, and a poem written at that time offers a splendid image of the complexity of these forms of free expression. The author is the Conceptualist poet Vsevolod Nekrasov, and it is one of his typically gnomic short poems. The text consists of little more than the Russian word for freedom, *svoboda*, plus the verb "to be." Nekrasov does an immense amount with these meager lexical resources:

> freedom is
> freedom is
> freedom is
> freedom is
> freedom is
> freedom is
> freedom is freedom[14]

> свобода есть
> свобода есть
> свобода есть
> свобода есть
> свобода есть
> свобода есть
> свобода есть свобода[15]

Nekrasov often took public slogans and made them into poetic utterances. Here, familiar Soviet assertions about its free, strong people create a repeating six-line foundation for a poem whose seventh line appears to round out the repetition. Nekrasov transforms the hammering repetition that freedom exists into a tautology. That closed logical loop might hint that freedom is its own dead end, but it also asserts that freedom becomes freedom by means of being repeated: its meaning accumulates, intensifies, even accelerates.[16] Neither possibility can be excluded. There is an ambiguous stance before freedom, at once affirming, insistent, and wary that freedom may be a fantasy no more real than the word that asserts its existence.[17]

That ambiguity was turned into a visual image in the artwork of Erik Bulatov, a Conceptualist painter (and friend of the poet), who used Nekrasov's poetry to create a memorable set of images.[18] There are several of these paintings, one of which is shown in figure 1. Bulatov repeats the lineation of Nekrasov's poem, seven iterations of the phrase "freedom is" (svoboda est'), but he repositions that last word, "freedom" (svoboda), moving it from the end of the last line up into a skyward overlay, so that the word is aimed, arrow-like, into

FIGURE 1. Erik Bulatov, *Freedom Is Freedom II* (2000–2001). Artists Rights Society (ARS), New York

a blue distance of ever-receding space. Bulatov lifts that last word of the poem off the text, creating a grid of identical lines of poetry, rather than replicating the text's asymmetry of that extra word "svoboda" in l.7. Those repeating words, "svoboda est," become a grid-like background onto which the blue sky of freedom can be painted.[19]

I placed Bulatov within late Soviet Conceptualist work, entirely appropriately, but his visualization of Nekrasov's poem was completed in the post-Soviet period, at the dawn of the apparent new freedoms of the early 2000s. Tellingly, his grid-like arrangement of repeating letters layered beneath a blue sky penetrated by the word for "freedom" yields neither the dream that freedom will hurtle into space unfettered, nor a grim reality that it might be an entrapping, empty repetition of sounds. Bulatov, like the poets I study here, is committed to getting his viewers to *think* about freedom, to enter the space of the picture. In his theoretical statements about painting, he contrasted the surface spaces of an artwork with its depths. Bulatov explained that in the history of painting, there had been an expectation that a canvas was either surface or depth, but he sought a way for the artwork to be both. The use of words, he claims, lets a painting exist as both surface and depth, enabling the viewer to "enter the space beyond the window" and "change from being a non-participating viewer to a participant in the events in the picture."[20] Bulatov wants the participation of the viewer. He seeks engagement, conversation.[21]

The doubled example of Nekrasov and Bulatov shows how that engagement might work between art forms (a conversation across media reprised here in chapters on poetry and music, and on poetry and photography). Bulatov in 2000 draws on a poem from 1963, but his picture can bring us directly to the present. In this contemporary moment, an unlikely and unfree moment, we can rethink and refine our ideas of how freedom gets used. An older idea of free speech as practiced only by a small minority of dissidents or innovative artists is ripe for reassessment. The stark division between loyalists and critics lost its salience after the fall of the Soviet Union; with the demise of state censorship and the explosion of venues for creative expression, free speech seemed available to anyone. By any standard, the 1990s, a chaotic time in terms of social structure and economic security, was a high point in the free exchange of ideas and the expression of dissent. Yet all of this has many gray areas. Current histories associate diminishing freedoms with the return of Putin to the presidency in 2012, but as Daphne Skillen has demonstrated in her excellent history of free speech in Russia, the legal groundwork for curtailing and regulating speech was laid in 2000 (and thus Bulatov's picture catches that transitional moment with uncanny precision). Skillen assesses the surprising lack of resistance from journalists in the Putin years, but the measurable decline in unregulated free speech does not mean its absolute curtailment. She notes that "as free speech declines from the 2000s, protest spread in the arts, which have always played an oppositionist role in Russian and Soviet society."[22] I share her view of the arts as an arena for free speech but want to challenge an idea that only a few lone artistic voices use their freedom to speak up. Free speech is generative. Expressive free speech can inspire others to know better their own ideas and to express them. Even as the state's brute force made protest within Russia rarer, it did not quell it entirely. The continuities across the post-Soviet period remain telling, as does the reverberating effect on social media of photographs and videos from protests.

Let the young woman in figure 2, who carries a Russian flag and a sign that declares, "Russia Will Be Free!," stand in for the millions who spoke out in praise of freedom and demanded it for themselves. They marched in cities across Russia, protesting manipulated elections, the war in Ukraine, a culture of corruption, the arrest of Aleksey Navalny, the mobilization of soldiers and reinstatement of a draft, and much else.[23] The image is from a day of nationwide demonstrations in 2017 and a day of brutal arrests; it is an emblem of confidence and calm.[24] Everything in the marching woman's posture and demeanor conveys a sense of patient optimism, which is all the more astonishing when one realizes that she is also being escorted in arrest. The image teaches a political reality as much as a moral truth. It is a moment when the state seeks to curtail speech, but a citizen affirms her right to display her inspiring hope for a better future. Like the artist Bulatov's use of words, this photograph layers a written speech act onto an image of bodies moving toward a different space (in this case, detention rather than the endless blue sky). But it is her calm confidence that lingers from this photograph. How to learn that lesson in courage and clear-sightedness? How does one become that woman? This is the same question one asks of Polina Barskova's poem "The Battle": how does one gain the freedom to write such a poem?

The questions are even more pressing in the face of violent efforts to curtail such independence and optimism. This did not begin in 2022. News reports in the 2010s regularly testified that the state was clamping down. Human Rights Watch noted in its World Report 2017 that Russia's "government tightened control over already shrinking space for free expression and stepped up persecution of independent critics during 2016."[25] Pussy Riot's performance and trial in 2012 was a signal moment in this clampdown. The band's choice of the canonical, controlled cultural space of a church for the disruptive performance of punk rock music by masked women challenged the Orthodox Church, but once on trial, when they read philosophical lectures to stone-faced judges in the courtroom, they were challenging the state. They weren't the first, but their colorful masks became an emblem of free expression and theatrical acts of collective resistance.

The masks, used in other actions by the group, were meant to mark the women of Pussy Riot as bandits and to preserve their anonymity. That they needed the protection of anonymity was a nod toward the dangers they were courting, a danger that was expressed fiercely with the more disturbing 2012 image of performance artist Petr Pavlensky's face with his lips sewn shut (figure 3). The photograph was taken as he looked on at protests in support of

FIGURE 2. "Russia Will Be Free!," unnamed woman, detained in
St. Petersburg (2017). Photo: George Markov

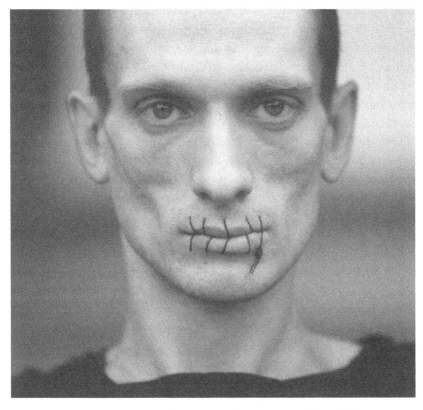

FIGURE 3. Petr Pavlensky, photograph, REUTERS / Trend Photo
Agency / Handout (2012)

Pussy Riot near Kazan Cathedral in St. Petersburg. Pavlensky's self-abusing gesture was directed against his body, a trademark of his performances. It defied Russia's apparent permission of free speech: what that freedom is good for, he proclaimed with his lips stitched shut, is the demonstration that Russia's citizens are being urged not to speak. The government that seems to grant freedom in fact forecloses it by punishing free speech whenever it suits them, including in the Pussy Riot trial and conviction.

Many other examples could be given that use verbal as well as these stunning visual means, some with as much ambiguity and irony as Pavlensky.[26] Writers, whose insistent freedom—both political and aesthetic   challenged the narrative of an adored authoritarian leader in a state where all is well, often participated in demonstrations and at one point staged a "Stroll with Writers."[27] They insisted on freedom of expression on the pages of their books, in blog posts and online publications, and in performances of their work. In their writings, they were doing something more than resisting capricious regulation of public assembly, although they did that, too: they were modeling the process by which one thinks and acts freely. That is the quality that makes their words into a superlative, into the freest possible speech—not because they have more daring or always utter more radical thoughts, but because by their words, they set the example for how minds might be ever more unfettered. Their rhetorical performances are doing the work of co-creating freedom, as Svetlana Boym would say.[28] By writing poems that follow ideas, themes, or images along pathways of freedom, Russia's poets are sharing with their readers the pleasures and dangers of free thought and free speech.

Forms of Freedom

What does freedom mean more broadly in the context of contemporary Russian poetry? Why exactly have I emphasized so sharply the modeling function of free speech, a speech situation that always imagines the presence of others? How exactly does the co-creation Svetlana Boym championed come into being, and why does it matter?

We can find answers to these questions in the writings of several thinkers in and beyond Russia, and I begin with Svetlana Boym, both to use her idea of freedom as co-creation and to take a step back from her work to ask why this pioneering thinker in literary and visual studies, who had written for several decades about patterns and puzzles of cultural life in modern Russia and about individual writers and artists, would write an entire book on what she called *Another Freedom*. As the subtitle had it, her book was meant to be "the alternative history of an idea." I cannot hope to reproduce the dazzling sequence that traced this alternative history—through etymologies, architectural spaces, and literary texts. But I do want to take her work, highly individual though it is, as a symptomatic turn to a conceptual framework, that of freedom, which has untapped potential to assist our understanding of cultural expression and cultural history. As she put it, there is a discourse of "Russia's 'other freedom,' which was to be found not in the country's political system, but in its artistic and spiritual heritage."[29] She foregrounds "the dialogic encounter that fosters free speech," an encounter that for her has to do with freedoms in the plural and with cross-cultural encounters in philosophy and aesthetics.[30] An important turning point in her study is a powerful critique of the most productive account of dialogism and freedom: Bakhtin's reading of Dostoevsky. Svetlana Boym insists that the heart of Dostoevsky's "freer freedom" is suffering, not liberation. By refusing to downplay the role of violence in his work, she brings into relief the political disaster that looms when a "philosophy of suffering" becomes "a proof of authenticity and a foundation of moral authority."[31]

My thinking was clarified by the reorientation in *Another Freedom* toward Dostoevsky. Russia's contemporary poets do not turn their gaze away from suffering, but even so, they create spaces for free expression in which connections to others opens out a more generous and more creative form of subjectivity. They are building on the foundations of phenomenology and ontology: their forms of lyric expression constantly return the poet to the question of who one is in the moment of free expression. Those subjectivities are grounded in possible communities and in conversations with others.

This notion of personhood is also crucial in the work of a thinker very different from Svetlana Boym, Vladimir Bibikhin. Less well known in the West than he should be, Bibikhin was trained as a linguist under the formidable Andrei Zalizniak, and the nature of the word was always at the center of his work as a philosopher and as a translator. He wrote often on literary texts, including a volume on the diaries of Lev Tolstoy (which won him the Piatigorsky Prize) and a long meditation on the poetry of Olga Sedakova.[32] Bibikhin taught at Moscow State University, the Institute of Philosophy at the Academy of Sciences, and elsewhere, and was a beloved, inspiring teacher. He lectured on topics few others were willing or able to treat at the time, including the thought of Martin Heidegger and Ludwig Wittgenstein, both important sources of his own thinking, as well as the philosophy of law, the origins of Christianity, and the significance of the forest (*hyle*).[33] Bibikhin was deeply knowledgeable about Orthodox and Christian theology, and during the Soviet era, he published on theological topics under the pseudonym Veniaminov. As a translator he was also drawn to the significant thinkers of secular modern thought like Heidegger, Derrida, and Arendt.

His work on Hannah Arendt merits closer attention. He translated a portion of her book *On Revolution*, and he left an unfinished translation of her essay "What Is Freedom?" in his archive.[34] In writing about Arendt, Bibikhin has an interesting point of intersection with the theory of freedom advanced by Svetlana Boym, in whose work Arendt also figures prominently: Arendt is a key thinker for Bibikhin because she was sensitive to the ambiguities of freedom and understood it as a "miracle of infinite improbability."[35]

Bibikhin, too, conceives of freedom as historically located in modernity, and there are important points of intersection with Arendt's essay "What Is

Freedom?" For Arendt, the "field where freedom has always been known" as "a fact of everyday life, is the political realm."[36] She finds the search for an idea of inner freedom more problematic than do several of the poets read here, and she insistently puts politics back into the discussion of freedom. Bibikhin, in writing about her and translating her essay, similarly sought to open a space for discussion of that political order whose founding was the guarantee of freedom to its citizens.

Bibikhin moved away from Arendt's insistence that freedom is to be measured by action, not by thought or word (a surprising assertion from her in any case, since she wrote eloquently in *The Human Condition* of words as a form of action). For Bibikhin, our world can never be any better than our conversations.[37] In his writings, great freedom is opened up, and one is left able to see the world as possibility rather than as a time grid or schedule.[38] It is like the world of uncertainty that Svetlana Boym called a requirement for co-creation, a human condition in which change is possible. Imagining change as possible was a startling fact and potent political force after the collapse of the Soviet Union, and it also affected one's sense of personhood and identity. The potential moral, personal, and spiritual growth is suggested by theorists like Bibikhin and Boym; it is an opening about which many poets treated here are curious, giving a provisional feel to some of their most interesting work.

A rather different thinker can sharpen the ethical edges of these possibilities, as well as the potential for social and political implications. How we use language is a measure of our moral and spiritual growth for Bibikhin, an idea that also echoes throughout the vast work of the American philosopher Stanley Cavell. For Cavell, moral perfectionism is the work of free societies, and the capacity of individuals to talk to one another—to truly hear one another—is a measure of their freedom.[39] To be open to the discourse of others is to be open to change. That openness is important in moral terms, amounting to a measure of one's recognition of imperfection. His notion of identity formed in conversation with others is not unlike the co-creation championed by Boym, different as their writings otherwise are. But they would meet at the point where encountering an other and allowing for the other's difference is a value of the highest order—recall Fanailova's insistence that her podcast guests value others' freedom as much as their own. There is an intonation of what neither would call enthusiasm but which both exude, alongside an extraordinary, improbable sense of optimism. Cavell would advocate for what he called "passionate utterance," which he deems successful when it constitutes an "invitation to improvisation," something Boym also embraced in her scholarship and in her artistic practice.[40]

That optimistic belief that one can catch the intent of the other even when belief systems and local idioms are at variance is a notion of dialogue very far from the definition that has long prevailed in Slavic scholarship, that of Mikhail Bakhtin. Bakhtin's sense of conflicting voices and his high valuation on aesthetic texts that can maintain the separateness of the distinct voices come from a different way of thinking about language and indeed about freedom. I am trying to create an opening for a different point of view, one not meant to displace Bakhtin's significance but one that, I believe, has more potential to help us understand poetic discourse. Bakhtin's theories were built on the foundation of the novel, and although some intriguing work brings his theories toward poetry, his point of origin in the novel and his emphasis on conflict limit his theory's perspectives on poetry.[41]

Cavell's chatty self-conscious ease and his agile movement among melodrama, Shakespearean plays, and Hollywood films measure the very great distance between Cavell and Bakhtin. Yet both value the utterance that is not meant to be a final word.[42] Cavell has elucidated a category he calls passionate utterances, which he defines as "an invitation to improvisation in the disorders of desire."[43] The improvisation he has in mind can be shown as a form of artistic expression—a Fred Astaire dance sequence, for instance—but Cavell uses those examples to press for philosophy to open itself to account for what the improvisation can mean, particularly to persons on some kind of path toward understanding themselves and others. As David Rodowick put it, an opening is created for "acknowledging how we may again become present to ourselves."[44] The unfinalizability so prized by Bakhtin is at work here— Rodowick words this acknowledgment carefully, for it is the process of becoming present that is at stake for him. Elsewhere, he draws on Cavell to fashion this idea in somewhat different terms, referring now to ontology: "Ontology in Cavell's sense is therefore not about an attained existence for either objects or persons," he writes, stressing the complex temporal structure that results on screen—and, to return us to Russian poems, also obtains in poetic texts.[45] The kind of poem that interests me here is one in which an improvised subjectivity emerges on the page, emerges out of words that may remember their own earlier poetic contexts but may also change—in Cavell's terms, are transformed—by the contact they have with others.

Cavell finds his most abundant examples in the intensely talk-oriented Hollywood comedies of the 1930s and 1940s, or in opera, with its complex back and forth of voiced emotion.[46] The self-realizations of those films, often mutual discoveries by women and men, are liberating, with characters pressed to recognize past strictures as so many unreasonable obstacles. Russian examples cannot easily find their way to the optimism that is so distinctly a part of American culture—moral perfectionism is nearer to hand in US traditions, Cavell might say—but the process of walking down the pathways of an experience (and it is often a matter of walking, quite literally) toward others who may prove complementary or revelatory is more at stake now than has been the case for Russian poetry in the past.

On such a reading, poetry can contribute to the collective project of enabling freedom by showing how free thought works and how it feels to risk such freeness. This is language not as a form of sublime communication between poet and muse, but as an exchange of ideas among imperfect mortal beings.[47] The openness to other persons is like the openness to the environment and the surrounding world: barriers are down, sensibilities and minds are open, and the possibility that one might connect across stark differences or even become different oneself is an important affective charge of the poetic text.

I have largely relied on philosophical discourse to set out these ideas of freedom, but we might also turn to sociologist Boris Dubin, whose work assessing public opinion led him to emphasize the capacity to recognize difference in others as a mark of free society. In 2014, Dubin was trying to understand the insistence on Russian exceptionalism that his public opinion surveys were affirming. He writes: "The figure of a meaningful 'other' or 'others' arose in the late 1980s and early 1990s when Russia was trying out all possible forms of freedom. The other was understood as a partner to whom you are connected, one who does not offend because of that difference, but on the contrary is made interesting as a result." For Dubin, the real effect of this encounter with an other is that one considers the possibility of becoming different oneself, recognizing that "you are not the best, the smartest, the strongest."[48] The same ambition motivated Boym's observation that "only a person who can change his or her mind can be a free thinker."[49] In an era when sanctioned public discourse is ever more chauvinistic and aggressive, such rueful self-recognition sounds a discordant note, and poetry is one place that can accommodate that kind of introspection and even resistance to chauvinism and warmongering. Dubin's writings increasingly reflected his pessimism that Russia would find its way back to the freedoms once promised in the 1990s.[50] The poets I am writing about can exude their share of pessimism but keep to the hope that personal freedom enables a readiness to struggle for political freedom and the hope that openness to others deepens an understanding of who one is in a changing world.

For poets writing in the years after the collapse of the Soviet Union, then, all these forms of freedom—inner freedom and political freedom, freedom of speech and freedom of action—can emerge in their poems and public performances. Not all the results are explicitly political (although I take up the more openly political possibilities in the first chapter of this book): Polina Barskova's freestyled performance of "The Battle" is one manifestation of that freedom. Pavel Arseniev's 2013 recitation of a poem containing an obscenity just after the law banning obscene speech is another.[51] Arseniev had gained fame the previous year as the author of a political slogan that may be his most memorable line: it puns on the verb that means both "to represent" and "to imagine" and thus means either "You don't even represent us" (in a legislative sense) or "You can't even imagine us" (in a cognitive sense): "Vy nas dazhe ne predstavliaete."[52] Arseniev caught the rebellious spirit of a moment when it seemed possible that resistance was sufficiently widespread to force the government to grant greater freedoms. What keeps the slogan relevant is its implied rejoinder: we will represent ourselves to your imagination, just as we will do the work of making our claims known. A central claim of this book is that this rejoinder has persisted, despite the successive crackdowns, in the work of poets who are political (like Arseniev) as well as of those whose topics seem quite far from politics, topics like music or photography or religion.

It is that liberating set of possibilities that I take as my subject here, as I seek to capture a dominant element in contemporary Russian poetry and perhaps to provoke a rethinking of poetry's work more broadly. Freedom in poetry is hard to define, as the eminent Slavist Vladimir Markov noted in an essay first published in 1961 and still compelling reading decades later. It encompasses a lack of constraint, a sense of lightness as if in flight, of being untethered from the maxims that would seem to govern poetic composition. There's a wonderful moment when he defines Mikhail Kuzmin's poetry as full of freedom and air.[53] If we look back at figure 1, Erik Bulatov's *Freedom Is Freedom*, we might now be struck as well by the way that freedom flies on currents of air. By projecting that line from Nekrasov's poem into the sky, Bulatov also launched the word for freedom into the atmosphere, into the space where air grows thinner and thinner until it is no more. The word itself narrows down to a point of near invisibility, creating the sense that "svoboda," which is to say, "freedom," depends on air for its very existence.

On Air

In 2006, on one of my trips to Russia to collect material for this book, I met a well-known poet, translator, editor, and, as I discovered that day, the creator of a new journal, *Vozdukh*. The title, *Vozdukh*, means "air," but I will call it by its Russian name as we conventionally do with journal names, like *Novyi mir* or *Ogonyok*. I could see quickly that this journal, *Vozdukh*, was unlike those well-known publications: at once a personal project, with a wish to set the record straight and right the wrongs of other journals and critics, and a porously open new space for poets of multiple generations, theoretical orientations, aesthetic sensibilities, and geographical locations. A sharply confident attitude immediately gave *Vozdukh* its distinctive energy, and all who know him recognize that attitude as belonging to its sassy, brilliant, and indefatigable editor and creator, Dmitry Kuz'min, whom I first met on that day in Moscow in 2006.

Vozdukh has rubrics that play on the metaphor of its title. There is the "long breath" of one section, the "changed breathing" of another, the "distant wind" of translated poems, the "ventilation" of a discussion section, the "atmospheric front" of the review section (here I translate names for various regular headings). In the early issues, there was a section on those "who have spoiled the air," which, after a certain point was renamed "Airless Spaces."[54] The journal is made up like a volume of poetry, its self-conscious internal classification system a way of foregrounding what Roman Jakobson called language's aesthetic function. Every issue begins with a "declaration of love" from one poet to a featured poet, in a rubric meant to deliver pure "oxygen." The featured poet is interviewed (by Linor Goralik, herself a premier writer, editor, and creator of collaborative cultural projects) and then described and praised by several poets. A selection of new work by the featured poet follows. In the first issue, the featured poet was Gennady Aygi, a major poet far better known in the West than in Russia and a representative of an earlier generation, even though most poets published in *Vozdukh* are younger. If there was canon formation in the works, it was done in defiance of most expectations.

Vozdukh displays a multitude of traits that characterize poetry written in Russian since 1989. Its strong stamp of Kuz'min's personality is exemplary: in contemporary poetry, personal visions of what counts as poetry are supremely important; there are strong bonds of affinities within communities of poets and readers; aesthetic preferences and notions about poetry's civic responsibility vary widely, but amid lively communication across boundaries and borders that are named and interrogated. The journal's section reporting on the poetry culture in a provincial city pushes back against the traditional dominance of Petersburg and Moscow and reminds readers that a significant proportion of major new poets hail from the provinces and have lived outside Russia—this was true even before the urgent migration of 2022. Poems in translation appear in all issues of *Vozdukh*, signaling openness to other traditions.

But most important to my argument is the metaphor of the journal's name. Kuz'min found a felicitous and multivalent metaphor in putting air at the center of the journal's self-conscious gestures of organization. He has featured an epigraph from the writings of Osip Mandelstam on the first page of every issue. It appears as follows, flush right as if lineated, and positioned to emphasize the end stop after the first sentence. As I do for all quotations in this book, I precede the quoted Russian with an English equivalent:

> I divide all poems into the permitted and those written
> without permission.
> The first are trash, the second stolen air.

> Все стихи я делю на разрешённые и написанные без разрешения.
> Первые—это мразь, вторые—ворованный воздух.

The journal has slightly altered Mandelstam's actual words, as they appear in his "Fourth Prose" ("Chetvertaia proza," 1929–30): instead of "all poems," Mandelstam divides "all the works of world literature" (vse proizvedeniia mirovoi literatury) into those two categories, written with or without permission.[55] The change aligns the quotation with the journal's mission, and the phrase "a poetry journal" (zhurnal poezii) follows the name of the journal on the title page. Kuz'min may simply have been quoting from memory, as poets are apt to do. The key phrase in any case is "stolen air," which defines genuine art as an act of stealth and theft.[56]

An additional argument may be made, however, to emphasize not the theft but the air, associating stolen air with freedom, which is meaningful for the journal, with its insistent unfettered self-definitions. This emphasis on freedom can be traced to Mandelstam's work as well. Discussing this phrase in Mandelstam, Irina Surat has written that its meanings far exceed the scandalous context that gave rise to the essay where it appears: "'Fourth Prose' consolidates a hierarchy: the artist's feeling of freedom, which cannot be taken away, but which is not available to just any artist: this is what 'stolen air' is."

And Surat adds, "the word 'air' means something that belongs to anyone and everyone, from which free discourse flows."[57] Surat's emphasis on the accessibility of freedom's air and on its necessity suggests what in US political discourse would be called an inalienable right. It is a right not given by the state but by nature, so the metaphor of air as the site of that freedom signals its pervasiveness, its status as something necessary to life itself.

The association between freedom and air comes from the words of a poet, and it is in poetry (and to some extent in other forms of art) that the possibilities of that freedom can be deeply explored. Some of the poems discussed in this book write directly about air, breath, or the liberating mental experience of spaciousness that comes from breathing deeply or gazing out into an expanse. And some confront the converse, the stifling denial of what is most precious to creative work.

Some poems ask what it means that air is a medium on which language hangs or depends. One poem that makes that point directly appeared in 2020, by Kira Freger:

> not wind
> it's just
> all
> the deaf
> are speaking
> the same
> language
>
> не ветер
> а просто
> все
> глухие
> говорят
> на одном
> языке[58]

Freger creates a memorable miniature that perfectly emblematizes the potential for air to serve as both the medium of poetic language and as a metaphor for its insubstantiality. Her slightly off-balance lines, with no patterned alternation of one or two words per line, constitute an utterance that is also not really a sentence, although it suggests a complete thought. That thought creates the illusion that users of sign language, a form of communication that varies across national languages, have reversed the fall of the Tower of Babel. In speaking simultaneously, they have unified language with a force that gives their talking hands the power to alter currents in the air.

To say that air is the medium on which poetry's words are carried is also to remind Freger's readers of the precise cultural and technological moment in which she is writing, and we are reading (or listening, or deciphering gestures and signs). The institutions that make literary culture possible have the solidity of bricks and mortar when they are publishing houses, salons, universities, writers' unions, or bookstores, and they have the lesser but no less tangible material status of paper when they are books, journals, manuscripts, or other documents. Tellingly, I began writing about the metaphor of air by writing about *Vozdukh,* which exists both in print and online. Contemporary poetry has thrived in a more digital and performance-oriented cultural moment, and the metaphor of air can also be a way to register those affordances. There is an emerging notion of air itself as a substance on which language might be carried, exemplified in Kira Freger's small poem—whether as an image of the human breath moving outward in an exhalation of spoken words (think of the etymological richness of the term *inspiration,* also true of Russian *vdokhnovenie*) or as the medium through which radio waves or digital signals might carry language across great distances. Some poems thematize this possibility for us, as hers does; others associate the oxygenating potential of air with poetry's freedoms or create a more embodied experience of the air-filled environment.

Freger begins by saying that the air's motion is not wind, but of course currents of air are felt as wind, sometimes with an intensity that seems to drive air into the body's very pores.[59] Tobias Menely has called this "the phenomenology of air": he describes air as "a substance pervasive but perceptually elusive, life-giving but ghostly, occasionally felt as pressure on the skin and only rarely made visible as smoke or mist."[60] Registering something so subtle as air's pressure on the skin or as barely seen mist is metaphorically a task that contemporary poets have taken up, often by the deceptively simple labor of noting down the impressions of the surrounding world. That is hardly a new task for a poem, but it has a dramatic potential that marks the poetry of the present in surprising ways.

Staring at the Present

Russia's self-referential poetic tradition, the tradition that was shaped by modernism and that gave rise to remarkable poetry criticism, has taken some fresh turns in the post-Soviet period. This tradition elevates poems about poetry making; it potentially orients poetry, poets, and readers toward the past. It was most famously studied by Harold Bloom, focusing on the English-language tradition. Such metapoetical poems, as scholars call them, continue to be written, and subtexts, intertexts, and conversations with earlier poets can be detected; in many of the pages that follow, I note such details when they are pertinent to a poem. But they tell an ever-smaller part of the story of poetry today, and in the gaps left in their wake, some intriguing new possibilities are apparent.[61]

New spaces have opened up, spaces where poems and poets have sought an unmediated, fresh, and often tactile connection with the world—that feel of air on the skin Menely was writing about. This subtle shift in aesthetic priority toward an engaged form of alertness to the outer world intensified in the late 1980s, especially after 1989, as the world itself grew more chaotic and more difficult to grasp. Something was happening in poets' minds that gave a new primacy and a new pleasure to the joys, distractions, and disturbances of the visible or imagined world. More and more, poems began to record the experience of physical and mental aliveness—not the past, lost or irretrievable, and not some utopian fantasy of the future, but the immediacy or inchoate flux or flickering possibility of the present. Mikhail Iampolsky has written eloquently about this tendency in the work of Arkady Dragomoshchenko, but it defines a far broader sweep of poets whose ways of registering that exterior world can be quite varied. Iampolsky's observation that it is not some other text but the surrounding world that enables the act of writing opens out a new way to see contemporary poetry, even by those who are otherwise far from Dragomoshchenko in aesthetic orientation.[62]

To record that external world of changing experience was also to reimagine the interior worlds of poets. Barriers between inner and outer experience were lowering. That potent metaphor, of walls torn down, broadly names a set of important traits in contemporary Russian-language poetry. Yes, it is first suggested by the fall of the Berlin Wall in 1989, and the general sense of walls coming down around the former Soviet Bloc, but walls were also coming down around the poetic subject. Even in the very late Soviet period, poets were less barricaded against the world, less urgently defended against the onslaught of stimulation and even harm that daily life might deal out. They began to peer out more intently, to hear all kinds of unearthly, repeating sounds, and to touch, smell, and even taste a world that yet had many powers to surprise them. That world might also have the force to shatter them—let it not seem as if all was rosy in the realms they regarded. For many poets, to look outside was also to look past the material, physical reality into metaphysical possibilities that far exceeded the mind's ability to grasp them fully. Poems of chaos and unbalance, or those in which the poetic subject seems frighteningly untethered, were written as often as poems that experienced the pleasures of being. Across this huge range, poetry as a form of imagination and discourse sought to grasp and respond to a vividly changing world, no matter its disturbing or stimulating or numbing features. This attention to the present was already detected by Mikhail Epstein in the 1980s, in an essay that became famous for its opposition between Conceptualism and Metarealism. More important than that antithesis, though, is the way that poetry flourished, as Epstein put it, when it was about both presence and the present.[63]

Russian poetry is not unique in this intense attention to the present, and a similar poetic turn toward the outside world could be detected as early as the 1970s. We could think of the emerging New York school, where a poem by James Schuyler or Barbara Guest or Frank O'Hara might be content to list the sights and sounds of a summer day. This kind of gorgeous poetry was perhaps less radical in the American context, with precursors like Wallace Stevens and Walt Whitman. In Russian poetry, however, something rather new was happening, sometimes fueled by fresh encounters with poets from the American and European traditions, but just as often inspired by a reordering of the canon and by the distinctive, idiosyncratic personalities of several poets, Dragomoshchenko among them.

In turning their gaze to the outside world, poets have not jettisoned all sense of poetic traditions. Dragomoshchenko's engagement with the poets of OBERIU or with American L=A=N=G=U=A=G=E poets is a case in point. My example of Barskova sampling the lines of Janequin in "The Battle" shows another approach; in a poem by Grigory Dashevsky treated below, images and forms pioneered by Mandelstam and Velimir Khlebnikov are clearly felt. Significantly, earlier poets are mostly invoked in gestures of similarity.[64] Their presence is affirming, and they are conversation partners rather than troubling ghosts.

Contemporary poets' focus on the world around them also has historical and generational contexts. Poets knew the terrors of Stalinism and the losses of the Second World War from family stories and, in the 1980s, from the flood of new publications about the traumatic past, but these histories were increasingly seen from a vantage point of greater personal liberty. The post-perestroika and post-Soviet eras contributed to loosening the hold of poetic traditions and gave poets greater confidence in taking their own impressions of the world in which they were living. Alertness to the sensory impact of daily life, to the details of felt experience as they accumulated in the mind, became a basis on which poems were built. The sheer fact of feeling oneself mentally freer created an opening toward new and perhaps conflicting impressions, and for many poets it meant a greater ease in living with those contradictions.

The historical underpinnings of contemporary poems, then, are important, and how we understand this history is itself still very much a work in progress. Mikhail Iampolsky has argued that our entire framework for understanding temporality, divided into past, present, and future, has effectively shifted into a different triad, or, as he calls it, a different regime of historicity: memoir, event, and enthusiasm.[65] Iampolsky stresses the ethical consequences in such a shift, a topic I take up in chapter 1. His analytical framework also draws our attention to the ways in which contemporary poets have focused on the event: their investment in its affordances, we might say, is what gives the poems their intense affective charge, and what makes them feel consequentially different. The resulting poems are themselves events, as Jonathan Culler would say, as they record a sensory documentation of some present experience and/or some experience of presence. For Culler, this kind of poem is not something new, and he gives as an example our one complete poem by Sappho, which he calls "lyric as performance and event."[66] True enough, but what is different is the capacity of such poems to define an era. Registering the experience of the event has afforded new possibilities of disrupting the conventions of poetic utterance.

Changes like this do not happen overnight; they accumulate and at a certain tipping point come to feel definitive. The virtue of a term like contemporary, in fact, is its flexibility, its capacity to move its own boundaries forward as time itself unfolds.[67] One poet who had a similarly uncanny ability to adapt to the exigencies of time and place is Joseph Brodsky. No contemporary Russian poet has been so richly studied, but his astonishing readiness to record in his poetry the sensory impact of the world has been underestimated, and one instance of this work is studied below in the chapter on music. He led the way in this changed consciousness of what poetry might do, and he led by subtle example, not by manifesto or direct argument. We can see instances of such poetry very early, even during his 1960s internal exile (there is no paradox in this, since the poet himself was the first to claim that the exile to the far North brought extraordinary inner freedom). But we really see it in the work after he leaves Russia. In 1972, he in effect becomes Brodsky as we now know him and as his fellow poets apprehended him. The distance was oddly canonizing, and it pushed the poets left behind (in Leningrad particularly but also elsewhere) to reshuffle allegiances and reestablish some sense of a local hierarchy. Some were liberated by the departure of a charismatic master, and younger poets felt freer to keep his potentially overwhelming influence at bay.

Brodsky was a touchstone, and when the journal *Vozdukh* made its debut in 2006, a questionnaire asked poets about their attitude toward him.[68] It was entitled "Ten Years Without Brodsky" (the issue came out a decade after his death in 1996). The answers range tellingly, with some poets helplessly exhibiting a certain amount of defensive swagger in the master's shadow, others proclaiming indifference to his legacy, and still others unafraid of saying that Brodsky was simply the foundation on which all else has followed.[69]

To give that kind of emphasis to Brodsky should not deceive us into imagining that he defines the post-Soviet period. It takes away nothing from him to claim, as I do, that other constellations are possible and revealing, or to observe that many exceptionally fine poets now writing in Russian have radically different notions of poetic achievement and experiment. Other contemporaries of Brodsky might also be named as important points of origin, and recent work has productively pinpointed the delayed impact of Leonid Aronzon.[70] Among the many virtues of his poetry is an orientation toward setting, so that what defines the lyric subject is often the setting in which an experience crystallizes, which Aronzon can evoke in considerable tactile and emotionally rich detail. I turn now to one final example from a very different poet. It lays out the terms for the kind of poem that sets forth a distinctive relationship of self to external world, which is then more fully explored in later chapters.

The Self in Space: Maria Stepanova, Grigory Dashevsky

In the last several decades, poets have productively interrogated the place from which a sense of self emerges. Spatializing subjectivity is but another shift in the paradigm of poetry without walls; it shows the ruptures between genres of poetic utterance, and it imagines a position from which the poet peers out into unaccustomed space.

Work inflected by phenomenology can especially help us understand these disoriented subjectivities. In seeking a theoretical model for the multifaceted, ambivalent subjectivities in contemporary poetry, I am following a trend advanced by leading scholars of English-language poetry, among them Susan Stewart and Charles Altieri.[71] In a post-Structuralist and perhaps not entirely post-psychoanalytical moment, when critics are suspicious of notions of identity as coherent, knowable, and fixed, projections of a self persist in poetry. Phenomenological arguments offer a sense-based account of the experience of selfhood in the world, and they alert us to the complex ways in which sensory information at once confirms and disturbs our perceptions of language, self, place, and others. They help us read the instabilities and shifting impressions of lyric poetry and track how those instabilities have led not to paralysis but to new forms of freedom. When Maria Stepanova publishes a volume of poems with the title *Not Lyric Poetry* (*Neliricheskaia poeziia*, 2017), she is not just reminding her readers of her virtuoso skills as a narrative poet. She is also saying that her storytelling always stands adjacent to lyric poems, and that the states of mind of her personae, including her lyric personae, are also always her subject.

Stepanova's naming her poetry as nonlyrical signals a broader rethinking around first-person utterance. Her 2014 essay "One, Not One, Not I" ("Odin, ne odin, ne ia") calls poetry a form of extreme tourism that ventures toward secret knowledge. Such poems forge an identification between reader and poetic speaker—she speaks my feelings and makes them seem real, thinks the reader—but also a sharp differentiation: she is "not I," and her pain or joy or capacity for empathy far exceeds my own.[72] Stepanova's trademark narrative lyrics project a parallel relationship between poet and speaker: there is lyric, there is voice,[73] and a poet's consciousness is engaged in acts of considering, deciding, discriminating, or identifying. That awareness of speaking at once as self and as other is not always experienced by the poet as salutary— Stepanova has called it a danger signal in the public space of poetry.[74] But in the terms I am advancing here, it opens a space for poetic utterance to chart its own progress. It is a space of freedom. Stepanova has gone so far as to suggest a thought experiment: what if the first-person pronoun were prohibited from poetry? She writes, "For a poem to be good, the author has to peek out of every pore, share space with every cell."[75] Where there is no pronoun, there is still that speaker. Stepanova's poetic practice and that of many peers show that even in poems bereft of pronouns, there is an abiding, intriguing presence of the lyric subject.

Stepanova's revisionist lyric subject is treated in chapter 1. Here I want to offer an example of complex subjectivity in a poem by Grigory Dashevsky, to whom she dedicated her book of essays. A reticent and perfection-driven poet, Dashevsky wrote in one of his tightest little lyrics the following meditation on being, nonbeing, and subjectivity. He begins with an emphatic denial of the first-person pronoun—we would call it extravagant were it not for the poem's refusal of all rhetorical extravagance. It is a poem of concentrated minimalism in tone, lexicon, and sound orchestration:

No self, no people,
not here, not ever,
The commandment brings light
to goutweed, burdock, gnats.

Singing faintly whines,
a gnat buzzing unseen:
as if a villain saws back and forth
yet the innocent feels the pain,
turns pale, turns white.

But law without people
shines light on personless space:
here there is no evil, no patience,
no face—just the flickering light
of tiny wings, tiny gnats.

Ни себя, ни людей
нету здесь, не бывает.
Заповедь озаряет
сныть, лопух, комара.

Ноет слабое пенье,
невидимка-пила:
будто пилит злодей,
а невинный страдает,
поблсднсв добела.

Но закон без людей
на безлюдьи сияет:
здесь ни зла, ни терпенья,
ни лица—лишь мерцает
крылышко комара.[76]

No translation into English, which takes more words for any utterance than does Russian, can replicate this poem's compactness, nor can one fully re-create the density of negation and sound repetition Dashevsky achieves in these fourteen lines. Most of the lines have a negating adverb or a noun asserting a lack, the most striking of which is "personless space," a single word in Russian (*bezliud'e*) and a very striking one. I at first took it for a neologism, but it is attested in Dal's dictionary.[77] Still, Dashevsky's usage is unusual, meant to apprehend the space in which no persons can be found—but not in a sense related to, say, physics: this is not a vacuum, as the wild plants and insects make clear. The contemplation is instead ontological: what is the nature of being in a space without people?

The poem's task, then, is both an ontological form of contemplation— what is the being that is constituted by absence—and an ethical account of where that ontology might lead: is such a space lawless, asks the poem, or, rather, can there be law without persons?[78] The answer seems to be that there *must* be law: even without persons, there is always evil and suffering, and law must regulate that harm. Even in such personless space, there are those who do evil, and those to whom evil is done. Dashevsky, so knowledgeable in English-language poetry, echoes the line from W. H. Auden's poem "September 1, 1939," "those to whom evil is done, do evil in return," but Dashevsky's poem does not lay out the political or history-tinged territory of Auden's searing response to the start of the Second World War.[79] Nor does he accept its ethical principles: in his poem, the innocent victims of evil suffer and turn pale; the evildoers make the only noise heard in this deserted space, a whining insect buzz.[80]

Sound is the poem's defense against emptiness, not the conventional beautiful sound that Romantic and modernist poets loved to offer as their allegories (Keats's nightingale, Stevens's blackbird), and not even the "dull rustle of a thousand deaths" (smutnyi shorokh tysiachi smertei) in Nikolai Zabolotsky's poem "Lodeinikov" (1932–47), because the crowd of weird presences in Zabolotsky's landscape is here reduced to a few common plants and bugs.[81] What fills in the vacant space is the poem's astonishing linguistic performance: its lines of anapest dimeter, tilted to lightly add stress in some initial syllables; its clenched sound repetitions; and its obsessive rhyming based on only four possibilities—the poet has every line conclude either with an end-stressed -*a* or -*ei*, or a two-syllable rhyme sound, either the verbal ending -*aet* or the noun ending -*en'e*. The sound repetitions are tight but unconsoling, for their pattern is irregular, ragged. Grammar and morphology serve the sound orchestration, and the syntax is relentlessly simple. The stanzas are not symmetrical—four lines, then five, then five—and the one reliable pattern is that each stanza ends with the end-stressed *a* sound, a further indication of language stripped down to its most elemental sound, the first letter of the alphabet, that open "ah" sound that is the opposite of the buzzing, whining insect hum.

Dashevsky begins the poem with a grammatically strange renunciation of self, almost a renunciation of the underlying logic of grammar—in Russian, it sounds weird to launch a poem with the pronoun *sebia*, which is not so much a freestanding notion of a self as it is like the *-self* in *himself* or *herself*, a half-word that feels like it is missing its defining first syllable. As a pronoun, *sebia* normally comes after the noun for which it is a substitution. So when he negates *sebia*, the poet sets off from the renunciation of reference and pronoun substitution more generally: the poem evokes a deserted space not by means of description, but by pulling out from space the persons and the grammatical hierarchies that could populate it.[82] The word I have translated as "face" (litso) intensifies that depopulation, for it is a word that also means person in the grammatical sense, as well as an individual, a person. Emptied of personhood, we might say, the space is also unnamed, and not just in the sense of not having a name (there are no proper names of any sort here, and no title). A hint of a category name is also taken away: the "commandment" of l.3 is the word "zapoved'," a meaningful word in the poem because the law, and lawlessness, will be taken up in stanza 2. But in stanza 1, the word "za-poved'" reverberates like a truncated version of the word for a preserve, for a parcel of land that has been set aside, shielded from further development, *zapovednik*. It is such a preserve that one expects to be the source of illumination for the plant life and insect life named in the stanza's final line. That unspoken word stands behind the poem's opening as surely as does a fixed expression, "ni sebe, ni liudiam" (of no benefit or use), flutter in the background of the first line.[83]

The poem becomes a kind of primer in how not to say things in poetry, how to pull back even from renunciation, that "piercing Virtue" in which Emily Dickinson specialized, and how to scrape away at the poem's own language.[84] Dashevsky pares away at form itself, reducing to a concentrated set of phonemes even the possibilities for rhyme, denying rhyme any sort of regular pattern yet getting readers to hear it in every line.

That form of condensation, of eliciting from readers a kind of intensified alertness, has a well-established point of origin: late Mandelstam. And it seems to me that Dashevsky has built this poem with reference to the last of Mandelstam's "Octaves" ("Vos'mistishiia," 1932–35).[85] I want to cite the poem and comment on those references to further open out this difficult, beautiful poem of Dashevsky's, and because the eight-line form, including Mandelstam's legacy, will figure in chapter 3. Introducing this striking example here will allow that chapter to close a circle I now wish to open. Here is Mandelstam's poem:

> And I emerge out of space
> Into the neglected garden of magnitudes
> And I tear through imaginary constancy
> And the internal harmony of causes.
>
> And your textbook, infinity,
> I read alone, without people—
> A leafless, wild book of cures,
> A problem book of enormous roots.
> *November 1933*[86]

> И я выхожу из пространства
> В запущенный сад величин
> И мнимое рву постоянство
> И самосогласье причин.
>
> И твой, бесконечность, учебник
> Читаю один, без людей—
> Безлиственный, дикий лечебник,
> Задачник огромных корней.
> *Ноябрь 1933*[87]

We might first note the semantic connections, particularly Mandelstam's striking phrase "without people" (bez liudei), which Dashevsky rewrites as "ni liudei" in l.1, then gives as "bez liudei" in l.10, both times in rhyme position. Dashevsky intensifies the emptying out effect of Mandelstam's poem with his doubled use of the noun for "people" in genitive plural (liudei), and with his noun "bezliud'e," a word that gathers up the imagined space without people as if it were a collective.

This first connection between the poems, then, projects an idea of absent personhood to ask what subjectivity in a poem would mean in a space without persons, and the second connection has to do with space itself. Dashevsky's poem stays with the work of representing that peopleless space (Mandelstam's "prostranstvo") and like Mandelstam's, gives us concrete points of reference (a garden gone wild, a place of "goutweed, burdock, gnats") and strangely awkward abstractions (imaginary constancy, infinity's textbook, law without persons). Both poems create a space where the cultivations of land have ceased, where gardens have gone wild, but Mandelstam moves that fantasy toward infinity, even as he brings it back to the culture of books (textbook, mathematical problem book, book of cures).[88] Dashevsky is content to stay in the peopleless space, to consider it sufficiently expansive for a long pause, where the poet can listen for what might otherwise go unheard.

There are implicit contrasts of scale as a result, and here the poem is pointing us in several directions, to be taken up in chapter 3, on magnitude and size in contemporary poetry. Dashevsky is playing with scale in a punning way, as if it were its own musical instrument—his poem is longer than Mandelstam's, yet his lines radically shorter. His choice of fourteen lines feels significant, a wafting gesture in the direction of the sonnet, just as Mandelstam's eight-line form could be read as a truncated sonnet. But still, where Mandelstam reaches for quantities (another translation for the "velichina" in his l.2), or for massiveness (his "huge roots" in the final line), Dashevsky has things get smaller and smaller. Rather than Mandelstam's magnitudes, Dashevsky attunes the poem's ear to a mosquito's whining buzz. And what flickers in the poem's last visual image is the moving light radiated by insect wings. It may be that the last line shows a will to temper Mandelstamian grandeur with the whimsy of Velimir Khlebnikov (the wings recall the great first line of his "Grasshopper": "Glitter-letter wing-winker," in Paul Schmidt's translation; Russian "Krylyshkuia zolotopis'mom").[89] And the idea that the sources of poetry are not sublime but mundane is furthered by Dashevsky's evocation of Akhmatova's poetic disclosure that poems grow out of debris; his use of burdock inevitably echoes hers in "Secrets of the Craft" ("Tainy remesla," 1942).[90]

But I want to pause the backward motion toward subtexts and return to the poem's present moment, asking how it shapes that relationship to the present with its first modest present-tense verb, a habitual form of the verb "to be," "byvat'," which appears in l.2. Mandelstam also stayed with the present tense in his choice of verbs, but they began with a sense of adventure, of drama, of discovery (vykhozhu, rvu). Dashevsky prefers usualness, where the drama that unfolds is itself a kind of back-and-forth sawing motion, a buzz of gnats or mosquitoes. Writing about Dashevsky's poetry, Anna Glazova observed its pattern of repeatedly approaching the point beyond which speech and thought become impossible.[91] But he does not give up on language, and that is the element in Dashevsky's work that makes him surprisingly emblematic. There is an evocation of public speech here—in the commandment, in the law, and in the way that law illuminates that dark space where there are no persons.

Dashevsky's poem shows how it is possible, even in a poem that begins with a negation of the self, to create a sense of engaged subjectivity, and in his move toward the law, he brings back the problems of a populated world that the poem's opening cast away.

The work of the poet, living in the contemporary world's darkness, is the work of "recovering the public world," as Robin Blaser put it.[92] Grigory Dashevsky addressed himself directly to that work of recovery, and we can find in his critical writings an expressive and useful account of what a recovered world might feel like. Dashevsky's writings about poetry were often practical, the kind of reviews that fellow poets were writing in the 1990s, 2000s, and 2010s as they created a kind of real-time guide to the poetry being made around them. Mikhail Aizenberg is another splendid exponent of this genre of writing, and one can read grateful comments about his discerning work by his fellow poets.[93] Like Aizenberg, Dashevsky stayed close to the texts, teaching his readers how to understand them. And so, when Dashevsky strays toward generalization, readers take note. In 2012, he published a remarkable short essay, "How to Read Contemporary Poetry," which sets out the terms of speaking in the context of contemporary darkness. Here his metaphor is not light but warmth, or its lack. He invites both poets and readers to imagine what it might mean to speak freely in this context. If I translate his words into my own terms, then Dashevsky is showing us how contemporary poetry is finding new ways to register its place in the world. Poetry is finding a public voice.

The example he gives is of the poet's use of free verse, which was still a sore subject in Russia, with squawking denunciations and intemperate reviews persisting in the 1990s and 2000s—even though there had long been significant and innovative poetry in Russian that did not depend on rhyme or meter. But free verse was on the rise in the post-Soviet period, and not every critic was pleased. Dashevsky in 2012 was keen to move past any sense of grievance and argue that free verse is the metrical formation for public speech, and that its rise—like the decline in a poetics of quotation—signals a shift in poetry toward the challenge of speaking not to a cozy elite, not to like-minded initiates, but to an audience of others. He is returning us to the idea of poetry as conversation associated in my argument with the thinking of Bibikhin and Cavell. But for Dashevsky, no philosophers or theorists impinge at the moment when he describes in his own words the absolute otherness that confronts the poet who steps out of the underground, out of the kitchen, out of the *tusovka*, and onto the square. I would add that this is also a step into the virtual reality of web journals, social media, and blogs. Dashevsky first published this piece in the web-based journal *OpenSpace*.

His idea about free verse and public address is breathtakingly optimistic. His insight opens a radically new sense of poetic audience, and of poetic speech itself. Dashevsky explains that when a poet speaks to this "utterly other person" (absoliutno chuzhoi chelovek), poetic speech becomes an interiorized conversation that carries with it this otherness. Metrical, memorized poetry is what one intones to oneself, but free verse is what one speaks to another. When the poet speaks in free verse as a form of address to someone utterly other, here is what happens:

> You will no longer be speaking with yourself in the meter of a rhythmic womb-like lullaby, but instead as if the cold and hunger of public space were inside you. And as a result, this public space—hungry, cold, and well-lit—will begin to be created in parallel: in the public arena, in the courts, in the parliament, inside a person and inside poetry.[94]

Dashevsky, as demonstrated vividly in his poem "No self, no people," was also an adept practitioner of metrical poetry (and of the poetry one can memorize), so he is not so much advocating the abandonment of that poetic practice as he is using free verse as a metaphorical category: a poetry that advances the cause of freedom. His is not an idealized account of the space in which such poems are spoken—just as the expanse created in "No self, no people" is made out of negations, so the public arena that concludes this essay is marked by a lack of warmth and nourishment. But speaking into that bleak space is the work of poetry. Speaking into that bleak space creates ideas for readers of what free speech sounds like, what kind of sustenance it might offer, what courts or parliaments—which is to say, what public institutions—it might amplify.[95] To create this space as one's internalized audience is the fundamental creative gesture of the contemporary poet. In the chapters that follow, I propose to test its possibilities, beginning with poems that present themselves as politically and ethically engaged.

PART I

Forms of Free Speech

1

Politics

WRITING POEMS IN A WORLD OF HARM

Medvedev • Golynko • Arseniev • Fanailova •
Stepanova • Rymbu

A work of art, after all, is one of the few spheres in which human freedom is
realized—even in those societies where such freedom is essentially unknown.

—MIKHAIL IAMPOLSKY

Maybe poetry isn't so helpful out on the square, during protests or in the
technical political sense, but it's needed so that revolution is born within us.

—GALINA RYMBU

RUSSIAN POETRY HAS A long history of civically engaged poetry, what is
termed *grazhdanskaia lirika*. Its origins came earlier, but Vladimir Mayakovsky
charted a revolutionary pathway that influenced twentieth- and twenty-first-
century poetry. He showed how to energize the poetic line and electrify a vast
readership. His suicide and the subsequent political course of the USSR also
show the risks of political poetry, and socially engaged poetry seemed more
programmatic than energizing from the 1930s onward. Engagement with the
present was a requirement of socialist realism; its seeming opposite, undue con-
cern for aesthetics or form, was taboo. Many unofficial poets in the late Soviet
period fled obviously political topics, but they could not flee politics, and some
did not even want to. Their work was regarded as suspect for its free-thinking
ethos and for its very resistance to ideologies and political idioms.[1]

Reassessment by poets and critics of their legacy has recognized that their endeavors were profoundly political and ethical.[2] As practitioners of what Foucault called fearless speech, unofficial Soviet poets have remained vital in the post-Soviet period.[3] In search of ways to continue their practices of fearless speech, contemporary poets have built on their legacy, particularly since 2000.[4] Many saw the reinvention of political poetry as an urgent task, and their work has flourished to considerable critical acclaim within and beyond Russia.[5] For left-leaning poets, talking about the language of poetry was a way to talk about political change, and many poems self-consciously ask how to widen their audience. Some who learned lessons of mimicry and mockery from the late Soviet Conceptualists have found other ways to make language matter, as they layered the discourse of the other into lyric poems of impressive eloquence and force. Key figures here include Pavel Arseniev, Keti Chukhrov, Dmitry Golynko, Kirill Medvedev, Roman Osminkin, Galina Rymbu, Alexander Skidan, and Evgenia Suslova.

These poets have been leaders in what is sometimes called a new social poetry (novaia sotsial'naia poeziia).[6] They are most invested in the middle term of this name, the social. That is what counts as political in their work: social relations, and the production of a communal ethos in which relationships of equality can flourish.[7] Most have worked together in varying combinations. Some have been associated with the Chto delat' (What Is to Be Done) group, and their work has appeared in the journal [Translit] and in the Kraft poetry series of the Free Marxist Press.[8] Several of them actively edit these publications.

Their important work, though, is not centrally my subject, although I treat some of it briefly and then devote considerable attention to the work of Galina Rymbu. I am more interested in some questions that are not always theirs: what happens at the border zones between narrative and lyric, between the impulse to tell a story—about injury or war or a disturbing encounter with an other—and the readiness to let that story unfold in the deformations and disturbances of language and selfhood. This political poetry, as Kirill Korchagin has written, "proposes a special status for the subject, whose duty is to express correlation between collective unity and the emancipation of the individual."[9] I also look elsewhere because I am concerned about a particular ethical commitment: the refusal to turn away one's gaze from harm. Mostly that refusal has to do with the harm of the present, although repairing the traumas of history, both collective and personal, is here as well, best exemplified in the work of Maria Stepanova. Two recurring scenes in this work are those of war (the ongoing war in Ukraine and the Chechen wars) and of sexual violence.[10]

Before focusing on these poets, however, I want to introduce a few of the new social poets, because their work has created a crucial context in which poets are testing the boundaries of what counts as political poetry. They set forth a whole host of new ways in which poetry can engage with politics and can reflect on its own politics, and several of them have become known outside Russia through excellent translations and collaborations with international cultural enterprises.

To Start: Kirill Medvedev, Dmitry Golynko, Pavel Arseniev

Of the new social poets, Kirill Medvedev is the best known both in Russia and in the West.[11] He is a well-published poet and prolific activist, a strong voice for a revived Marxist politics, who can anchor a political event with exhortation and song alongside his band, Arkady Kots (named for the translator of the "Internationale" into Russian). His renunciation of copyright in 2003 and temporary refusal to publish his works gained him a different kind of fame, as he sought to wed the politics of popular uprising with a critique of the post-Soviet marketplace. He returned to publishing in 2007 with the founding of the Free Marxist Press (Svobodnoe marksistskoe izdatel'stvo). His poetry has ridden the crest of free verse with a strong lyric voice and a compelling ability to mesh seemingly very personal poems with political invective. As a Marxist, Medvedev can offer a utopian glimpse of the changed world to come, and his poems seem designed to chronicle the steps toward that transformation. They can sound almost entirely prosaic, as if their only goal is to report the experiences and observations of a poet walking through urban or pastoral space. Somewhat like the poets of the new epic poetry (novyi epos),[12] Medvedev is a storyteller, committed to teaching readers to notice the political impact of the minutiae of daily life, and committed to showing what it means to be the kind of person who can advance the socialist project in post-Soviet Russia.[13]

Vivid examples of poems that strive for those goals appear in his book *It's No Good* (*Vse plokho*; OGI, 2002), including one that begins "I really like when" (mne ochen' nravitsia kogda). It starts as a stroll through Moscow, reflecting on the kinds of labor he has performed in the past and present. Placing persons in terms of their jobs is also the mental gesture that will end the poem. But at the halfway point, when the poet's mind is most engaged with noticing and estimating the significance of various subject positions, he insists that his is the point of view of someone who does not have a job. The poem unfolds at a slow pace, the pace of the poet's own self-reflections.

I walk further,
thinking about how
my poems
are the poems of a *nonworking* person
(as opposed to, say, the poems of the poet
Stanislav Lvovsky,
which he sent me not long ago:
his, in my opinion, are
the opposite—
a person in his poems is always
returning from work
moving around the glaring twilit
cityscape
given shape by information streams—I don't know
how things are in reality, but
that's the feeling you get
reading these poems).
I think about how
self-sufficiency
and dignified aloofness are qualities foreign to me
I think
I need involvement;
I thirst for some kind of solidarity;
having forgotten that tunnel
(which stirred in me, by the way,
in addition to everything else,
a kind of fixed, if not ruinous
obsession,
evoking the image
of some cheerful, ruinous chill
of a cool freedom taking in breath
of some kind of heavy, low flight
a feeling that
comes over me pretty often of late
it's a kind of knowledge
that lies like a lump
in my soul;
I sometimes wonder

where it comes from
and cannot understand;
in the end I think
it's the kind of knowledge
that comes
from without)[14]

я иду дальше,
думая о том,
что мои стихи
это стихи *неработающего* человека
(в отличие, например, от стихов поэта
Станислава Львовского,
которые он мне недавно прислал:
у него там, по-моему,
наоборот—
человек всё время
возвращается с работы,
передвигаясь по какому-то сумеречному,
прорезанному информационными токами
бликующему городскому пространству—не знаю,
как там на самом деле, но
стихи оставляют
именно такое ощущение)
я думаю о том,
что мне, в каком-то смысле,
несвойственна самостоятельность
и исполненная достоинства отрешённость,
я думаю,
что мне нужна вовлечённость;
я жажду какого-то слияния;
забыв об этом тоннеле
(вселяющем в меня, кстати,
помимо всего прочего,
какое-то глухое, чуть не погибельное
наваждение,
навевающем представление
о каком-то весёлом гибельном холодке,

о дышащей прохладной свободе,
о каком-то
тяжёлом низком полёте,
ощущение которого
довольно часто охватывает меня
в последнее время—
это какое-то знание,
которое лежит комом
у меня на душе;
я иногда думаю о том,
откуда оно,
и не могу понять,
откуда оно у меня взялось;
я думаю всё же,
что это какое-то наносное
знание)[15]

These short lines give a good example of the way Medvedev builds a dynamic of self-description and self-projection in his poems. The reference to Stanislav Lvovsky invokes a poet known for his innovative use of free-flowing conversational verse lines, and thus a model for the kind of poetry Medvedev writes.[16] But Lvovsky is also a point of contrast: not for Medvedev is the position of aloofness and distance, of purposefully moving through space *on the way to work*.[17] He seeks instead the attitude of absorption, of fierce attention to the surrounding environment. He wants it to surprise him, even to scare him.

The psychic pleasure of this relationship to surrounding space is associated with freedom: he thinks "about a cool freedom taking in breath" (o dyshashchei prokhladnoi svobode). A kind of sensory enrichment accompanies this metaphysical widening. Freedom brings a cooling surplus of oxygen, and the poet implicitly breathes in that cooled air as if it could carry into his body a form of being not shuttered by the limiting visions of success and failure vividly represented by the workers' fates he lists in the poem's ending.[18] Medvedev's poems can reach for a kind of freedom that comes from a new relationship to one's surroundings, then, and he represents that freedom by the expansive metaphor of oxygenating air. But his poems are not without some limitations on the capacity of others to share that freedom, and here one could argue that his real model is not Lvovsky, but Mayakovsky.

That lineage is keenly felt in a later long text, *Live Long Die Young* (*Zhit' dolgo umeret' molodym*, 2011), about a failed interview with the filmmaker Claude Lanzmann in Moscow.[19] The poem uses changing font sizes to convey the rising frustration and intensity of the questions left unasked (about what the poem calls "the Holocaust industry," for example). The illustrations by Nikolai Oleinikov that accompany the poem show a grinning, armed version of Medvedev and another figure aiming a rifle.[20] The small book packs a big punch, and it prompts a question about the place of aggressiveness in poetry. Is hectoring or rage-filled, invective-laced work likely to inspire the progressive social change Medvedev seeks? Such aggressive poems with a pointed political orientation surfaced elsewhere, including in feminist poems written in the wake of the #MeToo movement, and in response to the Russia-Ukraine war. How do we read their anger and their angst? What are the ethical implications of responding to harm with a readiness to inflict pain in return? And what are the consequences for a political project that emphasizes not social transformation, Medvedev's goal, but the rising sense of human dignity and freedom in every individual? Those are questions to which I return below, grateful to Medvedev's poems, even when they are problematic, for pressing them upon me.

A related angst is conveyed with more indirection and more of a high-theory intonation in the poetry of Dmitry Golynko, who published prolifically until his premature death in January 2023. He wrote what he called as of 2012 applied social poetry, suggesting his orientation, like Medvedev's, toward the social order.[21] His base was Petersburg (compared with Medvedev's Moscow), and, especially earlier on, he could savagely parody a recognizable Petersburg poetic tradition.[22] Without Medvedev's programmatic Marxism, and with a broader range of philosophies and theories as well as a deep interest in cinema and the visual arts, he cast a no less critical gaze on the world around him. He brilliantly remixed the discourses of the present, as Kevin Platt has put it, writing "a poetry that is capable of channeling the raw energy of contemporary language towards its own critical self-disclosure."[23] The element of critique was a late-blooming feature of the work, which in the 1990s re-created the voices of hip urban youth.[24] In translating Golynko, Eugene Ostashevsky gently reproached himself and his collaborators for not drawing on something close to hip-hop discourse (they chose more neutral styles).[25] Yet the undertone of disgust and the overtones of bravado easily recall hip-hop, as does the mix of found language and clashing stylistic registers. By 2016, Golynko could insist that poetry must be "severe, embittered, and cruel."[26] In 2018 he oriented himself toward the uncertainties of a postapocalyptic future; he claimed that in our post-truth and posthumanistic era, poetry becomes the instrument of cynical gossips, but also the only possible way to react to an anemic, stagnating social model.[27] These observations were grounded in the terms of social philosophy and political theory, operating as abstractions but charged with a relentless insistence that there was no way out of the closed space of global capitalism.

This account could leave the impression that the poems are meant to prove the theories, but the rigidity is illusory: Golynko was ever transforming himself as a poet, and his lines are dynamic, charged with energies and shifting valences. Like Medvedev, he could write poems riveted to the oxygenating scenes of the present, and his piercing attention to phenomena and to language itself is perhaps his signature. He was invested in what one poem called, in its title, "Looking at the Around" ("Ogliadyvaia vokrug," 2010).[28] The poem is long (twenty-five five-line stanzas) with an ironic, droning repetitiveness. All stanzas start with the title phrase and proceed to list observed phenomena. The lines are more or less equal in length, but the verse is free, so what organizes the poem is the syntactic pattern of a list. The observed phenomena are without hierarchy: a woman darning a sock appears in the same stanza as a peasant living through the Holodomor famine. A tour operator merits the same mention as economic default; the Orange Revolution is mentioned alongside the ultrasound of a fetus. The experiential impact of economic crises or political movements is no different from an overheard conversation between two women about love. Because so many kinds of persons are integrated into the list of things seen "in the around," it is hard to know who precisely is experiencing all these sights. Does the leveling extend to the poem's attentive subject—could this all be observed by anyone, everyone?[29] Whose attitudes are encoded in the poem's discourses, we are pressed to consider, by a poetic text that uses pronouns or missing grammatical subjects to keep in abeyance any commitment to a lyrical subject? Platt argues that the result is to make it everyone's experience: we are all implicated in the ugliness and injustice that give Golynko's poems their distinctly uncomfortable feel. But political discussions are sometimes at their best when one also asks how that *we* is constituted, and what it does to account for radically different subject positions in terms of power or privilege. To take only one difference, what happens to gender when such a collective is created? Quite apart from the poems themselves, Golynko's statements about poetry and responsibility suggest that he fully recognized a less than level playing field.

Golynko's theories draw a line between the privileged position of the poet and the voiceless, downtrodden subject position of "the masses," and that difference motivates his turn to an applied social poetics.[30] His poetry thus presses readers to ask how a poet can faithfully transmit what would otherwise be silenced. Does Golynko's often allusive, cleverly compacted diction channel or transform the voice of the other? Or does it transmute it to make it more like poetry? Moreover, are there really no differences in the potential for self-recognition in the poetry? To answer those questions too quickly feels to me like a mistake, all the more so in the wake of Golynko's early death; there will be a much fuller sense of his work as archival materials are published.[31] But let the questions of gender linger, alongside the ways in which Medvedev's poetry urges us to reconsider the role of anger and invective in political poetry. Both topics are foundational for the longer treatments of Fanailova, Stepanova, and Rymbu to follow. But first, one more example of the new social poetry.

Pavel Arseniev relies on found language and ready-made materials, which undergo little hammering or distortion in his nearly documentary poetic texts.[32] In the volume of his work that appeared in English with facing Russian texts, *Reported Speech* (2018), Arseniev assembles poems out of found bits of language, with a political charge racing through familiar words. He tells stories of how poems are created and performed, and he lets language laugh at its own seriousness. That laughter is a key factor in Arseniev's success and in his specific challenge to the conventions of political and civic poetry. In "Mayakovsky for Sale" ("Prodaetsia Maiakovskii," ca. 2008–12), the poem's eight lines are built out of internet terms in links that appear after an announcement that a set of Mayakovsky's writings is for sale. A video of the poem shows the cursor moving across a changing computer screen to assemble the poem's words as they appear serially. One takes the video as an estranged representation of the act of poetic composition and its dissemination, for the video ends with the poet clicking on the links in his email app that will send the poem to *[Translit]* for publication and will presumably post this very video.[33] The legacy of political and avant-garde poetry signaled by the name Mayakovsky seemed to be a trigger for a potential commercial transaction, with books for sale; writing and publishing the poem became a performance in the age of digital reproduction.

In "Forensic Examination," ("Ekspertiza," ca. 2008–12), Arseniev goes one step further, building the poem around declarations of thematic and self-referential content. It begins:

This poem is yet another specimen
Of how inserting
Political declarations
Into works of art
Flattens
And simplifies them

На примере данного стихотворения
Мы снова увидим, как
Политические декларации,
Включенные в произведения искусства,
Распрямляют,
Упрощают[34]

The poet declares that the voicing of political views impoverishes the poem, that art and politics are incompatible, which the poet ironically declares he would have learned if only he had studied in a Department of Comparative Literature; the poem announces that it betrays the great poetic tradition by its failure to use familiar meters, and that it violates the Russian criminal code by inciting extremist measures. The poem prophetically makes a joke out of Arseniev's later arrest for reading a poem in public with an obscenity (that event is the subject of another poem, "Russia Day" ["Den' Rossii," 2013]), but its association of poetic ready-mades with violations of both poetic tradition and civic law raises the stakes for the kind of poetry at hand. There is disruptive potential here beyond the jokes.

The joyful quality persists, however, and this trait distinguishes Arseniev's poetry from that of Golynko—intonationally, it can bring it closer, in this one sense, to the performance-oriented work of Roman Osminkin.[35] The exuberant pleasures of the poetic act particularly show through in some of the actionist gatherings, installations, and internet-oriented videos created by Arseniev. The wry sense of humor marks even the political slogan for which he is perhaps best known: his punning sentence that means both "You can't even imagine us" and "You don't even represent us" (Vy nas dazhe ne predstavliaete), which dates to the mass protests in 2011 against the falsified parliamentary elections. It is certainly a splendid pun, but the real cleverness here may be the adverb "even" (dazhe), which adds just the right fillip of invective and taunts elite officials for being unable either to represent or to imagine their fellow citizens.

What place is there in politically charged poetry for such humor, such lightness? Some ethical conundrums can spring up as a result: mockery is rarely a way to connect across differences, so such poetry, if it is aimed at persuasion, must rely on a kind of triangle, where one group is to be wooed at the expense of another. Arseniev's poems build on the ready-made, the quotation, the borrowed or mimicked discourse of the other, and derision can be an intonational side effect of the method. Is there any place for ambivalent, complicated connections across such differences? And is connection to the other even valued as a political or ethical act?

Let that be our last lingering set of questions, as we turn now to a different set of possibilities for what might count as political poetry in contemporary Russia. One of the issues that has figured in some corners of the new social poetry—particularly the work of Suslova, Chukhrov, and Rymbu—is gender, and it could be argued that in the late 2010s and particularly in 2020, struggles around gendered identity overtook the discourse around social and economic class in Russian poetry. Women poets, among others, have reminded their readers that there can be no freedom without bodily autonomy. Poetry about women's bodily freedoms and vulnerabilities is my next subject, where I reorient that work on bodily harm toward the poetry of war. The questions raised above—about anger, about gender, about connections across differences—are rewoven into a different fabric, one that can also take on questions of nation and destiny, and of the state's violence.

By writing about Russia at war (including the memory of the Afghanistan campaign that began in 1979–80, the First and Second Chechen Wars in 1994–96 and 1999–2009, and the Russia-Ukraine war that began in 2014), poets have forged a new form of political poetry. It is a poetry of the body, and of resistance against an authoritarian state that has failed to make good on the post-Soviet promises of equality, rule of law, justice, and human dignity. Some poems offer testimony of a defiant individual in the face of the repressive and dishonest state. Some poems are committed to making memories that can bind citizens together, memories based on experiences and losses that the state would cast as false (what in a short time would come to be known as fake news). The ones that interest me the most have taken up an ironic challenge, formulated succinctly in 2014 by the Minsk poet Dmitry Strotsev in his poem "Shame" ("Pozor"):

Shame

what has been done by Russia
what has taken place in Ukraine = in Crimea
is unworthy of a poem

March 18, 2014

Позор

произведенное Россией
произошедшее в Украине = в Крыму
недостойно стихов

18.03.2014[36]

Strotsev builds this minimalist, koan-like poem on a memory of the shameful moment on March 18, 2014, when the Russian Federation annexed Crimea, taking it from the independent country of Ukraine. That bloodless action plus the relentless assault on eastern Ukraine led to horrific destruction and bloodshed across Ukraine as of February 24, 2022. Strotsev's poem feels almost prescient, as it challenges the capacity of poetry, perhaps especially of Russian poetry, to respond to the shameful actions of the state. But even as he says that the annexation is not worthy of poetry, he accepts the ethical imperative that one not turn away from wrongdoing. Strotsev inverts Adorno's assertion that writing poems after Auschwitz is barbaric: to be a poem worthy of poetry's calling is to make the poem respond to such horror, whether it is the war on Ukraine or, as other poets will take up, the violence perpetrated by individuals in domestic and public spaces.

Several poets have risen to this challenge and done so in a way that remakes the politics of nation and military violence through a politics of gender. I closely consider three of them, Elena Fanailova, Maria Stepanova, and Galina Rymbu, starting with Fanailova.

Elena Fanailova and the Politics of Intimacy

In 2020, Elena Fanailova wrote a searing attack on a new antiabortion law in Poland, drawing on her medical training and journalistic practice and making broad comparisons to the situation in Russia.[37] For all the nuance of her poems, Fanailova is adept at political invective. She offers in the essay about Poland a list of topics that belong in her poems: the wars undertaken by her country (open, secret, and hybrid); widespread violence in prisons and the army; horrifying poverty in provincial Russia; and discrimination against those over sixty-five during the pandemic. It's quite a list, but it's the first item on the list that has increasingly become her subject. The way in which the topic of war has organized her poetry since 2014, when Russia's invasion of Ukraine began, is a fascinating study in one poet's evolution and an exemplary reconfiguration of the relationships among politics, ethics, and violence. The poems of war are considered as a performance in chapter 2; here the broader political context and ethical implications of this work are treated.

Retrospectively, her poem ". . . Again they're talking about their Afghanistan" (". . . Oni opiat' za svoi Afghanistan," 2002) looks like a turning point, and it may still be her best-known poem. Fanailova found a language scaled to the human but able to address post-Soviet Russia's grotesquely normalized culture of violence.[38] That violence also defines her poems about Moscow's streets in her 2008 book *Black Suits* (*Chernye kostiumy*). But it is the Afghanistan poem, reprinted several times, that first got readers to sit up and take notice.[39] The poem also epitomized her practice of speaking through others' voices, particularly women's voices. In her 2002 book *Transylvania Calling* (*Transil'vaniia bespokoit*), where the Afghanistan poem appeared, readers would have also found her "Jataka about a Woman" ("Dzhataka o zhenshchine") dedicated to the experiences of Mary Shelley, Yoko Ono, and Marina Malich.[40] Fanailova was doing something more than throwing her own voice: she was also listening for entirely other linguistic registers that she could draw into her poetic universe. And she was practicing what Namwali Serpell has called "oscillations of identification and distance," which would come to define her poems about the Russia-Ukraine war.[41]

Several poets and critics, reacting to this strong turn in her work, linked it to her long-standing journalism for Radio Svoboda.[42] A valid observation, especially epistemologically, in that her journalism, like her earlier work as a doctor, oriented Fanailova toward scrutinizing the self-presentations of others. But in a poem, her principal task is to transform the language of the other: Fanailova has said that the poet's work is registering the history-defining moments of the present in language.[43] She listens to speech acts as distinctively revealing, making what she hears into a larger poetic whole.

It was language—in fact, a simple rhyme—that gave rise to ". . . Again they're talking about their Afghanistan." Fanailova has recounted the poem's origins in an almost cinematic scene: she is relaxing with a friend at a riverbank, and a man is overheard talking about his time in the military: "The training was in Grozny, and the roses there were big and black." The poet admits, "I was hooked by the combination of sounds in 'roses and Grozny.'"[44] Grozny is the name of a city in Chechnya, founded in the early nineteenth century as a military outpost in the Russian empire's expansion into the Caucasus. The name means fearsome, menacing, and terrible, the same epithet as in Ivan the Terrible (Ivan Groznyi). But the resonance in Fanailova's poem is more modern. The time is 2001, and the conversation is occurring on the second anniversary of the start of the Second Chechen War, so the coincidence of a man's training place in Grozny (the capital and the scene of brutal fighting in both Chechen wars), launches a comparison between the 1980s Soviet war in Afghanistan and the horrific efforts to subdue Chechnya.[45] What begins as a grotesque rhyme that matches poetry's most cliché-ridden flowers, roses, with a toponym associated with carpet bombing and mass graves ends in a reflection on the multiple forms of violence endured and perpetrated by people of her generation: Fanailova recognizes in this small family group her own contemporaries. The violence they recount is horrifying, but almost worse is their weirdly neutral tone. That strange absence of affect marks the overheard conversation as an exposed wound from which the speakers have no way to heal. What her poem reports is at once intensely personal and horribly public. At that implausible border zone between the intimate and the civic, Fanailova found the poetic strategy that sustains her work to this day.[46]

The cool tone of this poem is a signature for Fanailova, as is the mix of pathos and irony. She has associated the coolness and the irony with several poetic models. To her surprise, she saw similarities with Timur Kibirov's work: his methods let her "fix a quantity of historical material in poetic form."[47] Kibirov's adept mixture of civic criticism, folkloric elements, self-irony, and linguistic acuteness may have attracted Fanailova, but like him, she was listening for the speech markers—the language—that could define a worldview. It is a world of harm, for which public discourse has no remedy. She translates the lack of an agreed-on language into fragmentary accounts of experiences, emotions, sights, and sounds that make up the inscrutable present.

The result lets Fanailova load into her poem the "unbearable, bitter pain of daily life in this country."[48] Grasping the realities of these people's lives, their memories and their blinkered state in the present, the poet senses their indignities and suffering but also their unthinking aggressiveness. Their casual moral indifference leads to the poem's wrenching conclusion:

> Now they're at the river getting soused
> And reminiscing about the good old days.
> And it's as though a strange chill tugs
> Against their corporeal flesh.

Now the lovers are both forty.
Or, more precisely, the husband and the wife.
The kid is ten, they had him late by Soviet standards.
Their scars speak for themselves.

I'll never find another country such as this.

Теперь они бухают у реки
И вспоминают старые деньки.
И как бы тянет странный холодок
Физическим телам их вопреки.
Теперь любовникам по сорока,
Сказать точнее, мужу и жене.
Ребенку десять, поздно для совка.
Их шрамы отвечают за себя.

Другой такой страны мне не найти.[49]

To write about daily life in this prosaic way became another hallmark of Fanailova's work, as did the undercurrent or explicit account of violence. This poem, despite its placid and summery ending, recollects war, disease, rape, and abortion. Because the poem is presented as the fruit of eavesdropping, it penetrates a zone of secrecy.[50] That quality may remind us of Fanailova's work as a journalist, where she is often interviewing public figures and testing their guarded self-protection.[51] Her journalistic work never probes for the sake of some salacious revelation, never goes after the personal in a way that disrespects an individual's right to privacy.[52] Instead, Fanailova asks after personal experiences that have broader cultural meanings, seeking out the traumas shared by a nation that has yet to find its language to name that pain. The scars on the sun-bathing bodies at the end of ". . . Again they're talking about their Afghanistan," in other words, are not just the scars of their surgeries (which Fanailova, a former doctor, decodes expertly); they are also the scars left by a history of subjugation and dehumanization.

Exploring those zones of intimacy is the fundamental political gesture of her poetry. She is laying out new possibilities in a lyric subjectivity of revelation and disclosure. Presenting the words of others transforms a poetics of self-revelation into an accounting of multiple forms of collective trauma. She is modeling a form of dignity and freedom in self-exploration that, in her view, is a necessary but often wanting component of post-Soviet subjectivity. She repudiates the hectoring, preaching voice so often associated with political poetry in the Russian tradition.[53] By speaking through others' voices, Fanailova charts an unusual rhetorical pathway: civic poetry often speaks in the first-person plural, but she often writes in the third person, if within a first-person frame. That crossing of lyric and narrative is another Fanailova signature, one with political and ethical implications.[54]

Nowhere is that seen more clearly than in two poems, companion pieces: "Lena and People" ("Lena i liudi," 2008) and "Lena and Lena" ("Lena i Lena," 2010).[55] To use her own name (Lena being a common nickname for Elena) in the poems' titles and as a character in the poems is to do with a proper name what might otherwise be the substitutional work of pronouns. Both poems poke fun at a reader's desire for confessional poetry and the poet's own ambivalence about privacy.[56] The boundaries between public and private are crisscrossed, and the poems encode themes of empathy, solidarity, readership, and human rights, as well as sexual desire, friendship between women, and women's health.

The first poem, "Lena and People," narrates an encounter between a poet and a clerk in an all-night convenience store. Both are named Lena. The clerk recognizes the poet from the Culture channel on TV, asks to read one of her books, and eventually judges the poetry as elitist. The poet is surprised by that label and presses Lena to admit that, well, yes, she did understand this figure or that text. But it's an unrewarding conversation that leaves the poet reflecting on what she calls her wish to be liked (a whorish wish, she had called it, earlier in the poem—"akterskoe bliadskoe / Stremlenie nravit'sia").[57] The poem does not idealize Russian readers, and it ruefully recalls a scene of reading an anti-Putin poem before an audience of icily hate-filled students. But Lena the all-night cashier is the kind of reader the poet cares to reach. The poem ends:

> And of course, she's right:
> It's a complicated text,
> Even when it pretends to be simple,
> Like now

> Ну и, конечно, она права:
> Это сложный текст,
> Даже когда он притворяется простым,
> Как сейчас[58]

In acknowledging the poem's ironies, Fanailova unmasks any pretense of simplicity and asserts that Lena the cashier is more than up to the task of discerning poetry's complexities.

The superb Moscow journal *New Literary Observer* (*Novoe literaturnoe obozrenie, NLO*) created a forum around this poem, asking contributors to reflect on its politics, ethics, and aesthetics. Mikhail Iampolsky reformulated those terms as "the absolute interdependence of 'ontology' (in the widest sense of that word), ethics, and politics," on which any productive analysis of cultural formations, including poetry, depends.[59] Iampolsky's insertion of ontology into the journal's proposed triad of terms is especially pertinent to Fanailova's poetry, where the meditation on who or what one is frequently intertwined with assertions about what is wrong or right, and about Russia's history and its violence. In "Lena and People," Fanailova meditates on what it means to be such a poet, distancing herself from the familiar model of the intelligentsia poet.[60] Readers will hear in the poem an echo of Pushkin's "The Poet and the Crowd" ("Poet i tolpa," 1828).[61] His account of a fraught encounter between the poet and the people becomes Fanailova's recollected auditorium seething with angry students. But her poem stubbornly retains its faith in Lena the cashier. Dmitry Golynko, another participant in the *NLO* forum, seized on the significance of Lena the cashier's presence in the poem. He took a Levinasian approach and located an understanding or apprehension of the self through this encounter with the other.[62] Golynko took what would for Levinas be ethical as sharply political, and this, too, is persuasive. The old vertical positioning of poet towering over a public is rendered horizontal in "Lena and People"; the democratizing gesture asserts dignity and respect for both Lenas.[63]

The companion poem, "Lena and Lena," slipped under the radar a bit, eclipsed by Fanailova's widely read poems that charted the street violence, erotic adventures, and economic uncertainty of the early Putin years.[64] But the poem merits real attention: it maps the foibles of international power struggles onto experiences of grave illness and intimate relations, and it contrasts sexual encounters with enduring friendships. It blends the national and military framework of the Afghanistan poem with the personal encounters of "Lena and People." As its title announces, "Lena and Lena" also tells a story of two women with the same name. The first Lena is a human rights worker, headed to Belgrade for a rendezvous with a Palestinian lover who works for the Red Cross. Their respective occupations open the poem out to an international scene of life-saving interventions in times of conflict. It is at once a hopeful and a danger-ridden backdrop. The other Lena is a Belgrade scholar and translator of Russian literature recuperating from chemotherapy treatments. Hers is a tale of healing—the cancer, the doctors tell her, is in remission. Because of her profession, she brings a self-consciously literary context into the poem, but this is not a text about a poet and her readers. What matters here are friends and lovers, or, as the feminist slogan says, pleasure and danger.

The narrative unfolds out of order. The Belgrade encounter between Lena and her lover occupies part 1, ending at the airport as she departs. Part 2 looks back to the other Lena traveling to Hungary for cancer treatment. Quick summaries of her marriage, movements around the world of central Europe and the Middle East, literary interests, and the cancer discovery ensue, leading back to Belgrade, where she lives, and where she will meet up with the other Lena who is there to see her lover. So, part 2, after a kind of backstory, joins the time frame of part 1 when the two women reconnect. Evocations of intense sexual encounters and warm friendship contrast sharply with the poem's many references to violence, harm, and risk.[65]

History bears down on the poem in references to the 1990s civil wars in former Yugoslavia.[66] The Communist past is literally on display in the poem: Lena and Lena visit an exhibit of gifts bestowed on Comrade Tito. The war's destructions have been cleaned up: "The center is good for long walks in September / You can't see the effects of the bombings" (Gorod khorosh v sentiabre v tsentre dlia progulok / Ne vidno sledov bombardirovok).[67] But Lena the scholar remembers bombs falling in Belgrade, and the destruction and fear linger as palpably felt traces. That sense of a strong aftereffect also influences the references to cancer, linking disease to political conflict: the war, we are told, led to more cancer diagnoses. The poem does not assert that Lena's cancerous lump was from exposure to wartime chemicals or war's dangers, but cancer is contiguous with those horrors: "in former Yugo there is a lot of oncology" (V byvshei Iuge mnogo onkologii).

The body is felt in this poem not just as a site of disease (although it is also that: true to her frankness about all things somatic, Fanailova includes the moment when the lump is discovered). The body is also a means to pleasure. Lena the human rights worker speaks her desires frankly: "fucking, pure fucking," as an "instrument of cognition" (Eblia, chistaia eblia do sinikh ognei / Kak instrument poznaniia). Enthusiasm for sexual pleasure is another of Fanailova's signatures (compare the line in "Lena and People": "I love fucking, pure and simple" [ia liubliu chistuiu beskompromissnuiu ebliu]).[68] In "Lena and Lena," that pleasure has a tremendously human tenderness or earthiness, as when things go badly, and Lena tells her lover to slow down, do it again, because, after all, they're not making a smutty film. That kind of joke is common in Fanailova's work, where humor can lighten fraught political poems. A borderline between comedy and terror is treaded ever so lightly in "Lena and Lena": the Palestinian lover has a visceral and (to Lena) unpleasantly harsh reaction to hearing Hebrew spoken at a nearby café table. This is as close as the poem gets to politicizing his nationality or mentioning what are surely brutal experiences in his work for the Red Cross. Instead, his contorted face speaks volumes. Fanailova excels in this kind of psychological characterization via concrete, memorable details (as if, like Akhmatova, she had absorbed the psychological lessons of the nineteenth-century novel).[69] The comparison to Akhmatova is worth keeping in mind: Akhmatova's late, long project to write a poem without a hero as well as her lifelong ability to juxtapose the personal to the broadly historical, as in her poem "Requiem" ("Rekviem," 1935-61) are an apt model for Fanailova's large and still growing collection of poems about Ukraine.

Starting with the war's inception in 2014 and gathering intensity after 2017, Fanailova had been writing these poems. She developed some elements of the Afghanistan poem, "Lena and People," and "Lena and Lena," especially themes of bodily and verbal frankness; an ever-present sense of the remnants of historical traumas; and quotidian interpersonal exchanges offered as the small dramas in which a broader historical crisis can be felt. Fanailova's response to what began as a hybrid war was to create a hybrid text, blasts of poetry shared on Facebook and marked with hashtags to signal the accretion of something larger than any single poem. I explore this large project as performance more fully in chapter 2. Here, I zero in on the political positions taken in this work, and the poetic means for getting those positions to reverberate with readers.

Both political and aesthetic principles are already clearly laid out in "Lines for Sasha Kabanov" ("Stikhi dlia Sashi Kabanova," 2014), a poem dedicated to one of the best-known Russian-language poets living in Ukraine who, like Fanailova, took a strong pro-Ukraine position from the start. It shows how quickly she found a set of promising rhetorical features and intonations for this topic. The traits include a loosely meditative structure, as if the poet is thinking out loud; irregular but sometime intensely echoing rhyme that binds the lines together and suggests folk poetry; direct address (the poem's first word is "you" / "ty," and words are spoken to Sash, a direct-address form of the name Sasha); reliance on easily found and often pop culture sources (in this case, poems by Kabanov mentioned in the headnote to the poem); easy, even jocular self-reference alongside the harsh realities of war; and, repeatedly, the firm assertion that Russians and Ukrainians are connected by history and by blood. Toward the end of the poem, Fanailova writes:

> Sash, I am thinking today about wounds.
> As a former doctor, thinking about our countries,
> About our mutual scary wounds, which run deep.

> Саш, я сегодня думаю о ранах.
> Как доктор бывшая, о наших странах,
> О глубине взаимных страшных ран.[70]

We recognize the will to see and to read wounded bodies from "... Again they're talking about their Afghanistan," but here the poet allows the wound to be more broadly metaphorical, a wound that comes from historical injuries that fester. Fanailova is diagnosing historical trauma as a source of the violence in Ukraine and recognizing the fresh wounds that invasions and occupations will inflict.

Another key trait is Fanailova's awareness of what it means to write these poems as a woman, and sometimes to speak directly to women, as in the framing remark for a 2015 poem that begins "The flame burns blue, ice fades out" ("Sineet plamen', ugasaet led"). That poem responded to the capture and imprisonment of Nadiya Savchenko.[71] Because Savchenko was one of the first women in Ukraine to be a fighter pilot, reference to her undercuts a patriarchal pattern (men fight, women provide comfort to the fighters) that these poems can also ironically evoke. By August 2016, Fanailova would begin to use references, often as hashtags, to Lysistrata to mark these poems.

Something potentially magical or demonic exists in the power that women might exercise. In the poem inspired by the capture (more like a kidnapping, actually) of Savchenko, Fanailova writes of the Valkyries, those Norse figures of legend who have the power to decide who will live, who will die, in battle:

> The Valkyries make their nighttime flight.
> Bodies are in the prison.
> But for a good witch there is no barrier
> In her mind.

> Валькирии идут в ночной полет.
> Тела в тюрьме.
> Но для хорошей ведьмы нет преград
> В ее уме.[72]

Fanailova associates women's power with an ethics, an ability to know right from wrong, and that, too, is a consistent and unsentimental theme in the work. The poet takes positions that ally her with principles like fairness, justice, human dignity and even love (any number of poems include open assertions that love is the one thing that can save). The personal is inextricable from the political, which is to remake another old feminist slogan into a principle for a writing practice, as Fanailova has said: "The author has always been interested in the way that the personal is connected to the political and the historical."[73]

In political terms, that means that Fanailova is not analyzing the war in Ukraine as the product of global forces, of capitalism or imperialism. Instead, her purview is specific to the history of Russia, Ukraine, the USSR, and the great traumas of the twentieth century—Holodomor, the Nazi invasion, the incursions into Afghanistan and Chechnya, the rigged elections of the Putin years. She registers this shared history—shared across multiple former Soviet republics—on persons, one at a time or in small groups, and in families who bear the scars of this violence. Fanailova embeds stories of her own family. In effect, through her family, "the personal is connected to the political and the historical." Many poems include references to her brother, her mother, her father, and she turns their stories toward memories that her readers will recognize—leftover weapons hidden in a basement, a grandfather who escaped during transport to Solovki.

Fanailova signaled this direction in her work when she published two poems in 2014 entitled "My Ukrainian Family" ("Moia ukrainskaia sem'ia"), about her two grandmothers. The title was picked up by the editor (Dmitry Kuz'min) to head the whole selection of Fanailova's poems, as if he understood the significance of this gesture of affiliation with the country Russia had attacked in a hybrid war of annexation, disinformation, and military conflict. The publication also featured two poems dedicated to one of Ukraine's premier contemporary poets, Serhiy Zhadan, an important model for Fanailova's poems.[74] In the second poem to him, Fanailova lists a set of traits that Zhadan, standing in for all Ukrainians, will see as horrifyingly Russian:

This (my) country will be the death of you
Its military mathematics
Its secret services
Its illusions and constructs
Its lack of scruple
Its mendacious depravity[75]

Тебя погубит эта (моя) страна
Её военная математика
Её спецслужбы
Её иллюзии и конструкты
Её беспринципность
Её лживое гадство[76]

The characterization is harsh, but there is a marked ambivalence in the way that Fanailova inserts herself into the equation: the phrase "this (my) country" finds her acknowledging reluctantly and parenthetically that as a Russian citizen, she is responsible for this image, for these behaviors, even as she affirms her Ukrainian genealogy.

That genealogy is at the heart of the two poems to her grandmothers. Fanailova places "Second Grandmother" ("Vtoraia babka") first and finds her fearful and gloomy. The expectation of sentimental attachment to a grandmother is jettisoned, and the poem begins with a memory of not liking her. The details about food (even her cooking is bad) and physicality are strong:

Her hands were dry and sinewed
She never hugged me
And when she did, it would have been better she hadn't[77]

Её руки были сухими и жилистыми
Она никогда меня не обнимала
А когда обнимала, лучше бы этого не было[78]

But later, the poet comes to admire this grandmother's fortitude, her ability to put men in their place. The poem ends with a dreamlike memory of traveling along the Don River, itself a microcosm of the region's history, to visit her.

In the second poem, Fanailova turns to her "First Grandmother" ("Pervaia babka"), considered first because she's her mother's mother. The contrast is apparent from the start: unlike the culinary failures of her second grandmother, this one makes exemplary borscht.

I still cook borscht from her recipes.
She was my goddess. I was incapable of criticizing her.
Even with cause. Today, she would have been in favor of Crimea.
As, in her day, she was for Stalin.
You can understand her.

Её борщи я варю до сих пор.
Она была моей богиней. Я не могу её критиковать.
Хотя есть за что. Сейчас она была бы за Крым.
Как в своё время за Сталина.
Её можно понять.[79]

That last sentence carries the ethical weight in this poem: Fanailova shows by example how one understands someone whose politics are anathema. The poem is loving in a way that is stunningly wholehearted, a physical and earthy love that includes caring for this grandmother as she ages and ails. The poem ends in a dream that the grandmother has bequeathed her house to the poet. It is a fantasy of receiving some physical, tangible evidence of all that she has inherited from this forebear, and a fantasy that puts the poet's origins again in Ukraine, where the house lies. To end with dreams is to show how these poems, for all their reference to the current political turmoil, rely on the unconscious, on the desires that are repressed in daily speech and on the traumas suffered and repressed.

The dreams in both poems have a hopeful narrative of homecoming. Fanailova's Ukraine poems would come to have Homer's *Iliad* as one of their sources, but at this moment in 2014, her inspiration is the *Odyssey*, its enactment of a journey home. She has the memories of a family's past to inspire her own identification as Ukrainian and to set the stage for an act of writing about this war that would urge her readers to inhabit the hearts and minds of those who fight, as well as those whose lives are maimed by the violence. Fanailova would go on to write dozens of poems about the war, and she reposted links to "My Ukrainian Family" after Russia's February 2022 invasion.[80] That metaphor of family is one that never leaves her, and I would speculate that the rhetorical residue of her political judgment is that the violence in Ukraine as well as the escalating repression in Belarus are seen as forms of civil war. She leaves no doubt which side she is on.[81]

Maria Stepanova and the Ruins of the Body

The poet Maria Stepanova has a set of formal skills and a vibrant poetic imagination that earned her immediate and sustained attention from readers and prize-giving juries alike. Admired initially for her ballads, she essentially reinvented this nineteenth-century form for postmodern audiences. But her wide-ranging oeuvre includes work in expressive prose, as well as a distinctive reinvention of the lyric as a kind of epic folk narrative that is capacious enough to unfold subtle political and ethical arguments.

Stepanova's sheer virtuosity could make her seem a poet's poet, but she has also emerged as a commanding public intellectual, a rare attainment for women in Russian public life. Most important here is her work as chief editor for the web-based journal *OpenSpace* (2008–12) and for its successor, the vibrant and crowd-funded *Colta*.[82] With these platforms, she created sites for essays and reviews of cultural innovations and events, as well as for freedom-loving writers and thinkers to share fresh ideas. Like Fanailova at Radio Svoboda, Stepanova became an important figure in journalism, if largely working behind the scenes. That work's ripple effects are great, and it should change how we view Stepanova: she brings a nuanced, well-informed sense of Russia's history to all that she writes.

She is particularly adept as an essayist, often taking a text or event as a jumping-off point for a broader statement about Russia's past and present.[83] Stepanova's leading cultural position was solidified when she published the genre-defying book *In Memory of Memory* (*Pamiati pamiati*, 2017); it won prizes in and out of Russia and appeared in foreign translation in multiple languages at high-profile presses. Many parts of this huge book began as separate essays published on high-traffic online sites, teaching an audience how to read its excavation of the poet's family history. *In Memory of Memory* was oriented around the process of discovery rather than the facts uncovered. There is a moment when Stepanova lists the traumatic historical events of the twentieth century thought to have spared her family: Revolution and Civil War, the Holocaust, the Terror, the War. But she discovers that images of her family's safety were largely illusory.[84] That realization lets her inscribe her own family into the shared cultural memories of her generation.[85] None of us is untouched, she suggests, as she draws on Marianne Hirsch's work with post-memory.[86] Stepanova thus has another thing in common with Fanailova: a readiness to probe the stories of her own family as a means to rejigger the common language for understanding identity and history. That labor can be seen quite early, in a poem she wrote about her great-grandmother, "Sarra on the Barricades" ("Sarra na barrikadakh," 2005).[87]

Still, something changed when Russia annexed Crimea in 2014 and went to war with Ukraine. Like Fanailova, Stepanova let the violence of the war into her work, but rather than the centrifugal and generative energies of Fanailova's many poems, Stepanova concentrated the topic into individual long poems, or cycles. Her subsequent work shows that this is a sustained, generative development in her poetry.[88] Here I focus on two long poems that mix epic and lyric: "Spolia" (2014) and "War of the Beasts and the Animals" ("Voina zverei i zhivotnykh," 2015), published together in her book *Spolia* (2015). Each is complicated in its own way, and they are tightly bound to each other. These complementary poems pushed Stepanova's poetics in new directions. Some elements build on her earlier work, including the guiding rhetorical practice that gave the small book its name: *spolia* is an architectural term, designating the stone bits of a ruined structure or monument repurposed for new building. These are the spoils of warfare, for it is in conquest that the practice finds its origins, and Stepanova surely intends the martial resonance by taking the Latin word as the poem's title. But the rhetorical practice of citation and redirection was hers from the start. To call this practice *spolia* is to emphasize how much the source material is itself in ruins; thus her citational practices are different from, say, those of the Acmeists. Mandelstam could boast of his freedom to rearrange the gods in an early poem as an allegory of his transformation of the poetic tradition, but his rearrangements were stabilizing rather than explosive.[89] Stepanova preserves the ruination, using deformations and fragmentations of language to stake out the limits of language to convey war's violence.

The poet finds other rhetorical means to firm up the authority of the text. With peerless irony, she writes in "Spolia":

if you gather it all up
here's what was said:

she is incapable of speaking for herself,
so she is always ruled by others

that's why her story is full of repetitions
and the outmoded forms are fake

and there is no telling where the quotations come from
is it nineteen thirty or nineteen seventy
because she quotes it all at the same time

and not so as to remind us, but just to fill the holes

(which is especially awful)[90]

если собрать в точку
было сказано вот что:

она не-способна говорить за себя,
поэтому ею всегда правят другие

потому в ее истории столько повторов
и фальсифицируются отжившие формы

и не понять, откуда какая цитата,
из тридцатого или семидесятого года
потому что она цитирует всё одновременно

и не чтобы напомнить, а чтобы наполнить дыры

(что особенно жутко)[91]

Mixing up the citations from the years 1930 and 1970 signals that history itself creates frightening points of similarity and contiguity—and Stepanova's final parenthetical observation about the horror of what she has done registers history's assaults, especially in this poem of war. In the lines that follow, the referent for *she* switches to Russia or to the country, both grammatically feminine nouns. Each acts as a clear subject for the "material"—the diamonds, the forests—that the poem will go on to list. If Stepanova were a different poet, say, Galina Rymbu, this list would lead to an argument about materialism, dialectical or otherwise. And there are glimpses of that economic argument in fact, in an image of natural gas, so desired on the international market, that follows the passage I cited.

But for Stepanova (and for Rymbu as well), materiality is a philosophical category. It is, like *spolia*, an essential building block of creative work. As in the lines of "Spolia" that artfully name poets from Innokenty Annensky to Anna Glazova, what is being built is an edifice of culture, one with a spoiled history but also with secret recesses poets can pry open, tugging at the edges of forgotten words and obscure persons. Those discoveries are born of repetitions and of patterns that also make the wars of the 2010s legible through references to other conflicts. The philosophical and aesthetic work being done in the poems, in other words, means that the Ukraine war is analyzed for its aftershocks, rather than as unfolding narrative, even of the fractured sort we might find in Fanailova's poems.

"War of the Beasts and the Animals" is built somewhat differently from "Spolia," relying on the deceptively simple genre of the fable to create a meditation on history. In effect, imagery and lexicon are deployed to show how the contemporary war has reenacted military invasions of the past, going back to the Igor Tale.[92] The poem boldly names the fable's central conflict as a civil war, likening Stepanova's point of view to Fanailova's. She, too, inscribes her personal history into a larger public history. Earlier, Stepanova had been quite reticent about family stories or any other self-reference.[93] But much had changed by the time she wrote her two Ukraine poems. She probes her family's history material deeply in *In Memory of Memory* (written at the same time) and dedicates "Spolia" to her father. "Spolia" recalls the factory accident that maimed her great-grandfather, a cousin Lyodik who dies in the war, and many others. These are fleeting references, yet they do the work of inscribing the poet's personal history into the moment when a nation goes to war.

The use of place names is similarly oblique. Whereas Fanailova uses recognizable contemporary place names to anchor her Ukraine poems, Stepanova once again chooses a less direct path. She keeps open "the imagination's supply lines to the past," in Seamus Heaney's resonant phrase.[94] Thus, for example, Stepanova embeds two place names from the Igor Tale early in "War of the Beasts and the Animals," Korsun and Surozh (the ancient name for present day Sudak).[95] From the many place names in the Igor Tale, she pointedly selects two in Crimea, an allusion to Russia's 2014 annexation. Similarly, in the photography section of "Spolia" mentions a 1938 image of Crimea. The poet sees the past as if it predicted the present violence. Connecting Russia's incursion into Ukraine with the failed battle commemorated in the Igor Tale is also a prophecy of Russian defeat.

Stepanova's use of those distant place names calls attention to language itself. When we speak of a hybrid war in Ukraine, we name its mix of military violence with disinformation campaigns. It is a war that recruits language to its cause, and a war that distorts and defiles words in the process. Stepanova's poems find a way to fight back through language. She is trying to wrest back words from a language that has been used to wreak violence, to show us that language itself already holds the tools for political resistance and repair.[96] For the twentieth century, the most resonant example of that project was Paul Celan's poetry, written in the aftermath of the Nazi exterminations. Stepanova would presumably not object to the association: her *In Memory of Memory* references Celan, although her model is more closely W. G. Sebald, another brilliant re-creator of a new German literature that never loses sight of the Nazi horrors. But whereas Sebald pushed linguistic disassembly in the direction of narrative prose fragmentation, Stepanova, like Celan, lets the poetic deformations do their damage to individual words. Here, too, Heaney's writings about poetry are unusually apt: he describes the "cultural depth-charges latent in certain words and rhythms" as including the "energies beating in and between words."[97] One could argue that nearly every line of Stepanova's poetry generates those energies, to the point where meanings are blown apart.

An especially radical example occurs in "War of the Beasts and the Animals" when she spaces syllables from recognizable words across the line, inviting us also to recombine them into new words as if the lines could be read against their own semantics. The nod to Celan or Sebald may be in the mention of Germans in the first line (itself motivated by the poem's allusions to the USSR's enemy from the Second World War). The claim, in effect, that "we are not Germans" is succeeded by assertions that we are not people or fish or things or broken bits of pottery or starlings or a cherry tree. The choices may sound arbitrary in English, but in Russian, the diction is motivated by sound repetition. The lines culminate in a passing abandonment of the negations to assert that we are, in fact, two things: bears (that emblematically Russian beast) and music, two words that also recombine each other's sounds (heard almost jarringly in the instrumental plural: *medvezhami* and *muzykami*). In some lines, then, the sounds cohere as words; in others, they are broken into syllables. This passage is twenty-six lines long, and here is a sample of it:

> we no germ ans
> not us germ ans
> furry hided
> infant young
>
> no man wo man we
> no be coming
> we no germ ans
> clack ing blood
>
> мы не нем цы
> не мы нем цы
> шерстью крыты
> их младенцы
>
> не лю ди мы
> их становья
> мы не нем цы
> цы кать кровью[98]

No translation into English can do this sound play justice, although the division of "Germans" to "germ" and "ans" at least shows the disruptive potential of the split. In Russian, rather than a suggestion of disease or infection, and rather than a syllable split that goes against morphology, the word's root lets the language itself do the poet's work. By splitting the word for Germans, *nemtsy*, into two semantically resonant syllables, readers first get *nem*, meaning "without speech" or "unable to use language." That makes the first three syllables of the line "my ne nem tsy" into a fierce assertion, effectively, that "we will not be silent." Then, the second syllable of *nemtsy* becomes the root of the verb heard in the last line cited here, *tsykat'* (again, like *nemtsy*, split into two syllables, *tsy* and *kat'*). The onomatopoeic verb *tsykat'* has a whole host of semantic possibilities, including the making of the sound "tsy" to get someone (often an animal) to stop doing something. But here Stepanova is surely also alluding to birds aggressively making a sound to warn off predators, as if the bloody ways of warfare (including war with Germans, what the Soviets called the Great Patriotic War) underlie these lines as well.

The poet is redirecting her poem's theme of a war in the animal kingdom, reminding us not that animals have no access to language—the *we* of these lines insists repeatedly on the capacity to use speech—but that the language available for use must be re-created from the most basic sounds. Mikhail Iampolsky saw this passage as evidence that war's killing reduces persons to animals, to beasts, to decaying matter.[99] Intriguing, and an argument about animals and decay also appears in the political poetry of Galina Rymbu, but I read Stepanova's philosophical underpinnings here somewhat differently from Iampolsky: these lines that grope toward language are also the words of the dead. Those who have perished in war are the ones refusing to be silent, so that this text, like so much else in Stepanova, is haunted. These ghosts' fractured language has given a paradoxical life force to the poet's own language.

In a 2017 interview, Stepanova said that the two poems in *Spolia* were "written during the start of the war in Ukraine, which shook me to my core. I tried to deal with a reality unfamiliar to me in the way that a ruined pagan temple was wildly incomprehensible to Italians in the tenth century. I tried to understand how words were changing, how the relationships between words were changing."[100] What she found was a way to use language's potential to become a mass of ruins, not as a static outcome, but as a form of endless ruination. Bad news kept coming, she said in that same interview, and her poems became large shape-shifting vessels that could accommodate its endless destructions.

The political project of these poems, then, goes even beyond resisting the Ukraine war.[101] The poems want to jolt readers into an awareness of their power to take back control of the relationships of words to things, their capacity to live at a tempo of their own choosing even in an era of such overwhelming chaos and violence. The critic and philosopher Alexander Markov has written that "Spolia" constitutes "an insistent demand to be free, to carry out judgment as a free person." For him that is "the very air of this poetry."[102] It is striking that he uses the metaphor of air here, as Stepanova did in that same interview, describing her ambitions for these poems to enable freer breathing.

"Spolia" and "War of the Beasts and the Animals" push a familiar metaphor of the poet's breath as a measure of speech and of artmaking in new directions: Stepanova specifies the ethical implications of her long-standing practice of speaking in the voices of others. That had been the trademark of her ballads, and it was perfected in the lyrics of *Kireevsky*, her 2012 book of poems. In "Spolia," however, the first voice that the poet mimics is that of some imagined critics, who wonder why she doesn't just speak in her own voice; they cast this refusal as if it were an aesthetic flaw. Stepanova mocks their criticisms in the emphatically ordinary image of a bagel: her voicelessness is like the bagel's hole. That apparently empty space, however, is filled with the air of potential utterance, filled as if with the recollected citations that later in the poem she stands accused of conflating.

The lines of "Spolia" spread down the page in ways that open a different kind of space, which is why Mikhail Iampolsky observed that the world of this poem "finds itself in an extreme metaphysical state of fragmentation and objectification."[103] He compared the cited words of others to old photographs, and reminded us that photographs, "that technological and metaphysical means of pausing, fixing reality," are used repeatedly in the poem (and, I would add, extensively in *In Memory of Memory*).

When photography appears in "Spolia," in a passage of some seventy lines, the technology of the camera is foregrounded: the passage begins with the camera's "click" (shchelk), and what follows is a linguistic registration of the fragmentation and ruination Iampolsky observes.[104] The click elicits similar sounds, including the click of a gun trigger, and similar-sounding words. But then we get a series of internally divided words, with the prefix "trans" (Russian "pere") separated out. A linguistic as well as spatial and temporal transformation is being enacted by the broken transfers of the lines, and the dead mix with the living. Stepanova's family members make their appearances, turning up as if preserved in snapshots. The poet integrates her process of studying these images into the descriptions, very much as she would do in *In Memory of Memory*. There is a group of Jews who are oddly described as unassigned or unattached ("ne pristavlennye"), as if apart from the usual flow of history, but the poet quickly attaches herself to them in the next line, a parenthetical comment "(we are Jews)" ([my-evrei]). There is a grandmother seen at an age only a little older than the poet, one of two old women seated on a bench. And there is her mother, aged five, wearing a silk hair ribbon. There are relatives from Saratov, Leningrad, Khabarovsk, and Gorky and an image of all these dead relatives gathered around a May 9 Victory Day celebration, all temporal boundaries breached in a kind of photographic act of *spolia* creation.

Most important, though, is a little girl who will remember this all ("devochka, kotoraia vse eto zapomnit"), an echo of the reference to her mother, shown as a young child. But just as surely, the little girl who will remember is the poet herself, a fully grown adult woman of magnificent powers to comprehend and transmit complex ideas, but also someone who can be taken back to the past by the imaginative leaps of the poems. A beautiful example of this transport appears in "War of the Beasts and the Animals":

> sing to me of how, in an alley of two-hundred-year-old trees on a
>   family estate,
> the bones lay under a birch tree, catching the light, turned bare,
> as if glad to be there, spread out, chattering like girlfriends
> there was no point to us, we didn't lend each other our hands
> we are as if again in the nursery, tightly swaddled

> спой мне о том, как в усадьбе родной, в двухсотлетней аллее
> кости лежат под березонькой, отсвечивая и голея
> любо в рассеяньи быть, подруге стрекочет подруга
> мало от нас было прока мы не поддержали друг друга
> снова мы в комнатке детской лежим, спеленуты туго[105]

It is characteristic of Stepanova's transformations of time that the bones of the dead would be like the swaddled babies of the living, chattering like old friends, so that the bones are also like the adults caring for those infants. That the poet would revive the bones of the dead is not new. As Mikhail Iampolsky articulated brilliantly in his reading of *Kireevsky*, Stepanova showed early on how to revive the voices of the dead.[106] But bones offer a different set of figurations from voices. By the end of the 2010s, partly because of the ways that war sharpens the focus on the potential harm to bodies, and partly because of a deepening commitment to the politics of the body, Stepanova was writing more compellingly about the way that voice emerged from a body, and what it means to affirm the enduring nature of both body and voice.[107]

I thus end this discussion of Stepanova with a text that takes the identification of poet with young girl found in "Spolia" toward a politics of the body. In 2020, Stepanova published "Girls Undressed" ("Devochki bez odezhdy").[108] Like the pairing of "Spolia" with "War of the Beasts and the Animals," this poem has a companion piece: "The Body Returns" ("Telo vozvrashchaetsia," 2018).[109] The latter imagines a woman's body safely buried, deep in the earth as the source of language, but "Girls Undressed" stays steadily above ground in a world of harm. It is one of Stepanova's most explicitly feminist poems, and a leading poet of the younger generation of feminists, Oksana Vasiakina, said it was the most important poem to her the year it appeared.[110]

"Girls Undressed" is a long poem: 150 lines, fifteen ten-line stanzas. It is compulsively readable and totally unnerving. Here is its beginning:

> There is always something that says: undress
> And show, remove and set aside, lie down
> And spread out, let me look,
> Open, touch it, did you look?
> There is always a room with a horizontal
> Surface, you always stand there like a tree,
> Always lie there like a felled tree,
> With toneless branches thrown back,
>
> Between fingers the earth, the mouth full of fingers,
> Apples left unguarded, done for.

> Всегда есть то, что говорит: разденься
> И покажи, сними и положи, ляг
> И раздвинь, дай посмотреть,
> Открой, потрогай его, ты посмотрела?
> Всегда есть комната с горизонтальной
> Поверхностью, всегда стоишь там как дерево,
> Всегда лежишь как дерево, как упало,
> С глухими запрокинутыми ветками,
>
> Между пальцами земля, во рту пальцы,
> Яблоки не уберегла.[111]

"Girls Undressed" is about a structure of violence and humiliation inflicted on women. The poem's intensity comes from its litany of harms, from the endless forms of dread and shame, and from the fact that the violence is inflicted not on adults but on the young. The age of fifteen recurs in the poem and is formally allegorized in its fifteen stanzas. The number fifteen (piatnadtsat') is surely chosen because of the sonic waves that can spin out of its sounds (the word for spot or stain, "piatno," or for heel, "piatka," seem to emerge from its first syllable, "piat"): the poet writes early on, "Fifteen—this is the number for a stain" (Piatnadtsat'—eto chislo piatna).[112] But that tender age of fifteen also lets the poet record the mix of curiosity and shame experienced by someone having a first sexual encounter in a way that is imposed rather than freely desired.

This is how it begins, the poet seems to say, and once begun, how it lives in the world of eternal repetition. Thus, the temporal adverb in dozens of lines of poetry is "always" ("vsegda," repeated thirty-three times over 150 lines).[113] "Girls Undressed" is marked by a high degree of syntactic and verbal repetition, creating the sense of a closed and unchanging world. Rather than the layering of literary and cultural allusion that marks her other texts, particularly "Spolia" and "War of the Beasts and the Animals," this poem lets Stepanova obsessively tread back and forth over the same terrain of exploitation, injury, harm—but also recovery.[114] She writes as if compelled, and to do so in a poem about forms of compulsion, of force, is paradoxically bold.

That possibility for repair reverberates in the title of the book where "Girls Undressed" appears, *The Old World. Life Repair*. In this poem, "life repair" emerges not in the lexicon (the phrase does not appear here), but in its images. They are developed through repetition and limited to two semantic fields. The first has to do with food, specifically fruit, beginning with the apple in the first stanza and then in terms for body parts that use the image of the apple (Adam's apple, and the Russian word for eyeball, "glaznoe iabloko") or of pears ("grushi," slang for breasts). The apple inevitably conjures up the temptations of the Garden of Eden, and Stepanova's revisionist attitude toward myth has her exposing the fake lure of forbidden knowledge—what looks like seduction becomes the violence it veils.[115]

The other metaphorical field is the tree, born of the same myth but bringing the knowledge of sexual violence. The tree's woodenness, its stolidity, its long-lived thereness (as if an emblem of that eponymous "old life") are repeatedly invoked. It is a tree to which the girl's body is compared again and again, as early as the second stanza's parentheticals: "(she was like a log) (why are you so wooden?)" ([ona byla kak brevno] [chego ty kak dereviannaia?]).[116] But what seems wooden and unfeeling is alive to the insult and pain inflicted. The tree's status as living matter is emphasized in the image of bark opened out to reveal the wood within, as if it were the musculature of a body:

> And if he wants to, he can look into the very
> Center of the wood, where the flesh
> Is still moist and seems to smolder.

> И тот, кто хочет, может заглядывать в самую
> Середину ее древесины, туда, где плоть
> Еще влажная и кажется, что дымится.[117]

Trees also suggest a setting in the woods, the woods of folktales, where danger lurks. The trees lead to a hunter, a woodcutter, and a fisherman, predators all. In the final stanzas even a soldier turns up, consolidating the masculine force that brings harm—and shame and silence—into the poem.

The poem destroys that silence, speaking forth the ungraspable nature of a world in which girls are treated like trees, their limbs splayed out like branches, their bodies numb with the relentless gaze and command of the other. What Stepanova has achieved in her merciless representation of the subjective experience of that numbness is to show that she who is treated so brutally can yet speak. A girl who is turned into a tree is always in some ways repeating the salvation of Daphne, turned into a laurel tree to save her from rape. Stepanova, who has thrown her voice in so many ways, here offers it up as the speech of one who may be physically and emotionally numb, but who will not be silent.

F Letter: The Example of Galina Rymbu

Alongside Stepanova and Fanailova are a group of poets associated with the web journal and platform *F Letter* (*F Pis'mo*), which takes its name from the seminar in feminist theory and philosophy that Galina Rymbu initiated in 2017. Key figures have included Elena Kostyleva, Yulia Podlubnova, Ekaterina Simonova, Oksana Vasiakina, and Lida Yusupova. It tells us something about the broad cultural impact of the group to note that before 2022, they lived in cities as different as Petersburg, Moscow, Ekaterinburg, Lviv, and Toronto. In 2020, the Andrei Bely Prize jury gave *F Letter* an outstanding literary project award. The jury singled out their "collective creation of new political languages for poetry" and noted their collective work as a new model for what, during the days of unofficial poetry, had been largely author-driven innovations.[118] It is fitting that this chapter conclude, then, with the political and aesthetic innovations made possible by this new wave of feminist poetry.[119] By treating these mostly younger poets after the work of Fanailova and Stepanova, I want to be careful to avoid creating a clear genealogy or straight line of descent.[120] There is evidence of affinity and respect in both directions.[121] An impressive group of younger poets is also emerging, particularly in the aftermath of the new phase of the Russia-Ukraine war. Activist and poet Daria Serenko is perhaps the best known and is likely to be still more prominent because of her leadership in the Feminist Antiwar Resistance.[122] But she is far from alone, and establishing the lines of affiliation among these poets is ongoing and compelling work.[123]

The scope of the poetry of *F Letter* poets, however, is often distinct. The orientation toward activism and the readiness to call out offensive, inappropriate, or condescending statements is much more concentrated, exemplified by highly charged statements that refused the Andrei Bely Prize outright.[124] Each editor of *F Letter* wrote an individual statement to explain their refusal. In her statement, Rymbu pushed back against the praise for their collective work, because, as she put it, the award could have also named the editors in the award statement and thus reject the long-standing cultural practices that have left women anonymous or nameless.[125]

Rymbu wrote in her introduction to the bilingual anthology *F Letter* that theirs are not the first feminist voices in Russian poetry.[126] She named Anna Al'chuk and Marina Temkina as forebears (one might also mention Nina Iskrenko, a major figure still not fully appreciated, and elsewhere Rymbu has put forward Elena Shvarts as a model for writing the body, at once ecstatic and ungainly).[127] But it is telling that Rymbu would single out Temkina and Al'chuk, clear models for current work. The latter was adept at conceptualizing the cultural work feminists needed to undertake.[128] Al'chuk's palindromes, morphological play, and artfully laid-out poems offer a fine juxtaposition to the post-Conceptualist, historically rich work of Temkina, which can be in turns funny, sad, wry, and expansive. Her poems readily take on the cultural legacies of major literary figures as well as the traumatic memories gathered from her work with refugees and immigrants.[129]

Temkina's best-known work for many years was the poem "Category of the Brassiere" ("Kategoriia lifchika," 1994).[130] The explicit body imagery of that text, its long conversational lines, mocking lists, and readiness to send up a sexist culture that objectifies women's bodies are all features that Galina Rymbu adapted in her poem "My Vagina" ("Moia vagina," 2020).[131] The controversy it generated threatened to overwhelm the poem itself. It was first posted to Facebook, where a portion of the comments, including from some other poets, were so demeaning that Rymbu used them to create a new poem, "Great Russian Literature" ("Velikaia russkaia literatura," 2020).[132] But many rose to Rymbu's support, both creating poem responses of their own and stressing that "My Vagina" originated as a means of supporting the body-positive feminism of artist and activist Yulia Tsvetkova, whose persecution is directly mentioned in the poem.[133] This poem, then, much like the poem Rymbu wrote in solidarity with protests in support of Aleksey Navalny in 2020, was conceived as a political act.[134] She spoke not as an orator proclaiming truth, but rather as a person seeking to understand political injustice. As she wrote in her poem of solidarity with Russian protesters:

> I write long poems,
> long, like the endless hours in a jail cell,
> because I always get confused about what I wanted to say,
> as if I were giving testimony
> and not certain precisely
> about what happened.

> Я пишу длинные стихи,
> длинные, как сутки в ментовке,
> потому что всегда путаюсь—что хотела сказать,
> как будто даю показания
> и не уверена точно,
> в том, что происходило.[135]

Rymbu's lengthy poems allow her the mental space to think through an experience that, like feminism's enduring slogan, is political and personal at once. Her poem "My Vagina," after all, took as its subject, signaled by the possessive pronoun of its title, the impact of having a body part regarded as if its representation, integrity, indeed its very name were controlled by a patriarchal social order. And yet her poem insists not that body parts lack social meaning, but that she can decide how to frame that meaning—not the state, the medical industry, her parents, the church, or strange men, all of whom she lists as having an interest in her vagina.

Her purview in "My Vagina" is large, beginning with the opening of the poem, "a son came out of my vagina" (iz moei vaginy vyshel syn); that miracle of birth is like Courbet's painting of the origin of the world, which Rymbu seems to refer to in one of the poem's closing lines, "my world is a vagina" (moi mir—vagina).[136] In addition to childbirth, multiple sexual acts and menstruation come into the poem, evoked with enthusiastic frankness. The poet doesn't just insist that she should be the one to lay out the meanings of her bodily orifices; she also insists on owning that discourse—the possessive pronoun of the poem's title is made meaningful throughout. But so are the public, political meanings of women's bodies, and the poet makes clear the vulnerabilities of the body subjected to a male gaze or to the state's control. Those vulnerabilities are physiological as well, and the poem is written against a background where the body is conceived as a site of suffering, another reason it opens with a scene of childbirth. The birth itself becomes a form of wounding, as the poet records having been stitched up after the tears of labor.

One question to be asked, based on this poem and on the work that Rymbu has published since her move to Ukraine in 2018, is how her poetry has changed. In her first three books, she wrote in ways that allied her with the new social poetry of the *[Translit]* group, and she had an explicit and personal view of how its philosophical and theoretical accounts of the political could make their way into her poetry. As she put it, in an interview that focused on the poems of her book *Life in Space* (*Zhizn' v prostranstve*, 2018): "For the last few years, I have been trying to work with something like a phenomenology of political reception, with complex political (and not just political) affects. I'm interested in understanding and studying a different type of political sensibility, one which doesn't reduce to simple, recognizable affects and images (anger, deception, the crowd, etc.)—or in uncovering behind these recognizable images a multiplicity of dimensions and meanings."[137] In 2020, Rymbu restated this principle, using a concrete series of questions to elucidate how that "phenomenology of political reception" could work. She wrote, "I call my writing political because, as a feminist and leftist, I seek answers to complex questions in my poems, questions that have disturbed me since childhood: 'why are there haves and have-nots?'; 'why do people hate each other?'; 'is a world without violence and wars possible?'; 'what is freedom?'; 'how to be together, as one, and what is the feeling of shared solidarity?'; 'how to move forward and imagine a better future, in spite of pain and suffering?'; 'why is our thinking so catastrophic, and is it possible to live as if accustomed to catastrophe?' etc."[138]

Many of the poems that make up her 2018 Russian-language collection *Life in Space* follow almost uncannily on that last question: they unfold a set of meditations on living in a post-catastrophic world.[139] A profound irony of Rymbu's work and one of its deep strengths is that she is determined not to deny the end-of-the-world feel that attaches to far too much of contemporary

life (and thus can write poems that have a kind of sci-fi quality in their imagina-
tion of environmental and social catastrophe), even as she refuses to give up
on utopian dreams of what she calls "a better future," or a "world without vio-
lence and wars." A concrete instantiation of this doubled refusal turns up in
the specifics of poetic subjectivity as she projects it, and this particularly shows
up in terms of sexual politics: without diminishing the reality of sexual harm
and sexual violence, she calmly creates a poetic speaker who affirms the iden-
tity positions of queer, trans, and nonbinary people.[140] An important political
position is staked out by the neutral intonation in such inclusiveness.

Rymbu's affiliation with *F Letter*, her advocacy for feminist causes, and her
efforts for women's education in feminist thinking have thus not changed her
poetic direction so much as confirmed certain tendencies, allowing a more
explicit politics of gender. I want to stay with that neutral tone for a moment,
because it can feel quite different from the exclamatory rhetoric of some poems
(I think of the sequence, in all caps no less, of "FIRE! FIRE! FIRE!" [OGON'!
OGON'! OGON'!] in a poem of 2014).[141] I am reminded of a description
Eugene Ostashevsky offered of the changes in Elena Fanailova's writing, which
he called an experiment with neutral intonation, seemingly stripped of rhetori-
cal features associated traditionally with poetry—not just meter or rhyme, but
also metaphor and other tropes.[142] There is a density in figuration in the poems
in Rymbu's first book, *The Moving Space of Revolution* (*Peredvizhnoe prostranstvo
revoliutsii*, 2014), which includes the poem I just mentioned, but in the later
work, unusual, striking images are sparser, if more striking still.

Any rejection of poetic affect is more apparent than real, because the poet
(as is true of Fanailova) continues to use lineation, repetition, and irony in
meaningful ways, and even the poems that seem most extravagantly to repro-
duce an unpoetic public language are rife with irony and juxtaposition.[143] She
relies on the parataxis of lists, laden with nouns in a way that will remind
American readers of Walt Whitman or Allen Ginsberg; it would not surprise
me to learn that some of this technique was indeed learned from Ginsberg's
Howl (1954–55), although there has been a pull back from the high-pitched
rhetoric of a poem like *Howl*.[144] Rymbu seems to be trying to awaken from the
dream described in a 2018 poem, "The Holiday" ("Prazdnik"), "I dream that
we / will never know: what is *writing accessible to all*?" (mne snitsia, chto my /
nikogda ne uznaem: chto takoe—*pis'mo dostupnoe vsem*?).[145] Even the phras-
ing here shows how Rymbu can make meaningful, small choices that distance
her poetics from what might be understood, pace Jakobson, as everyday com-
munication: italics mark the phrase "*writing accessible to all*" as borrowed, pre-

sumably from the theories that inform the work of *[Translit]*. Its reinvigorated Marxism is likely an ideology Rymbu supports, but one whose principles she interrogates. How to make a poetry accessible but preserve its sense of mystery and authority, its ability to embed subtle political analysis into its scenes of reported events and of scenes of daily life? That might be understood as the driving force of much of her work in and after 2018, and the poem I have just cited, "The Holiday," could read as exemplary in retaining some of the dense metaphoricity of earlier work but resolving, in its last lines, into a scene of delicate negotiation among friends and a celebratory sharing of food.[146]

Food as sustenance plays an outsized role in Rymbu's poetry, and precisely because her metaphors can generally be so lush, one senses a strong contrast with traditions of writing about foodstuffs in a context of plenitude. The pastoral traditions of writing about harvest come to mind here, like Keats's great ode "To Autumn" (1820). His "mellow fruitfulness" feels worlds away from the hunger that marks more than one of Rymbu's poems, and not just because Keats was writing two hundred years ago in England.[147] An exemplary modernist revision of Keats's poem might be Seamus Heaney's "Blackberry-Picking," which has in common with Rymbu's poetic world an emphasis on a remembered childhood memory and Heaney's own marked awareness of the hunger and deprivation of Ireland in his young years. But Heaney's poem retains Keats's rhetoric of plenitude even as he strips away his idealism: the vast quantities of picked berries get hoarded in a bath and begin to rot. Heaney can lament "a rat-grey fungus, glutting on our cache," so that "all the lovely canfuls smelt of rot."[148]

Rymbu would surely love that flickering suggestion of rats glutting on berries because the fungus is as if colored by their fur. This metaphor of decay finds resonance in her work, but the disturbing plenitude does not. She writes of food largely as lack, a gaping absence that is not unique to her own childhood memories of hunger. In a 2020 poem, "Summer: Gates of the Body" ("Leto: Vorota tela"), she writes:

and my head is like the head of a large restless bird moving left to right,
thinking of what to do and how to do it:
he's hungry, I'm hungry, they are hungry.
almost the whole world is hungry.[149]

а голова как у большой тревожной птицы вертится туда-сюда,
думает, что сделать, как сделать:
он голоден, я голодна, они голодны.
почти весь мир уже голоден.[150]

In this poem, the body's dysfunction (the poem's term is *dysphoria*) corresponds to a broken system of nourishment or sustenance: the kitchen is filthy, the berries are tasteless, dead-looking mint and cold dill are spread on the table, and there is only tepid water to sip as if after an illness or milk straight from the cow that turns bitter in the mouth. Unlike the autumn harvest celebrated by Keats, this hot summer makes the body feel swollen, covered by a layer of fat that itself seems revoltingly edible. But as the poem progresses, as often happens in Rymbu's poetry, utopian dreams reverse the negative valences of specific images, so that even the association of a bodily surface as edible is transformed into a beloved son's tiny blemish that is so sweetly appealing one wants to taste it.[151] The food gradually becomes a bit more appealing but still teeters on the edges of ambivalence: sour soup in a familiar old pot, sausage made with cellulose, towering stacks of tortes pictured in a fancy magazine that urges the Mediterranean diet, as if mocking the straitened circumstances in which such journals are read. In the end, there is a walk home carrying cellophane packages of berries, a form of consolation. Not the hand-picked berries of Heaney's memories, but also not their rot. Instead, the image dissolves into berry juice, the color of menstrual blood, and once again food and body conjoin, this time not in disgust but in that same calmly neutral intonation, describing bodies marked by time.

Rymbu's most extensive meditation on food is aptly named "Poem for Food" ("Stikhi dlia edy," 2020). It opens with a child's acquisition of the most basic food, bread, as if the rhythmic engine of the poem needs this food/fuel to be set into motion. The motion is the child's, too, as she walks, and munches, and thinks about how foodstuffs combine to make nourishment, to make that which tastes good:

White with rye, bread dear, bread—
my warm god,
I eat, I bite it from all sides
on the way from the store,
my warm god
feeds me, mom, and pop.

    a bag of flour, great wealth.
    a bag of flour, a lick of luck.

sugar, too.[152]

серый хлеб, хлебушек, хлеб—
мой тёплый бог,

я ем его и кусаю со всех сторон
по дороге из магазина,
мой тёплый бог
кормит меня, маму и папу.

   большое богатство—мешок муки.
   большая удача—мешок муки.

и сахар.

The poem is quickly weighed down not by these sacks of provisions but by surreal combinations of objects and abstractions as if all could be consumed and used by the body to provide energy for life. The fantasies of food include a torte made of desires, a sense of community gathered from every empty dish, endless days of eating only macaroni, marinated capital in jars of cryptocurrency, eyes that figuratively gobble up all sights, and eyes that are themselves turned into food. Such images recall Rymbu's signature combinations of the material and the abstract, a valuable reminder of her [Translit] days.[153] But there is a difference, shown vividly later in the poem's recipe for the soup of mourning; it draws images from Celan's "Death Fugue" ("Todesfuge," 1948) and Nazi gas chambers, and from the horrible foodstuffs of the Leningrad blockade, when wallpaper glue was consumed in desperation:

my recipe. sorrow soup
black dumplings
ashes for seasoning
smelling of gas.

my reality. sweet funeral porridge
glut in the throat.

the words of my dead. edible clay of the steppes
boiled wood pulp
sweet wallpaper glue.

мой рецепт—суп скорби
с чёрными галушками
с приправой из пепла
с запахом газа.

моя реальность—поминальная кутья—
прилипла к горлу.

слова моих мёртвых—съедобная степная глина,
варёная древесина,
сладкий обойный клей.

The poet claims one of these substances, clay from the steppe, is edible, but these are not images that nourish or sustain life. The poet's recipes can tip either way, however, and the "sweet funeral porridge" listed here (kut'ia), commemorates the dead but is also part of the Christmas feast in eastern Slavic cultures. Food can give rise to obsession—that is the note in fact on which the poem ends—but the obsessive fantasy of plenty reads as a mark of undiminishing hunger. There is always an underlying sense of indicting the broader society, unable to provide sufficient food for its citizens, but the poems keep the focus on what that scarcity feels like, how it forms the psyche and makes satisfaction seem always out of reach.

"Poem for Food" is not included in her 2021 book, *You Are the Future* (*Ty—budushchee*), where a different poem of hunger takes the poet back to her own teenaged years.[154] The volume's title poem, addressed to her young son, finds Rymbu feeling her way toward an idea of childhood imbued with optimism. The optimism is not sentimental, and it does not dispense with her trademark political acuity. Also striking is "Her Guy Is an Enforcer" ("Ee paren' rabotaet vyshibaloi," 2020), with its fifteen-year-old speaker and uncanny combination of sexual naivete and a jaded view of sexual acts as paid transactions. Like Stepanova in "Girls Undressed," Rymbu is writing about a teenager finding her way through a world of sexual exploitation and menace. What she learns is mediated through others: the friend of the poem's title, who is only fourteen; a prostitute who ends up in their car (she is thirty); and the enforcer, the quasi-boyfriend who drives the car. He's a fixer and finds his clean-up work coolly funny. But there's a crying woman in this image who isn't laughing:

he showed us a video on his phone
with a cool situation as he put it
two drunk men naked in a bath house
with their bellies hanging out
they didn't want to let the woman go although
she had done her work
and they're grumbling
while the woman is crying
but he'll handle it straight away
still it's funny right
says the guy the guy the guy

он показал нам видео на телефоне
где прикольная ситуация так сказал он
два пьяных голых мужика в бане
с обвисшими животами
не хотят отпускать женщину хотя она уже
своё отработала
и мычат
а женщина плачет
но он щас разрулит
всё равно смешно же да
говорит парень парень парень[155]

The poem's young speaker gets a lesson about male power from the video and from the guy's amusement: a humiliated woman, who did what she was supposed to, is more vulnerable than the slightly ridiculous male patrons, exposed in their nakedness. The poem makes manifest the force of that male gaze by the repeating last line, even starker in Russian where there is no article to distract from that word for "guy."

The poem uses repetition in several ways, repeating the girls' ages, repeating the word "mama." But the most expressive and dramatic is the verb heard ten times: what in English takes three words, "they are hammering," in Russian is a single word, "dolbiat." That word strikes against the consciousness, again and again. It ostensibly refers to icons that the speaker fantasizes they are also delivering in their car, and she compares the women they are moving around the city to icons (one is even fetched from a church). But the word also conveys a physical sense of being struck (something in that awful repetition helplessly recalls the title of Freud's essay "A Child Is Being Beaten"). The same verb is repeated in the poem's ending, when the guy, the enforcer, hammers at the fourteen-year-old friend of our speaker, equating sex with physical violence.

Rymbu gives a kind of weird postapocalyptic quality to the poem's ending, when the enforcer's car cruises along an avenue that has both "peace" and the "whole world" in its name (Prospekt mira). There's nothing original in making use of the doubled meaning of *mir*, but our speaker is very young. Rymbu repeats *mir* in different forms, reproducing the mindset of a young teenager turning over the double entendre in her mind—she is finding her way with language and with a complicated social scene. As she puts it, a lot happens on this street they are driving along, "this street named for the fucking unfair world" (po prospektu ebanogo nespravedlivogo mira).[156] The vulgar phrase could be another overheard bit of language she tries out, and almost immediately she willfully sees beauty instead, praising the coral-colored sun as it rises over this very street.

The poem ends with a one-line statement that puts the possibilities of beauty and of violence into a grimly realistic statement of what the prospects for the future really are (and it is likely that Rymbu, who has some knowledge of English, means that pun for the Russian "prospekt"): "in our town all the avenues lead nowhere" (v nashem gorode vse prospekty vedut v nikuda).[157] That ending, "nowhere" (v nikuda) is all the stronger because the poet has made the adverb into a kind of noun and put it at the very end of the sentence and of the whole text. For a poem that occurs almost entirely in a car, with its speaker always in motion (or proximate to motion: sneaking out to get into the car, or just being dropped off), there is a circular, pointless quality to the motion, which is another way that repetition is such a strong trope in the poem. Rymbu has taken a moment in a young person's life when there should be so much possibility and filled it with the affect of being lost in endless pointless motion.

To see too much despair here, though, would be a mistake. It is more than an irony that this poem appears in *You Are the Future*, where "you" is a child. Rymbu gave some further context in comments linked to the journal publication of some of these poems. She wrote that they represent the speech "of a range of imagined subjects from within political experiences like resistance, repetition, catastrophe, reaction, (self-)organizing, transformation." She adds that the poems show how "reigning ideology influences speech, but also about the way that within 'ossified' language and absurd speech formulas the thought of liberation can begin to move."[158] And there we see the opening created by even her bleakest poems: the thought of freedom is starting to be sensed, perhaps by the young teenager who rides around in the closed-up space of a hatchback car, rescuing sex workers and taking in cautionary lessons about commerce, desire, and friendship. Mark Lipovetsky, writing about Rymbu's earlier poems, found in them a longing for freedom, "uncomfortable, painful, but freedom nonetheless."[159] He catches the paradox of her work extremely well with that observation.

Rymbu's poems are a good place to end this chapter on political poetry: she is relentlessly following the many pathways along which poetry can investigate the bounds of the political.[160] She brings a subtle, smart understanding of gender dynamics into her account of politics. She refuses to let go of poetry's liberatory potential even as she charts the obstacles to freedom and the harm done to individuals by those obstacles. In a 2016 interview, she pointed to the still valuable Benjaminian model of the revolutionary potential held in that which oppresses or traumatizes.[161] There is something at once prosaic and sublime in her work, which means that she is staking out a terrain remarkably close to what Jacques Rancière found in the work of Rimbaud.[162] The magic of language—the possibility that every once in a while, signs are not arbitrary—means that we even hear Rimbaud's name paronomastically in Rymbu's.[163] In that magic, as well as in the clarity and optimism of her thought processes, Rymbu finds her way to a poetry that imagines freer futures. She seems to follow Rancière in seeing poetry's liberatory potential.[164] But it would be a mistake to imagine her as following anyone. Like the other poets treated in this chapter, and most especially like Stepanova and Fanailova, she is blazing a trail that beckons readers to follow her.

2

Performing Poetry in the Age of the Internet

Fanailova • Doubled Performances • Skandiaka • Prigov

LIVE POETRY READINGS can be magical, leaving new readers with a fresh sense of how poems might sound, and reminding longtime fans why they cared about a poet's work in the first place. The words of a poem can be linked to a body and to a face, to a set of gestures and speech patterns that listeners may recall when the poems are reread on the page long into the future. In post-Soviet Russia, readings brought people to cozy bookstores and cafés that sprang up after 1989, and they created and amplified a poetry community that found further support by burgeoning online communication, including LiveJournal blogs, Facebook pages, shared projects, and the possibilities of uploading or livestreaming recorded readings. The start of the pandemic in 2020 strengthened the online connections and provided a peculiarly controlled experiment for comparing live gatherings with virtual ones.

Both formats proved that the hieratic aura long surrounding Russian poets was not diminished by greater familiarity and accessibility. What I saw in live readings in Petersburg and Moscow, well into the 2010s, and even more what I witnessed when online readings became a source of solace during the isolation of pandemic lockdown, convinced me that the aura wasn't incompatible with the close-up. The readings were still performances, and performers cultivated porous boundaries, setting them off against their audiences by their cool (or coolly indifferent) clothing, by their polished or self-consciously rumpled styles of reading, and by the visible affiliations with other poets who were also in the audience and who got more of the in-jokes and warm dedications. Beyond my memories of live performances, I draw here on recordings that readers can find—as audio, video, or poems that perform in unusual ways on the page or screen. My hypothesis is that the poet's aura has not just survived but flourished in the age of mechanical reproduction. Walter Benjamin asked the right question, decades ago, but we have arrived at a point in the twenty-first century that has changed the terms of the answer.[1]

The change might be rendered in this way: rather than the uniqueness of a one-time live event, and rather than the authenticity of a singular poetic personality guaranteed by its difference from all others, performance in the age of the internet depends on forms of multiplicity. This is not just because recorded events can be viewed more than once, although this iterability is an important component of the new performance culture. Rather, the numerical orientation of performance has moved the needle more subtly, from one to two. It is as if the binary code at the heart of the internet allows ideas of performance to vacillate between one and two. But something inherent in the logic of Russian grammar is also at work here: the counting system relies on not just the distinction between singular and plural, but also a remnant of the old dual designation.[2]

Whatever associations we choose for this phenomenon, whether grammar or digital coding, forms of doubling have marked some significant poetry performances. In the examples that follow, I distinguish among the doubles created by pseudonyms, iterative online publication, and performance styles that create a kind of double for the poet. I begin and end with the work of Elena Fanailova and Nika Skandiaka, with the middle of the chapter focused on two anthologies of contemporary poetry readings; key examples there are performances by Dmitry Kuz'min, Olga Sedakova, and Mikhail Gronas. I begin with Fanailova, whose political poetry is treated in chapter 1. Here, we will watch how she channels Russian poetry's long tradition of persona poems, a form of doubling, in order to perform on screen the process of poetic creation itself.

Elena Fanailova's Lysistrata Poems

Fanailova's Lysistrata poems are a vast and unfinished body of work, and as a performance, the incompleteness indexes an act of creation. The tradition of writing poems that thematize their own creation is long, in ways that are pertinent to Fanailova's performance. In the Russian context, creative self-consciousness has long been associated with a pause or rupture in composition,

at least since Pushkin's unfinished poem "Autumn (A Fragment)" ("Osen'
[Otryvok]," 1833).[3] Contemporary poems have recombined those two
gestures—stopping short of the end and creative self-referentiality. The
political and ethical invitation created by openings in Galina Rymbu's poem
"An Offense to Power" ("Oskorblenie vlasti," 2020) is one possibility: Rymbu
addresses her reader with a list of "the arrested and persecuted" and asks for
additions and suggestions:

> And for those arrested in the *Seti* case. And for the historian Dmitriev.
> And I also think that others could finish writing this text,
> For example, adding to this list of the arrested and persecuted.
> Right here. Propose ideas for actions
> of the most radical nature.
> Here, in this piece of writing, right now. **It's a beginning**.

> И за тех, кто по делу "Сети" сидит. И за историка Дмитриева.
> А еще я думаю, что другие могут этот текст дописать,
> например, этот список сидящих и преследуемых дополнить.
> Прямо здесь. Предложить идеи для действий,
> самого радикального характера.
> Здесь, в письме, это возможно. **Это—начало**.[4]

Rymbu establishes her own "piece of writing" as an opening, a "beginning." It
is not broken off, like Pushkin's "Autumn," but rather strategically left as if in-
complete to invite readers to propose their own "ideas for actions / of the most
radical nature."

In Fanailova's Lysistrata poems, though, interconnected pieces seem to
change dynamically as new poems emerge. I treat a few of these texts from a
political perspective in chapter 1 (and give an account there of the poems'
themes and range). This massive work merits fresh attention here because its
sprawling, slow growth in real time constitutes one of the most interesting
performances of freedom in Russian poetry. It has been public, mediated by
Facebook posts and by some online journals (where possible, I cite published
versions). There is something rhizomatic in the shape of this work, which sends
out new shoots at intervals and grows in unexpected directions, surprising even
the poet, to judge from her comments along the way. The poems, themselves
often very long, mostly have hashtags rather than titles, signaling their geneal-
ogy within a searchable electronic medium. Rare is the text that has only one
hashtag. Poems are complexly interrelated by familiar poetic means, like repeat-

ing phrases, quotation or allusion, and rhetorical devices, and the intermingling of hashtags, toponyms, and personal names from public life and from the poet's friends also signals that they are parts of a larger whole.[5]

If Fanailova assembles and reorders the texts in book form, a new double for the Lysistrata poems will be created, one reshaped by the exigencies of print publication and the finite nature of a bound book. But in its open and unstable form, this work is already reaching a public: her Facebook page has over six thousand followers and two thousand friends, and it is public. The amount of material is substantial, with more than 115 poems between 2014 and 2020.[6] At various times the posts have been preceded by comments that the cycle is winding down, or that a new text is a postscript.[7] Fanailova can comment, when posting a new poem, that she thought she was done with this, and her Lysistrata hashtags can joke that "she's at it again" or "taking a rest," only to return.[8] But in 2020, the most common hashtag was simply that Lysistrata is writing (#Лисистратапишет), which begins to suggest that writing is compelled, unrelenting, so long as the falseness and violence of Russian public life endures. In 2022, after February 24, texts appeared and reappeared ever more often.

The amplitude of this project is modeling a radical expansiveness in how a poem might be created before the readers' eyes, with new themes and personae added as historical events evolve. The context of the poem is Russia's war in Ukraine, with reference as well to the conflicts in Syria and in Georgia and to ongoing political protest, as the poet has noted explicitly.[9] Of the multiple hashtags, the most expressive and the ones that set the agenda for these poems use the name Lysistrata, who will surely be Fanailova's most famous double, whatever else she goes on to write.

Named for its heroine, Aristophanes's *Lysistrata* (411 BCE) is a comedy, and male characters deride the women who are ready to withhold sex to stop a war. Full of sexual innuendos and puns, the play makes for high entertainment. The popularity of *Lysistrata* for performance and imitation rose in the twentieth century, as a good vehicle for an antiwar agenda as well as a platform for the fantasy that women have the power to stop male violence.[10] The war it registers is the Peloponnesian War (431–405 BCE), between Athens and Sparta, but Fanailova, in her use of hashtags, often aligns it with the legendary war for Troy, which occurred hundreds of years earlier (archaeologists believe that ancient Troy was destroyed ca. 1180 BCE). Her reasons, I would conjecture, have largely to do with the genres associated with the Trojan War. To write of Troy is to invoke Homer's *Iliad* and *Odyssey*, and thus the epic account of

battles that could lay the foundation for Western European culture's under-
standing of itself.[11] The oral origins of Homer's poems, their having been
woven out of different layers and dialects of ancient Greek, and the fact that
behind that name "Homer" are undoubtedly multiple poets and scribes whose
contributions shaped the poems—these traits are also reflected in Fanailova's
Lysistrata poems. The poems abound in multiple speech registers and draw
on sources from folklore, Europop music, and popular cinema, as well as from
Russian high modernism, and some include phrases in Ukrainian alongside
the Russian.[12] The multiplicity and variegation of input material is one of these
poems' defining traits. Many of the texts have a vivid, spoken quality, and while
the fixed epithets of the Homeric epic are not here, phrases and images recur
within and across texts, establishing a sense of potential oral performance and
reaffirming the poems' recourse to folk culture.[13]

Performance is thus at the very heart of the Lysistrata poems. Fanailova
models them on dramatic elements of Aristophanes's *Lysistrata*, including its
bawdy comedy and innuendos, as when she laces her lines with casual obsceni-
ties. She channels the possibilities of drama in her creation of multiple char-
acters for these poems, sometimes using the structure of a chorus followed by
individual voices. For example, the set of poems published in *Snob* in 2017
features a merchant, a diplomat, a spy, and the leader of the chorus, with a
postscript that brings Ivan the Terrible back to life to issue a lover's complaint
to the English princess who spurned him.[14] That publication intriguingly in-
cludes the opposition of Troy vs. Lysistrata in its title, as if the battles at stake
are not just those of Ukraine, the Balkans, the Spanish Civil War, Russia's civil
war, and the Trojan War itself, all mentioned in the texts, but also a conflict
between the aesthetic modes that the names Troy and Lysistrata stand in for.
In that "vs." in the title, then, the poet acknowledges a disparity between a
nation-creating set of epics like Homer's and a titillating ancient comedy like
Lysistrata. Her poems accommodate both ambitions.

To layer echoes of *Lysistrata* over those of the *Iliad* and the *Odyssey* is also to
push the Homeric epos in a decidedly feminine direction. One of the central
performances in the Lysistrata poems is that of gender. It is as if Fanailova is
doing something uncannily in kinship with the first complete translation of
Homer into English by a woman, Emily Wilson's *Odyssey* (2018) and *Iliad*
(2023), or the brilliant project of reclaiming Homer that has yielded Alice
Oswald's books *Memorial* (2011) and *Nobody* (2019).[15] I am not suggesting that
Fanailova was influenced by or even knew Wilson's and Oswald's work, for
which I have no evidence, but there is a striking similarity in the cultural reso-

nance achieved by radically rewriting the Western tradition's most prized high-culture texts to expose and challenge their masculine aura. Interrogating the experienced realities or imagined absences can mean paying attention to seemingly peripheral details, as Oswald does with the dizzying accounts of heard sounds or watery depths in *Nobody*. Highlighting the grotesque violence of the Trojan War, in both Oswald's *Memorial* and in Emily Wilson's unsparing, vernacular translations, can intensify an antiwar argument, too. It is an argument that Fanailova, in her own way, seeks to make (although she does so without showing brutality up close or in detail, emphasizing instead the harms of violence on the psyches of those who perpetrate, witness, or survive these acts). She introduces women speakers and addressees, creates family contexts in which war's losses are felt, and sets poems from the perspective of men in or near battle. The fundamentally dramatic structure of the work is fully in view here: the poet creates figures whose politics she clearly does not share (a Russian fighting in Ukraine, for example).[16] The imagined characters are a mix of the heroic and the pathetic, tragic and comic, and their feelings of terror are articulated as fiercely as their bravado or fortitude. Fanailova blurs the boundaries between masculine and feminine attributes along the way, even as she writes poems that send up the association of masculinity with clear reason and women with clouded emotion.

Fanailova wrote in a poem to the Ukrainian poet Serhiy Zhadan that she admires his cold reason.[17] She has in fact translated some of his poems into Russian (the only poet she has translated, to my knowledge), and Galina Rymbu rightly noted that Fanailova is in dialogue with Zhadan throughout her recent work.[18] I would suggest that some of that dialogue has to do with how a poet projects an image via performance. An extraordinary description of a performance/poetry event by Bob Holman shows us one possibility: Zhadan presides over a table of twenty men, in military uniforms, who are disassembling and then reassembling rifles, one at a time, each time in under a minute, each time passing the gun to the next man, who does the same thing. As this repeated action of unmaking and making the machinery of war goes on, Zhadan reads his poetry, paying no attention to what Holman calls a "macabre spectacle"; Zhadan's poems were "holding their own against this violence," Holman judges, but he finds that the poems seemed, in their own way, "rooted in the male war dance assembly line."[19]

Fanailova's poetry in a way reimagines this bizarre scene into one that is not 100 percent male: those who are creating the violence to which poetry speaks are not all men, and the poet making this work is not a man. But her work also imagines that the scene, twenty-one people sitting around a table, is more than the juxtaposition of war making and poetry reading. For Fanailova, neither is separable from the daily lives of people sitting around any table to eat or to do schoolwork, or a table at which a radio host, as she also is, conducts an interview. That connectedness to multiple forms of life—a trait her work shares with that of Zhadan—means that war is not some event apart from daily life. It is, as C. D. Wright once said (about art, in the context of writing about US prisons), not apart, but a part of.[20] Creating a sense of proximity to distant violence is thus a further aspect of the work Fanailova's Lysistrata poems are meant to perform: to make the apprehension of war a part of daily life, a regularly repeating experience with a very low bar for admission—one has only to check in on Facebook to encounter a new installment. Of course, once the war in Ukraine became an all-out invasion, there was no need to do any work to suggest that proximity. The curious thing about the Lysistrata poems is how Fanailova was doing this work from 2014 through and beyond February 2022.

As innovative as Fanailova's Lysistrata poems are, and as tied as they are to the technologies of the twenty-first century, they do have one completely traditional model, an unexpected one: the work of Anna Akhmatova. I know, comparing the two risks seeming gratuitous, as if every contemporary Russian woman poet must withstand comparison to the standard bearers. The connection is all the more counterintuitive because when it comes to women poets, Fanailova has aligned herself with Marina Tsvetaeva. In her youth, she recalls, she preferred Tsvetaeva's open expressions of sexuality and her spiritual openness (what she calls Tsvetaeva's "chistaia dusha").[21] Fanailova also surely still prefers an earthier idiom to Akhmatova's patrician tone, but her Lysistrata poems have a deep affinity with Akhmatova's modes of self-creation.

Three elements in that self-presentation are important: first, a pattern of lyric ventriloquism, where speech is routed through other women (Akhmatova's Dido, Lot's wife; Fanailova's "Jataka about a Woman," "Frida's Album" about Frida Kahlo, and now Lysistrata); second, a use of first-person utterance to take civil or public (grazhdanskii) positions (Akhmatova's war poems and "Requiem"; Fanailova's poems of post-Soviet violence and war poems); third, and perhaps most strikingly, a sense that the poet is haunted by a death of someone beloved, a death that is personally traumatic but has some larger public consequences (for Akhmatova, the death of Nikolai Gumilev in 1921; for Fanailova, the death of someone mostly unnamed or called Sasha).[22] The obsessive returns to private mourning as the wellspring of public speech mark both their poetics.[23]

Akhmatova may be a model for Fanailova's Lysistrata poems in a fourth way: her lengthy composition process for "Poem without a Hero" ("Poema bez geroia," 1940–62). Akhmatova cast a retrospective glance in "Poem without a Hero," re-creating the earlier era from which her poetics took shape. But her *poema* is also a record of the present, its hauntings and its terrors, and like Fanailova's Lysistrata poems, it is a matrix of quoted material that mixes multiple forms of aesthetic expression (ballet libretto and harlequinade for Akhmatova; popular song, the visual arts, and cinema for Fanailova).

The gender politics of Akhmatova and Fanailova remain quite distinct. Akhmatova's elevated status was at least partly built on a foundation of rather patriarchal gender arrangements, and even feminist scholars have acknowledged that she established an early image as a passive victim of masculine dominance.[24] But Fanailova is more likely to represent herself as a fully formed and independent adult, one prepared to steady a nervous lover with light-hearted jokes, her eyes open to all his flaws. And to her own: rather than the pride we associate with Akhmatova, Fanailova's later work has so little self-idealization that one of her signature vulgar self-reproaches is to tell herself not to lose heart in the face of danger with a word that literally means "don't piss yourself" (ne ssy).

Here we see how Fanailova distinguishes herself from Akhmatova, and the difference shapes the range of roles the poet performs in the Lysistrata poems. The same reproach not to chicken out is repeated to imagined soldiers on the field of war or to those traveling to Ukraine's battle zones. It is one way the poet establishes equivalences between herself and soldiers (on both sides of the war), or herself and family members of those sent into battle. Several poems are in fact spoken in the voice of a man involved in or observing military action. Fanailova emphasizes having thrown her poetic voice to a male speaker by including words of affection or longing or reproach to an absent female lover.

This crossing of gender lines is emblematized by a hashtag that mashes up personal pronouns, #онаонаони (which means she + she + they); it can appear on its own, or in combination with the Lysistrata hashtag.[25] The hashtag #онаонаони fixes through an absolute minimal number of phonemes the possibilities of a mutating gender identity. It does so by means of the personal pronouns, a part of speech that in Russian, as in many Indo-European languages, carries the mark of gender. The minimalism is even more stark in Russian than in, say, English, because so few letters are involved: one consonant, one constant vowel, one changing vowel. Thus, *he, she, it*, and *they* are in transliteration *on, ona, ono, oni.* An underlying exclamation of "oh, no" almost leaks out of these recombining phonemes. And the sequence itself is meaning-ful: for the hashtag, Fanailova chose two iterations of the pronoun that means "she," followed by "they" (#онаонаони), as if creating a formula for what it would take for individuals of the feminine gender to become plural, and a suggestion that in the plural (where gender is not marked), some residue of the feminine, for this hashtag, has been imported.[26]

The formula of two feminine pronouns also encodes brilliantly the femi-nine doubling that defines so much of Fanailova's work, including the poems "Lena and Lena" and "Lena and People" (featured in chapter 1). In the Ly-sistrata poems, she stages fresh encounters with women named Elena, each studied for signs of similarity despite obvious differences. Lena the Slavist, from "Lena and Lena," reappears.[27] The poems add other doubles, inspired by psychoanalytical and anthropological theory (the poet mentions Otto Rank and Dr. Freud, as she calls him, as inspirations), and Fanailova also invokes the specific use of poetic doubles in the Russian tradition.[28] She considers Marina Tsvetaeva a double in a poem that opens with the line "I encounter my double" (ia vstrechaius' so svoim dvoinikom).[29] Tsvetaeva appears in a dream here, such an appropriate site for a double, and she is distorted into a one-dimensional parody of her poetic persona: all ego, all self.

> this double is deranged
> wearing a winter coat and insisting
> that she is Tsvetaeva, the maniac of literary egoism
> and ten times right there in front of me she repeats
> that there is only I and I means only she

> этот двойник невменяем
> одета в зимнее и утверждает
> что она Цветаева, маньяк литературного эгоизма
> и десять раз на моих глазах повторяет
> что есть только я и я это только она[30]

The double repels Fanailova, who tries to ward off the harmful vision with prayer. She awakens and sees the dream as a set of hidden desires: she is firm in her resolve, casting its demonic allure as something that is not to be feared but met with cold clarity. The dream signals the self-analysis and broader social analysis that these poems are meant to perform. Fanailova is reconstructing what Seamus Heaney would call the theater of our dreams, and like Heaney, she is doing so in part to explore how history reenacts itself in the political misadventures of the present.[31]

For Fanailova, the unconscious of individual psyches and the unexamined history of a people stand not just as inconvenient obstacles to getting our desires fulfilled, but as the very material of which genuine freedom can be built.[32] That work requires an examination of how violence became a condition of life in Russia.[33] And the drama of doubles, performed in her Lysistrata poems and elsewhere, stages the process of working through that psychic history toward genuine freedom. The poet who entitled one of her early books *With Particular Cynicism* (*S osobym tsinizmom*, 2000) may seem the last person we'd expect to offer wide-eyed, sentimental paeans to freedom, but Fanailova's commitment to dignity runs deep and has been a powerful force in her poems for more than a decade. That project intensifies in the Lysistrata poems, and it is one reason she can admire, in a poem to Zhadan, that "good and evil are visible" to him (vidny dobro i zlo).[34] Zhadan stands to Fanailova as a beacon of moral clarity, one who knows how to choose between truth and shame.

The word Fanailova uses for "shame" in that poem is "pozor," a noun whose root comes from the action of seeing, from an archaic verb (*zret'*) meaning "to see." She has in mind the spectacle of shame in this poem and in dozens of other representations of war, including the Afghanistan war (as shown in her poem in ". . . Again they're talking about their Afghanistan"). Fanailova makes clear her feelings that her nation is behaving shamefully on the world stage and that as a citizen, she is free to say so in public. She can be no actual Lysistrata, with powers to stop men from battle. But she can show her readers how to take inspiration from Lysistrata's performance of courage and fortitude.

The poems often circle back to earlier texts, trying to shed fresh light on the same stories, the same heroes. Like her use of doubles in creating characters, the work itself loops back: Fanailova often posts poems a second or third time, and the Tsvetaeva dream poem is one such example. Those repostings are likely prompted by the Facebook reminder of something from a previous year, but Fanailova makes the repetition aesthetically meaningful, and she often adds a new comment when she reposts a poem. She also doubles back to her own words within a given post, reproducing in the comment stream some choice phrase.

What does it mean not only to be engaged in writing a vast text like this in full public view, but to be in the clutches, so to speak, of that very text, in the clutches of its images and stories and rhetorical patterns? As she wrote in a poem from 2018:

> I live in my head with this difficult singing
> With incomplete knowledge
> With ceaseless humming and sound
>
> Я живу в голове с этим трудным пеньем
> Несовершенным знаньем
> Непрекращающимся гулом и звуком[35]

The "incomplete knowledge" generates a ceaseless hum in the poet's mind that presses her to keep returning to the scene of poetic creation. What Fanailova is creating in these poems is as much a mood as it is a set of arguments. She engages her readers at the level of affect, as theater does at its best.[36] The repeated return to a matrix of sensations, observations, imagined or remembered scenes is itself the central work of the poems. One can see the consequences of this affective intensity in the Facebook comments from her readers, which are often exclamations of emotion so devoid of narrative shape that they are rendered only as exclamation marks ("!!!" is a frequent response, as is "Lena!"; there is even the occasional heart emoji). What the poems do to a reader is as significant as how the poems make their meanings. They stage an act of poetic rumination and reflection that takes full advantage of their digital medium, and that in turn can set the stage for what a host of other poets have been doing in performing for their readers online and in person.

Doubled Performances

Doubling takes many forms for Fanailova, but as soon as we shift from her publication practice as a kind of performance toward institutional structures for poetry readings, doubling can look quite different. The most interesting variant occurs when poets perform their work and that of others. Although I comment on several other reading series, I look most closely at two networked resources built around these doubled performances. Their goals, range, and formatting also sought preserve the aura of authenticity that marks so much contemporary Russian poetic performance. I begin with the older of the two.

On April 21, 2008, the editors of *OpenSpace*, then Russia's premier site for cultural and political news, inaugurated *Live Poetry* (*Stikhi vzhivuiu*). It would become a series of short videos by sixty-eight poets, each reading two poems:

their own poem, then one by another poet.[37] The series held many pleasures, perhaps none greater than the recording made by Dmitry Kuz'min. He read his own loose, perambulating verse account of three youths on the streets after a movie (Bertolucci's *The Dreamers*, 2003). The two boys steal an embrace in an entryway; a girl patiently stands guard.[38] As signaled by the mention of Bertolucci's erotic film, Kuz'min's poem celebrates a kind of sexual urgency that lines up well with the liberated poetics of his free verse.[39] His poem flashes a bit of English-language text and some choice popular cultural references, mixing irony and pathos. Kuz'min takes his readers on a narrative journey back to adolescence, to a moment when sex and love acquire their first meanings. These are the passions of youth, the quick embraces, the daring encounters that feel as cinematic as the cultural sources on which they are modeled.

Separately, Kuz'min reads sixteen lines from Olga Sedakova's cycle "Chinese Journey" ("Kitaiskoe puteshestvie," 1986). It is very different kind of love poem, and a surprising choice: Kuz'min has championed many young poets, yet he turned to a poem published decades earlier, by a poet who, although her work in the 1970s and 1980s was quietly fearless, by 2008 represented an established and more conservative verse style. Kuz'min recites her poem in a gentler voice than one hears when he reads his own poem, but the clarity of articulation, a trait of his spoken Russian whether he is reading poems or engaged in heated conversation, is unmistakable. He makes the poem his own, we could say, especially as his recitation is starkly unlike Sedakova's more musical and gentler reading style.[40] Kuz'min recites Sedakova's statement of loyalty and love from memory, offering it as a direct address to the camera. The poem begins:

> You know, I love you so much
>   that should there come an hour
> that leads me away from you,
> it will not take me away—

> Ты знаешь, я так тебя люблю,
>   что если час придет
> и поведет меня от тебя,
> то он не уведет—

And it continues:

> You know, I love you so much
> that I can't separate it from
> the wind's whistle, the branches' rustle, the rain's life[41]

Ты знаешь, я так люблю тебя,

что от этого не отличу

вздох ветра, шум веток, жизнь дождя[42]

Sedakova's poem creates a zone of almost wordless intimacy, which Kuz'min re-creates dramatically, meditatively, as if the feelings were entirely his own. He offers her lines as a man speaking directly to his beloved, to other poets, and to readers far into the future. As a gay man, he hears in Sedakova's poem a spirit of openness that is the pulse of nature itself—"the wind's whistle, the branches' rustle, the rain's life"—making his performance into an interpretation of her poetics. Inevitably, he also returns these words to the poet who wrote them, addressing her as a fellow poet he embraces as able to speak his own love.

Like Kuz'min, every poet who read for *Live Poetry* established a relationship to another poet because of the doubled format; all offered a gesture of affiliation, and all were exposed to their audiences as the creators of poetic texts and as poetry's readers. Each, in their different ways, created an authentic connection between poet and poem, and between poet and poet. As valuable as the curated series *Live Poetry* is as an archive of poets reading their own work, the poets' performances of others' poems may tell us even more. When poets speak in each other's voices, they embody acts of creation as they imagine them in other people's lives.[43] The defining feature of this series is the doubled reading, then, and in what follows I attend as much to the poets' performances of others' work as to their way of reading their own work.[44]

The modes of reading or reciting poems have their own history, one that can be specific to a cultural moment or a national tradition. I follow Christopher Grobe, a scholar of the performance practices of American confessional poets, in this historicized approach, and in arguing for archived recordings as invaluable material for studying performance.[45] Grobe zeros in on a cultural anxiety over the insufficiency of the poem as printed or scrawled on the page, but I do not find that tension within contemporary poetic practice in Russia. Poets seem more comfortable with a fluid continuum between poems as written and performed, as exemplified in Kuz'min's easy movement from reading his own poem from print to reciting Sedakova's from memory. Indeed, dramatic and performance-oriented texts are showing up increasingly in the work of key figures (for instance, Keti Chukhrov, in multivoiced dramatic reading and in song).[46] Spoken and printed words become mutually constitutive.

Readers in *Live Poetry* upheld the promise of bringing texts to auditory life that the series title offered, and their gesture of animating the written word was complemented by video's affordances with a physical embodiment.

These poets do not barricade themselves off from the poems they read, and their embodied performances show them taking on and absorbing a poem, whether their own or that of another poet. The spoken words are linked to a body and to a face, to a set of gestures and speech patterns that listeners will access as potential memories when later rereading the poems on the page. This observation would hold for any video of a poetry reading—and the historical moment when *Live Poetry* emerged saw ever more such recordings, on YouTube, Rutube, and some personal, journal, and otherwise aggregated websites. The *Live Poetry* series, like these other examples, counts as what Philip Auslander has called a "mediatized performance," an instance of a live performance that has been made available for repeated viewings and circulation.[47]

Live Poetry offers an expansive archive to study gestures of embodiment, largely because of the unchanging, doubled format. *OpenSpace*'s curatorial presence was felt in the uniformity of presentation: two videos for each poet, vertically stacked, each without links to printed poems and without an announcing voice, only a musical phrase as an opening tagline and a visual label with the poet's name on one side of the screen, the *OpenSpace* logo to the right. Each video used the same black and white format, tightly focusing on the poet reading, at most showing the poet from the waist up, with added close-ups. Different angles are edited in, rendering the fixed format dynamic, and many poets look directly into the camera. The videos were posted at spaced intervals, affording a focus on one poet, in two videos, at a time.

That oblique positioning of body or gaze as if focused beyond the camera's range allows each poet to suggest a larger poetic tradition, a cultural context felt just outside the video screen's boundaries. There is an otherworldliness to the readings, particularly when the poet reads another's lines. As Charles Bernstein noted, we rarely see or hear poets "covering" someone else's work.[48] For Bernstein, though, this gesture of voicing is a powerful metaphor for all acts of recorded poetry. To have a poet recite or read a poem into a recorded format is inherently weird, he suggests, creating a ghostly effect. Bernstein, a leader in creating the archive at PennSound, is chiefly concerned with voice. But *OpenSpace*'s recordings rely on video format, with a similar potential for uncanny frisson.[49] The *OpenSpace* editors and the performing poets used the physical presence of the body to suggest absent others. Some appear almost to bring back the dead. Crossing the boundaries between the living and the

dead, the present and the absent, the material and the spiritual, seems to mo-
tivate many choices about whose poetry to read. For many, including Kuz'min,
the crossing was toward intimacy, into a zone of contact with an inspiring
other poetic voice.

The format chosen by *OpenSpace* promotes that crossing, allowing future
viewers to sample performances of resuscitation, re-embodiment, ghosting,
and reimagining. The videos also let us study canon formation in its most
nascent form: which poets are worth keeping alive? Which ones need to be
brought back from the dead? How might performing space become elegiac
space? *OpenSpace* itself is no more, so anyone accessing this archived material
after 2011 would be retrieving something from a past electronic life. One of the
archive's many paradoxes, built into its use of a defunct computer program
(Adobe Flash), is its status somewhere between experiences that are live and
those that are repeatable, between those that live on past their moment and
those that are suddenly gone. This is another form of doubling built into the
project itself.

For a while in 2008, *Live Poetry* featured a short statement that set out the
principles behind its presentations. The key sentences were the first two:
"Contemporary poetry needs to be heard and seen. Sometimes it resembles
theater, or performance, or rap."[50] This statement emphasizes that poems are
not inert words on a page, but rather heard sounds uttered by a poet who is
seen. And it announces a diversity in performance styles. Fyodor Svarovsky's
reading style, to mention the poet who initiated the series, is noticeably neu-
tral and self-effacing—he reads fast and expects his listeners to keep up. His
breathless reading pace is unlike Kuz'min's forceful style, and his gesture of
affiliation is casual. He chose a short narrative text by his friend Arseny Rovin-
sky, and as he announces Rovinsky's name, he looks off-camera and grins.
Perhaps Rovinsky was present, taking pleasure in hearing Svarovsky read his
poem. The grin conveys the warmth of friendship with someone with whom
Svarovsky had just published a collective volume.[51]

That first choice showed the potential for *Live Poetry* to produce both su-
perb, expressive videos and records of poetic affiliation and canon creation
that both the editors' and the poets' choices might suggest. Some poets
violated the *OpenSpace* rule and did not choose a contemporary: Sergei
Stratanovsky read Pushkin, and Eduard Limonov read Gumilev. But most
often, the poets' choices allow us to infer bonds of friendship and loyalty
within the contemporary poetry scene; some poets are chosen more than
once, suggesting patterns in admiration and value.[52]

The poet whose poems appear the most (five times) is Grigory Dashevsky, briefly treated in the introduction to this book. Classical scholar, translator, editor, critic, and poet, Dashevsky was a teacher, and some poets who recited his poems were as if students, hoping to learn from a master whose words they savored and held close. Dashevsky was seriously ill for a long time, and he died at age forty-nine in December 2013.[53] The impulse to recite his work also seemed born of anticipated loss.[54] Dashevsky's poems were read by Elena Fanailova, Alexander Timofeevsky, Dem'ian Kudriavtsev, Marianna Geide, and Yuli Gugolev. Two read the same poem: Marianna Geide quickly, as if completely engrossed in the page of verse; Elena Fanailova deliberately, pausing between stanzas or between thoughts to look at the camera lens and beyond to an imagined audience. Here is the poem those two poets chose:

Quarantine

More courageous than Sylvester Stallone
or at least his picture above the pillow
is the one who stares in the nurses' pupils
    with no pleas nor fears,

but we scan those eyes for a diagnosis,
and we can't believe that under the covers
of that starchy robe there is almost nothing,
    at best—some undies.

Daily naptime, boys, oh that is your torture,
daily naptime sees you biting your blankets,
during naptime watchfully we examine
    the bars on the window.[55]

ТИХИЙ ЧАС

Тот храбрей Сильвестра Сталлоне или
его фотокарточки над подушкой,
кто в глаза медсёстрам серые смотрит
    без просьб и страха,

а мы ищем в этих зрачках диагноз
и не верим, что под крахмальной робой

ничего почти что, что там от силы
    лифчик с трусами.

Тихий час, о мальчики, вас измучил,
в тихий час грызёте пододеяльник,
в тихий час мы тщательней проверяем
    в окнах решетки.[56]

This haunting poem, dated 1996, mixes erotic desire with frightened watchfulness. As intense as the love poem chosen by Kuz'min, this text also lets readers affirm a connection to the poet. The poem's fantasies of an immobilized poetic subjectivity has that offbeat tonality that marks some of Dashevsky's short lyrics; also typical is the precise poetic diction that can spring forth into the wildest zones of freedom.[57] Dashevsky was known for his translations and transpositions, and this poem formally reads as Sapphic stanzas.[58] Dashevsky had two names for the poem: "Quarantine" ("Karantin"), which is how Fanailova and Geide read it; and, earlier, "Quiet Time" ("Tikhii chas"), the phrase repeated in this English translation as "daily naptime." Both metaphors—quarantine and a quiet hour of retreat—suggest conceptual contexts for how poetry performances on *OpenSpace* were meant to work: as separate zones for reflection, and as a mental space enclosed in the rectangle of the video screen, cozy enough to draw in viewers. Dashevsky's poem thus allegorizes the ambition of *Live Poetry* to create a respite from the crowded and ever-changing world. It was a poem before its time in another way as well: anyone reading a poem entitled "Quarantine" after 2020 will inevitably think of the COVID-19 pandemic, when respite became its own form of immobilization.

That association is of course anachronistic, but in the way of remarkable aesthetic achievements, an eerie prescience is at work. *Live Poetry* sets up paradigms (particularly the use of doubling) that would come into new prominence during the pandemic. A number of series of poetry readings began to occur in spring 2020, providing an important outlet for poets and readers in lockdown. After February 24, 2022, with the exodus of many leading poets and critics from Russia, and with curtailed travel into Russia from Europe and the United States, virtual spaces for poetry readings, as for symposia and conferences, remain vital. The readings dating to the first months of the pandemic thus created a set of new social practices for the large audiences enabled by the virtual environment.[59]

I will mention only two of them, both using notable forms of doubling.[60] Zarina Zabrisky of the San Francisco–based Globus Books created multiple events, including lectures and seminars. Many featured major poets who had published new books in translation.[61] These were often bilingual events, with poets and translators, and while the doubling was at one level necessarily linguistic, the events also had a twofold intellectual ambition, which included critics and scholars invited to comment on texts, poets, movements, and traditions.

In another valuable series, in spring 2020, Michael Kunichika, director of the Amherst Center for Russian Culture, and the poet Polina Barskova convened four readings that each paired two poets (for example, Linor Goralik and Maria Stepanova on April 26, 2020; Anna Glazova and Alexander Skidan on May 10, 2020).[62] The readings were also in effect bilingual, with translations projected on screen. That projection thus created a further doubling, between written text and heard poetry.[63]

That doubling of poetry seen and heard was a feature taken up by the project to create an anthology of women's poetry in 2021, organized through the Belinsky Library in Ekaterinburg, a city with a flourishing contemporary poetry scene at that time and a particularly strong group of women poets.[64] What one sees on screen is a poet reading; running alongside the framed video of the reader is the written text—again, a doubling of visible and audio poetry. In this case, the project did not ask poets to read something of their own, as *Live Poetry* had done; it simply asked for a poem by a woman, in any language, published before 1917.[65] Several poets went outside the Russian tradition, reading the original or a Russian translation, or both. Emily Dickinson was a popular choice, and among Russian poets, so were Marina Tsvetaeva and Elena Guro.

The ambitions of this series were highlighted in comments by one of the initiators, the poet Ekaterina Simonova. She reported the inclusion of seventy-eight women poets living in fourteen countries, reading the work of forty-four different women poets. The poets read between their day jobs and their work at home; they read in the living room and the kitchen, in studios or on snowy streets, and in more ways besides, all enumerated by Simonova. Her key point comes at the end: they read as only they can read, no one else.[66] As she suggests, though, most read in domestic settings, perhaps epitomized by Alla Gorbunova, who reads with her child on her lap and doesn't miss a beat as he comes, goes, eats candy, and plays with the foil wrapper. A few read out of doors: Nina Aleksandrova, reading Klara Arseneva; Yanina Vishnevskaya,

reading the poem that Lesia Ukrainka wrote in Russian; Olga Mekhono-
shina, reading Anna Bunina in air so cold you can see her breath; Lilya
Gazizova, reading Yasar Nezihe first in Turkish and then in her own transla-
tion. Gazizova is somewhere warmly sunny, presumably Turkey, where she
resides and teaches.

This is a compendium, then, not just of contemporary poets and pre-1917
poetic texts, but of the spaces in which poetry reading might happen in the
first place. The fact that the project was conceived and executed during the
isolation of the COVID-19 pandemic is nowhere stated explicitly, but it is felt
palpably as poet after poet sends in a low-tech recording with minimal props,
staging, lighting, or framing. Several read from a handheld telephone. Most
are straightforward readings into a computer screen, but some are thoughtfully
staged and playfully dramatic readings, like Alla Zinevich's reading of her own
translation of the eighteenth-century French poet Fanny de Beauharnais. Dana
Kurskaya expressively reads a Zinaida Gippius poem about a little demon,
bringing the strange narrative vividly to life. Some of the most striking
performances are not in Russian. Iya Kiva reads a poem by Lesia Ukrainka
("The Word," 1899), in wonderfully rhythmic, strong Ukrainian; Egana Dzhab-
barova beautifully reads the work of Ashug Basti in Azeri, although she warns
that her pronunciation might be wanting; Maria Martysevich provides strong
gestures alongside her assertive, impressive reading of a poem in Belarusian
by Aloize Pashkevich.

The most dramatically expressive and complexly engineered performance
is the reading of Cherubina de Gabriak's "The Double" ("Dvoinik," 1909) by
Alyona Ogneva, a performer and poet whose experience as a Moscow television
and radio personality surely contributed to the sophistication and high produc-
tion values of the video. She reads the poem in a recording studio setup that
makes her seem like a diva, a part she performs with enthusiastically cool erotic
pacing and a readiness to use her fingertips, lips, and facial expressions to reveal
the underlying drama of the poem. That image is layered over a cinematic repre-
sentation of a woman walking or standing, dressed drably, the double whose
words Ogneva recites. The poem describes and addresses itself to a double, to
whom Ogneva also speaks. The double's images are shown at the start and finish
of the video and interspersed along the way. The double is on the street, and
unlike the simple body-revealing costume of Ogneva in the recording studio,
the double is wrapped in layers of concealing clothing, shown alone, barely
moving, as if hiding from the social world. Toward the end of the video, the
double turns her face to the camera, and it is Ogneva's own face (figure 4).

FIGURE 4. Screenshot, Alyona Ogneva performing Cherubina de Gabriak, "The Double" (2021)

"The Double" emerged from the most famous mystification in Russian poetry: Elizaveta Dmitrieva (1887–1928) was turned into Cherubina de Gabriak by male poets in the Silver Age, chiefly Maximilian Voloshin, who was eager to play tricks on a rival poetic grouping, the Symbolist journal *Apollon*, headed by Sergei Makovsky. Twelve poems were published there in 1909, including "The Double," and another group appeared the next year.[67] Ogneva's choice of a poem not only about a double (and doubling was a great theme in Dmitrieva's work) but by someone who was, in effect, turned into a double, fills her performance with irony.[68] Ogneva exposes the persistent desire for woman poets with a sexy, romantic aura. That she does so in the guise of performing Dmitrieva's poem in no way lessens the irony, nor does the way she transforms the erotic desires into an exchange between two women. Her video challenges the fantasy that behind the alluring public persona hides a self-effacing, sad woman.

Ogneva's ironies suggest that when twenty-first-century poets embody the past, they can escape the manipulative world epitomized by Hitchcock's 1958 film *Vertigo*, with its doubled heroine and its glamour layered over a plot of murder, mystery, and glimpsed spirituality.[69] Spirituality, or a sense of aura, lingers at the edges of mechanical reproduction in a number of these videos. Some suggest that the reader is inhabited by a ghostly voice from the past, as with, for example, an Elena Guro poem read by Ekaterina Boiarskikh, or a poem by Olga Rozanova that Tatiana Danil'iants reads (intensified in the latter case by the mirage that the poem describes).

Although the format is different, several of the *Live Poetry* videos similarly use intonation and tempo to create an otherworldly impression. The most vivid example might be Mikhail Gronas's performance of a poem by Olga Sedakova, the same poet read by Kuz'min. Gronas chose a poem from "Old Songs" ("Starye pesni," 1980–81), a cycle he called "the highest achievement of late twentieth-century Russian vers libre."[70] He selected the one poem in the cycle written in metered verse, "Marching Song" ("Pokhodnaia pesnia"). Gronas's style of reading could not be more different from Kuz'min's dramatic style, or from Sedakova's, with her lucid, lightly musical lilt.[71] Like Kuz'min, he makes her poem his own: eyes closed, his mind turned inside toward the memorized, internalized poem. The slight angle of body and head enhances the ghostly effect. He is as if inhabited by the poem, and in the other video, where he reads his own poem, he recites at ever-accelerating speed, playing at his beard with one hand and swaying. He recites an untitled poem dedicated to Grigory Dashevsky: "All movements, sounds surrounding and through"

("Vse dvizheniia, zvuki vokrug i cherez," 2007).[72] When he finishes, Gronas opens his eyes and looks out at the camera, as if he has let himself be caught in the act. This most reluctant of readers performs in a way most like the hieratic, keening poet.[73] One of the archaic meanings of performance is a rite or ritual, which is what this reading resembles.[74]

Several other *Live Poetry* performances reach toward a spiritual world. Sergei Stratanovsky's Pushkin recitation is one kind of conjuring ritual; Anna Glazova's intense and precise recitation of her own poem and of one by Gronas stands as another (as does the quietly forceful recitation by Dashevsky). The visual elements chosen by *Live Poetry* can accentuate that spiritual quality: Olga Sedakova and Arkady Dragomoshchenko, for example, wore very dark or black clothing, so that their heads loom out of the black background eerily in the videos, as when Sedakova is in a three-quarters shot, reading her own poem (figure 5). The effect intensifies in close-up, and all the *Live Poetry* videos mix in such extreme close-ups. Sedakova also recites Elena Shvarts's "Short Ode to Hopelessness" ("Malen'kaia oda k beznadezhnosti," 1998). Her choice thematizes the spiritual longing that the video evokes: the eloquent poem was written in memory of Shvarts's mother, Dina Shvarts.[75] Sedakova's reading contains its own proleptically memorial gesture because Shvarts was mortally ill at the time she made this video. It was published the day after Shvarts died.[76] Across *Live Poetry*, the dead live on as readers (among its performers, Vasily Borodin, Grigory Dashevsky, Arkady Dragomoshchenko, Mikhail Eremin, Natalia Gorbanevskaya, Mikhail Gendelev, Victor Koval, Eduard Limonov, Lev Rubinstein, and Aleksei Tsvetkov have since died), and the words of deceased poets resound in others' voices. This palimpsestic presence of the dead underlies the power of *Live Poetry* to literalize the metaphor of its name, and to materialize a kind of spiritual afterlife for poetry itself.

The iterability of recorded poetry readings gave *Live Poetry* the potential to become interpretable and legible as canon formation, and as a window into the nature of contemporary poetry creation itself. Surely the creators of *Live Poetry* had something of this potential in mind when they named the series. It signals that *OpenSpace* is itself opening a window onto the life of poetry. The site participates in the cultural work of keeping poems and poets vividly alive in our imaginations. *OpenSpace*'s archive also lets us study performance as recorded, framed, and electronically delivered. I have been referring to it as an archive, but it is in effect also a repertory, in Diana Taylor's terms. *Live Poetry* constitutes an act of engagement as well as a repository of performances—one

FIGURE 5. Olga Sedakova, *Live Poetry* reading (2010)

poet reading another's work demonstrates that the canon is created by active engagement and physical presence: in contributing to this repertoire, "people participate in the production and reproduction of knowledge by 'being there,' being a part of the transmission."[77]

The doubled performances, which make the work of another poet equal in status to one's own work, remind us of the ghosting of voices inherent in a poet's performance, and of the ways that subjectivity and reperformance (or mimesis) are always entangled.[78] These readings let us study Russian poetry in its current state: poetry as embraced by digital media, made available as video and audio and archived for repeated viewings; poetry as a connective tissue among poets who read each other's work and who dedicate poems to one another; poetry reading as the visible embodiment of a human being's work in creating poetry; and poetry publication as a curated activity, selected, sequenced, and framed by editors, translators, and other poets. All these actors are involved, as are we, in another cultural performance—the practice of making what we read our own, and of transmitting texts we most love to others.

That activity was also richly on display in the anthology of women's poetry created in Ekaterinburg, in performances that sought to come at the question of canon formation from a different angle: to insist that even in 2021, a site for women's poetry as presented by women poets could find an audience. Two weeks after the project was unveiled to the public, it had more than 1,200 visitors. This website attests to the prominence of women's voices in contemporary poetry, and it sought to draw attention to the poets who read and to those whose works are performed (it has separate pages with bio-bibliographical notes on them all, thus encouraging visitors to read more). The videos offer a capacious archive of performance styles and modes of self-presentation by dozens of poets young, old, and everything in between. The readings can be focused more on the music of the poem, where one palpably hears line or stanza breaks, or declaimed in a dramatic style, where the pace is entirely determined by the psychological portrait drawn by the lyric.[79] One comes away from the anthology with a richer sense of how women make poems their own and model for their readers a range of affective responses to the poem's music, its insights, its linguistic magic. Many of these same things can be said about the *Live Poetry* archive, where one has the added benefit of seeing the poet read a poem of their own. Sometimes, though, the poet's performance practices are resolutely hidden. What happens when the poet writes and writes and writes but will not read—on screen, in person, anywhere, anytime?

Nika Skandiaka, Who Cannot Be Seen or Heard

If performance is an embodied practice, as many have theorized, then the enormous poetic output of Nika Skandiaka presents the ultimate test case for a performance where the body has been withheld.[80] We have a 2007 Moscow book of Skandiaka's poetry, several journal publications, and (until she took most of them down in 2022) hundreds of poems and dozens of translations published on several websites she established.[81] But no one in the world of Russian poetry will say that they have met Skandiaka face to face.[82] Skandiaka's decisions to withhold all personal encounters, to have all connections to others mediated by email or blog comments, and to use what is an obvious pseudonym have created a palpable distance between the poet and her readers. There are no recordings, either audio or video, of readings. This is its own kind of performance, I believe, and it should not be regarded in the same way as the many mystifications or hoaxes that have dotted the history of poetry in and beyond Russia. One of the mystifications, the most famous one, Elizaveta Dmitrieva writing as Cherubina de Gabriak, was mentioned just above, as the author of a poem in the anthology *Women's Poetry*. But Skandiaka's extensive writings point in a different direction: this performance is a rejection of the figure of speech "a body of work," for here, the work itself commands all attention. The name Nika suggests that Skandiaka is a woman, and the performance behind this work reads as a radical act of resistance to the whole history of women's poetry, where personality, biography, and physical presence have been enormously consequential. That this act of resistance has been structured by the creation of a double, an alter ego who writes and translates poems, lines Skandiaka up with the other poets treated here so far, for all the ways in which she is radically different from them.

Skandiaka is not entirely a poet to whom no story of any kind can attach. But there isn't much. A minimal biography of Skandiaka has been present from the start. For example, an early set of texts by Skandiaka appeared in Kuz'min's enormous anthology of Russian poetry as world poetry; the biography offered at the back of that book specifies a poet born in 1978 in Moscow, reared in the United States, and living in Edinburgh.[83] These sparse details are repeated verbatim in other places, and they are enough to suggest a life of emigration and movement between countries (she now lives in the United States, to the best of my knowledge). The physical movement between countries has a complement in Skandiaka's writings, for she is a formidable translator, particularly between English and Russian.[84] Translation itself occurs often within her texts, as the poet freely inserts words in English into a text in Russian, as well as transliterated Russian into a text in Cyrillic. The poems also move seamlessly among multiple discourses—the worlds of machines, particularly computers, and urban environments, as well as the sensory and cognitive experiences of those worlds.

Skandiaka also records sounds and sights of the natural world. In one early poem, an amoeba is seen under a microscope, and the poet notes that surely it feels horror; in another, ivy grits its teeth and seems to verbalize its presence ("i tut! tut! tut!"); in a third, the call of a cardinal is reproduced.[85] That last poem ends with questions about what the bird is thinking or desiring, and thus sets out a task for poetry, making palpable—in a sense, performing—the cognitive activity of another, not just another person, but another being of an entirely different part of the natural order. This is its own form of doubling, allowing the poem to imagine itself as a vehicle for the subjectivity of another. In a 2005 poem, Skandiaka produced her own "Mutabor," or incantation that turns humans into animals and vice versa.[86]

Later work takes up this project of transformational subjectivity far more extensively. Although invocations of the natural world continue, even more prominent is the lexicon and signaling of computers and machine learning. One of the poet's avatars, to use the term for doubling born in the virtual world, is "System for Machine Dialogue," in fact.[87] The visual layout of the poems engages with the reader's imagination to suggest that we are in the presence of a text permeated by coding—its punctuation marks, its syntax, its specific organization of the world as a series of commands. Rather than the conventions of lyric apostrophe, which imagine a world of persons and things who might respond to the poet's acts of address, Skandiaka's texts rely on the conventions of computer coding, which imagines a world based on algorithms. It is not that feelings, affective responses, and ideas of something non-material or spiritual get swept to the side. Rather, the branching syntax of cyber communication means that the texts offer themselves up as a series of self-modifying propositions, constantly challenging their own assertions, as if pushing the reset button to go back to premises or promises that hold out further meanings.

Repetition thus becomes a chief rhetorical trope of the texts, but it is repetition at the level of sound and morphology as much as it is a set of repeated lexical items. Writing with this high level of repetition and patterning makes Skandiaka like, rather than unlike, many others writing in Russian today. What is distinctive, although not unique, is the use of these unfolding patterns of iteration to enable a kind of rumination as the central subject matter of the poems. I say it is not unique because we can find the self-correcting, self-observing utterance as a key feature of Arkady Dragomoshchenko's work, writing very much in the spirit of American L=A=N=G=U=A=G=E poetry.

Skandiaka's orientation is different, however, in part because she has no interest in the social poetics that were crucial to L=A=N=G=U=A=G=E poetry.[88] She also tends not to create the kind of dense-on-the-page texts brilliantly exemplified by Dragomoshchenko's writings, whether in prose or in poetry. Her work has a strongly visual orientation toward open space, and although there are some print publications, so much of the work appeared only in her blogs that we need to think of the open space of the screen, not the page.[89] To understand that orientation, I propose a somewhat counterintuitive comparison, one that gets us closer to apprehending the specific kind of creative performance that Skandiaka's texts enact.

The comparison is to how the American poet Jorie Graham thinks about creating poems. And to the experience of reading Graham's poems. There are staggering differences, of course: Graham is a great inheritor of the Anglo-American lyric tradition, a poet whose range of reference and whose own models for creative work run from Italian Renaissance painting to Wallace Stevens, from Keats to A. R. Ammons or her own teacher, Donald Justice. The intensity of lyric expressiveness in her work is utterly unlike the withdrawal into a puzzling collocation of words that marks the surface of Skandiaka's poems. But there is a strong lyric undercurrent in Skandiaka, and the comparison to Graham can help make it palpable.

They also share a commitment to making poems that create the "mind in action," as Helen Vendler put it, in writing about Graham's 2002 book *Never*, the mind "pushing and pausing, cresting and deepening."[90] Vendler was perhaps Graham's best reader, and certainly the one most keenly attuned to her poetics of thought. In writing about *The End of Beauty* (1987), Vendler explained that "the lines ripple and pause, utter and subside. The poems are often long, like sonatas, carrying the musical moment of process through its hurry, its delay, its fears and repentings," but she also notes that Graham is "determined to track ongoing mental action even at the risk of diffuseness" and that the progress from thought to thought can be halting.[91] The language of description has a loveliness appropriate to Graham's gorgeous, post-Romantic poetics, and although that beauty may feel rhetorically far from the cyberworld of Skandiaka, the observations are uncannily apt as a way to understand the rhythms and the mental orientations of Skandiaka's texts.

What is perhaps not so much uncanny as totally to be expected, given the finite resources of graphic signs, is that both poets have brilliant recourse to marks of punctuation as a way to speed or slow the tempo of reading, and as a way to signal to readers patterns of subordination, alternation, revising along the way, as well as moments when thought comes right up to the edge of its own possibilities. In the poems of *Never* especially, but also elsewhere, Graham uses a dense overlay of parentheses and brackets, the roundness and squareness of which seem to enact how ideas tightly fold into themselves as the sentences unfurl. In *Swarm* (2000), spaces open between words. Still earlier, in *The End of Beauty* and *Regions of Unlikeness* (1991), Graham was using the dash repeatedly as a form of both interruption and connection and employing a blank underlined space where an absent word had been, as if pushed out of the poems. The dashes persist throughout her work, including in *Materialism* (1993), which also has an admixture of texts in changing formats, including words in columns, prose extracts, and time-stamped notations. The dashes can still be found as a signature in Graham's 2017 book *Fast*, but there are also arrows between words that seem almost to propel readers ever faster through the lines, even where the density of thought and image slows us down.

I could go on, for Graham has been prolific over a long period, and as in Skandiaka, the ways of using punctuation markers have been manifold and changing, but those arrows are a good place to stop because they show Graham in effect inventing her own punctuation. Skandiaka hasn't invented punctuation marks so much as absorbed them from the worlds of mathematics and computer science, and she has foregrounded her readiness to draw on those worlds, for instance, in using numbers as if they could be markers of identity. The title of her published book, for example, is a bracketed date, [12/4/2007], which for US readers might need to be translated given conventions for writing the date in Russian: those numbers signify April 12, 2007, presumably the date the book was finished. I presume that because each of the book's nine sections is designated by a date given in the same numerical style and enclosed in brackets: the first is November 27, 2005, and the last is April 3, 2007, which puts the book title shortly after the dateline or title of the final text. Or not exactly final, since the book concludes with Skandiaka's translation of Randolph Healy's long poem "Arbor Vitae."

The translation is far from an afterthought. Healy's poem may have been a model for Skandiaka in how to incorporate computer language and its signs, but he also showed ways to use numbers and a whole range of language games (anagrams, acrostics, formulas). In his case, the variegated surface of the poem was in the service of telling a story about brain chemicals, sign language, and the miseducation of the deaf, whereas for Skandiaka, the overall project is something closer to what I have described in Graham: a record of thoughts rippling across the mind, of cognitive processes recorded. Sometimes this comes across as a record of how a poem is made, as when Skandiaka posts a word or two, then in a few hours, posts a small elaboration of those initial utterances, and in a few hours, expands still further. Or a larger, complex text might be posted to one blog, and then in another text or set of texts, one finds lexical alternatives, as if different forked paths have been taken.

The excellent criticism on Skandiaka has focused on the textual qualities that enable the processual orientation of the poetry. Some of that work has pointed to the mix of languages, and to a bilingual foundation of the poems.[92] The fragmentary nature of the poetic lines has been studied, as have the consequences for a kind of dispersed subjectivity, or a sense of the subject that changes across and within lines.[93] The punctuation, as noted here, contributes to the sense of rupture within lines, and to that end Skandiaka can even mobilize the asterisks often used to separate parts of a text; in the book publication, little square boxes are varied in shape and number, suggesting a kind of syntax created by the devices of book design.[94]

In the extensive material once freely available on her various websites, graphic signs, design elements, and punctuation were increasingly aimed to direct the reading experience, to make the texts perform rhythmically and visually. For example, line spacing or layout on the screen were used expressively, and poems presented as charts or data sheets especially invited the eye to read both across and down, disrupting semantic connections almost as soon as they are made. The vertical double bar || was often seen. The symbol itself comes from computer science: it is a logical operator meaning "or," and the poet can use it syntactically to organize the logic of a line. But it is also found between texts as a design element. Within a line of poetry, it can simply demarcate elements of the line. Another kind of punctuation from the language of coding are square brackets. In Python, square brackets enclose a list or an array, with items separated by commas. At other times, the brackets work like parentheses, denoting parentheses within parentheses, or offering visual variety in lines where there are multiple parentheses. The same observations could be made of curly brackets, recognizable from mathematical set theory. Let me give just one visual snapshot of how this might look, four lines at the end of a sequence in which the poet basically signs off. The Russian words mean something like, "okay, I'm off" followed by "and this is always." It's the mix of brackets and slash marks, as well as the lineation, that make that prosaic utterance interesting.

$\{[\text{всё,}]$
убегаю$\}/\{[$

и это
всегда$\}/\{]$[95]

The irony of signing off even as the texts will continue feels entirely consonant with Skandiaka's erratic on-screen persona.

All of these graphic and punctuation elements constitute Skandiaka's performance practice on page and screen. Much of the rhetorical surface of the work—the signs from coding, the idiosyncratic graphic signs, the affordances of digital technology—presses us to imagine the poetic subject as an emerging hybrid of the human and the machine, as a cyborg whose capacities are comprehensible essentially as the generation of new poetic material. Such a conceptualization of Skandiaka's project aligns it well with digital poetry, a burgeoning field in multiple poetic traditions.[96] But that alignment, while significant, cannot fully comprehend this body of work. What distinguishes Skandiaka in this field is the nature of her poetic practice, one shaped by the poet's renunciation of a biography or knowable identity, and by a continuation of just enough elements of the predigital, precyborg poetic tradition to create what one of her most astute readers, the late poet Aleksei Parshchikov, called an unmistakable aura.[97]

At the start of this chapter, I invoked Walter Benjamin's claim that, in the age of mechanical reproduction, art's aura would necessarily dissipate, and Parshchikov makes that same observation when he writes about Skandiaka. But he adds that the distinction between an original and a copy disappears in the virtual world, and in the widening space created by vacillations between those two poles, digitally enacted poetic texts like Skandiaka's have the potential to reestablish that aura. Parshchikov lists several ways in which Skandiaka seizes that potential, and one of his most memorable is near the end of the essay, where he moves from the formal fragmentariness of the texts to an insight into their apprehension of the whole natural world: "The fragmentary and sporadic qualities of the texts create a portrait of the natural world as if before the appearance of its first classifiers."[98] Parshchikov had pointed to the significance of translating Healy for Skandiaka's poetics, and there is a whole deep layer in Healy's "Arbor Vitae" of something like evolutionary and somatic biochemistry, of the creation of the world from chemical elements, or of neurotransmitters, which are the building blocks of his acrostics, too. Skandiaka's re-creation of the natural world can feel more lyrical, as in a set of texts that invoke hills, valleys, a lion, an apple, and sheafs of grain; the first poem begins by asking how those things, out there in the fields—they are as yet unnamed—how they are, how they rustle in its dark shadows.[99] In another poem, the poet imagines a reader who would take a printed version of her poems out into a sunlit apple orchard.[100]

These are evocative images. We might say that the aura of this poetry is found not in its creation of an authentic individual poetic subject, but rather in the impulse toward vividness, toward vivacity in its poetic lines. Similarly, Ilya Kukulin admired as the most salient trait of her work its "pathos for the *rehabilitation of reality*," its creation of what he called "the effects of presence." He explains these effects as a state of direct, unmediated, and intensive experience of the world.[101] And in that kind of performance, Skandiaka is in effect showing us how the example of a poetic world like Jorie Graham's is not so far away after all. One of Graham's key terms, the soul, turns up in an early Skandiaka text, and as if aware that her pathway toward that term would be through the poetic tradition, this sequence of lines also quotes Marina Tsvetaeva, the celebrated interrogator of what she called the "hour of the soul."[102]

One crucial difference, however, bears remembering: Jorie Graham's storied biography has attached to her considerable fame as an American poet.

One can find videos and audio recordings of Graham reading at multiple stages of her career, and she has done countless live readings and recorded dozens of memorable interviews. Her distinctive voice long resonates in the mind of anyone who hears her read.[103] But in Nika Skandiaka's work, whether read on page or on screen, none of us has any idea how the poet would perform it. I began here by talking about the poet's decision to take a pseudonym and not meet any readers or other poets in person, not to give a body or a face to the poetry, but I want to end by reflecting on the equally consequential decision not to give the work her voice. Remarkably, Oleg Dark, in a penetrating essay about Skandiaka's 2007 book, tries to argue that this is *oral poetry*—the emphasis is his, and he claims that the written presentation is merely its means of transmission. But when he adds parenthetically that it would be interesting to hear how Skandiaka reads the poems, he is acknowledging the desire to hear that voice, even as he admits that whatever else this is, in our experience of the text, this will not be orally performed poetry, not by the poet herself.[104] Dark goes on to draw on the Healy translation to claim that the poetry is voiced as something like the sign language of the deaf, that it performs a language of mimicry and gesture. But to my mind, Skandiaka has refused the language of gesture, with its requirement of an imagined or present body, as fully as she has refused to give readers the timbre, pitch, and rhythms of her own voice. She keeps our attention fixed on the visual arrangement of letters, design elements, and punctuation marks, pressing us to puzzle out the significance of these many signs and to do so on their own terms, whatever they may be.

At a conference in March 2020 on contemporary poetry and translation, I spoke about Skandiaka's work, and there was a lively conversation about why a poet who was such a prolific translator would refuse all requests to translate her work (all of her blogs had a statement asking that the work not be translated). Matvei Yankelevich suggested that her intended audience was the world of Russian poetry, period. Perhaps, since the refusal to permit translation means that the poems, as poems, will not reach readers who have no Russian. She also sets some real challenges to those who write about her work when they cannot translate quoted extracts and make them more accessible (thus my reliance here on paraphrase rather than translation for quoted lines). That further guarantees that the critical work on Skandiaka will be largely in Russian.

The orientation toward Russian speakers is another element of her unique performance, one with lessons for translation theory. Considerable pathos-laden work has criticized what is seen as poetry written for export, poems with enough local color to raise the flag of their native culture, but also as if written for translation into languages with a wider readership than their own (most often English).[105] This criticism is meant to take down an idea of "world literature." Skandiaka stands as a defiant point of resistance, even as her work displays many forms of internalized translation. Her existence as an unknowable individual person, as the creator of texts that can only live in the languages in which she writes them, and as someone who made hundreds of texts unavailable and untraceable intensifies the aura of both poet and text. For all who do read them, these poems are one of the most distinctive poetic performances in the twenty-first century.

To End: Prigov

I argue in this chapter that doubling is a distinctive feature of performances of contemporary Russian poetry, across several sets of recorded performances and in the work by Fanailova and Skandiaka to perform acts of creation before their readers. The doubling works differently in each setting: it can involve speech and writing (in the women's poetry anthology), personae or pseudonym, bilingualism, among other formal devices and themes. An open question is whether this doubling is inherent in performances of poetry, or whether there is some point of origin or exemplary poet initiator of the trend. In an earlier version of this chapter, I had planned to write about the wide-ranging performances of Dmitry Aleksandrovich Prigov, but I pulled back from that idea largely because his performances have been well discussed by others.[106] And a shorter account of his singing appears in chapter 4. But Prigov's example remains an appropriate way to conclude this chapter, not least because he had so many doubles, from the Soviet *militsaner* to the spectacular photographic series where he poses, hands folded, eyes behind sunglasses and head framed by an admiral's cap, next to monuments to Russia's classic poets (figure 6). In each of these photographs, the base of the monument is visible, with the name of the great writer clearly shown (Pushkin, Lermontov, Mayakovsky, or, in this case, Gogol).[107] The posed poet in effect replaces the writer known to be towering above the pedestal. The pose, particular because of the grandly ironic effect of the hat, positions Prigov as the honored writer's double, sharing monumental space.

Prigov's performances—in person, in recordings, in photographs, in his series of self-portraits—include the wide range of his performances on the page. They blazed the trail for poets to see performance as constitutive of the poetic

FIGURE 6. Dmitry Prigov, photographed by Vikenti Nilin for *The Monuments* series (2006), Courtesy of the Moscow Museum of Modern Art

act itself. Critics and scholars are giving us ever more to work with in understanding Prigov's legacy, including the huge five-volume edition of his works published in Moscow.[108] It is especially clear that his legacy extends far beyond his foundational participation in Conceptualism.[109] And as more becomes known, I suspect that many more aspects of his work will start to seem prescient. One discovery, given the strong presence of women poets in contemporary poetry, was his having understood and then demonstrated, in a remarkable series of poems, that writing in a woman's voice could offer a whole range of new forms of resistance to the many kinds of hegemony his poems react to.[110] A different aspect of that prescience can be found in the small-scale video GIFs he made as a web-based project called "Public and Private in Contemporary Art" ("Obshchestvennoe i privatnoe v sovremennom tvorchestve"): it is as if he proleptically participated in the world of TikTok poetry videos.[111] Each of those GIFs bears a sentence or two joking about the content; each is signed with the poet's initials, DAP, and most include a light-hearted word of farewell ("Poka"). In that signature, one senses yet another kind of performance: the light touch, the self-possessed irony, the awareness that for all the jocularity, the aura would ever linger. The association between Prigov and performance will also be as indelible as his thousands of printed poems. A rare gathering of poets in Moscow post–February 24, 2022, was at the Nonfiction Book Fair in December 2022, for a wake in Prigov's honor. The participants recalled previous Book Fair competitions for the loudest recitation of a Prigov text; those earlier competitions in turn were meant to recall Prigov's own "Kikimora shriek" performance. He was seen as the ideal poet to commemorate the enforced silences of Moscow in the period of the "Special Military Operation."[112] They read poems based on his work that doubled as bitter attacks on the prowar atmosphere in which they were living. Prigov's work made possible a performance that showed a new generation of poets already looking back to earlier eras for a model for reviving Russian poetry. That small Moscow performance was a promissory note for the future, and a way of resisting the terrifying present.

3

On Magnitude

POETRY IN LARGE AND SMALL FORMS

Rubinstein • Gronas • Eremin • Sukhovei •
Simonova • Grimberg

Breathe in deeply, hold onto the air, blue sky is in your head.
—MARINA TEMKINA, 2020

HOW MUCH space does an expression of freedom need? The question might seem one of form, asking how the space on the page is organized, and what meters and formats the poets rely on. Many poets treated in this book write mostly free verse, departing from several centuries of a tradition dominated by poems shaped by familiar metrical patterns, stanzaic organization, and especially rhyme. Those elements have not disappeared, but they coexist with more free verse, and all of poetry has absorbed more aesthetic elements associated with prose—everyday language, speech rhythms, and a logical flow often like that of cognition or meditation. Free verse brings important possibilities for liberation, where formal expansiveness can allegorize other forms of freedom.

Form matters, but an equally telling development in recent poetry has to do with size. Play with a poem's magnitude can be as telling as its play with form, especially fixed form.[1] The last several decades have seen poets define their work in these terms. Some work takes up long poetic lines and extends the traditions of prose poetry, and other texts are written in ever-smaller, tighter forms. Magnitude, in other words, stretches in both directions, sometimes simultaneously. This chapter leads up to the narrative orientation and long-form prose-like poetry of poets like Faina Grimberg and Ekaterina Simonova, but it begins with the intense minimalism of Mikhail Eremin, Mikhail Gronas, and Daria Sukhovei. Others are drawn in along the way. It's a group of otherwise dissimilar poets, all of whom are interrogating the imaginative possibilities of size and scope.

These poets take up problems of space, including the space of the page in books or on screen. Unlike the performances of those who seem to write in the moment we are reading them, like Nika Skandiaka and Elena Fanailova (both of whom work at once on a grand scale and as if with smaller forms), these texts catch a different kind of present moment, something directly experienced or from a meticulously re-created past (the latter brilliantly exemplified in Maria Rybakova's long poem *Gnedich* [2011]).[2] Much of this work, whether large or small, has elements of minimalism as art critics define that term: they use it for artwork that eschews the high-class status, high-flown rhetoric, and ornamented loveliness associated with Art, capital *A*, in favor of a prosaic, down-to-earth composition derived as if from everyday life. But as in the visual arts, some of the smallest poems strive to re-create a vast sense of interiority replete with metaphysical desires, or to suggest a whole cosmos through the briefest of poetic texts. It is in this aesthetic largesse, I believe, that small-form minimalist work crosses paths with more maximalist projects. Size and scope become what Caroline Levine would call "colliding forms," an expressive textual element that can show us surprising sides of several poets.[3]

Many of the small-form masters accumulate their short texts: this serial impulse does not produce a progressive sequence that builds to a single larger whole (a model for which might be a crown of sonnets), but the sheer accumulation of examples can build toward the kind of vast project epitomized in the work of Conceptualist Dmitry Prigov. None of these poets has sought to write 36,000 poems, as Prigov was said to have done by 2005, but some are following a modified Conceptualist pathway. The smallest bit of poetic text can do double duty as a building block in an impressively larger edifice.

A quick example might be useful here before I turn to sustained readings of several poets. Leonid Schwab, a master of startling, mysterious stories in his small poems, wrote this four-line poem as one of his most minimalist statements, and he dated it to 1995:

Very old man, waiting for Kaminsky.
Very old man, waiting for Kaminsky.

Kaminsky is delayed at the airfield.
Kaminsky is delayed at the airfield.[4]

Глубокий старик, поджидая Каминского.
Глубокий старик, поджидая Каминского.

Каминский задерживается на аэродроме.
Каминский задерживается на аэродроме.[5]

Schwab's full-sentence repetitions mean that the four-line poem is built out of a mere seven words in Russian (ten in my English), and the repetitions intensify the mood of delay and expectation that is the poem's subject. What makes this minimalism so telling is that Kaminsky appears in other short poems by Schwab. So do other proper nouns and place names. They all remain slightly mysterious, even as the additional texts put new brush strokes to an incomplete portrait. The small world of any one poem, in other words, builds a precarious bridge to other poems, conjuring a larger story or world that can barely be glimpsed.

In this paradoxical bridge between large and small, contemporary poets have achieved the greatest possible freedom. It is as if they have found an exit strategy between the twin temptations of saying as little as possible and taking up all possible air space, as the maximalist projects can do. My mention of Prigov here should alert us to the legacy of the late Soviet period on which so many of these poets are building. Vsevolod Nekrasov is another important precursor, as is Genrikh Sapgir, particularly for the aesthetics of minimalism. Sukhovei draws on these exemplary figures from the Conceptualists and the Lianozovo school in her work.

One further preliminary, to mention the briefest of all possible forms: the one-line poem, or monostich. Maximalism might have no absolute upper limit, but it is fair to say that smallness can be taken down to a quite specific degree of tininess, a poem that starts, then need go nowhere. It is complete in and of itself. The one-line poem (in Russian, *monostikh*) has been a particular form of fascination for Dmitry Kuz'min, who wrote a four-hundred-page book on the topic.[6] Kuz'min has also published the one-line poems of others in his journal *Vozdukh*.[7] One of them, by Marina Temkina, is the epigraph to this chapter: "Breathe in deeply, hold onto the air, blue sky is in your head" (Vdokhni gluboko, derzhi vozdukh, v golove goluboe nebo).[8] This line compresses into its small space many traits typical of small texts: a tightly organized orchestration of consonants (*vd/kh* in the first and fourth words, *gl/b* or *gl/v* in some combination in words 2, 6, and 7, with the equivalent sounds g/k also well distributed); some repetition and development of a single image, in this case that of air, drawn in in the first phrase, held in the second; and an illusion of large space within a tiny verbal artifact, here the sky drawn into the small space of the head. The text does not use internal rhyme, a frequent feature in monostich poetry, but its repetitions and sound echoing bind its words together as tightly as rhyme might achieve.[9] The poem is written as a sequence of imperatives uttered without urgency, as if the tone had absorbed the gentleness of breath itself.

Kuz'min, not only as a fan of one-line poems but as the editor of a journal, *Vozdukh*, whose title means "air," must surely have felt the special loveliness of this poem. It pauses for the length of time it takes to inhale and creates magic in that single breath. Its promise of enlargement makes it a perfect text to launch this chapter, where poems shuttle internally between their contrasting magnitudes. Poets also build larger forms out of small pieces and create illusions of expansion within constricted formal spaces. Or the reverse: poets use large form to burrow into the tiniest kernels of an idea.

Lev Rubinstein and the Gentle Expansions of the Prosaic

One poet who modeled precise shuttling between large projects and small forms is Lev Rubinstein. He remained a vital presence long past the Moscow Conceptualist movement that brought him fame, particularly through his spirited essays and public statements.[10] His prose is an example of how to write poetry by other means, and there are important parallels between the two forms of expression.[11] But the impact of his poems written on library cards came first, and it is a pleasure to reread them and to reexperience the thrill of what he was able to achieve with minimal material. Rubinstein showed the potent force of single poetic lines, sometimes even single words, collected into a sequence that could be hilarious and profound. One can re-create that sense of reading off cards through facsimile editions, and the website *Vavilon* has a section in which fourteen of his texts can be read by clicking on each "card" to move the text along.[12] In performance, Rubinstein typically read quickly and dryly, barely looking up. The rhythm is seemingly structured by the requisite time to move from one card to the next, and the poet has confirmed that the card is itself a unit of rhythm.[13] But the pacing in performance was controlled by Rubinstein with masterful understatement and accompanied by his inimitable, subtly changing facial expressions.[14] These gestures are a source of humor as well as pathos.[15] And it would be a mistake to underestimate the pathos. Earlier on, when Rubinstein was read firmly as a Conceptualist and most often compared to Dmitry Aleksandrovich Prigov, there was a sense that he was creating a "museum of linguistic models," and that his own subject position was lacking—in an important early statement on Conceptualism, Mikhail Epstein compared him to a tour guide whose opinions simply would not be appropriate.[16] There is something appealing about that museum metaphor, especially as Conceptualists worked so often in alliance with visual artists. But particularly now, when we have so much more of Rubinstein's writings, he seems less like an anonymous museum curator or guide than like a poetic version of the artist Joseph Cornell, the creator of framed collections of tiny objects sprinkled with bits of language, assembled with a distinctive and idiosyncratic flair.[17] No accident that the metaphor of the frame has such deep associations with Rubinstein's work: one of his best-known texts is "Mother Washed the Window Frame" ("Mama myla ramu," 1987), and he has said that the contemporary author "corresponds with the frame of the text."[18]

Unlike the ornamental, sentimental material to which Cornell was often drawn, however, Rubinstein used the plainest possible language. Some texts organize that unpoetic language into familiar forms.[19] Other discourses are mixed in, from the bureaucratic to the academic. But most often, the texts are built out of fragments of spoken dialogue, particularly the utterances that work as a kind of social glue, saying nothing in and of themselves but moving along the speech acts of the other. Those seemingly empty comments are filled out and defamiliarized by easily recognizable poetic quotations, often altered in misquotation or by a dramatic lowering in pitch.[20]

Rubinstein's decision to write poems on library cards, one line per card, was his early signature, a reference to his former job as a librarian and a way to reuse available paper in a time of chronic shortages. Some of those cards bare the device, as the formalists would say, of the library card format to offer an apparent bibliographical entry and nothing more. Yet there is always something more: some data in the citation have gone awry, like the reiterating page numbers, pp. 12–21, for four different scholarly articles "cited from" the same volume in "It's Me" ("Eto ia," 1995). Or the attribution of one of the poem's exaggeratedly casual lines, "Well then, I'll be on my way" (Nu chto zhe, ia poidu) to a character presented as if an entry in a bibliography: Golubovsky, Arkady L'vovich.[21] The effect of the pauses between lines gets lost in my paraphrase, but the sequences, however seemingly plain their language, always have what Gerald Janecek called an "inexplicable musical aura."[22]

That music is created by the poems' stark juxtaposition of their often lengthy list-like quality—the numbered cards can add up to more than 170 (in the early text "Autocodex 74," the first in the 2015 retrospective collection). Even the shorter sequences produce more than an additive effect as line follows line. A splendid example is the fifty-eight-card text "And On and On" ("Vse dal'she i dal'she," 1984), whose title self-referentially denotes the text's own forward movement. It proceeds by making an assertion, then warning the reader or listener to beware of what might come next. For example:

3

Here respiration is easy and free.
The best respite—is here.
But one most go on.

4

Here no matter where you look—it's all charming, no matter what the ear picks up—it's all a sweet refrain, no matter who speaks—it's all true.
But let's go on.

3

Здесь дышится легко и свободно.
Лучший отдых—это здесь.
Но надо идти дальше.

4

Здесь куда взгляд ни упадет—всё прелесть, что ухо ни уловит— всё сладкий напев, кто что ни скажет—всё истина.
Но пойдем дальше.[23]

This passage has the association between freedom and air that I have noted in so many other texts. There are faint and funny echoes in the diction, as when the root that means "breathing" is in both the first two lines quoted here (the translation suggests the echo differently, with the visually similar "respiration" and "respite"). The changing rhythms are artful, as the text moves into a visually very long line to start card 4 but one that is broken up syntactically, creating the illusion of the text's usual short segments.

Later cards continue to use the same rhetorical devices—lists based on syntactic similarity and internal segmentation. They combine forward movement, "and on and on," with a slowdown created by repetition. In the middle of the text are nine cards that create unnamed characters beset by unhappiness and incomprehension, and again the syntax keeps to unnervingly fixed rhythms, the tone flat. We are very much in the world of Daniil Kharms's "happenings" (sluchai), but as if imploded by internal repetitions.[24]

24

Here is someone depressed by what has happened. The attempt to explain what exactly has oppressed him leads to nothing. One pities him;
Someone surprises by the paradoxical nature of his judgments. But one pities him too for some reason;
Someone consoles himself with the anticipation of something different. His path is bleak. Does he realize this?
Someone doesn't see or hear himself. It's a shame: he would have looked at a lot of things differently;

24

Вот некто удручен происходящим. Попытка выяснить, что именно его угнетает, ни к чему не приводит. Его жаль;
Некто поражает парадоксальностью суждений. Но и его почему-то жаль;
Некто тешит себя ожиданиями чего-то иного. Его путь уныл. Знает ли он об этом?
Некто сам себя не видит и не слышит. И напрасно: на многие вещи он стал бы смотреть иначе;[25]

The text exudes Rubinstein's typical gentle humor, with the speaker swooping in to introduce a kind of quotation from nineteenth-century elegiac poetry ("ego put' unyl") next to the acerbic observation that he is missing the chance to view the world differently. Multiple unnamed individuals endure woes that elicit pity. As throughout Rubinstein's work, very little here adds up to quite a lot.

In what follows, I take Rubinstein's extraordinary agility in moving between the large and the small as a point of departure for several poets, none of whom writes texts that resemble his. He was inimitable, but some later poets pick up on the possibilities of creating the illusion of minimalism and maximalism at the same time. And several have something in common with his signature tone—a remarkably gentle kindness (in this, deeply unlike Daniil Kharms) and a winning pleasure in the small coincidences and juxtapositions that his very plain language surfaces. Figuring out a way to be so acutely perceptive and nonviolent is one of the major projects of this poetry.[26] The poet who is most like him in this regard is Mikhail Gronas, to whom I now turn.

Mikhail Gronas, Master of Understatement

It may be hard now to re-create the sudden intensity of attention to the poetic achievement of Mikhail Gronas when his poems appeared in the early 2000s, because his prominence and impact seem so obvious twenty years later. One measure might be that he was awarded the Andrei Bely Prize in 2002 for his first book, and he was chosen over short-listed books by very highly regarded poets: Aleksei Tsvetkov, Sergei Timofeev, Kirill Medvedev, Sergei Zav'ialov, and Sergei Kruglov.[27] Speaking for the jury, Elena Fanailova singled out the poems' extreme economy of form (her phrase was a "restricted palette"), and although she emphasized his orientation toward the European poetic and intellectual tradition, she also saw links to the work of Olga Sedakova, Mikhail Kuzmin, and the poets of Lianozovo and OBERIU.[28] Gronas, a scholar himself, builds on a tradition he knows extremely well, yet his work sounds like no one else's. One has the sense that he found a way to boil down traces of others' work into a powerful, nearly vanishing concentrate.

The texts are small, as is the body of work (two slim volumes in two decades). His ability to work with extremely meager formal elements and with the theme of lack make the idea of magnitude a valuable way into his poetics. Gronas often writes of those pushed to the margins by a social order they find incomprehensible—orphans, prisoners, the poor—and then translates this sense of human smallness into a set of forms, and then, as if out of nowhere, introduces a kind of sublimely vast sense of space or mental reach to render the smallness astonishingly paradoxical.

Gronas made even a comma significant in the title of his first book: *Dear Orphans,* (*Dorogie siroty,,* 2002).[29] The poem in which the book's title appears is exemplary of his ways of making poems out of meager means. Note that comma in the first line, and then the refusal of other punctuation in the clauses that follow:

> dear orphans,
> your graves are dug
> in greenest pastures
> into the graves you lie down
> and oblige us greatly
>
> oblige us greatly

> дорогие сироты,
> вам могилы вырыты
> на зеленой пажити
> вы в могилы ляжете
> и очень нас обяжете
>
> очень нас обяжете[30]

Like all texts built out of a restricted lexicon and soundscape, this one loses some density in translation, although the alliteration made possible by "green," "grave," and "greatly" helps, and I have taken the liberty of turning "green" into a superlative (which it is not in Russian) so as to echo the *st* sound of "pastures" in "greenest." The Russian binds these six lines together more tightly. There is one rhyme pair for ll.1–2 and then a quadruple and dactylic (three-syllable) rhyme for ll.3–6; all six lines have an unstressed *ti* sound at the end of the rhyme word (or *ty* or *te*, which are similarly sounding unstressed syllables). The implied poverty of orphans whose only home is the grave is allegorized in the exceptionally constrained sonic orchestration of the poem. It also makes unusually expressive work of a very simple childlike meter (trochaic tetrameter).[31]

This kind of doubled-down simplicity works as well at the level of its individual words.[32] Anna Glazova has compared Gronas's diction to a double that is returned to its own identity, pointing toward the double entendre that layers over the word "oblige" (ob"iazhete): those who descend into the grave make space for the living, in a sense having made their lives possible as if engendering them.[33] Gronas intensifies the completely impossible obligation—how would the living repay this debt to the dead?—by addressing the request to orphans, themselves by definition having lived to bury those who engendered them.

Not all of Gronas's miniaturized poems are so formally constricted, and he uses some kinds of repetition to open out a poem as if from the inside.[34] In this poem, l.5 is repeated as l.6, save its opening conjunction. Elsewhere, whole lines can consist of a word or phrase repeated multiple times, again contrasting minimal lexical variety with maximum expressiveness.[35] These repetitions stand out as a rhetorical feature that gives shape to the poems, but behind the striking repetitions is a dazzling variety of formal features, compactly surveyed by Dmitry Kuz'min in 2002 as mixing free verse, rhyme, refrains, and prose: the versification, he said, is marked by an absolute and resolute sense of freedom.[36] What Kuz'min pinpoints as extraordinary formal freedom in the first book recurs in Gronas's second book, *A Short History of Attention* (*Kratkaia istoriia vnimaniia*, 2019). Lev Oborin was right in his review to say that the only reason it did not seem to be as mind blowing as the first book is because, in the intervening seventeen years, other poets had started to do similar things in their own work.[37]

Yet the secrets of the poems' success are as hard to successfully imitate as to divine (surely one reason Igor Gulin, an astute critic of contemporary poetry, found these poems difficult to write about).[38] The magic or alchemy (both words turn up in the reviews) derives from the brevity of the spells. And from the many indicators of smallness besides length, thematized psychologically as a focus on marginalized persons or formally by how many of them use little punctuation, and no capital letters, even to start sentences. There is also a greater concentration lexically of what Jakobson called shifters, the pronouns and adverbs whose referentiality is entirely dependent on context (recall that Rubinstein, for all the ways these two poets differ, was the master of using shifters, epitomized in his poem "I Am Here" ["Ia zdes'"]).[39]

Consider how Gronas uses numbers. Here are two examples, the first from the book *Dear Orphans,* and the second from *A Short History of Attention.*

no one picks up but she's there yelling and losing it can you imagine?

but no one

actually I was calling to say just

what the phone said:

four six eight twelve sounds

not distinct one from the other

one not more important than the other

just this—nothing else

трубку никто не берёт а как она там орёт надрывается
представляешь?

а никто

собственно я звонил сказать именно то

что сказала трубка:

четыре шесть восемь двенадцать звуков

не отличных один от другого

один не важнее другого

только это—ничего другого[40]

And, from his second book:

This poem was written by the author at night.

It is the twenty-three million nine hundred fifty-three thousand
one hundred and eighty-sixth poem after Auschwitz (the figure is
inexact).

In it are expressed such feelings as longing for the homeland, love for
the beloved, and friendship with friends.

All of this is expressed with words.

Это стихотворение написано автором ночью.

Это—двадцать три миллиона девятьсот пятьдесят три тысячи сто
восемьдесят шестое стихотворение после Освенцима (цифра
неточная).

В нём выражаются такие чувства как тоска по родине, любовь к
любимым и дружба с друзьями.

Всё это выражено словами.[41]

The second poem claims that the large number is inexact, giving the lie to its
precision, and the elaborate spelling out of the number, the way it is "expressed
in words," just as the tautological feelings of love for the one who is loved,
friendship for friends, get spelled out with words, designates rather than acti-
vates the emotions mentioned. It resembles the instructions for a poem that
a Conceptualist might write. The earlier poem is a good example of the mourn-

ful poems that Gronas more typically pens, in fact, but it, too, literalizes action—reporting the phone's sounds rather than establishing the phone as a way to communicate. The "four six eight twelve sounds" are heard by someone counting out the rings on the other end. No one is answering.

The sounds are interrogated as if they were phonemes, examined to see if they are distinct and meaningful, leaving the speaker to conclude woefully that there is no differentiation, no "otherness" (the word "other" ends the last three lines) to be had. A poem written after Auschwitz carries the special burden, as Adorno's famous saying had it, of overcoming its own barbarism, and thus its own otherness, but it fails in that mission because it has only cliché and tautology to express. It laments a failure very similar to that of "no one picks up," where there is sound and speech as if on a separate plane of reality— yelling and losing it, someone calling to say just that, someone counting the phone's ringing sounds—and no possibility of speaker and listener connecting. The numbers in the latter poem grow grotesquely large, magnifying the smallness of the poem itself, while the multiplying numbers in "no one picks up" create a kind of lesser internal counting, like small and nimble poetic feet.

The second poem has a further trait that codifies Gronas's improbable and consistently successful way of invoking smallness and largeness at the same time. It consists of what we could call four lines, although the way it is spaced on the page makes them read as four stanzas. Either way, the middle two are long sentences that read as prose, in one case taken up almost entirely by the written-out number 23,953,186, in the other, by a list of topics that point toward some of poetry's most clichéd themes. The incursions of prose-like sentences into Gronas's poetry are frequent, and they often introduce an antipoetic intonation, as here, but they are more like "imaginary prose" than actual.[42] The text uses the lineation of poetry and reads very much as a poem, but it is sucked into its own gravitational force field, or perhaps the reverse: made massively larger from within. The "inexact" number 23,953,186 is the poet's way of signifying that mass.

Why that number? Why, indeed, a number at all? As a scholar, Gronas is interested in quantifiable elements of cultural production among other highly original topics.[43] And among his many gifts as a poet is an ability to write poems that subtly push back against the scholarly work he has done (one of his great topics is memory, including a brilliant study of the formal elements of poems that make them easier to retain in memory; compare his own unforgettable and repeating line about forgetting, with its morphological pun, "to forget is to start to live" / "zabyt' znachit nachat' byt'").[44] But this is not a precisely countable phenomenon, how many poems were written, nor is the time period "since Auschwitz" something to be pinned down. What matters is the mismatch between the precision of numbers and the seemingly immense amount of poetic production over many decades. The poem's quiet horror is its ability to remind us of a different kind of counting, the victims of genocide and mass murder, where the larger the number, the less likely its precision. The grotesque observation attributed to Stalin, that one person's death is a tragedy but the death of millions is a statistic, also reverberates here, as does the Nazi practice of tattooing identification numbers onto the skin of people in concentration camps. In its "inexact" and huge number, this small text maps itself onto orders of magnitude involving poems and persons, history, and ethics.

If we return to "no one picks up," where the phone number would seem to have no such connection to a history of human suffering, we will notice a different affordance of the minimalism of Gronas's poetry. The speaker who ends a poem by saying "just this—nothing else or other" is occupying as little discursive space as possible, exploring what has been called in quite a different context a poetics of precarity.[45] Sarah Dowling would label this as "repetition and annihilation," and Gronas makes their convergence as rhetoric and lived experience the basis of his precarious expressions of subjectivity.[46] He is as if listening to an interior poetic voice that is muttering incomprehensibly. Other Gronas poems can shout out to language, hoping for an answer, but getting only the sound of a ringing phone or perhaps the recording that invites one to leave voicemail; they can work spatially as well, creating a hole through which consciousness looks at nothing more than empty worlds.[47] Words stay stuck in the throat, and the eyes do not know where to look to begin taking in the outlines of an object.[48] Such poems take up the familiar work of lyric poetry in creating a sense of interiority, and they align with the aesthetic observation made by Susan Stewart that miniaturized aesthetic objects exaggerate interiority.[49] Stewart writes that this interiority, because compressed, is unrecoverable; Gronas's poems document that experience repeatedly.[50] That interrogation of interiority opens out to a metaphysics, which is another instance of the small growing large. But most striking is how that cosmos can seem to grow out of essentially empty space, or unspoken words. Or an unfindable word, because the concept or loss for which words are sought is too large.[51] Like the poetry of Paul Celan, whom Gronas has translated, this is a metaphysics of loss. And it is a poetics of holding on to that loss, and making its magnitude felt in the smallest of forms.[52]

This chapter might naturally turn next to the poetry of Anna Glazova, a subtle reader of Gronas's work and a masterful creator of miniatures. I write about her extensively in chapter 5, so here only briefly mention her creations of tiny spaces within her poems. Those spaces lock themselves down the better to be penetrated, and she in fact has more than one poem with a keyhole in it. Consider the compressed spaces in these lines from a poem that begins "woven from leftover string—something" (splelos' iz ostatkov strun—chto-to):

—no right to a voice, mouth,
lock, seal the lack of clarity
of what obviously happens nearby.

—без права голоса, рот,
замкни, запечатай неясность
того, что точно случается неподалёку.[53]

Glazova invokes something that the poem cannot quite absorb, a vagueness that "obviously happens nearby." That is one of her ways of making her small poems open out to what they cannot contain, and although the philosophical and ethical agenda of her work is ambitious, she is not a poet who, like Gronas or, the poet to whom I am about to turn, Mikhail Eremin, sharpens the paradoxes of large and small by invoking vast worlds within the tiny spaces of the lyric. She is rather one who burrows—tellingly, this poem appears in a volume called *For the Shrew* (*Dlia zemleroiki*, 2013). And that is a reason I defer discussion of Glazova, to let photography open up her poetic practice: how to photograph with words that which is buried? Let that aura of photography linger, as I turn to a poet of boundless curiosity about the capacity of words to fix evanescent worlds as if a shutter clicked on them.

Mikhail Eremin, Eight Lines Open to the World

Mikhail Eremin appears here with several other poets, but the idea for this chapter originated with him. He committed to writing in short poetic form to a degree that almost defies belief. What would it mean for a poet to devote all creative energies to a single poetic form? What possibilities for free expression could there be within such limitations, and how might the poet introduce variety into the same poetic form, again and again? How might the smallness of the form be opened to larger themes? The intensity of Eremin's commitment to this form is amplified by the length of his career: he wrote poems for more than five decades. Born in 1936, and an active poet by the late 1950s, he was allied with what was called the Philological school. In unofficial circles in the late Soviet period and especially in the post-Soviet period, he remained an admired and closely read poet, winning an Andrei Bely Prize in 1998 and a fellowship from the Joseph Brodsky Foundation that got him to Rome for two months in 2014. In 2022, only months after his death, he was awarded the Grand Prize by Moskovskii Schet for his volume of collected works, published in 2021. He has been called a quintessential modernist, and yet his poetry never stopped seeming utterly idiosyncratic. Reading it was compared by Lev Loseff to the experience of getting on an escalator for the first time.[54]

Beyond some exceptions in his very earliest work, Eremin's poetic output is entirely confined to poems that are eight lines long, a form called in Russian *vos'mistishie*, the term I use.[55] In English it can be known as the octave, or sometimes the octet, although the latter term is usually reserved for eight lines of a sonnet. Either way, eight-line poems may take the sonnet as a point of origin, seeming a truncated sonnet depending on how the form is set up and whether it leads to an especially sharp point. The form has a currency in Russian that it does not in English; Russian varieties, unlike the English experiments, are also largely unrelated to Italian ottava rima.[56] Eremin's extraordinary exploration of the form represents a burrowing into language that led Mikhail Aizenberg to call him a poet of the dictionary.[57]

The greatest *vos'mistishiia* in Russian were written by Osip Mandelstam in 1932–34. Although he is said to have written these eleven poems as if unwillingly, feeling them as failed pieces of something that should have been larger, his eleven poems retain an incantatory and inspirational power.[58] They have already come up in this study, in the analysis of a poem by Grigory Dashevsky in the introduction. They have generated impressive readings by scholars and critics, often with a focus on them as an ars poetica. A superb study of Mandelstam by Andrew Kahn sees them as a "cycle about the formation of meaning and the meaning of form."[59] They lay the foundation on which a thematic of magnitude and miniaturization is mapped onto a short-form poem: they are "an attempt to grasp the inner excess of space" and include such images as "a minuscule appendage," "a countlessly huge number of eyes," "small magnitudes," "a big universe sleeping in a cradle / at the edge of a small eternity," "an overgrown garden of multitudes," and "a textbook of enormous roots."[60] The imagery reaches across the discourses of biology, botany, evolution, architecture, textiles, mineralogy, music, religion, geography, childhood, metaphysics, and writing itself.

Some of these topics turn up in *vos'mistishiia* by other contemporary poets, and the form has generated important cycles by poets as different as Andrei Rodionov, Sergei Magid, and Natalia Gorbanevskaya.[61] They, alongside Aleksei Parshchikov, Olga Sedakova, and others, differ from Eremin's example not just in their having written eight-line poems among other forms, but also because the thematics are largely truer to their own oeuvre and continue lines of development from *vos'mistishiia* in earlier traditions.[62] But Eremin picked up pretty much where Osip Mandelstam left off: his *vos'mistishiia* extend all the discourses explored by Mandelstam. Some poems also probe at the morphological associations between words that define Mandelstam's late cycle. The "enormous roots" in Mandelstam's image of a textbook link tree roots with the morphological elements of words; that allegorical potential between botany (and scientific fields) and linguistics is essential to Eremin's aesthetic.[63] Ilya Kukulin has also argued in a penetrating essay that Mandelstam's aesthetic credo in his "Conversation about Dante" ("Razgovor o Dante," 1933) underlies Eremin's.[64]

Mandelstam is the foundation for Eremin's *vos'mistishiia* in multiple ways, then.[65] But what was one cycle of poems for Mandelstam generated more than 346 instances of the form in Eremin.[66] What Eremin has done is necessarily more varied than Mandelstam's single cycle in both theme and form. Rhyme and metrical variety mark Mandelstam's *vos'mistishiia* (amphibrachic trimeter for eight of them; iambs, mostly pentameter or hexameter, for the other three). Eremin's poems avoid rhyme and use varying line lengths, sometimes radically so, but his lines mostly scan as iambs, with an illusion often of free verse.[67] That illusion is more than a flickering detail, for it formally signals the feeling of immense freedom that Eremin is able to create despite so rigidly limiting himself to eight-line poems. Other formal ways of opening out the poems are similarly liberating, as we shall see. There is a further noteworthy uniformity within Eremin's publication practice: every one of his books of poetry has the same title, *Poems* (*Stikhotvoreniia*), followed as of 2002 by the specific volume number.[68] In 2021, when a huge volume collected his work, it, too, bore the title *Poems* (*Stikhotvoreniia*). The poet Sergei Zav'ialov noted a further gesture of self-limitation at work: there is no lyric in which the first-person pronoun appears, nor any instance of a verb conjugated in the first person.[69]

The formal restraints find their parallel in the poems' themes. As with the closed-in spaces of Anna Glazova's short poems, Eremin's work is rife with semantic clusters and lexical items that denote closure, and more than a few of the poems, even on repeated readings, suggest a world closed in on itself.

Some critics have read Eremin's hermeticism as closing out a reader.[70] But this is an overstatement: the many signs of closure are deceptive and largely un-done by multiple subtle indications of openness, some of them semantic (for example, images of windows).[71] The syntax, too, can go to great lengths to maximize the ways in which words comment on themselves, as if challenging their meanings. This is one source of the tremendous irony in the poetry and a reason many poems use parentheses multiply and idiosyncratically.

How, then, to open out a form that is strictly limited to eight lines? Not by giving the poems expressive titles, it turns out. The poems never have titles, another instance of an absolute rule. Anne Ferry has subtly analyzed how poem titles can be a sign of ownership and self-presentation; when a text has no title (or a generic one, like *Poems*), she sees these "evasions of the title space" as a kind of "withholding."[72] But Eremin creatively exploits all other possible paratextual additions, including epigraphs, dedications, datelines, and footnotes. A date of composition, usually only the year, concludes every poem. The dedications, either to persons designated by initials and thus with their identities concealed, or to recognizable names, including that of the poet's wife, Iraida, project an idea of an author who lives and works embedded in relationships with others. Just as the datelines place the author into human history, dedications put him into community. The dedications move the poems into a far less sealed-off enigmatic space of utterance, linking the speak-ing poet to other persons. Dedications refer us to a biographical subject, a person living outside the poem's world. This personal quality contrasts with other poetic features of the poems, like the renunciation of first-person utter-ance. The dedications are referential in a distinctly human way.

The epigraphs and the footnotes—and they are foot-of-the-page notes—by comparison intensify the poems' relationship to other texts (some notes give sources, or explain a term by way of a source, as when Hogarth is cited as the source for the phrase "line of beauty").[73] Many, as in "line of beauty," draw in words or texts from other languages. Occasionally foreign words are translated in the notes, and a whole series of poems in the later work have biblical sources. But more often, enigmatic linguistic commentary fills the notes, sometimes defamiliarizing a Russian phrase by putting it into a foreign context. For ex-ample, in the poem that begins "From the naming of the constellations, con-ditioned" ("Ot poimenovaniia sozvezdii, obuslovlennogo," 2001), Eremin links the phrase used in the poem to mean the play of imagination ("igra voo-brazheniia") to a German original, "Spiel der Einbildung," and he names Kant as the source.[74] The notes, the epigraphs, and the dedications all serve to vary the presentation of the eight-line poem on the page, enlarging its visible appearance to the world.

These are all texts that reward very close reading, so I want to linger on two examples, one of them written earlier. As is true of some other poets (Aygi and Mnatsakanova, for instance, among poets treated in this book), Eremin's texts written before the end of the USSR are a literary fact of post-Soviet life.[75] He included examples of the earlier work in several of the books he published with Pushkinskii fond as of 1998. So, in a book that appeared in 2005, he preceded new poems with eleven poems from the period 1962–85.[76] His previous book, from 2002, in turn began with eighteen poems dated 1959–89, after which it jumped to 1998 and beyond.[77] These are poems that the poet wishes his contemporary readers to have, and because they would have been so little known in the pre-1989 years, these poems become a part of poetic culture at the time of their publication.[78]

That delay allows us to see even more vividly Eremin's consistency. The impulse toward freedom was always there. He wrote, speaking of the philological school poets with whom he was associated, "As people, we were absolutely free and inquisitive. Knowledge and freedom were supremely important to us."[79] It is that performance of freedom and inquiry that his eight-line poems repeat, one after another. One expression of that freedom is how the poems, for all their images of small objects and small worlds, can open out to far vaster themes. The intellectual scope widens precipitously. An inquiry into dramatically different fields of knowledge can almost weigh down the poetic lines with information.[80] Poems can thematize the idea of large magnitudes of ideas, or of large spaces, as in the beautiful 2005 poem about the crystal world hidden inside a geode, "Geodes with amethyst granules; caves" ("Zheody s ametistovymi druzami; peshchery").[81] Through linguistic investigations into fields like botany or architecture, Eremin assiduously draws orders of magnitude into his small poems.[82]

Here, then, is a 1972 poem, published in 2002.

> I behold the sculpted idols . . .
>
> — G. R. Derzhavin

Hardly the most deserving of fame
Like a bronze orchid,
Its scaly root made of air,
Twisted and poisonous.
As between prefix and suffix,

The snake is between πετρος and Peter. Evergreen—
Not chlorophyll, but $Cu_2(OH)_2CO_3$—
Its laurel graft arose.

Зрю кумиры изваянны . . .

—Г. Р. Державин

Едва ль не самый достославный
Подобен медной орхидее
С чешуйчатым воздушным корнем,
Изгибистым и ядовитым.
Как между префиксом и суффиксом,
Змея меж πετρος и Петром. Вечнозеленый—
Не хлорофилл, а $Cu_2(OH)_2CO_3$—
Вознесся лавровый привой.[83]

1972

This poem collects several characteristic ways of opening out the eight-line poems, starting with its epigraph from the poetry of Gavrila Derzhavin (his 1810 "Procession of the Russian Amphitrite along the Volkov" ["Shestvie po Volkovu rossiiskoi Amfitrity"]). The epigraph does some of the work that a title might otherwise do, in that it sets up one of the poem's themes, that of public statuary. Citing Derzhavin draws into this small poem the grand rhetoric and poetic ambitions of Russia's court poet, and one of the tradition's great poets of the sublime.

Yet the poem proper begins with a deflated claim, of some object that deserves none of the fame that is accorded to monuments. If we read down to line 6, we find the first noun that is in the nominative, thus the barely famous object, a snake. And it is specifically the snake that sits at the foot of that most famous monument, Falconet's Bronze Horseman, the snake whose appearance is presumably what caused the statue's horse to rear up. The snake is compared to a word's root, that meaning-carrying part of a word that occurs between prefix and suffix. In its shape, the snake is also like the roots of an orchid, which reach out into the air for moisture. To paraphrase the poem's similes in this way is to bypass its considerable linguistic play, but this first step is an important way to dispel an idea of Eremin as so erudite as to be opaque.

It is in the linguistic play that Eremin introduces further openings into his otherwise closed-off poetic form. The poem includes the Greek word for "stone" (πετρος), its sounds apt to conjure the name Peter, which in fact follows immediately. The snake appears, as it does in the physical space of Falconet's statue, between the stone (the cliff) and Peter. Eremin also takes up the language of science in this poem, including a set of symbols as foreign to Cyrillic Russian as were the Greek letters: $Cu_2(OH)_2CO_3$, which is the version of copper carbonate commonly known as malachite. The vivid green color of malachite works metonymically to suggest the green color of the copper statue, and in a different, earlier version of the poem, the formula that appeared, $CuCO_3$, is indeed the kind of copper carbonate that gives a green tint to monuments like the Bronze Horseman.[84] By indirectly sending readers toward that green color via a reference to malachite, Eremin fortifies other references to stone in the poem, and he draws in another semantic field, that of art and interior design: malachite is famously on display in a room named for that stone in the Winter Palace, a room that centers around a magnificent malachite vase designed by Montferrand. Our small eight-line poem, then, has built on the discourses of sculpture, chemistry, botany, and cultural history, showing not that they are similar—that word occurs in line 2 of the poem, and similarity is a constant source of investigation for Eremin—but that poetry can synthesize their principles and assumptions.

I want to stay with botany for a second example. It is a poem dated 1997, published in 1998.

Not to dwell in loneliness, but at oneness
In that unremitting, in which
The raven, in his previous life a *corvus*,
Also drinks the eye of something that was once sentient,
And *Paris quadrifolia**,
True to the behest of the protophyte,
Out of ashes, waters, and sky creates
Its own organism.
1997
*Paris quadrifolia—the four-leaved "raven's eye"[85]

Не одиночествовать, а единствовать
В той непрерывности, в которой
И ворон, в предыдущей жизни бывший враном,
Пьет чье-то око, чувственное искогда,
И Paris quadrifolia*,
Завету протофита верен,

Из праха, вод и неба созидает
Свой организм.

1997
*Paris quadrifolia—Вороний глаз четырехлистный.[86]

This poem returns us to the fascination with numbers that defined Gronas's "This poem," but rather than unimaginably large numbers, Eremin starts from the number one, offered in the first line in two forms. Counting does not go very far, though, and by the outmost point of the poem, which is its foot-of-the-page note, he has only reached the number four. Formally, this poem is very much like the preceding one by Eremin, although instead of an epigraph, it has a footnote as a way of expanding the space occupied by an eight-line poem. Both consist of iambic, unrhymed lines of varying length, with extreme options explored in both cases. "Hardly the most deserving" has the challenge of its chemical formula (although if one transposes the formula to "malakhit," the line scans perfectly as iambic tetrameter).[87] And this poem has a last line of only two iambic feet.

The footnote is the place to start in comprehending this poem: it glosses the botanical term but fails to explain a biological designation that is likely to be at least as unclear, protophyte. Reading the poem requires that we put these two terms into alignment, in effect to ask how a protophyte (a unicellular organism) can coexist textually with a plant species whose name points to its four leaves. The poem asks how to connect the oneness of the protophyte with the fourfold structure of the *Paris quadrifolia*. It poses the question of how to get from one to four, and whether a poem could privilege one of these numerical notions at the expense of the other. In fact, the flower's name, *Paris quadrifolia*, is itself a conflicted classification when it comes to counting: the name Paris refers not to the French city but to a pair, which is to say, to the number two.[88] Eremin's poem sets out the contrast between oneness and fourness by asking how both these options take definitive form in terms of the basic unit of binary pairing.

The opening line, and thus the poem's premise, is an instance of binary pairing: a grammatical choice of infinitives, where becoming solitary is put aside in favor of becoming a one-cell entity, something entirely reproducible on its own terms, thus the kind of protophyte to be named in line 4. In line 2, the poem places both activities in the uninterrupted flow of nature and language, where a raven drinks from an eye and when the word for raven, in an earlier life, was spelled differently (what is now *voron* was once *vran*). Oneness is created out of a plant whose botanical name mentions its four-leafed form.

FIGURE 7. *Paris quadrifolia*, Kew Botanical Gardens

The berry-like center of the plant, which is its flower, provides the visual equivalent of the eye that is part of the Russian name, *voronii glaz*, which literally means raven's eye. Oneness, we might say, is conjured from this fourness, visually in the way that the plant's central spherical dot unites the four leaves, and in the way that the blue berry in the center rises from the leaves, acting as the plant's bloom (figure 7).

The botanical image shows itself to be deeply true to the semantics of naming—the epithet *vernyi*, meaning true or loyal—which the poem will use semantically, presented in another recombination of the $v/r/n$ consonants that give us the word for raven, *voron*. Equally true to the protophyte's unicellular nature, then, is the flower or the bird that can create its organism as if out of the elements of the universe—the dust, waters, and sky listed in line 7. And the act of creation is one of the poem's deep themes, as we might say of "Hardly the most deserving" or indeed of many Eremin poems. The poem also suggests, given the look of the *Paris quadrifolia*, the image of a bird "drinking" in the flower or center of the plant. To imbibe the berry at the plant's center and carry it off is also to propagate the plant, which is what the poem will go on to describe in the creative activity of a one-celled organism. In that tiny image, Eremin has ostensibly imagined the origins of all life, once again demonstrating for us the enormousness that a small poem can contain.

Daria Sukhovei: From Eight down to Six

One of Eremin's most insightful readers has been the Petersburg poet, cultural leader, and critic Daria Sukhovei. She was born nearly forty years after him, in 1977, and is one of many in her generation who sought out poets who quietly thrived in the late Soviet years. Her 2014 interview with Eremin makes for great reading, even though his meager answers re-enact the brevity of his poems; her reviews of his work, and the comments she has made elsewhere, show her careful study of the internal organization and rhetorical tropes that mark his *vos'mistishiia*.[89] Sukhovei was also a significant figure behind the scenes in promoting other poets' work. She founded an online guide to literary events in St. Petersburg in 1999 and curated a festival of new poets as of 2001, the same year her first book of poems, *A Catalogue of Random Notes* (*Katalog sluchainykh zapisei*) appeared.[90]

In later work, Sukhovei published her own *vos'mistishiia*, and her approach to this form is more minimalist than Eremin's. Like him, she uses some para-textual gestures to slightly open out the poems (including titles, unlike Eremin). She also creates sequences of *vos'mistishiia*, so that position in a larger sequence compensates for the texts' brevity.[91] But the thematic or material orientation of the poems could not be more different from Eremin's: her poems are caught up in the stuff of daily life, making poetry out of housecleaning, a flag seen out the window, loud music in a bar. When there is a metapoetic element, and there often is, the rhetorical gesture has a parodic quality (what she called her three "antiflarf" *vos'mistishiia* exemplify this well).[92] Sukhovei's poetics have a strong admixture of Conceptualism and reflect her admiration for the Lianozovo poets (she has written about Genrikh Sapgir and singled out Vsevolod Nekrasov as the key figure in advancing the Futurists' work of freeing poetry from many shackles).[93] It is very tempting to include some of her *vos'mistishiia* here, hard as they are to translate (most rely on rhyme, regular rhythms that may be in jarring contrast to the poem's themes, and considerable word play), but what is even more interesting about Sukhovei is that she has turned instead to an even shorter form, six-line poems.[94] She publishes them on her Facebook and LiveJournal pages, with the hashtag #shestisti (which shortens the Russian word for a six-line poem, *shestistishie*, so as to get the visual and sound echo of *stisti*). In presenting one poem at a time on Facebook, and in the sheer quantity of the work, Sukhovei has engaged in a Conceptualist project; in October 2020, she noted that she had been writing them for five years, 1,550 poems to date.[95] By early 2024, there were more than 2,300. She published a large selection in her 2017 book, *In Essence: Selected Six-Line Poems* (*Po sushchestvu: Izbrannye shestistishii 2015–2017*).

Why six-line poems? It is a marked and unusual choice. Even more than with eight-line poems, there is a problem in English of what to call them. *The Princeton Encyclopedia of Poetry and Poetics* lists several possibilities, classed under the term *sexain*, but even English professors might be hard pressed to recognize that term (spellcheck thinks it's a typo).[96] What we know more familiarly would be *sestet*, the designation for the six-line portion of a sonnet. It is an interesting detail, telling us that this form, like the *vos'mistishie*, has some connection to sonnet form.[97] There is something fragmentary about the six-line poem on its own. *The Princeton Encyclopedia of Poetry and Poetics* says that it is a form almost as frequent as quatrains, and the Renaissance form of the sestina was revived by modernist poets in English.[98] But Sukhovei is not using the six-line form to build a sequence. These are not stanzas but freestanding poems, and they can read like quick snapshots from a daily life built on a single aperçu, or like small bits of language into which another poet's work has made some significant incursion (like the "antiflarf" *vos'mistishiia*). Or both, and that combination of a prose-like recording of life's mundane events with a critical engagement with the poetic tradition makes these poems distinctive and telling.[99] Her poem that begins "when we first rode through lianozovo" ("kogda my vpervye proezzhali lianozovo," 2016) is a good example of deft usage of the place name as a reminder of a poetic tradition, in a poem that is otherwise a run-on sentence describing a railroad travel experience of little interest.[100]

One of her six-line poems from the "Incursions" ("Vtorzheniia") group is explicit in its engagement with the poetics of Vsevolod Nekrasov. Many of the "Incursions" poems riff on some other poet's work but indirectly. Here, Nekrasov is named:

> if "sea repair"
> were written by
> vsevolod nekrasov
> it'd be
>   "sea
>   repair"
>   22dec18 (1108)

> если бы "ремонт моря"
> написал

всеволод некрасов
было бы
   "ремонт
      моря"
         22дек18 (1108)[101]

Sukhovei is playing here on the reiterative quality of Nekrasov's poems (as in his poem about freedom, cited in the introduction). An extreme example, and possibly the one she has in mind, repeats the phrase "Water at night" (Noch'iu voda) in each of its eight lines, with a space between lines 4 and 5. No title, nothing else.[102] Sukhovei is calling attention to this extreme minimalism as poetic practice. Nekrasov wrote many poems with only one word per line (hence Sukhovei's imagined version of his text "sea repair" has it spread over two lines). His poetry also uses the space of the page in multiple meaningful ways, and Sukhovei alludes to that practice when she makes the split of two words into two indented lines, producing a poem that occupies more space in our imaginations than the few words it encompasses.[103] And yet, the phrase "sea repair" is very much her own. It is as weird in Russian as it is in English, not a phrase found in Nekrasov. That's the kind of incursion her own poems perform, putting two words together that are lexically and semantically unlike but linked aurally (in Russian, "remont moria," the *r* and *m* consonant sounds repeat, and the sole stressed vowel is *o*). Sukhovei makes poetry out of such small bits of linguistic play, and then assembles her poems into a record of daily creative work and lived experience that adds up to an outsized and memorable impression.

Ekaterina Simonova: Toward Openness and Irony

To turn to the poetry of Ekaterina Simonova moves us into a poetic realm so completely different in magnitude and project as to seem a world away. Simonova's distance from the capitals is in fact a key part of her poetic identity. She was born in Nizhny Tagil and lives in Ekaterinburg in the Urals. These places define the locale of many poems, which have resonated with readers near and far, epitomized in the decision to award her one of the inaugural Poeziia prizes for 2018. The poem honored by that jury, "I was glad when Grandmother died" ("Ia byla rada, kogda babushka umerla," 2018), has many qualities for which Simonova is known. These include the clear-eyed recognition of material things in all their expressiveness, which suggests a lineage derived from the Acmeists, alongside a fascination with time and timelessness that connects her to the Symbolists.[104] Other key traits are this poem's expansive, prose-like lines; an underlying narrative that mixes concrete everyday details with bits that are so little made of matter as to seem spiritual; recollected scenes of life from her family, neither sentimentalized nor distanced; a Dostoevskian sense that death can define what a life means, alongside a clear-headed and nearly Tolstoyan optimism about the way in which lives change.

There is as much love as irony in her poems, and an openness to the world that, since about 2018, has found a capacious, extended poetic form. Simonova dates the change to February 2018, when the poet and critic Yulia Podlubnova invited her to co-create an anthology based on the travels of Silver Age poets.[105] She wrote something that was entirely different from her work to date and says that when she read it, she shrugged her shoulders, and then the next day, and the day after that, kept writing in that mode. Simonova has conceded that the poetry of the Silver Age, especially that of the Acmeists (Akhmatova, Gumilev, Kuzmin, Mandelstam, for example), was a deep source of inspiration in the poetry she had written to that point, and most reviews of her work mention that connection. She has a whole volume of poetry that stylizes the literary lives of poets from the period.[106] So why would an invitation to think about that same period provoke a dramatic change in her writing style? The answer must have to do with the subject matter, travel, and I hypothesize that perhaps this narrative element made all the difference.

Simonova's poetry in fact turned decisively toward narrative, becoming a kind of record of daily life. Formal changes were also afoot, perhaps the easier to tell stories. The pre-2018 work is often metrically regular, arranged in stanzas, and dependent on rhyme; there are many nature poems, elegies, and quasi-love poems. Olga Sedakova, in introducing the poems in *Elena: The Apple and the Hand* (*Elena: Iabloko i ruka*, 2015), had admired the "precise wording, the pure sound orchestration, the natural changes in rhythm, like spoken words."[107] Sedakova would surely have recognized her own poetry as the source for the wild rose of this short poem in that volume:

> you don't know it
> don't speak
> words are wounding like a wild rose
> let the silence remain
> turned into a bit of smoke
> a shroud of a past day that never came to pass

a burial shroud
smelling like the wild
flower of the rose

не знаешь что
не говори
слова ранят как дикий шиповник
пусть молчание остается
подвернуто дымкой
несбывшегося пеленой прошедшего дня
погребальной
пахнущей диким
цветущим шиповником[108]

An unusually successful instance of a contemporary poet building on Sedakova's legacy, this poem also shows us the subtle means by which Simonova is making things smaller.[109] Although the poem reprises several metaphors from Sedakova's poem "The Wild Rose" ("Dikii shipovnik," 1976), including the image of a wound and the deeper silence that contemplation of the rose enables, missing is one of the most striking words and concepts in Sedakova's poem, an Old Church Slavonic–based word that means all of creation (mirozdan' e). The omission makes Simonova's poem smaller in scope. Sedakova's poem, only fourteen lines, uses longer lines, and indentations of several parts of lines make it seem to occupy more space on the page. Hers is an example in fact of the kind of enlargement from within that I have traced in several poems above, intensified thematically by the theological diction and references in her poem.[110] Simonova makes for a much smaller poem by evading those references, and she keeps the semantics steadily focused on the verbal. In her poem, it is words that can wound, whereas in Sedakova's, it is the rose. As if in compensation, her poem gives the rose a trait that Sedakova, in turn, had not included, the possibility of fragrance. But the smell is associated with smoke and death, with the accoutrements of burial rituals (which in turn could be another intertextual engagement with Sedakova's poetics: her study of the burial rituals of the ancient Slavs).[111]

Thus, the reason I include Simonova here is not just because she has emerged as a superb creator of expansive texts, but also because the question of size may give us a way to understand the transformation in her work: she moved from work that had elements of miniaturization and compression toward a poetic that is open and spacious. In that newly large work, a striking element of restraint persists, as if even in the expansive texts she has retained an element of the miniature, the small. In commenting on the poem about her grandmother's death, in fact, Simonova resorted to the idea of size to describe the poem: "the small woe of a small person speaking from a small point on the map" (malen'koe gore malen'kogo cheloveka, govoriashchego iz malen'koi tochki na karte).[112]

The suggestiveness of that map might be best imagined in Simonova's largest cycle, thirteen texts grouped as "The Departed, the Exiled, the Disappeared, and the Dead" ("Uekhavshie, vyslannye, kanuvshie i pogibshie," 2018).[113] These are the poems that were prompted by Podlubnova's invitation to think about the Silver Age in terms of travel; Podlubnova is the cycle's dedicatee and figures in the fifth poem, gently teased for her disdainful reports on travels to Paris, which makes her a modern-day Blok, the poem says.[114] The cycle mixes in the voyages, real, imagined, and canceled, of Simonova, Podlubnova, and others in the present but it is held together by its re-creation of the experiences of literary luminaries from the Silver Age.[115] While it is largely about the poets' material circumstances, the physical details of travel, and the spiritual and cultural consequences of those movements through space, the poems reflect repeatedly on whether these consequences are significant or trivial, at one point musing on the outsized role played by "little Romania" in journeys by several members of the Potemkin family, at another observing drily that "Sometimes a little trip / leads to big consequences" (Inogda malen'koe puteshestvie / privodit k bol'shim posledstviiam).[116] The big consequences in the latter case are that Elizaveta Dmitrieva (Cherubina de Gabriak) stopped writing poems for five years, and she is one of the several women of the Silver Age whom Simonova features prominently in these poems (also Nina Berberova, Nina Petrovskaya, Sofia Parnok, Elena Guro, Marina Tsvetaeva, and briefly Zinaida Gippius). These women figure in stories about the poems they wrote or failed to write, and they also figure as lovers, as agents of their own desires, even when those desires seem improbable or wrongheaded (one of the poem's great moments is the tirade against falling for a straight woman, Tsvetaeva's mistake with Sonia Holliday). Simonova shows that a travel narrative—replete with arrivals, departures, vacations, emigrations—is also an apt framework for love stories.

How love stories came to be a part of Simonova's writings is itself a tale that remains to be told. Lesbian desire was clear in Simonova's poetry from the start. *To Be a Boy* (*Byt' mal'chikom*, 2004), her first book of poems, opens with an apostrophe to the naked body of a woman whose nipples are, at that moment, more important than all poetry. In these playful poems, crisscrossing

languages allegorize and report on erotic encounters, and the poems move
quickly. In her next books, the poetry of nature and mood takes a more com-
manding role, in work that shows another side of her absorption in the poetics
of the Silver Age, focused on Mikhail Kuzmin.[117] Particularly deft are the
personae poems, some of the richest in contemporary poetry after those of
Elena Shvarts.[118] But irony hovers inevitably in Simonova's poetry, even in the
love poems. Her poems that tend toward the spiritual have a materiality on
which dust can visibly settle, yet they concede nothing in their images of spirit.
It is as if the objects described have been made up not of the molecules of their
substances, but of the glances and touches that have left traces on their sur-
faces. The earlier work can make whole poems of these impressions, but the
later work slides away toward a specificity and material density onto which air
itself seems to descend. Air is a frequent presence in earlier work, and it mate-
rializes as dust in a memorable later poem that begins "Recently I learned that
in domestic dust / There is always a little cosmic dust" (Nedavno uznala, chto
v domashnei pyli / Vsegda est' nemnogo kosmicheskoi pyli).[119] Like Gronas's
poem about writing poetry after Auschwitz, where numbers stand out as gro-
tesquely precise, this text allocates percentages to the sources of various par-
ticles (hair, skin, pollen, smoke, textiles, paper), only to insist that a significant
percentage is left over for what comes "from that star that was just to the right
over the house across the way yesterday" (Chto-to ot toi zvezdy, kotoraia
vchera byla sprava nad domom naprotiv). Its temporal distance—the star is
said to have disappeared ten thousand years ago, another approximated num-
ber—is also a residue of something that has been lost. The poem goes on to
list the foodstuffs that the poet's parents brought, stuffs to which the parents'
labor has also stuck, just like the lingering dust. In the last lines, the dust that
remains after beloved friends and family guests have departed lingers as if with
their presence, and the poet materializes loneliness as the moment when the
percentage of her own hair strands hits nineteen percent. Numbers resurface,
including the ten thousand years after which a burned-out star's remains can
be felt between one's fingers. These numbers are doing work like that of the
material objects themselves: concretizing what is otherwise entirely spiritual
or mental, dreaminess or memory.

The poem's free verse creates an expansive, domestic feel, one that contrasts
bookshelf dust and stardust to suggest both the tiniest of particles and the vast
cosmos. As her poetry is developing, Simonova is using large form less to ex-
plore largeness (or smallness) itself than to tell stories of love and loss, and to
tell them in the first person, as if they are her own stories, even as the contra-

dictions among them make clear that these are at the least different hypostases of a self.[120] She has particularly made interesting the idea of what actually is one's "own" story when it comes to love, and the generous imagination of possibilities across different stages in one's life as a lesbian gives this poetry a bracingly political underside.[121]

Simonova's Anna Arno poems are the most radical example of this adoption of a persona. She has found an alter ego that lets her write a different kind of poetry. The second group of these poems, published in 2020, thus after Simonova's poetry had moved in a direction of longer and more prose-like lines, let her write shorter, evocatively post–Silver Age poems once again.[122] In a sense, adopting a mask as a lyric poet is itself a form of expansion—an expansion of the very idea of subjectivity, a rhetorical move that lets a poet imagine the felt life of someone else, usually wholly invented. In addition, then, to the formal and thematic expansiveness (and contraction) seen so far, Simonova's work points in a further direction, that of the poetic self as a source of enlargement. I turn to one further and final example of that possibility, the work of a poet who has had multiple alter egos, but in prose.

Faina Grimberg, Returns without End

Faina Grimberg fits almost no categories of contemporary poetry. Her stature within the poetic community became somewhat more assured after about 2000; but she has put off more than one reader and even admirer.[123] Grimberg was born in 1951 in a small town in Kazakhstan and educated in Tashkent. An outsider in Moscow literary circles in the late Soviet period, she did not find her way easily to publication, although she is now widely published.[124] Her work as a poet is dwarfed by her flood of publications in historical fiction, many of them elaborate authorial mystifications. These are not just pseudonyms or masks, of the sort used by Kirill Reshetnikov (Shish Briansky), or by Elena Shvarts in creating Lavinia or Cynthia, and this is not the disappearing act performed by Nika Skandiaka. It is much more like what Simonova would go on to do with Anna Arno, but many times over: Grimberg tells stories through fully imagined individuals with biographies she stands ready to recount.[125] She presents herself as transmitting historical fictions that might otherwise be lost, updating the found manuscript topos, as did Simonova in "translating" Arno. In many cases, she lists herself as the translator, not the author, and most of her alter egos are not Russian. But some historical fictions are signed with Grimberg's name, and she has also translated several books.

Grimberg has tried to make the impulse to create these personae seem simple: when she was a little girl, she said, she didn't understand why she had to be a single person with a distinctive name—why not have multiple selves, multiple lives? Writing lets her live those alternative lives. Before there was Facebook, many Russian poets were active on LiveJournal (and a few still are). Grimberg had two LiveJournal accounts, one as Villon-14.[126] The mask was chosen to highlight another of Grimberg's alter egos, this one in her poetry: she has written a remarkable book-length poem as if by the daughter of François Villon, the great French fifteenth-century poet.[127] And in 2014, she published a set of poems as if they were written by Villon himself.[128]

In creating so many alter egos, she takes the further step of not just transmitting a world but inventing it. She re-creates herself as a German, Bulgarian, Turkish, or Hebrew writer, to give the national identities of several pseudonyms, in effect transporting herself outside the physical space of Russia.[129] There is an enlargement of the very idea of being a writer, in other words, one that moves outward to fresh identities and multiple nationalities. The psychic dimensions of this mode of self-invention should be understood as the foundation on which Grimberg has constructed her poetic world. It is never enough to have one self, she seems to be saying. And when she writes a lyric poem, it is doubly curious to see how she handles the notion of subjectivity and individualized expression.

Grimberg fled lyric individualism in her best-known poem, "Andrei Ivanovich Comes Home" ("Andrei Ivanovich vozvrashchaetsia domoi," 1997).[130] Its roots are in folk lament, and its chronotope is a timeless space of war. The text may have particularly pungent associations during Russia's bloody war of aggression in Ukraine, and when it appeared, the losses of the Chechen wars would have seemed to hover above the text. But the poet is writing at some distance from any specific conflict, and Andrei Ivanovich appears in other Grimberg poems and in other eras.[131] Hers is the realm of folklore and myth, not politics. Andrei Ivanovich is every soldier who has departed into senseless battle, every missing son or husband. The collective voice of this first-person narrative represents two women, an utterance that is always spoken by *we* rather than *I*. Although it is not spelled out, readers come to understand that one is the mother of Andrei Ivanovich; the other, named Marina Markovna, is his wife. The poem's ending rises to a surprising conclusion. Andrei Ivanovich's mother and wife recover a child from the waters near the gravesite, and when they say that bringing home this child means bringing home Andrei Ivanovich, they wrest an improbable and astonishing affirmation from the insistent elegy of this poem. They transform its sustained lament into an announcement of renewal, and they do so in the last pages of a fourteen-page text.

This long poem demonstrates a wavering between small and large impulses by its use of a refrain. Structurally, the refrain is its most important element, as is often true in Grimberg's work. The refrain, heard again and again, creates the impression of a poetic text that occupies a small space on the page—even though the physical motions of its protagonists are considerable. The refrain is all the more striking because its negation reverses the poem's title: "Andrei Ivanovich is not coming home" (Andrei Ivanovich ne vozvrashchaetsia domoi). It is repeated so often that it seems to emanate from the landscape through which the two women move. How could anything, even the poem title's affirming claim, undo its negation? Yet the refrain may sow the seeds of its undoing. A multiply repeated sentence with its hammering emphasis can seem an unchanging truth. But doubt can also be an effect of repetition, as if the utterance holds true only for as long as it is spoken, and then needs to be repeated. The contrast between title and refrain, in other words, means that both assertions—Andrei Ivanovich is returning home, Andrei Ivanovich can never return home—become the foundation on which the poem is built.

The refrain thus gives the poem a circular motion, which is intensified by the many instances of verbal repetition.[132] Yet the circularity and verbal constraint mean that many images and phrases in the poem's ending are also heard from the very beginning. Here is the poem's opening, couched not as a beginning but as an ending:

Life grows dark,
        It turns into a prison;
Everything in this life will turn to petty chaos.
It's all over.
        And there is no way forward for us.
Andrei Ivanovich will not come home.
In the beginning, he was a round-faced little boy.
But there came a time when he left,
                when he sailed off.
On a river steamship, he sailed off.
And now he is no more,
          but he existed. He lived.
He was young and handsome.

He was handsome, he was fair-haired—
                           we say in tears.
He was handsome, he was speckle-eyed,
            he had such gray, speckled eyes,
So handsome,
             so beloved was he!
Andrei Ivanovich is not coming home.

Жизнь затмевается,
                        становится тюрьмой;
Всё в этой жизни станет мелкой кутерьмой.
Всё кончилось.
                 И больше нет для нас пути.
Андрей Иванович не возвращается домой.
Сначала круглолицый мальчик был.
Но он ушёл однажды,
                   он уплыл.
На пароходе по реке уплыл.
И больше нет его совсем,
                    а был.
Потом он молодой красивый был.
Красивый был, светловолосый был -
               мы приговариваем со слезами.
Он был красивый, пестроглазый был,
            с такими серыми и пёстрыми глазами.
Такой красивый был,
              такой любимый был!
Андрей Иванович не возвращается домой.[133]

These lines are rife with verbal repetitions, including a refrain that recurs throughout the poem. The rhetoric of repetition takes on the role of a psychic structure: if one human being cannot return, then how can experience be ordered to compensate for that loss? All the poem's search for meaning is pulled back into a tiny orbit of possibility. Imagining human return is all that matters. But return is impossible. We know that from the start.

Could substitution work as imagined return? A child comes home in the end, with a vaster task: to replace the dead warriors from all the world's wars.[134] That child will implicitly live to repeat the pattern of travail and death. Grimberg's poem becomes an archaic ritual enacted by lamenting words of its female speaker. She does not provide the consolation of a list of mourners, nor is nature much of a consolation—indeed, the natural world is the embodiment of the dead Andrei Ivanovich, another way in which the poem's seemingly vast space tightens in on itself. Rather than trees bent over in sorrowing comfort, the tree becomes a spectral transformation of the missing man. All the world is a representation of what is lost, even the waters that send forth the child who is fated to die in turn.

All this constraint is the counterbalance to the poem's maximalism, which arises from its length, from its long lines, and from its plural subjectivity. The maximalism also has an emotional and affective force that spreads across space and time. As the poet Galina Rymbu said of Grimberg's work, this is the opposite of the fragmented or ruined world created by other poets writing in a similarly historical mode (Rymbu's example is Sergei Zav'ialov, chosen well). Grimberg's work is what Rymbu calls a "totalizing" intentionality.[135]

Grimberg's poems suggest that there is no limit to the intense pathos language can contain. The vastness of the poem's emotion is meant to be commensurate with the tragedy of human experience. In an astute essay that draws on both her poetry and her historical fiction, Stanislav Lvovsky says that Grimberg finds the full sweep of history (what he calls "Bol'shaia istoriia") frightening because it is a history of slaughter, and repeatedly she affirms that it is overwhelming and impossible to grasp at an individual level.[136] She actualizes this hugeness in the poetry by mixing chronotopes and temporalities, so that a character like Andrei Ivanovich can reappear in her texts.[137] The rhetoric of repetition thus works across multiple levels of the text, from the individualized heroes to the language itself.

Grimberg is a poet who, as much as anyone discussed in this chapter, embodies within her work the tremendous pull of both the large and the small. To have traversed a mental space from Rubinstein to Grimberg is not just to have moved from smaller to larger forms, but to have probed the potential for contemporary poetry of capaciousness as an idea. Poems, whether large or small, whether prose-like or intensely formal, and whether restricted or extravagant in their diction, engage with the affordances of both restriction and largesse, and in the process open themselves out to new freedoms and ever-present constraints.

PART II

Free Speech and Freed Minds

POETRY AND ITS OTHERS

4

The Music of the Present

Brodsky • Aristov • Malanov • Aygi • Mnatsakanova •
Chukhrov • Borodin

MUSIC HAS LONG STOOD AS AN emblem of art's aura, its ability to take the imagination places where words or pictures cannot go. There is a perceptible shift in contemporary poetry away from the imagined, unheard music celebrated by the Symbolists toward the noises and rhythms of the surrounding world, which can push poems in decidedly unpoetic directions. Some musical sounds represented in poems or created as the poem's own rhythmic signature are not aesthetically harmonious, and just as classical music in and after the twentieth century has explored multiple forms of dissonance, so Russian poets have been drawn to a very wide range of sound patterns. Poets have broken down the boundaries between music and other sounds, following pathways laid down by contemporary composers.

Even so, many contemporary music poems build on the traditions they are questioning.[1] The earliest poetry may have emerged when people put words to music, but poems often use their words to lament that words are not notes, and speech is not melody. Romantic poets like Keats could dream of unheard sweet melodies in "Ode on a Grecian Urn" because the best music seemed inherently imaginary (Keats's urn depicts musical performance, rather than reporting on harmonies or rhythms).[2] This idealization of music's bliss has lingered in poems that hold out melody, rhythm, and musical form as supreme artistic ideals.

Modernist poets built an implicit argument about poetry's primacy by worshipping the gods of music. In no other art form did they find so congenial a spiritual partner: music could set out the ideals to which poems should aspire and save the poet listening to its melodies from the worst defeats of daily life.[3]

Some of those satisfactions linger for later poets who sought music-like poetic forms, but others spurned the implied aesthetic hierarchy and drew on the elements of music to make emphatically noisy poetry.

Contemporary poets have inherited other myths about music, including its potential for harm. A dangerous association with the passions was an important topic in Renaissance poetry and rhetorical theory, and the ancient Greeks believed that music shunned reason. There were melodies thought to cause a dance to the death, or to lure dazed listeners down some treacherous path. We associate ecstatic dance with Dionysus, and fatally beautiful singing with the Sirens, but Orpheus best represents this danger and most often appears in music poems: his music could tame wild animals, but his own passion cost him Eurydice when he could not refrain from looking back at her. Even excelling at music had its dangers, as shown by the fate of Marsyas, who dared to best Apollo in a musical contest.

These myths are one vehicle through which poems reprise the temptations and dangers of music. Elena Shvarts opens her "Elegy on an X-Ray of My Skull" ("Elegiia na rentgenovskii snimok moego cherepa," 1973) with the flaying of Marsyas, and she tersely notes that his fate awaits all earthly flutists. Each will hear the fatal words someday: "You have licked at the honey of music, yet you are covered in mire" (Ty medu muzyki liznul, no ves' ty v tine).[4] Shvarts steps into the territory of synesthesia here, not uncommon in music poems: the ecstasy of musical perfection sticks to the tongue like honey, and perhaps because it tempts the tongue to adds words to the music, the poet is left covered in unpleasant mire. For Shvarts, contact with the earth was a source of satisfying poetic inspiration, but in this elegy, with its plot of drunken blasphemy, that mire becomes a source of shame.

Elena Shvarts's poem moves between the positive and negative valences of music's lure with the starkness so typical of her work. Sublime and potentially elevating, music can also be associated with what we might call the ugly passions, and it is this territory that contemporary poets explore more boldly than their predecessors.[5] Although some poems take up music from earlier eras, many are attuned to contemporary music in multiple forms—classical, hip-hop, jazz, operatic, folk, liturgical, and rock and roll—and some particularly seek out dissonance and clangor.

That daring sense of movement into unexpected places defines the new poetry of music. The poet's ear is newly attuned to the music that can be heard anywhere, anytime—in performance, in the car, in the park, in your headphones—all layered over the music imagined in the mind. To pull the music of daily life into poetry is to compare it to the sounds of the imagination, and to allow the imagination to be stimulated and changed by these myriad external pleasures and distractions. For Shvarts's elegy, music was an idea. But in the poems treated here, music can be experienced in real time, part of an event around which the mind wraps itself in pleasure and in pain. All these sources coexist, not always in conflict with one another. Far be it from me to stage a contest—we know from Marsyas's demise what happens even to successful contestants.

Contemporary poets are listening to the music of the surrounding world and, as if it were entirely new, to the music of the past. In these acts of attention, they are breaking down the boundaries around the poetic subject yet again, and they are also demonstrating that the path to poetic innovation can run as surely through a wide variety of musical forms as through the sacred groves of Russia's own poetic tradition. The examples here are varied and multiple, taken from the work of seven poets as different in generation and temperament as in poetic style and, perhaps most intangibly, intonation.

First, a coolly sublime study in jazz by Joseph Brodsky, a poem that uses profoundly un-Russian music to set standards for engagement across aesthetic modes. Second, poems by Mara Malanova and Vladimir Aristov represent the music of the overstimulating, quick-changing urban environment. Whereas variation in pitch defines Brodsky's orientation toward music, rhythm is the crucial element for Malanova and Aristov. Next, the poetry of Gennady Aygi, which is shaped as a form of rhythmic improvisation; his use of silences is akin to musical rests. Rhythm also defines the work of Elizaveta Mnatsakanova. Her poems mix music's history with innovative rhythms and unusual visual arrangements on the page. They take the poet back to an idea of childhood, when music makes its first impressions on the psyche. The music of the mind remained an ideal to Mnatsakanova, linking her surprisingly to the Symbolists. The chapter concludes with two poets who have created striking musical performances. Keti Chukhrov uses her beautiful, classically trained voice to transform an audience's understanding of her pain-ridden poetic text, and Vasily Borodin uses his skill as a guitarist in songs that intensify but also challenge the emotional tenor of his poems.[6]

Brodsky to Begin: Jazz Seen, Felt, and Heard

Joseph Brodsky spoke about music in many interviews, and he named poems after musical forms ("Songs to No Words," "Aria," "Cape Cod Lullaby," "Bosnia Tune," "Taps"). Poems often referred to instruments and melodies, from the grand piano to the tango.[7] But Gerald Smith, an expert on classical and jazz music as well as on Brodsky, thought that the poet actually knew rather little about music and didn't much care for the details of performance or innovation.[8] In fact, Brodsky, who was an autodidact in literary matters, seems to have had the same laser-like ability to home in on the metaphors and tropes that music could bring to poetry, sometimes with eerie precision. His taste was eclectic, including his Soviet generation's respect for Baroque music. He valued jazz alongside the music of Henry Purcell for its spirit of "cold negation," and he associated jazz with "a feeling of cold resistance, irony, estrangement."[9] Temperature is a distinctive measure of music's power, and it defines the poem to which we now turn.

"In Memory of Clifford Brown" ("Pamiati Klifforda Brauna," 1993), presents the passionate, hot musician Clifford Brown as if he were maximally cool. Brodsky thought of Brown as "the greatest jazz trumpeter ever," not an implausible claim.[10] Brown died in a car accident in 1956 at a tragically young age, and Brodsky likely heard Brown's music and the news of his death on the American radio program *Time for Jazz*.[11] Written more than three decades later, his poem enacts a remembered return to that act of listening. It is a memory of what music does to the mind, and it is a metaphysical and speculative poem about death. More than that, the poem seeks to comprehend melodic intensity and harmonic balance not as loss, but as intense forms of presence.

"In Memory of Clifford Brown" searches for words to describe Brown's music. The poem resembles a definition or riddle poem, like Pasternak's "Definition of Poetry" ("Opredelenie poezii," 1919).[12] But it begins by arguing against identity. Negations launch each quatrain in a direction from which it must be quickly diverted—a swerving gesture not unlike the provocations of a jazz trumpeter playing against other instruments.[13] This poem is arranged in quatrains with end rhyme and uses *taktovik* meter as Brodsky often did; those formal regularities accentuate the syntactic and metaphorical repetitions.

In Memory of Clifford Brown

It's not the color blue, it's the color cold.
It's the Atlantic's color you've got no eyes for
in the middle of February. And though you sport a coat,
you're flat on your naked back upon the ice floe.

It's not a regular ice floe, meltdown-prone.
It's an argument that all warmth is foreign.

It's alone in the ocean, and you're on it alone,
and the trumpet's song is like mercury falling.

It's not a guileless tune that chafes in the darkness, though;
it's the gloveless, frozen to C-sharp fingers.
And a glistening drop soars to the zenith, so
as to glance at the space with no retina's interference.

It's not a simple space, it's a nothing, with
alts attaining in height what they lose in color,
while a spotlight is drifting into the wings,
aping the ice floe and waxing polar.[14]

[February] 1993

Памяти Клиффорда Брауна

Это—не синий цвет, это—холодный цвет.
Это—цвет Атлантики в середине
февраля. И не важно, как ты одет:
все равно ты голой спиной на льдине.

Это—не просто льдина, одна из льдин,
но возраженье теплу по сути.
Она одна в океане, и ты один
на ней; и пенье трубы как паденье ртути.

Это не искренний голос впотьмах саднит,
но палец примерз к диезу, лишен перчатки;
и капля, сверкая, плывет в зенит,
чтобы взглянуть на мир с той стороны сетчатки.

Это не просто сетчатка, это—с искрой парча,
новая нотная грамота звезд и полос.
Льдина не тает, точно пятно луча,
дрейфуя к черной кулисе, где спрятан полюс.[15]

Февраль 1993

Definition poems switch metaphors frequently, trying first one, then another in an attempt to fix a rhetorical equivalent, in this case for Clifford Brown's trumpet playing. Brodsky limits his metaphors to a few semantic fields (color, water, temperature, bodies, clothing, and fire or light), with temperature predominant.[16] Each stanza has some mention of cold (or its opposite, heat), and the main metaphor, the ice floe, appears four times. Repetition is intense, a clue that the work of metaphor relies on density rather than variety.

Coldness has a positive valence in Brodsky's poetic world: it is associated with the North, with Leningrad, and with the satisfactions of enduring harsh circumstances; it suggests a metaphysics of absence and deprivation.[17] Curiously, the best counterpart for Brodsky's juxtaposition of solitude and cold northern geography is found in the radio work of pianist Glenn Gould, even though Gould's collage of voices makes his theme of solitary journeys turn into something surprisingly communal and shared.[18] Brodsky's poetry performs a more intense act of solitary expression (as we find in Gould's studio performances). We hear the terse exclamation "time equals cold" (vremia est' kholod) in Brodsky's long poem "Eclogue IV: Winter" ("Ekloga 4-ia [zimniaia]," 1977), a meditation on cold itself.[19] That insistence on an implausible equivalence, "time equals cold," turns a metaphor into an absolute claim. In such equations, and Brodsky loved to make them, all differences fall away—differences of language, meaning, matter, and time itself.

The tone of frigid rationality is heard elsewhere in "Eclogue IV: Winter" in the language of comparison: "In February, the later it is, the lower / the mercury. More time means more cold" (V fevrale, chem pozdnee, tem men'she rtuti. / T. e. chem bol'she vremeni, tem kholodnee).[20] The poem has a refrain, "My life has dragged on," which in one of its iterations prompts the added reflection: "One cold resembles another / cold. Time looks like time" (Zhizn' moia zatianulas'. Kholod pokhozh na kholod, / vremia—na vremia).[21] No longer can the mind pick out the specificity of an experience or say what makes it matter. No longer can the exhausted mind come up with terms for comparison, which is to say, with metaphors. Time looks like nothing but time itself, and if we widen our gaze to Brodsky's body of work, then this is true even of time demarcated by music's rhythms. The state of mind induced by music has no particularity of its own: music, like so many other experiences charted in the poems—gazing out at a South American river, standing before the ruins of a church, watching a beloved get out of bed—throws the mind back on itself, repeatedly trying to come up with stable points of reference and of memory.

It may seem as if that cosmic quandary has strayed far from music, but it is also the point toward which "In Memory of Clifford Brown" rises—or slides, depending on how we read the images in the final quatrain. Brodsky changed these lines rather dramatically when he translated the poem, and I have quoted his translation here. But a literal translation of the last quatrain shows what a difference his adherence to the poem's rhymes (his constant point of orientation in his self-translations) made.[22] The Russian lines mean: "This isn't just a retina, it is brocade setting off sparks, / a new musical document of stars and stripes. / The ice floe does not melt, it is like a patch of light, / drifting to the wings, where it is dark and where the pole hides." One can see why Brodsky reinvented the lines, but in the literal version, we detect his salient description of jazz as "a new musical document of stars and stripes," which emphasizes the American nature of the music as well as its newness.

The key thing here is the sense of freedom this music represents, a freedom so profound that it is registered as a kind of physical unmooring, the body set afloat on an ice floe. In the Russian original, the rhyme scheme pairs "l'din" with "odin" (effectively, *ice floe* with *alone*), and both words are repeated in their respective lines to move them into final rhyme position and to make the rhyme a kind of echo. The body is like the ice floe, cold and unattached. As it floats horizontally, the sound of the trumpet rises vertically, affording "a glance at the world from the other side of the retina" (here I translate the final line of stanza 3 literally).

The poem's freedom with the way poetry invokes music rises forth from this image of the unattached body. The poem's references to cold are also references to the physical sensation of the body, which Brodsky invites the reader to experience from a position of lying "flat on your naked back upon the ice floe." Colder than that, one does not readily imagine. Brodsky translates audibility into tactile experience, reminding us that we listen to music with our whole bodies.

To let the body estimate aesthetic experience is another of this poem's rhetorical gestures. Americans reading this poem might in fact think of Emily Dickinson's famous comparison—"If I read a book and it makes my whole body so cold no fire can ever warm me I know *that* is poetry"—and perhaps Brodsky knew this definition, living as he did each spring semester from the 1970s until his death in 1996 in South Hadley, Massachusetts, a mere half hour from Dickinson's Amherst home (and this poem, with its February dateline, was surely composed in South Hadley). For Dickinson as for Brodsky, body temperature measures aesthetic engagement, although Dickinson's next sentence switches to an idea of bodily integrity: "If I feel physically as if the top of my head were taken off, I know *that* is poetry."[23] Dickinson is describing the experience that in later years would come to be known as "mind blowing," an epithet that seems far more appropriate for a jazz soloist's effect. Which is, in a way, Brodsky's point. The mind grasps at possible definitions for the experience of listening to Clifford Brown's trumpet, drifting even as it reaches for something to hold on to. But in the end the drift is itself the effect, like that ice floe moving toward the pole, reconfigured as an outpost of the stars and stripes.

Brodsky's poem sets the body of one who experiences music, or, for that matter, poetry, adrift in a solitary experience of absorption. One takes in the art through the senses, especially in this case the sense of touch. In that moment of haptic reverence, one does not attend to music like what Elena Shvarts would later call a solo on a white-hot trumpet, but rather one translates a heated musical performance into frozen alertness.[24] Time may equal cold, but it is a cold that streams through the fingers of the performing sax player to all who hear the music.

In this memorial poem to Clifford Brown, music has given poetry an icy body of water on which to float, setting it adrift toward unknown possibilities. It is said of Brodsky that he was the last Romantic in Russian poetry, that he was an end to a certain form of high modernism rather than the beginning of all that came next. I don't entirely buy that, and we can look to later music poems to test the possibilities of a more generative legacy. How did his peers and later poets listen to his music? What did they catch—his warmth, or his icy touch?

We could also ask, though, a different question, one that "In Memory of Clifford Brown" helps us answer. Where did Brodsky as a poet find his freedom? In a trenchant essay on Brodsky's life and poetry, Keith Gessen positions him as something of an aesthetic conservative: compared to the American poets like Allen Ginsberg, who found freedom in "breaking the bounds of traditional prosody," Gessen says that Brodsky found freedom in "reestablishing a tradition that Stalin had sought to annihilate."[25] I think Gessen underestimates the innovation of Brodsky's prosody (typically *dol'nik* or *taktovik* rhythm, strong enjambment, risky rhymes, and elaborate stanza forms). But by that standard, "In Memory of Clifford Brown" is formally conservative (with no striking enjambment, and only one off-rhyme—*polos/polius*).[26] And yet the poem has a radical openness that Gessen points us toward when he quotes Brodsky's friend and biographer, the poet Lev Loseff. The first time Loseff heard Brodsky read his poems, he said, "It was as if a door had opened into a wide-open space that we hadn't known about or heard of. We simply had no idea that Russian poetry, that the Russian language, that Russian consciousness, could contain these spaces."[27]

That kind of opening out to a new space is achieved in "In Memory of Clifford Brown," and while this same ambition is realized in a great number of Brodsky's poems, what is distinctive here is the way in which the poet instructs his readers on how art—the jazz of Brown's trumpet, or the poetry of Brodsky's own lines—can open that vista. It is a vista that itself gazes down upon the earth from which it arises, as if seen from behind the retina. So much of this poem translates audial experience to touch that it is a shock to realize that the poem's final invitation is toward vision. That shifting boundary between the impressions of multiple senses is what makes this poem seem so contemporary.

Listening to Music in the Big City:
Mara Malanova and Vladimir Aristov

In Brodsky's poem, the drifting body is a remarkable contrast of fixity and motion: the body lies still, but the ice floe glides across freezing water propelled by music. In the less watery urban environment, where multiple poems about music are set, movement can have both propulsive force and its opposite, bringing all motion to a sudden halt. In the poems of Mara Malanova and Vladimir Aristov to which we now turn, the poets absorb the city's energy through its sounds, and like Brodsky's image of a coasting ice floe, the pulsating sounds of the city fuel physical movements through its spaces. How and when does that sound register as music? The idea of the city itself as a musical instrument has a long history, but poets hear what we might call "the instrumental dimension of urban space" differently in an age when performed music can come from many sources.[28] One enduring trait of music is its capacity to rise above other heard sounds. When set in the urban environment, poems more often juxtapose one set of sounds to another, with melody or rhythm shaping just about anything that is audible. Noise becomes its own form of music, or, as in work by such composers as John Cage, John Luther Adams, or John Adams, overheard or recorded sounds energize new forms of musical creation.

An untitled poem by Mara Malanova goes one step further, toward a reversal: here, the music has the properties of noise (including its absence), while the city transmits that noise's aesthetic beauty. Malanova's poetry is temperamentally and formally unlike Brodsky's—none of the frosty grandeur, and little of his stanzaic patterning.[29] She generally prefers inscrutable narrative miniatures, where human oddity is captured and held up for inspection, alongside short rhythmic poems of extraordinary, fleeting beauty. Born in Ulan-Ude, Malanova lives in Moscow, the setting for this poem.

It begins with a reference to a well-known avant-garde musical event, the four-minute thirty-three second performance of a work by John Cage, which bears the title of that length of time: 4'33". A pianist (David Tudor at the first performance in 1952) sits at the piano, puts the score on the stand before him, looks at a score, uses a stopwatch to time intervals of stillness, but does not otherwise touch the piano or make its strings resound.[30]

Radio *Cage* transmits 4'33" around the clock,
clouds curved outwards hang over the city,
you walk down the underground passageway and suddenly see
a geography teacher explaining to his fifth-grade girls
how to wash windows correctly using newspaper and spit:
his hair is wet and slicked-down,
his body motions are jerky,
and he chokes out his speech.
How rare it is that something springs to life, not exactly memories,
but something held, locked away God knows where
since the moment it happened,
and for a second Radio *Cage* goes silent.

Радио "Кейдж" круглые сутки транслирует 4'33",
облака, выгнувшись наружу, нависают над городом,
ты идёшь по подземному переходу и вдруг видишь
учителя географии, демонстрирующего пятиклассницам
с помощью слюны и газеты, как нужно правильно мыть окна:
мокрые прилизанные волосы,
судорожные движения,
захлёбывающаяся речь.
Как редко оживают не воспоминания,
а то, что хранилось Бог знает где
с момента своего происшествия,
и на миг замолкает радио "Кейдж."[31]

Rather than the famously bounded period of silence created by Cage in 4'33", Malanova posits a radio station that transmits the piece in an endless loop, creating a listening experience of nothingness attuned to the Zen aspirations of Cage himself.[32] Something is antiquated about the radio's presence in this poem, creating an apt analog for the vivid form of estrangement (*ostranenie*) that shapes the poem's every line. The whole point of Cage's composition was its live performance, where an audience sat in fixed rows of seats preparing to hear a piece of music.[33] They would be made intensely alert to the noises around them when there was no music playing. Malanova references 4'33" to model the intensified act of attention that the poem itself offers. It shows us incongruous elements of urban life (like a spectacle of mimed instructions for window washing), refocusing attention to the present in all its absurd happenstance. Whether she knew the poem or not, her readers might make the mental comparison to another poem about Cage's 4'33", by Viktor Krivulin, a leading figure in late Soviet unofficial poetry in Leningrad.[34] His poem uses the silence of Cage's composition to open a space in which memories of his generation's youth well up.[35] Malanova's poem by comparison refines that retrospective work—"not exactly memories, / but something held, locked away God knows where"—by means of the spectacle of the window-washing instructor. The performance of music wraps around the spectacle, holds it in its silence as the mind has held a memory, but the poem and the memory both end with an abrupt and enigmatic sign-off: the radio goes silent, a debased version of the hieratic "silence and authority" (tishina i gospodstvo) that conclude Krivulin's 4'33".

Silence fascinated John Cage: he called 4'33" his "silent piece," and he generally regarded music as "silent prayer."[36] In one version of the score for 4'33", Cage wrote the word "TACET" to mark each of the three movements—the word is "the instruction in a score that tells one instrument to be silent in the midst of the sounding of the other instruments of the orchestra."[37] What are those other instruments, though? One answer is material, the clicks and hisses of the sound environment; by design, the quiet induced by 4'33" would let those noises, those other instruments, be heard more fully. But another answer for Cage, practitioner of Zen Buddhism, is being itself. Our ears' alertness to sound becomes a metaphor for the mind's alertness to its own being, and full attention to the experience of the present would open out to a form of ontological revelation.

Does Malanova also use her poem to drive deeper into the mysteries of being? The whimsical tone of her poem, if not the downright silly sketch of a geography teacher instructing fifth graders in the art of window washing via pantomime, suggests that the poem doesn't want us to take it all that seriously.[38] But Cage repeatedly showed his irritation that audiences took 4'33" as a joke, and Malanova, whose poems almost always have this quality of quizzical lightheartedness, is surely daring us in her own way.

Malanova's work recalls the poetics of OBERIU, the loose affiliation of Leningrad writers in the early Soviet period who created poems, stories, and dramas with improbable plots and caricatured actors; many wrote for children (and there is a childlike quality to Malanova's work, which often re-creates scenes of childhood and projects a seemingly naïve intonation). For Daniil Kharms and Alexander Vvedensky, the antic resistance to cause and effect long distracted readers from sensing the philosophical and theological underpinnings of their work, which Vvedensky called "a poetic critique of reason."[39] Scholars have begun to assess their work differently, however, and we can learn a great deal about how to read OBERIU-like texts from the performance-based approach advanced in Branislav Jakoljevic's book *Daniil Kharms: Writing and the Event*; from the philosophical emphases of Vvedensky's best translator, Eugene Ostashevsky; and from the learned theological arguments of L. F. Katsis.[40] They model for us ways to take seriously that which looks slight. Learning from this superb scholarship and theory, we should consider how a silent radio and a mimed demonstration of window washing could have philosophical significance. Even the connection to Zen is pertinent: the contemporary writer Victor Pelevin, a sometime student of Zen, observed that "Kharms is a mystical writer; his extreme isolation may have been involuntary, but his experience is all the more unique. His brief stories resemble Zen koans that halt the mind and destroy the world."[41]

Malanova is not going so far as to record world destruction, but she is drawing on a logic familiar from Cage's music, famous for chance operations, whimsy, and Zen, but always also deep attentiveness. Listen to Cage on Henry David Thoreau: "Each day his eyes and ears were open and empty to see and hear the world he lived in."[42] This is a fundamentally ethical project, for which there is supreme value in "a condition of responsiveness, of openness and reception as against grasping and penetration."[43]

What Malanova seeks and finds in her enigmatic vignettes of contemporary life is precisely this condition of responsiveness and openness, to a degree that, as she put it in a poem about "Flute and Drums" ("Fleita i barabany"), would drive the listener out of her mind ("Priblizhaetsia zvuk barabanov, svodiashchikh s uma").[44] The poet is led to a kind of mental disarray, but one in which perceptions are sharpened: she drily observes, "I am as if not here" and "I don't know myself what is happening to me" (I menia kak budto net; Chto so mnoi proiskhodit, ia ne znaiu sama).[45] What is attended to at such moments is described at the end of yet another poem:

And all will surround silence in twilight—
The unseeing music of ceaseless praise.

И все обступит сумраком молчанье—
Слепая музыка неумолкаемой хвалы.[46]

The poet describes what she is listening to in this "unseeing music" as an "endless conversation of whispers and sighs" (beskonechnyi razgovor iz shepota i vzdokhov).[47] The music of the universe is made of human sounds, as defined by its silences as it is by its noises, very much like the music of John Cage's 4'33". These other poems have taken Malanova out of the urban setting that marks her poem on instructional window washing and Cage's music of silence toward a greater freedom of imaginative setting. The inner freedom to see one's place in the cosmos, triggered by the sounds and the silences of music in the poem treated here, can be brought on in her other work by just about anything: industrial archives, bridal gowns in a magazine, excess drinking after a funeral, or children eating meat pies in the kitchen. Sensory impressions register lightly on the poet's consciousness, but to profound effect.

A similar layering of sounds occurs in the poem by a quite different poet, Vladimir Aristov. He is a physicist (and thus part of a great tradition in Russian humanistic culture, in which path-breaking scientists are also creative figures in the world of poetry, tracing back to the eighteenth-century poet Mikhailo Lomonosov). Aristov's poetry has connections to the trend of Metarealism, and the poem treated here shows the linguistic self-consciousness and dense metaphor associated with Metarealism, its capacity to find "modes of expression for the unity of distant things," as one translator of Aristov put it.[48] Aristov has written a play about the philosopher Gustav Shpet, and he is also a fine writer of prose; his poetry can display elements of dramatic encounter and narrative shape, revealing a scientist's and a novelist's eye for detail.[49]

The initial setting of Aristov's "Object Music" ("Predmetnaia muzyka," 2008), an underground passageway, may remind us of Malanova's poem in terms of location, but the volume of sound could not be more different.[50] The poem blends several kinds of music—the zither-like music heard in performance, the rhythmic sounds of city life, and the music re-created on a shoulder bag lain across his lap as the poet later sits in a speeding tram. Rescaling experiences of distance is one of the poem's tasks, exemplifying Metarealism's quest for finding the "unity in distant things." The poet's task of bringing together distant concepts runs parallel to the imagination's labor to bring music's sounds nearer to mind. The music is heard, felt as if physically, but also imagined (which is important—as Carolyn Abbate and others have shown, unheard or impossible music can loom large).[51] Even when the music is performed in the mind, it is enacted as if by bodily action, on the body addressed directly as "you" (ty).

The poem also asks us to imagine what it feels like in our bodies to make the city's music. Its sensory impact, then, crosses the tactile and the auditory, as in Brodsky's poem "In Memory of Clifford Brown." What is different here is a fleeting suggestion that the heard music is made not just by the surrounding environment, but by the listening poet's body.

Object Music

The distant urban drone
You started to listen on a winter morning
Eyes closed

You remembered: a magic gusli was also playing in the underground
    walkway

You ran past carrying your usual shoulder bag
                    and felt beneath your toes, at your fingers
        all the city's music, tremor, and human conversation

    you were its source, the weakly flowing spring of this droning sound

        you could feel that the world was playing, turning into a simple
            object

but there is no one to collect it, to create

the city everywhere and somewhere
    but you were not there

                    a head distantly aches

    at twilight you already made out that sound—a sudden woof in
        the distance—
            a pattern of mother-of-pearl, unfamiliar and vague

    you thought you could return that figure

And in the freezing tram
Where distant music
Glassed off by cold

Briefcase on your knees making sounds under your hands
As if you turned over the guitar
With the strings facing down
You hear the music in yellowed wood
It starts to tremble like a lyre in the fields

The surrounding city—does not see you
And you feel just barely the palms of its hands
     what's this . . . the light shiver of a banknote, a child's flag or a
       pennant in the breeze

    and snow, a ruin all around, is indestructible

  the city-world asks that you wander
        its streets and gardens
          giving its distant meaning as a gift

You play with your fingers
       on the edges of your shoulder bag
       or on the wood of the old guitar

And although the city with its every gesture
       races ahead of you triumphantly
    it will not happen without you.

Предметная музыка

Отдалённый города гул
Ты заслышал зимним утром
Глаза закрыв

Ты вспомнил: в метро-переходе играли так же гусли-самогуды

Ты пробегал с привычной сумкою через плечо
        и ощутил под пальцами
          всю городскую музыку, трепет и людские разговоры

  ты был его источник, слабый родник этого гула

    ты чувствовал, как мир играл, переходя в простой предмет

но некому его собрать, создать

город везде и где-то
  но там тебя нет

отдалённо болит голова

ещё в сумерках ты нащупал звук—внезапный лай отдалённый—
узор незнакомого смутного перламутра

ты думал, что сможешь вернуть тот рисунок

И в мёрзлом трамвае
Где музыка отдалённая
Остеклённая холодом

Твой портфель на коленях под руками звучит
Словно ты гитару перевернув
Струнами вниз
В жёлтом дереве музыку слышишь
Затрепетав, как лира полевая

Город вокруг—не видит тебя
И ты лишь ладонь его чувствуешь
что́ это . . . лёгкая дрожь купюры, детский флажок или вымпел
под ветром

и вокруг снег—руина, но всё ж нерушим

просит город-мир, чтобы ты бродил
по улицам его, садам
даря ему его отдалённый смысл

Ты играешь пальцами
на сумке своей
или дереве старой гитары

И хотя город каждым жестом своим
торжественно тебя опережает
он не произойдёт без тебя.[52]

Let's begin with the last line: the poet observes that urban life cannot happen without "you," a capacious pronoun that includes the poet himself. What is it that he is required to do? To listen, and with a special kind of alertness. In running past the sounds heard at the start of the poem, the poet comments on his own absence, and his head aches as if pounding with the failure to heed the music. But then on the tram, he begins to hear something, to be physically a part of the urban space, visible and audible to others as he rides along. He is no longer the invisible, absent body described earlier.

The poem suggests that the presence required is also metaphysical: the poet is the one who gives "distant meaning" to the streets and gardens. Conferring that meaning is performed by means of a musical performance, the poet drumming or strumming on the briefcase that he has rested on his lap during his tram ride. He uses it as a folk musician would use the gusli, a zither-like instrument that is one of the very oldest in Slavic cultures and an evocation of folk culture.[53] The poet heard the gusli during his walk through the underground passageway, in fact, and I translated it as a "magic gusli" to get the folktale resonance, but it is more precisely a self-playing gusli ("gusli-samogudy"), an instrument that makes its own music. It is uncannily like the radio in Malanova's poem—we don't see or hear a human person performing the music in either case. But the ancient folk origins of the gusli differentiate it from a modern mechanical invention like the radio, making it more like an Aeolian harp. Its sounds emit as if without human agency. The poem goes on to provide the image of a lyre in open fields, another way that music could be created by the wind moving along the strings. Both the lyre and the gusli motivate the poem's insistence that the music is distant: the epithet is heard five times, three of them referring to music. Mentions of the gusli and the lyre make the music come from afar not only spatially but temporally, from two distant moments in the cultural past, one specifically Slavic, the other more broadly European.

Collapsing these cultural and temporal distinctions is one of poetry's urgent tasks, Aristov has written, creating a "cosmos of time, where one can cite from the future, where one can not only see the deep past, but construct it."[54] That temporal openness is enabled by a poem's ontology, demonstrated well in "Object Music." What is it that makes music an object? The answer might be found through recourse to the writings of Timothy Morton, in what he has called object-oriented ontology (I resist following him in using the abbreviation OOO, although the specter of nothingness suggested by those zero-like gaping circles is awfully tempting). Morton has suggested that philosophy needs what he calls hyper-objects: objects that are nonlocal, foreshortened in time, and (metaphorically, I assume) viscous. These objects are too big to behold, and "the more you know about them," the more overwhelming they become.[55] They are emblems for the sublime, and Morton writes insightfully about the long tradition of the sublime. His examples tend toward phenomena like ecological crisis or "stolen objects" that act with what he calls "a spooky agency." I would argue that music, as Aristov represents it, is also such a hyper-object, and that its conceptual stickiness or viscosity is felt doubly: Aristov's "object music" is a pervasively affecting phenomenon that is at once outside the psyche and made within the body; it is an immediate and present experience but also something occurring at a distance. Even its status as an object is doubled and ironically rendered. At one point the poet calls it a "simple object" (prostoi predmet), but nothing could be less simple than this gesture of naming the object as simple. The phrasing calls to mind instantly both a children's song, the song of Winnie the Pooh as translated by Boris Zakhoder ("Vot gorshok pustoi, / On predmet pustoi"), and a definition of the object advanced by Ludwig Wittgenstein in the *Tractatus*, one whose parts are not themselves also objects.[56] For Wittgenstein, simplicity is a logical term, and its clarity would have attracted Aristov, who has written about the nature of logical equivalences as a mark of similarity between physics and poetry.[57] Morton's hyper-objects are an attempt to get beyond that logical simplicity, though, and while Aristov is drawn to the idea of clear equivalences in rhetoric and math, his own poetic practice, where metaphors can densely pile up, points toward a greater complexity. One pathway for those representations is the collision of sensory impressions, hence the intensely auditory and tactile realms of "Object Music."

Those practices of naming, unnaming, and sensory crossing also mark an earlier poem, also on music. In "Music" ("Muzyka," 1977), Aristov evokes a wasteland of sound made from stones and voices, and he utters an imperative not to carry these sounds into music ("ne unosi zhe v muzyku nash zvuk"). Holding on to the sounds, which alone seem capable of stopping the world short of complete emptiness, means holding music itself at bay. That sound may well be coming from the "ancient and nameless sea" before which the poet stands in its final line ("pred nashim drevnim morem bez nazvanii").[58] But can the poet or the poem keep music and sound separate? In calling the poem just "Music," Aristov seems to bring all the heard world into that capacious term. Whereas "Object Music" offered many terms for the heard sounds of the world ("gul," "lai," "zvuk") in addition to music itself, this poem loads all those possibilities into the poem's one-word unadorned title. The last metaphor for sound in a poem that has laid out a vast stony landscape is the sea, itself a metaphor for the kind of hyper-object Morton describes. Although it is said to be "our" sea, and an "ancient" sea, it eludes that most human capacity for naming.[59] It and the music it represents seem poised to take up too much space, to engulf the viewer or the listener.

Why is it dangerous? We know that music has historical and cultural associations with danger, but in Aristov's poetics, the danger is more narrowly specific. In a tantalizingly brief essay on free verse as a form of translation, Aristov commented on how translations done during the Soviet period, often by poets with no knowledge of the original language and relying on an interlinear text, in effect falsified the poem's music, not because their interlinear notes excluded comments about form but because the pressure to make the poem sound like mainstream Soviet poetry—metered and rhymed—far exceeded any expectation that the translation would convey the possibly stuttering, jangling, innovative, or plain-spoken textures of the original.[60] Aristov's plea at the end of "Music," then, has a local meaning—to preserve the harsh, even frightening sounds of a stony, windswept, sea-facing landscape that in turn image some of the craggy verse he was reading at the time (in his essay on translation, he mentions as venerable an example as Eliot's 1925 poem "The Hollow Men," and Aristov has translated the contemporary American poet Michael Palmer, to give a very different point of comparison).[61] Let us hold still in our contemplation of the hyper-object, the poem insists, however overwhelming it might be; let us not turn it into something smaller or narrower; let us not reduce all sound to music.

The more metaphysical and philosophical reading of Aristov's poetics is reinforced, then, by the specific historical reference, and we are left with multiple paths along which definitions of music run. Is music a threat? A trope for poetry itself, made on the body and made in harmony with the city's rhythms and spaces? The answers may include all of the above. That hypothesis will now be tested by a poet who stays quite far from the intensities of an urban environment, but one whose sense of spatial music is also richly philosophical.

Gennady Aygi: Rhythms of Performance and of Nature's Sights

Gennady Aygi is more fully available in English than nearly any other contemporary Russian-language poet, although his reputation within Russia was slow to emerge.[62] Born in the Chuvash Autonomous Soviet Socialist Republic, he published nine books of poetry in Chuvash, but it is his Russian poetry that brought him fame, if belatedly within Russia.[63] His first book publication in Russia came after twenty-five-plus years of publication abroad.[64] His work thus became another fact of post-Soviet cultural life, even for poems composed

much earlier. We have already seen this delay in the reception of Mikhail Er-
emin, but Aygi's reputation is more complicated. His position among Russian
poets was subject to intense argument, turning on perceptions of him as in-
sufficiently Russian and of his work as not really poetry. The paradox of his
reception is obvious. As Sergei Zav'ialov put it in response to Aygi's death in
2006: "Never before has a poet who wrote for nearly fifty years in Russian, who
was legally published in Russia (at least for the last two decades), and who was
recognized and translated throughout the world, departed this life in the face
of such utter indifference from both readers and the literary establishment."[65]
Olga Sedakova declared that Aygi was the most widely read of any con-
temporary poet, an exaggeration, perhaps, but not implausible—Aygi has
been translated into more than a dozen languages, for example, and many
volumes of his work were published posthumously in Russia.[66] The strangely
bifurcated reaction to Aygi was neatly summed up by Michael Wachtel: "Ad-
mirers consider him a genius (as numerous prizes attest), while detractors
dismiss him as a fraud."[67] The prizes were all given by European countries,
pointing to another distinctive feature of Aygi's work: he was inspired by
French poetry, from Baudelaire to Jacob, Char, and Deguy.[68] That engagement
with the French tradition is what likely made his work less legible to critics
within Russia (not unlike the way some were confounded by the work of
Arkady Dragomoshchenko, after his deep engagement with American
L=A=N=G=U=A=G=E poetry). Aygi warmly admired figures who were
themselves outsiders in Russian culture, a fact he noted proudly.[69]

The cultural world that Aygi himself most prized was that of music.[70] His
friendships with Andrei Volkonsky, Sofia Gubaidulina, Valentyn Sylvestrov,
and other composers are documented in the dedications of several poems.
Music is a frequent theme or point of reference, and the musical or rhythmic
features of Aygi's poems are distinctive and highly varied. They derive more
directly from the musical tradition than from poetic conventions. In a 2001
documentary film, Aygi explained that his fascination was with rhythm, not
meter—a distinction by which he means not the contrast of underlying and
realized metrical structure, as the two terms are technically used in philology,
but rather a rejection of conventional, regular poetic meter in favor of unpre-
dictable, changing rhythmic phrases as he sensed them in the natural world.[71]
In articulating and evaluating that contrast between meter and rhythm, Aygi
is approaching these terms as they make sense in music, rather than in poetry.
He sees meter as constraining, rhythm as expressive—and in the documentary
film where he is explaining these ideas rather tersely, his gestures dramatize

the difference. He demonstrates meter by tapping out a regular beat with his arm, something like the tick-tock of a clock or a nail being hammered. Rhythm, however, is enacted by his arm moving in a circular, widening gesture. Rhythm seems to have emotional and expansively spiritual potential, whereas meter is mechanical. In re-creating rhythm, he gestures broadly, embracingly, as if taking in the contents of the air; in mimicking meter, his body stiffly raps out a series of movements that are confining and regular, a series he seems eager to burst out from. In that urge to break out, Aygi's poetry comes into being. Attending to phenomena in the world, he is alert to the moment when the mind and the poem might leap toward something freer.

True to this principled quest for a more expressive poetic form, Aygi's poems eschew syllabo-tonic meters, an enduring foundation of Russian poetry, in favor of a freedom with verse line and shape that has few rivals even in a period dominated by free verse.[72] He was an inventor of many different kinds of poems, and what kept him looking for these new possibilities in poetry was a matter of music, specifically rhythm. Of course, he worked with such a restricted lexicon that one would almost have to think that his prolific work as a poet was driven by different rhythmic possibilities. We know that Aygi loved music, but we have not yet understood what it meant that he loved equally the harmonious, emotionally expressive music of Franz Schubert and the jazzy, percussive rhythms of his contemporaries, like Sofia Gubaidulina.[73]

Gubaidulina's music is heard in the documentary film about Aygi, in fact. At one point in the film, the poet reads this 1977 poem he dedicated to her.

mozart: "cassation I"

for S. Gubaidulina

mozart godlike mozart straw compass godlike razor wind paper heart attack madonna wind jasmine surgery wind godlike mozart cassation twig jasmine surgery angel godlike rose straw heart cassation mozart

моцарт: "кассация I"

С. Губайдулиной

моцарт божественный моцарт соломинка циркуль божественный лезвие ветер бумага инфаркт богородица ветер жасмин операция ветер божественный моцарт кассация ветка жасмин операция ангел божественный роза соломинка сердце кассация моцарт[74]

This poem, published in several places, is always presented as an indented paragraph and justified as if prose, with more or fewer lines depending on the page and margin size.[75]

The visual density of the poem (it looks like a dense brick of words), so unlike the airy, spaced-out lines of countless Aygi poems, is intensified by another feature of the poem, its rejection of conventional punctuation and of all syntax, which would be created by verbs and declined nouns. You could, for instance, create a poem almost entirely of nouns in Russian by changing the endings, to suggest relationships among the terms—this is something Marina Tsvetaeva did famously, and other poets have experimented with this possibility. But Aygi does not decline the nouns here: they are all in the nominative (and only one word is not a noun, "godlike" / "bozhestvennyi," heard four times). The poem, as an illocutionary act, is an announcement, a presentation of evenly cadenced lexical items. The Russian words are from two to five syllables long, and there is no regular pattern in the repetition of words by syllable or by lexical item. The visual density of the poem suggests simultaneity, as if the words were meant to operate musically as a chord. But to hear the poet read the poem, where he pauses after each word (not lengthy pauses, but distinct and equivalent pauses that suffice to separate each word), is to experience it not as a temporally collapsed text but as a sequence that unfolds in time.

Why these specific words? They create five semantic fields: musical genius (mozart, godlike); nature (straw, wind, jasmine, twig, rose); book or drawing (compass, razor, paper); religious belief (godlike, madonna, angel); and a medical understanding of the human body (heart attack, heart, surgery, razor). Nearly all these semantic fields, although not always in these words, appear in Aygi's poetry commonly, although this is the sole poem in which heart attack or surgery appears. There is a metonymic link, though, between the rhythms of a heartbeat, particularly one interrupted by a cardiac emergency or corrected by surgery, and the pulse of a poetic text. This poem, in its manifest difference from the hundreds of other poems Aygi wrote, establishes its own altered rhythm, where there is nothing but the even, forward progress from one word to the next. The effect is stabilizing, and from that position of strength, the poet can peer at the elements of the natural world, its tiny bits of blossom and twig, and peer out at the manifestations of a cosmic order.

Mozart presides over the poem as ruling spirit, both creatively and phonically. The epithet "godlike" grows out of Mozart's status as a divinity among musical geniuses, and it refers to his middle name, Amadeus, meaning "beloved by God." The consonants in his name generate some of the poem's other words. The final *t* sound recurs in the word for heart attack, "infarkt," and the *ts* sound in the Russian spelling "motsart" reverberates in "operatsiia," "tsirkul,'" and "serdtse" (respectively surgery, compass, heart). The *ts* sound is also heard in the title word, "kassatsiia" (cassation), a musical term now largely super-seded by the nocturne, or serenade. But the quotation marks in the title mean that the poem is presented as a "cassation" written by Mozart. In Mozart's lifetime, the genre designation was familiar: an "informal instrumental genre of Classical period, usually intended for performance outdoors as a kind of street serenade."[76] What kind of evening performance is this? The lack of verbs, including any imperatives, omits the expected appeal from the streets to come forth, which a cassation would normally feature.[77] Instead, the poem unfolds a sequence of nouns, an invitation for quiet contemplation.

The poem becomes its own form of musical performance, and performance is nearly always a part of an Aygi poem. Many contain instructions for how they should be performed, either in verbal form or as unusual punctuation markings that turn out to have rhythmic, which is to say musical, significance.[78] Words themselves can be stretched out internally to suggest an exaggerated form of enunciation and a deceleration in any imagined declamation. The slowdown inevitably involves not the consonants, as in "mozart: 'cassation I,'" but the vowels. In an expressive example from 1984, entitled "White Flowers at the Very Edge of the Motherland" ("Belye tsvety na samom kraiu rodiny"), Aygi opens the poem with lines that look like this:

they departed
then disappeared— ———————still fa-arther
———————————and here
also there's no one to see
that something happened: they will not now return

уходили
потом и исчезли——————все да-альше
————— ————————и здесь
тоже некому было увидеть
что что-то случилось: уже не вернутся

A few lines later, a woman is conjured up; we see only her hands:

hands to the window—but
on angelic-dead glass

only signs from fluent-vivid fingers will appear——————(the
    same coolness
cool-ness)

руки к окну——а будут
на ангельски-мертвом стекле
лишь знаки от пальцев истекающе-яркие——————(та же
    прохлада
про-хлада)[79]

The poem continues for another six lines, where there is another line interrupted by seven long dashes. In a note to the poem, Aygi explained, "The row of dashes found in this poem are expressed as equally measured, monotone knocks when the poem is read aloud, in accordance with their number." And the text contains multiple indications about the intended speed and rhythm of its performance (even more in the full text in Russian, where several words have extended vowel sounds to lengthen pronunciation).

The poem registers different forms of disappearance and absence, including finger traces on a window and, in the conclusion I did not quote, hills that cast no shadows. From the start, there is no one to see what has happened, as if the poetic subject were also absent. The white flowers in the poem's title appear nowhere in the poem, perhaps because they are the grammatical subject of the first word, "departed" (in Russian, there is no pronoun, just the third person past-tense verb). Even that is a bit jarring: normally, we would not think of flowers having the agency to depart on their own, but nature is animated in Aygi's world. In the last lines, the hills also turn and show themselves.

Aygi uses the musical aspect of this poem to counteract its multiple forms of absence: a set of performance directions are firmly present. Although we might think about performance as the most ephemeral of art forms, as having no material existence after it ends, Aygi's poem stakes out a more assertive claim, and he intensifies the assertion by giving even more duration to the poem itself. The knocking sounds denoted by those long dashes and the hyper-extended vowels slow things down, giving readers or listeners extra time to contemplate the scene evoked in this poem.

One can find other instances of this kind of punctuation in Aygi's work, for example, a poem of the same year, "hills-and-hills" ("kholmy-i-kholmy").[80] It combines an exclamation point and dash (!—) as a stand-alone line twice, essentially dividing the poem into thirds. Aygi can be heard reading this poem in a short film from 1998, and he knocked on the nearby table firmly at these junctures. To watch him read that poem, in fact, is to see how each word in the poem was like the knocking sound. There is a percussive force to his act of enunciation, and he gives emphasis with his body to each accented syllable. The poem gains a rhythmic force that is again much stronger than its imagery would suggest.

One of Aygi's most emphatically rhythmic pieces was dedicated to the percussionist Mark Pekarsky, and the dedication may have prompted the poet to see just how far he could go in re-creating percussive rhythms in a verbal text. Entitled "oasis of daisies in the field" ("ostrovok romashek na poliane," 1982), it is not often reprinted, but it can be found in a large-format, well-illustrated volume produced in 2001 in Petersburg.[81] The full text looks like this:

oasis of daisies in the field

To the splendid percussionist Mark Pekarsky

illumination
moving (. . . . .)—

!—

aaaáAAAÁaaaá
(voices voices voices):

:

–⓵–⓵–⓵–
illumination above (voices-and-flickering-and-voices):

:

. . . . (o radiance-drumming):

:

⓵

островок ромашек на поляне

Замечательному перкуссионисту марку пекарскому

озарение

двигаясь (. . . . .)—

!—

аааáААААáаааá
(голоса голоса голоса):

:

–⟨!⟩–⟨!⟩–⟨!⟩–
озарение вверх (голоса-и-мерцание-и-голоса):

:

. . . . (о сияние-дробь):

:

⟨⟨!⟩⟩

In this case, we do not, as far as I know, have a recording of Aygi's performance, so we are left to our own imaginations in establishing the respective loudness or rhythm of the symbols ⟨!⟩ and !—to say nothing of the colon that also appears and the lengthy ellipses. We know from other Aygi performances that these may be instructions to drum, or to beat, or to otherwise make a percussive sound. But we don't know that ⟨⟨!⟩⟩ is louder or longer than ⟨!⟩. The words, too, leave open some elements of any imagined performance. How to voice the difference between a phrase in parentheses and one that is not? Aygi here brings us right to the edge of imagined audio experience and leaves us to linger on the visual means of suggesting those rhythms and sounds.

As is often true in his work, we have a natural scene to which we are invited to exclaim in wonder—is that the reader's imagined extended *a* vowel sound, a reaction to what is seen and heard? The poet's word painting offers an entirely different alternative, that the huge clump of daisies surrounded by open field are themselves giving voice, as if articulating sonically the radiance made by their pure white light. As in Brodsky's poem "In Memory of Clifford Brown," Aygi crosses between sensory capacities, in this case sight and sound, as opposed to Brodsky's use of touch and sound. He does so in a poem that not only cannot be paraphrased, but exceeds the limits of alphabetic language to draw on the expressive force of regrouped punctuation marks. In that sense, the poem becomes an experiential record of an event, epitomizing that quality of hyper-attentiveness found throughout Aygi's poetry.

Elizaveta Mnatsakanova's Metamorphoses

Elizaveta Mnatsakanova's poetry shares intense visuality with Aygi's work. She ranges across musical forms and rhythms with a different breadth, drawing on her training as a musicologist. Like Aygi, she is one of a kind: her poems have a rhythm and sound structure unlike anything being written in Russian at the time she began in the 1970s. She creates sonic work based on repetition, paronomasia, and rhythmic variation. As of 1994, her work appeared in Russia in book form and in leading journals, as well as in Vienna, where she emigrated in 1972.[82] Mnatsakanova continued creating her self-published books of poetry well into the twenty-first century. She was awarded an Andrei Bely Prize in 2004.[83] So she shares another fate with Aygi: her readership in Russia was very much a post-Soviet phenomenon.[84]

Mnatsakanova used the term *visual poetry* to name her work. As the creator of handmade books and one-of-a-kind albums, and as a calligrapher and photographer who embedded snapshots and elaborate handwriting into her work, she transformed the look of poetry on the page. Her poems also often thematize music or derive from musical genres, and some passages leave all referentiality behind to become pure sound.[85] When her words are arrayed on the page as compositional elements, they become blocks of text whose meaning can also be musical, as Gerald Janecek has shown in his reading of "Das Hohelied" as graphic representations of the passacaglia form.[86] And sometimes the visual presentation can have clear thematic elements, as in her most famous poem, "Autumn in the Lazaretto of Innocent Sisters: A Requiem in Seven Parts" ("Osen' v lazarete nevinnykh sester: Rekviem v semi chastiakh"), which ends with lines arranged in cruciform fashion.[87]

The presentation of text in *Metamorphosen* (1988), the small book I concentrate on here, is daringly simple by comparison, and if the focus were on Mnatsakanova's visual art, other books, particularly *Das Buch Sabeth* (1988; "Das Hohelied" is the concluding part) would be far more apt.[88] But *Metamorphosen* is the ideal text for concentrating on Mnatsakanova's music. There is some visual adornment, but it is stern. Unlike the vivid blue cover chosen for her 2004 book *Arcadia* and unlike the bright, expressively colored images on the covers of all her other books, *Metamorphosen* is entirely black and white, as if encoding its visual restraint and mimicking the black and white look of sheet music. Even so, the imagery has many connections to her other work, including three versions of her trademark hand holding a pen (on the back, inside, and front covers). The book's cover is pictured in figure 8. Within the pages of the book, the chief ornamentation is the use of calligraphy borders, strictly sequenced to offer a border on one side of the page (top, right, left). The border is made of a row of cursive E's (the first letter of the poet's first name). Right and left borders are doubled, with a single long line of loops. On the title page (figure 9), there is a complete frame of the title (presented in nine iterations), with rows of E's and other kinds of decorative loops. The borders are all as if produced by the hand pictured, a reminder of the poet's compositional work creating the poems and the book that presents them. She is the composer, in multiple senses of that word, of a book that, like all her Vienna books, she personally assembled and formatted.[89] This visual composition presses us to read it musically. The title page's calligraphy, assembling all the visual variants that will be seen on pages of the book, turns the succeeding pages into a kind of minimalist reiteration of the title page's affordances. Verbal repetition, with fugue-like variations in the sound orchestration, is a signature of Mnatsakanova's poetry, and more than in any of her other books, repetition is an organizing feature of *Metamorphosen*.

Music is directly suggested by the volume's title. *Metamorphosen* may call to mind Richard Strauss's late, great work for strings by the same name, which Edward Said praised as an "unbelievable polyphonic invention."[90] Strauss's *Metamorphosen* has twenty-three musical lines, one for each string instrument. The shape of Mnatsakanova's cycle of twenty numbered poems, plus a prelude (or "motto," as she calls it), and a finale, is similar. She gives her *Metamorphosen* a subtitle, as the title page shows us: "20 Veränderungen einer vierzeiligen Strophe und Finale" (20 Transformations of a Four-Line Strophe and Finale).[91] Mnatsakanova has said that she did not think consciously of the connection to Strauss until after she finished her *Metamorphosen*, but she confirmed that it is an unavoidably pertinent text.[92] Her work shares its mournful tones and its evocation of happier memories from youth. Completed in 1945, Strauss's *Metamorphosen* was an elegiac tribute to the destroyed opera house in Munich, where he had spent his youth.[93] Mnatsakanova admired Strauss, particularly his *Alpine Symphony* (1915). Her love for the Alps informs her poem as well: halfway through her *Metamorphosen*, a walk in an Alpine landscape is evoked, and the cycle was in fact composed during one of her annual summer sojourns in the Swiss Alps.

Although the title and the poem's eventually Alpine landscape might suggest Strauss, *Metamorphosen* more fundamentally refers to the music of Johann Sebastian Bach, and formally the poem draws on his compositions' multiple separate lines of melody and elaboration to create the effects of polyphony.

FIGURE 8. Cover, Elisabeth Netzkowa, *Metamorphosen* (1988)

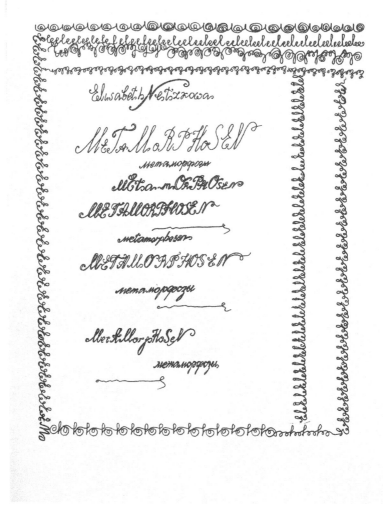

FIGURE 9. Title page, Elisabeth Netzkowa, *Metamorphosen* (1988)

Mnatsakanova has pointed to Bach's English and French Suites and his Partitas, especially BWV 826, as a point of reference, noting that she played these piano works as a child and loved Glenn Gould's performances of them as an adult. She emphasized Gould's versions in all her comments about Bach's keyboard writings, and she surely admired his technical mastery in conveying both the large ordering patterns in the pieces as well as the tiniest expressive details, all along keeping the separate melody lines distinct.[94]

Bach is frequently mentioned in *Metamorphosen*. He is called by his complete name, Johann Sebastian Bach, and by each of those names separately. Each name in turn generates whole sequences of words and associations, both of other persons (Johann becomes Ioann, or St. John the Apostle) and places (Sebastian becomes San Sebastiano). Bach's friend, the master organist Gottfried Silbermann, is mentioned, and his name substitutes for the organ he played. Phonetic sounds motivate verbal transformations, and the poem's lines create swift semantic contexts for these transformed sounds. Throughout, the poem interrogates the possibility that narrative flow can be created from these bits of sound—flow or current being a key motif in the poem and the form to which it aspires.[95]

Maintaining constant flow is repeatedly challenged, as the poem moves along from one set of sounds or motifs to another. The challenge is defiantly named from the start, when the prelude begins with an emphatic all-caps assertion:

NO, THE SIGNS OF DEAD WORDS WILL NOT FLAME UP
НЕТ, МЕРТВЫХ СЛОВ НЕ РАЗГОРЯТСЯ ЗНАКИ.[96]

This line asserts something entirely unlike Bulgakov's famous prophecy that manuscripts do not burn: instead, the failure of words to catch fire leaves the world darkened without their light. There is a reference to the poet's calligraphy, surely, in these "signs of dead words," and to her persistent project of creating requiems for those she has lost.[97]

The poem pivots toward a dreamed fantasy of a posthumous choral performance, resonating through the trees and pathways of an Alpine landscape. Although the poet said that it is her own death that is mourned by this dreamed requiem, she connects the melody and the vision to Bach by invoking his first and middle names:

ah, that melody
returns in dreams:
the death-defying melody
of ioann
the death-impending vision
of sebastian
the choral melody

of the organ is flying
is flying and dreaming
is filled with joy.

ах, все мелодия
та
снится: посмертная мелодия
иоанна
предсмертные видения
себастиана
летит мелодия
хоральная органа
летит и снится
веселится.[98]

These lines from part 14 of *Metamorphosen* inaugurate the dreamed sequence
of the rest of the poem. The tonality of the last third of the work is that of a
requiem. Mnatsakanova has said that the work's title, for all its rich verbal and
musical associations, is something of a "pseudonym," and she has urged atten-
tion to the text's hidden tragic side encoded in its theme of "farewell, farewell
to childhood, to one's home, to the Alps, which are my second home, and to
much else." She links that sense of farewell back to Strauss's *Metamorphosen*,
observing that motifs from the funeral march motif in Beethoven's Eroica sym-
phony were Strauss's musical encoding of that requiem.[99]

Poetic quotation further marks *Metamorphosen*, from Aleksandr Blok's
"Verses on a Most Fair Lady" ("Stikhi o Prekrasnoi Dame," 1905), Ivan Kry-
lov's fable "The Wolf and the Lamb" ("Volk i iagnenok," ca. 1808), a song based
on Nikolai Zabolotsky's poem "In This Birch Grove" ("V etoi roshche berezo-
voi," 1946), and the hymn "From Heaven Above" ("Vom Himmel hoch," writ-
ten by Martin Luther in 1534).[100] Several of the quoted phrases give rise to
extensive sound play. These are not the misprisions or competitive revisions
made famous by Harold Bloom, so much as demonstrations that distant poetic
texts retain their life-giving powers to inspire new work.[101]

Mnatsakanova uses the names of musical forms, some of them antiquated,
in much the same way (and this should remind us of the way that sounds heard
in the Russian word for "cassation," *kassatsiia*, inspired the sound orchestration
of Aygi's poem to Gubaidulina). She, too, is opening new pathways for inter-
twining verbal and musical thinking. Some of the resurrected forms she
mentions are the musical genres in which Bach excelled, including the dances

(allemande, courante, minuet) used to name the parts of his keyboard suites.[102] These words seem to call forth others in a flow of sounds that crosses languages: courante, for example, suggesting the calque *current* in English or *courant* in French, which in turn produces the verb *techet*; the minuet (in Russian, *menuet*) evoking paronomastically the verb *minuet* (from *minovat'*, to pass by). These words expand, opening out to morphologically and phonetically similar words and sounds, enacting at the level of language the metamorphosis that gives this text its name.

Bach's central presence in *Metamorphosen* provides the poet with something else as well. The sequence of parts for the partitas BWV 820–826 and the English and French Suites (the compositions from which she has taken the names courante, allemande, minuet), signals changes in rhythm, tone, and tempo that her own *Metamorphosen* mimics. I suspect that what drew her to these partitas and suites is their elaboration of dance music, their strong rhythmic orientation meant to capture different patterns and styles in which bodies might move to the music.[103] Mnatsakanova has said that the physical experience of her own body moving through the Alpine landscape was a source for *Metamorphosen*, and there is a kind of productive restlessness in the way that the energies grow and change in the course of the text. But this is mental as much as physical movement, and we can perhaps best understand it as a kind of musical thinking, to borrow a phrase that Christoph Wolff has used in describing the work of Bach.

Bach provides us with the best guidance for understanding Mnatsakanova's poetry as a whole, both its seriousness as an intellectual project and the contours of her texts. Although many scholars, performers, and devoted listeners regard Bach's writing for vocal ensembles, particularly his Mass and the St. Matthew Passion, as his supreme achievement, Mnatsakanova favored his suites and partitas for keyboard. It is an interesting choice. Perhaps a poet, whose art relies on words, might have more readily gravitated to the settings of hymns or the Passions, where words and music interact in ways that add so much complexity and intricacy to the compositions. And Mnatsakanova has commented on his Christmas Oratorio, to which her own *Metamorphosen* refers. But proportionally, the keyboard works are far more significant to the conception of the text. Perhaps the poet preferred wordless melodies as a structure that her words could fill, but the answer may be no more complicated than the fact that Mnatsakanova played the piano and loved the keyboard music. It has elements much like her own poetry. As John Eliot Gardiner writes, "Bach's keyboard works maintain a tension—born of restraint and obedience to self-set conventions—between form (which we might describe variously as cool, severe, unbending, narrow or complex) and content (passionate and intense) more palpably and obviously than does his texted music."[104] That contrast between stern form and intense content perfectly describes the inner dynamic of Mnatsakanova's writings.

Bach's meditations have an order and a shape that also deeply affected the poet. His first biographer, Johann Forkel, defined his music as shaped by "order, connection, and proportion in the thoughts," and Christoph Wolff emphasizes that these terms, along with coherence, continuity, and relation, are definitive in a way that genre and form are not.[105] This means that Bach created a cantata or a partita not on the basis of a received idea of these genres of music, but rather as if from within the forms, reinventing their parts in his own way. Similarly, Mnatsakanova's poetic texts conform to no received notion of lyric, dramatic, or narrative form. Instead, they proceed according to what always feels like an inner logic, with principles of order, connection, and proportion very like those in Bach. Her writings move according to a certain abstract idea rather than elaborating or unfolding narrative or other thematic motifs. Wolff explains that "what Bach dubbed musical thinking was, in fact, nothing less than the conscious application of generative and formative procedures—the meticulous rationalization of the creative act."[106] And there is indeed something procedural in the way Mnatsakanova unfolds her longer poetic texts. Her way of using repetition, patterning, splicing, and decomposing gives the appearance of turning over all possible modulations and configurations.

One dramatic instance of that procedure occurs at the end of *Metamorphosen*, where what is sequenced is pure sound. The lines are presented with such grammatical freedom as to have their own syntactical strangeness. The sound of the word "strangeness" (*strannost'*) phonetically underlies these lines, which feature a profusion of consonant clusters: *sn, st, str*. And there are verbs with no subject, creating another dream-like sequence in which the language itself has absorbed the displacements and condensations of dream work. Someone or something (the nearest subjects are house and street) is dreaming, standing off to the side (*storonitsia*), standing, groaning, and in the state of being incompletely built (*nedostroennyi*). Actions occur as if unrelated to agency, all of it physically static and slightly unreal. Lines of mangled, extended sounds interrupt periodically. These same *sn, st, str* sounds soon recur in a single line of three conjugated verbs four lines later: "groans stands guards" (stonet stoit storozhit), in which the new term, guarding, reinforces the sense of physical immobility.[107] When the next verb appears, it almost seems to be the movement that the words have been guarding against, for it is the verb "to wander" now spread across the stanza's longest line: "waaaandeerrrsssss—thi-i-i-s-s-s" (straaaanstvueiiittt—etttaaa). The letters of this word wander, we might say, although in terms of the poem's narrative, it is a street that wanders, if we read the short lines sequentially.

I want to end with an example that pulls closer to pure affect, as suggested in the line just quoted about wandering. It is part 20, the last before the finale. Here, as against my usual practice, I won't translate these lines, knowing that their sound patterns can be apprehended on visual inspection without much knowledge of Russian. This is not the reference-free experience of the signifier, though, and semantics continue to show Mnatsakanova's use of source texts. Two key terms, *street* (ulitsa) and *house* (dom) come from the short song "The Blue Balloon Is Whirling, Turning" ("Krutitsia, vertitsia shar goluboi"), a childhood memory for the poet. Notice how Mnatsakanova lays out the lines, essentially turning them into instructions for pronunciation:

ах—а-а-а-э-э-э
тт-ау—л-ии
ца-а-а—э-э-э
тт-аа-ттт дооо-ммм
-а-а-а-аааа
ах, а-эттааа
у-у-улиииии-и
ца-а-а-аах-эт1атт-доомм
дооомм-kathedrale
ах—а-а-а-э-э-э
тт-ау-л-ии
аах, этта ууулиится
снится сторонится
странно сторонится
дом стороною
стоит
недостроенный
стонет
стоит
стороною этт-ааа-т

дооом- ээ-тт-ааа

уууу-л-ииии-тттт-сааaa

стонет стоит сторожит

а-а-а—всеоооо—

страаaaнствуеииитттт—этттаааa

ууу-л-иии-ттт-сааa

всяа в голубом

вся в голубом

стонет и странствует

стынет и страшная

страаa-ааaaн—-у-е-иииитттт-эээт

и и-и-и-э-и-э-ииии-э-э-э-ттттааа a-

и-у-л-ииии-ииии————-ииии—и—--—ииии—[108]

Consider that last line, built out of the word for street (*ulitsa*). It is stretched out but also broken, all vowel with no final syllable. Language has been returned to its basic sounds, and what we have here is both a visual performance (where the hyphens between vowels function almost as musical rests) and the script for a spoken or chanted performance. To listen to Mnatsakanova read these lines is to realize that the text is in fact only a sketch on which the poet can improvise in performance.[109] The model is something closer to jazz than to the music referred to in the text. Mnatsakanova has produced a poem that has uncanny similarities to the poem Brodsky wrote in memory of Clifford Brown, even though his definition poem is very far indeed from the way her text moves toward the re-creation of purely affectual experience through sound.

I end with reference to Mnatsakanova's performances of her own poetry for one other reason: some contemporary Russian poets' performance work is similarly based on profound knowledge of the classical music tradition, using song as a pathway toward emotional richness. Mnatsakanova's *Metamorphosen* refers to choral music, but her orientation is not toward the power of song. Let me end this chapter with two poets who do sing. The first is Keti Chukhrov, rising to a register of fierce pathos.

Why Keti Chukhrov Sings

Keti Chukhrov's unusual poetic dramas might have been properly treated in other chapters of this book, given their performance histories and rich political implications. The political implications have been important in critical

treatments of her work, and understandably so: she is a prolific cultural theo-
rist and aesthetic philosopher, and her many interviews and essays show that
her thinking turns on urgent questions of inequality and social injustice.[110]
She has vented some frustration that poetry often lacks serious political and
social resonance, and discourses of materialist philosophy and aesthetics,
ethnicity, and gender are prominent in her poetic texts.[111] These texts are
structured as dramas that put into conversation clashing discourses and sub-
ject positions. The dramas translate conflict into a contest of voices, and as in
a polyphonic Dostoevsky novel, the characters can feel like stand-ins for ab-
stract ideas (one character, for instance, is named Diamara, a name based on
an abbreviation for dialectical materialism; there is a man called Hamlet, and
another called Platon, the Russian version of Plato). Chukhrov, a native Geor-
gian (she was born Ketevan Chukhrukidze), often creates characters from the
Caucasus. For example, she has pointed out that Hamlet is a common name
for men in the region; her text "Elpida and the 'Greeks'" ("El'pida i 'greki,'"
2006) is set in a part of the northern Caucasus where military conflict is rag-
ing. Sometimes this ethnic origin is realized as substandard Russian in the
texts (in "Med-Madonna" ["Medik-Madona," 2007]), and Chukhrov can ex-
aggerate ethnic stereotypes by these linguistic means, pressing her audiences
to confront their own assumptions and prejudices. The same hyper-
characterization occurs in terms of gender, and it can intensify into sharp
parody, best heard in *Communion* (*Kom'iunion*, 2009).[112] But gender and
erotic desire are also crucial in the text on which I focus, "Afghan-Kuzminki"
("'Afgan'-Kuz'minki," 2008), as noted in its subtitle: "Scene for an Attempt to
Initiate Sex" ("Stsena popytki pristupit' k seksu"). The clash of discourses, so
typical of her work, marks that subtitle's mix of nouns from formulaic or
public language to blunt direct speech. Polyphonic clashes of discourses and
subject positions occur throughout this short two-character play; Chukrov's
sung performances translate that multivoicedness into multiple musical reg-
isters.[113] Her poem-dramas often veer off into parody and dark comedy, but
Chukhrov uses melody, pitch, and rhythm to secure a lyric beauty for
"Afghan-Kuzminki" that shows us another side of contemporary poetry's
powerful engagement with music.

 The play consists entirely of dialogue between Hamlet (a purveyor of furs
in the open-air market nicknamed "Afghan" in the Kuzminki neighbourhood of
Moscow) and Galina (a seller of cheap undergarments in the same market).
The setting guarantees that a discourse of commerce will pervade all the back
and forth about whether these two will have sex, and the sexual act is itself

presented as a form of economic exchange: when Hamlet suggests within moments of the play's beginning that perhaps she'd like to trade up to selling fur, she asks if having sex with him is part of the deal. He's offended when she wonders if he'll keep his word, but his bravado speaks for itself, including his shouted responses into his cell phone as business problems keep interrupting. The plot unfolds as a series of delays (she checks her invoices, he smokes, they pause for food, he leaves for a bit); finally, they end up in his apartment, watch some TV, and fall asleep in different rooms. In between, they do "initiate" a sexual act, still in the market, but Hamlet recoils at the sight of Galina's body and zips up his pants after hurling a few choice abuses.

Their verbal exchanges are riddled with his vulgarities, and her language can descend quickly into common obscenity. It's as if she has no language for her longings, which have almost nothing to do with the sex on offer to her.[114] But there are several moments when she attempts to articulate her desires, not repeatedly deferring them the way the text defers the sexual act, but always adding some element of debasement to cast doubt on the lyric impulse. For example, when she comes home from the market, she says, she gets herself something to eat and sings to herself, until her off-key singing annoys the neighbors, but then she might go into the bathroom and sing some more. That singing is the first effort Galina makes to transport herself to a different emotional state, but the song offers little comfort, as if she does not know how to use her own voice to create loveliness. A second moment comes when she retells the plot of a TV film she's started to watch. It's "About a man's life, about his existence on earth. / He sort of lives but doesn't know / Whether he has everything or has nothing at all" (Pro zhizn', pro bytie cheloveka na zemle, / kak by zhivet on, to li est' u nego vse, to li net nichego). But this glimmer of a metaphysical musing is immediately darkened: "One minute he's told 'you're a fucking ass,' and then a broad licks him all over and lies beside him" (To emu govorit: "ty zapadlo," a to baba vse oblizhet i riadom liazhet).[115] He can't make up his mind whether he wants all of this desperately or is completely indifferent, and his anomie becomes a transferred expression of Galina's own state of mind. When Hamlet slaps her face in disgust at their one near approach to a sexual act, she has no reaction at all.

"Afghan-Kuzminki" keeps trying to break through that numbness, all the way through to its ambivalent ending. Chukhrov staged her own act of resisting the numbness by singing the text, and among the many ways her work has been performed, this musical rendering is perhaps the most revealing. As a singer, Chukhrov takes both parts, raising and lowering the pitch of her voice to differentiate the voices of Galina and Hamlet, and accompanying herself on the piano. That she ably both sings and plays the piano should come as no surprise, for Chukhrov had serious musical training and has described herself as taking up poetry the day after she abandoned music, as if one led inevitably to the other.[116] By singing the text, Chukhrov activates a subtitle that appeared on the recorded performances, "A Human Oratorio" ("Chelovecheskaia oratoriia").[117] The genre tells us something important about Chukhrov's decision to give musical voice to "Afghan-Kuzminki": oratorios are sublime musical compositions on religious themes, and even when their narrative is complex and their dramatis personae many, they are heard without costumes or staging. Chukhrov, too, renounces the theatricalization of the text, performing as if in her own clothes (in one version, where the room she performs in must be cold, she keeps on her jacket and gloves).[118] The text itself is a stripped-down oratorio, for two solo voices. She sings both parts, mostly a cappella, and for extensive passages she accompanies herself; in other passages, she plays lovely piano interludes. Those piano passages are largely free improvisations with generous samplings of the music of the Baroque, the period in which the genre of the oratorio flourished, and of the Renaissance (the composers include George Frideric Handel, Jean-Philippe Rameau, and John Dowland). The sung text is quite varied in its rhythms and suggested sources (they range from religious litany and chant to pop music), but it opens with the highly regular rhythm and reduced pitch range of religious chant, a rhythm to which it often returns.

The premiere performance at Teatr.doc in Moscow was recorded and can be seen online.[119] Chukhrov has explained that the Moscow performance was improvised by her, both piano and voice, and that she subsequently watched a recording to transcribe what she did.[120] This act of listening to herself is a remarkable element of the musical performance, as if the creator of the script had heard in it a whole set of musical polyphonies layered onto the play's words and brought them into being. It calls to mind the theoretical work of Peter Szendy, who has written of a desire "to share such-and-such sonorous event that *no one besides me*, I am certain of it, has ever heard as I have."[121] Chukhrov acts on such a desire. She is reimagining the possibilities for poetic lyricism by bringing "Afghan-Kuzminki" to voice.

We can see how important the beautiful elements of this singing are to the performance of this text by comparing a very different performance that she gave with the poet and critic Alexander Skidan in 2010. With him, rather than singing through the lines and including piano accompaniment, Chukhrov speaks Galina's lines in an expressive, conversational voice; Skidan reads Hamlet's with an eye to their humor, even cracking himself up at one point, and their joint performance conveys a lovely ease and intimacy that is very far from the interactions they are re-creating. Song, however, comes into this performance as well, near the end of the play, when Chukhrov sings an excerpt from Tsvetaeva's "Poems to an Orphan" ("Stikhi sirote," 1936).[122] She does so in a way corresponding to the childlike, one-syllable-at-a-time manner of the text's stage directions (pochti po slogam, po-rebach'i); her rhythmic, almost spellbound way of singing the lines captures Galina's enchantment with Tsvetaeva's poetry.

This singing happens in the final scene, which finds Hamlet and Galina in his apartment. The delays and interruptions in their ever-deferred sexual encounter include a televised address by Putin, and the TV also shows someone reciting from Marina Tsvetaeva's "Poems to Akhmatova" ("Stikhi k Akhmatovoi," 1916); Chukhrov includes a stage direction that this performance is "mannered, pretentious, and vulgar" (manerno, vychurno, i vul'garno).[123] Interestingly enough, one of the omissions in Chukhrov's performance of "Afghan-Kuzminki" is this televised bit of poetry, but the lines are important in the play's logic because they trigger Galina's recitation of Tsvetaeva, which ensues once she is sent off to sleep in a separate room. She begins with that passage from "Poems to an Orphan," and she then intones three excerpts from Tsvetaeva's "Poem of the End" ("Poema Kontsa," 1924).[124] The written text includes parenthetical identifications of the first two as Tsvetaeva's (and names "Poems to an Orphan" as the source of the second), but the selections from "Poem of the End" continue as if in Galina's own voice. Still, an audience will recognize Tsvetaeva's emotional intensity from "Poem of the End," one of the most passionate poems about a broken-off love affair in the language. Chukhrov's lovely performance of these lines reaccentuates the music of the poetry and even moves the word stress to give a rising intensity to the short bursts of lines. Whereas in the performance with Skidan, she reverted to a speaking voice for the passages from "Poem of the End," in the sung-through version of "Afghan-Kuzminki" these lines are a musical summit, allowing Chukhrov to move quickly among changing intervals in the most contemporary sounding of the performance's melodic lines. Piano accompaniment is used to vivid contrastive effect, as Galina laments that the world has cast her aside as if she were a material object: "To throw me away like a thing / When there is no thing I ever prized / in this empty world of things" (Brosat' kak veshch' / Menia ni edinoi veshchi / Ne chtivshei v sem / Veshchestvennom mire dutom).[125] Chukhrov has taken one of the central philosophical and political themes of "Afghan-Kuzminki"—

the treatment of persons as things, and the consequences of a market economy on one's experience of personhood—and redirected the poetry of Marina Tsvetaeva as well as the beauty of her own singing voice to reaccentuate that theme and give it great emotional force.[126]

The quotations from Tsvetaeva, however, do not get the last word, and the final note is not one of lyric exaltation. Instead, the next morning, Hamlet and Galina awaken. Her incantatory performance of Tsvetaeva's poetry has brought him a dream of a world without walls, and for a moment it seems as if the text will have a utopian conclusion. Then he tells Galina to get some toilet paper so they can wipe off the cheap lipstick and see her face. The music is over.

Vasily Borodin, Songs to Praise a World of Harm

Vasily Borodin is a fitting choice to conclude this chapter for several reasons, not the least being his growing significance as a contemporary poet. He was unassuming to an extreme degree and had a quiet voice that risked getting drowned out in the cacophony of Moscow, where he lived his whole life. But recognition, including an Andrei Bely Prize in 2015, came his way: when *Vozdukh* surveyed younger poets in 2012, he was named as an emerging leader by five of the respondents.[127] And when he died suddenly in 2021, the outpouring of grief and disbelief was intense.[128] Igor Gulin wrote that only at this moment of Borodin's shocking death could one see that he was the most significant poet of his generation.[129] Perhaps it should have been obvious earlier, as Borodin's output was prodigious: the 2020 publication *Cloud Nine* (*Klaud nain*) in the excellent Voznesensky Center poetry series was his eighth book to appear in just twelve years.[130]

Borodin also comes logically last here because his work draws together and reweaves many of the ideas pursued in this chapter. Like Aygi, he is attuned to the music-like offerings of the natural world and uses a restricted, deceptively naïve vocabulary to re-create the experience of that audiable and visible world for his readers.[131] Like Chukhrov, he has changed the valence of his written texts by his singing performances. In a surprising way, his work has also reimagined the radical simplicity of Olga Sedakova's "Old Songs" ("Starye pesni," 1980–81), and she saw his work, in turn, as an incantatory return to poetry's points of origin.[132] But the seeming simplicity of Borodin's small poems is only part of his achievement, and his muted music ironically amplifies the rhetorical and aesthetic project of the poems. Like the work of Mnatsakanova, his poems thematize music, and while he did not have the advanced degree she attained nor her extensive professional training, he knew music history, theory, and practice well.[133]

Borodin's relationship to music is but one feature of his work, although a defining one.[134] He has a further rather remarkable thing in common with Mnatsakanova: a long-standing artistic practice. But these are different practices. Borodin used to give away his work at poetry readings and exhibits, as if it were barely his, which is the opposite of her careful signing, dating, and archiving practices. Whereas Mnatsakanova uses her first name's initial, *E*, to create precise calligraphic borders, Borodin's artistic practice has a sense of spontaneity and freedom epitomized in the tiny book that included drawings made with his eyes closed, *Rain-Writing* (*Dozhd'-pis'mo*, 2013). Still, like Mnatsakanova, and like the books created by Futurist poets who influenced them both, Borodin sensed an enormous potential in aligning text with image. Sometimes the images punctuated poems, as in a 2011 group of poems that incorporated handwritten text into images.[135]

Other work fused poetry to image more uniformly, as in the beautiful sequence of seven childlike, resolutely simple watercolors, one poetic line to each image, beginning "where is lovely water?" (gde krasivaia voda?).[136] Here is the text of the poem written out in lineated form:

> where is lovely water?
> where are her edges? when?
> where is motionless Always carrying along in the sky?
> at the wise bonfire
> Here is walking and Yesterday sleeps
> round air hides in round bread
> and we're off

> где красивая вода?
> где края её? когда?
> где несущее в небе неподвижное Всегда?
> у разумного костра
> ходит Здесь и спит Вчера
> круглый воздух в круглом хлебе прячется
> а нам пора[137]

Figure 10 shows the penultimate image, where line 6 appears.

These colors are so beautiful, themselves the answer to the initial question of where one finds loveliness, and this particular page edges the words around

FIGURE 10. Vasily Borodin, "Where is lovely water?" (2011)

the central yellow roundness—a roundness that is both air and bread—so that there is a deeper fusion of image and word.[138] The poem has an uncanny connection to a poem by the English poet Alice Oswald, her "Sea Poem," which includes the line, "what is the beauty of water."[139] Like Oswald, Borodin is fascinated by the possibilities that plants, water, air, animals, insects, and birds can speak in poems, so that the poet's job is to listen. In his work, some of that attentiveness is to the world's music, and to reproducing the heard sounds in estranged linguistic form.

Here, for instance, is the intensely onomatopoetic opening of his "Dog's Song" ("Sobach'ia pesnia"):

ва в ва
в ва в ва
вы в вы
в вы Ы в вы в
ваАв в ав в а
вы Ы в вы . . . в ppppppppp[140]

It feels almost silly to "translate" these sounds, which would amount to a transliteration of them (the sounds are *v*, *a*, and a kind of hard back of the mouth *i* in combinations). The poem uses letters on the page to suggest a dog's growl, howl, and eventually soothed sounds of contentment.

Something similar happens in the poem "sleeps" ("spit"), but now the visual element comes to life in the poetic lines. The materials of image making themselves become part of the poem. In one poem, we see an ink blot crawling into the letters of a hymn ("vot chernil piatno / raspolzaetsia / v bukvy / Gimny").[141] Susan Howe, an American poet lauded for her experiments in sound and visual arrangement, has said that every mark on the page is an acoustic mark.[142] The apprehension of a move from marks on a page, whether poetic words or drawn figures, to a rhapsody of sounds becomes one of Borodin's signatures as a poet.[143] That expectation of a sound in a visual image is captured well in Lawrence Kramer's account of Rembrandt's painting *The Philosopher in Meditation*, which he connects to sensory hybrids of a particular kind: sounds that "can be heard, or heard well, only under certain visual conditions," as he puts it, or as if "sound were parting a curtain."[144] It is that sense of auditory expectation that Borodin's performances foster.

Because he sang his poems, often accompanying himself on guitar, Borodin was himself the instrument of transforming marks on the page into acoustic sounds. Igor Gulin offered an expressive view of his readings as performances: "Borodin did not read his texts, he sang them. In his shaman-like incantation the poems were almost impossible to understand but this was the only performance adequate to the poems. His poems are hymns. He sang, and by means of his singing elevated things: large and small, living and inert, ridiculous and grand. This singing took on physical power: it literally lifted things up; they floated up in the light, and the words that referred to them were changed as a result."[145] Gulin pinpoints the impact of singing on a reader's experience of the texts, the way that song floats words up into the air—like the round bread in "where is lovely water?"—and gives them both substance and lightness. Each word in the poems has a kind of potency that lacks violence or force.[146] Gulin hears that power in the way Borodin's "singing elevated things." As a result, he calls the poems hymns, catching not just the elevating capacity of Borodin's simple rhetorical gestures, but also the way in which his every poem resounds with praise.

An untitled poem—Borodin's poems are nearly all untitled—that has the word "hymn" in its last line begins by invoking a musical instrument invented about one hundred years ago, the theremin:

the theremin breaks down into measure and amplitude
its gold removed in error

and in the air the icon grows
into someone—anyone—walking this way
the rubber sole of crummy sneakers

parting, a hymn

2011

терменвокс распадается на мензуру и амплитуду
туда смыли золото по ошибке
и икона в воздухе обрастает
человеком—встречным, любым другим
поролон в подошве плохих кроссовок

расставанье, гимн[147]

2011

Borodin begins by naming an arcane musical instrument, the theremin, a kind
of precursor to the Moog synthesizer and an invention in post-Revolutionary
Russia by Lev Termen. Borodin suggests the two antennae or knobs of the
theremin, which control the music's frequency (here, measure) and volume
(amplitude). But rather than conjuring up a scene of performance, with a
player moving their hands around the antennae, he suggests that the instru-
ment is itself dissolving into these two points of control. It would have been
quite a compelling start to the poem to create that scene of performance, and
one in line with Borodin's usual imagery and poetics, because a player makes
music on the theremin without touching it. But the poet never specifies the
hands waving in the air, leaving it to readers to imagine them. The air is reserved
for the next sequence of images, where an icon materializes into a person. That
person is not necessarily the saint normally depicted on an icon but someone
so ordinary that their sneakers are badly worn at the heel.

That vertical descent, both metaphorical and literal, takes us with precipi-
tous speed all the way to the ground and down to a set of debased images that
seem impossibly far from the music-making theremin—until the poem's last
word, "hymn." That final word not only loops the poem back to the musical
references with which it began, it also transforms all the poem's lines into the
praise poem that constitutes a hymn. To quote Susan Stewart, praise in poetry
"reveals, augments, and at the same time creates surpluses in excess of what it
discloses."[148] The hymn, we might say, arises from the surplus Borodin has
created with the piteously few words of his poem. A spirit of glory arises from

the theremin and the icon, and rather than using the lowly sneakers as a point of contrast, the poet lets that glory cover the sneakers as well.[149] They march to the beat of the hymn as might any more elevated image or object.

A similar magic is worked when Borodin sings his poems. On one level, there is a sleight of hand made possible by the simple act of performance: the requirement that a performer believe in the performance translates into a palpable sense that when he sings his poems, Borodin believes in their power. In the wake of his death, we know all too much about his self-doubts, but that cannot diminish the deep conviction that emanates from his performances, especially the poet's absorption in the music he is making.[150] The magic of the sung poems, though, is also formal. Because he is creating his own musical settings for the poems, there is no sense of the music swallowing up the rhythmic elements of the verbal texts that aesthetic theorists have described in composers' settings of poetry.[151] Borodin can muffle some of the words, depending on the performance, but one hears line breaks in his settings, and conversely, the poems themselves often read on the page as if they were composed with a future musical setting mind (for example, when there are sequences of lines that syntactically stand free as if ready for musical phrasing, or when similar syntactic structures and verbal repetition make a song's rhythms feel complementary and natural).[152] The continuity between poems as verbal texts and sung versions of the poems with guitar accompaniment shapes this work, felt keenly when Borodin as a performer would pause in his musical renditions to read or recite poems.[153] But there can also be long passages in which Borodin simply plays the guitar, improvising his own melodies and as if following those melodies in and out of encounters with the poems.[154] The guitar work is beautiful and varied, doing more than creating a musical bridge from one poem to the next. It sets a mood, and it lets us witness Borodin's fierce attention to his music, which, in the wake of his early death, took on an elegiac air as of 2021.

It would be a mistake, however, to conceive of Borodin's poetic world as tragically earthbound, however unfortunate his untimely death and however profoundly he reflected multiple losses and impossibilities in his poetry. A structure of aspiration is constitutive of his songs' mood. Susan Stewart has said that moods are set by "the mind reaching after what it cannot grasp," and that structure is pervasive in Borodin's work, including his habit of reaching toward some sense of faith or apprehension of the eternal.[155]

The aspiration toward an ethereal lightness shown in the visual images for "where is lovely water?" is also a signal feature of the work. Even when a text suggests a somber mood, the poetry and the music can turn quietness toward

something like prayer. Any number of his poems in fact sound like prayers.[156]
The resulting attitude and affect creates a shared subjective state, what Charles
Altieri called "atmospheric landscapes" in which poet and audience may dwell.
Altieri is describing what we mean when we talk about a poem's creation of a
mood—a concept that, like Stewart, he richly theorizes. Their work helps capture
the paradoxical radiance of Borodin's poetry. As Altieri says, "Mood produces
overall affective coherence, and as such attracts subjects to make identifica-
tions with its insistent but ungraspable totality."[157]

That "affective coherence" aptly describes the powerful hold Borodin's
songs and poems have on an audience. The poems reach out to a listener, even
amid the feeling of solitude.[158] There is a paradox of solitude and community
in performances that mix spoken texts with sung versions, and in the poetry
as well.[159] That is to say, there is a great continuity between the aesthetics of
the verbal texts and the sung performances. Borodin's spoken renderings
exude an intense musicality and rhythm that lets the text embody myriad
subtle changes in pitch, rhythm, and pacing.[160]

Thus, even when he reads his work with no guitar in sight, music remains
a defining feature of the work. Borodin's readings blur the line between singing
and speaking, making his spoken performances of his poems into something
like opera's *Sprechstimme*.[161] A striking example of that gentle sense of perch-
ing his performance between song and speech is heard in the poem "Through
the skies' light-gray darkness" ("Po svetlo-seroi mgle nebes"), which also has
some beautiful guitar work. Sometimes there is only the faintest hint of pitch
variation, but the rhythmic performance retains the contours of song. By re-
moving the barriers—by breaking down the walls—that might separate ele-
vated music from ordinary speech, Borodin brings us full circle back to the
transformations of musical allusion in the work of poets like Vladimir Aristov
or Mara Malanova, where the source of music is a noisy urban environment.
They attune us to hear music where our minds might dismiss the surrounding
sounds as noise, but Borodin teaches us to hear the most ordinary chatter of
daily life within the sublime sounds of his poetry. In that ordinariness, lan-
guage reorients itself, finding a rare authenticity.[162] We are far from fully com-
prehending Borodin's contribution to twenty-first-century poetry and must
await fuller publication of his work. But one thing is clear: he found ways to
make poetry sing. From a paucity of materials, from a restricted vocabulary
rife with repetition, and from a range of expressiveness that can leap from near
muteness to loud exaltation, this poet built a one-of-a-kind body of work that
sings praise to a troubled, tragic world.

To end with Borodin is to end with a poet who both wrote about music in his poems and used his skills as a guitarist and composer to create sung versions of his texts. His versatility is shared with poets who have composed and performed musical versions of their poems (like Chukhrov) and with those who have seen their work set to music (like Aygi and Mnatsakanova; this is also true of Sedakova). Borodin's most distinctive feature as a musician poet, however, may be his own intense acts of listening, particularly to the silences that feature prominently here in the work of Malanova and Aygi. To hear the inaudible and to make it, as Lawrence Kramer would say, audiable, is to prepare readers and listeners for a future in which the sound might be heard.[163] In the end, that is less far from the orchestration of urban clangor found in Aristov's poem than it might seem, because for both poets, the speaker is remade by the acts of listening, bound over into new forms of experiencing the self in the world. We have come full circle to Brodsky's physicalization of that experience in the icy hot jazz of Clifford Brown and to his thrilling sense of the freedoms that music could bring. The examples in this chapter have wound toward less and less freedom, either because the poet exposes the structures of inequality that hold persons back (Chukhrov) or because the small glimmers of freedom offered up by the world feel so fleeting (Borodin). The reader is offered that small bit of freedom, however, as a prized gift, one that retains its powers to console, to inspire, and to sustain. The next chapter turns to photography and to documentary material that is balanced on the same paradox; it gets us closer to pure freedom of expression, even when constraints loom large.

5

Poems and Photographs

MATERIALIZING THE INEFFABLE

Yusupova • Svarovsky • Dragomoshchenko • Glazova

IN THE AGE OF smart phones and Facebook, we are all photographers, creating and sharing snapshots of daily life and ritual occasions. When poets take pictures, they can be just like the rest of us, performing an accessible form of artmaking that makes a memory. They record the present moment in anticipation of a retrospective glance back. They take cat pictures (figure 11). They capture a beautiful outdoor scene, filled with light (figure 12), or a quirky urban setting (figure 13). These photographs (by Fyodor Svarovsky, Anna Glazova, and Arkady Dragomoshchenko) all fit recognizable genres of photography, but each is also legible as an index of poetic practice.

The poet who held the camera assembled a picture out of elements that could have inspired a poem—if not the precise objects in the photograph, then some aspect of the picture's light or pattern or swoosh of movement. Svarovsky, known for his narrative poems about robots, time travel, and heroic exploits, photographed an animal in shock at the possibility of flight, held aloft by a barely seen person who perches the cat in the air. The image partially reveals a clock, as if the cat were traversing time itself. Glazova's photographs are mostly still-life arrangements of flowers and fabrics, but here she catches a shower of light, the light rays themselves taking on materiality; her poems constantly materialize substance out of the pockets of air between the objects or plants or burrowing animals she describes. And Dragomoshchenko creates a painterly composition that juxtaposes an urban receptacle for trash with a wall whose paneled coloration fashions a saturated, gorgeous backdrop. The composition seems to recycle the color

FIGURE 11. Fyodor Svarovsky, untitled photograph (2017)

FIGURE 12. Anna Glazova, untitled photograph (2014)

FIGURE 13. Arkady Dragomoshchenko, untitled photograph

field paintings of modern abstract art, as if creating a painted surface to match the abstractions that define his poems. Dragomoshchenko's recursive ironies, Glazova's airy expressiveness, Svarovsky's fantasies of transhuman time travel are all before us. Perhaps the poems have taught me what to look for in the images, but what the poets taught themselves in taking photographs—or in assembling or responding to the photographs of others—can also become transformative lessons for writing and reading poems.

Consider a fourth example, by Gali-Dana Singer (figure 14). She has lived in Israel since 1988, and this is likely a photo taken during a nighttime walk in Jerusalem. This photograph was posted to Facebook on May 16, 2018, with the tag "Good night" in three languages: Hebrew, Russian, then English. For several years, Singer regularly posted a daily good-night picture, her way of signing off for the evening, as well as a good-morning photograph, to greet each day. The good-night pictures were often nocturnal scenes, like this one of spiky flowers (which one of her friends identified as acanthus), and the mood is quiet even when the scenes are more markedly urban than these glowing flowers. Shalom, the photographs say, and with their trilingual tags, they send a message of peace into the troubled world that the poet leaves behind for the

FIGURE 14. Gali-Dana Singer, untitled photograph (2018)

day. Light and shadow enter the photographed scene, as is often the case in the images to be studied here, where the world of shadows is offered up to the viewer as a version of the real.[1]

In their photographs and writings, the poets are working through many senses of the real. Photography triggers these meanings, in part because the photograph affirms that some object or event existed. As Roland Barthes put it, a photograph shows "reality in a past state: at once the past and the real."[2] Barthes wanted to distinguish between a memory—what the mind holds as its own picture of some past event—and a photograph, which captured the moment as it really was. And in some of what follows, for example, the work of Lida Yusupova, that documentary sense of the real is at the forefront.

A different idea of the real, however, is also pertinent, to take a more Lacanian approach: the real as an order of thought that "lies outside the symbolic process, and it is to be found in the mental as well as in the material world," as Malcolm Bowie put it.[3] I like that definition because it indirectly resists Barthes's separation of the photograph from memory. It joins the mental world, where memories take hold, with the material world, where photographs are made. Bowie points us toward the rich aesthetic potential of the real as Lacan understood it. Photographs are a good gateway to that real, an order of thought that language (or the symbolic order) might foreclose. For my purposes, then, photography can offer word-dependent poets an alternative pathway toward the real. Along that pathway, the poet or the photographer might find the greatest freedom.[4]

The flowers in Singer's photography frame a gateway to such a poetic world. As a poet, she can exercise a kind of sleight of hand, often by forms of verbal dexterity that are deceptively casual. Here, the spiky flowers reflecting the light in multiple ways make the flowers themselves seem like lesser light bulbs. There is a self-conscious "meta" quality to the image, as was true of Dragomoshchenko's photograph of the garbage bin: if photography is light writing, as the etymology tells us, then the diffusion of light across the surface of the image makes the image itself tell a story of light. In the same way, Singer's poems can register as allegories about language and poetic playfulness, in a sense documenting the tonality of their own coming into being. The poems embrace the possibilities of language, while the photographs defy its limits.

Writing about garden photography (which we might say the image by Singer exemplifies), the English novelist Penelope Lively observed, "The photograph reports; the painting examines, interprets, expands."[5] In a sense, Lively's stark distinction between photographs and paintings is undone by Dragomoshchenko's urban image, and her emphasis on reporting, as if photography were only a record of what was (as in Barthes's definition), would seem like a retreat from the more capacious definitions enabled by the Lacanian real. But it can become a step forward if we use all of Penelope Lively's verbs—report, examine, interpret, expand—to build an account of what poems and photographs can do. These labors are inextricable, which means that we are well advised to enlarge such famous definitions as that of Charles Sanders Peirce, who called photographs indexical: signs that are "in certain respects exactly like the things they represent."[6] That likeness goes beyond what Lively calls reporting, even if it asserts some material truth.[7] It goes beyond reporting because, like poems, the truth claims of photography may include the fanciful, supernatural, fantastic, and visionary. In poems, the truth claim can even be a secondary realization for a reader. This event happened, this pattern of flowers and shadows existed, asserts the poem, but by means of sounds and signs, not light imprinted on a page. The density of verbal expressiveness may delay or intensify the moment when that realization dawns (meaning, we can read poems sometimes and not grasp at first what they are "about"). Of course, some poems resist these rhetorical strategies; they diminish what Jakobson called the poetic function. But all these poems foreground the moment of registering a set of impressions; indeed they create a verbal record of engaging with the external world, a visual complement to the orientation toward the world's sounds and music found in the poems of chapter 4. Just as unheard sounds or silences are a theme in music poems, photographs and poems may seek to register the unseen. In capturing the signs of invisible substances, this photographic work and the poetry that accompanies it can look for the imprints of air and its currents.

Some poems directly draw on the imagery of photographs, presenting forms of ekphrasis or using the terms and structures of photographic practice to frame their own aesthetic work. But equally significant are the poets who place poems alongside photographs or take photographs as part of their artistic practice. References to photography can create pauses in the sequence, as if the camera shutter is clicking for an instant, and the poem pausing to note down its own mental and creative work. Teaching the reader how to read both word and image can happen most intensely at those moments of lyric pause. As Alexander Markov put it, photography becomes not an image in a text but the poem's fundamental gesture.[8]

One last preliminary, having to do with time. Some assumptions about photography as a record of the past feel almost incontrovertible. For example, poems (like photographs) can assert their power to be an aid to memory that allows a past event to be called to mind, or the proof that something forgotten did, in fact, happen. For all the ways in which poems may seem to snap a photograph of a present moment, by the time one reads the poem or studies the image, the thing recorded has become part of the past.[9] Readers and viewers may be invited to consider whether this past is idiosyncratic or shared, whether it is personal or broadly cultural.

Theorists of photography and memory have asked whose memory is at stake. Particularly in studies of family photographs, they have argued that what may look to be a personal memory—a wedding or a birthday—is often layered over with signs of public shared history. The segregated classrooms of a first day in kindergarten, the background photograph of a president or general secretary of the Communist Party, or the looming billboard of the Marlboro man can all date and locate an event like a digital time stamp.[10] They mark the pictured events or persons as fixed in the past, but *fixed* is really the wrong epithet here. When photographs bring into the present an image from the past, they record time's flux as much as they fix any moment.

The poems treated here are in this sense like Gali-Dana Singer's glowing nighttime acanthus, registering a moment that is just barely gone, some elements of which might be repeated. The separations of past, present, and future are tampered with, so that poems that thematize photographs or that use techniques of photography challenge the assumption that a photograph is merely a record of the past. A more expansive affordance of photography was well described by philosopher Stanley Cavell, who contrasted "the reality in a photograph" as a "world past" with the way it feels intensely "present" to the viewer.[11] One of my goals here, then, is to chart the more complex ways in which the poems, in their associations with photography, register time's imprint. Some of the poems are themselves abstract philosophical meditations on time. They can do this work in a rhetoric of high theory (Dragomoshchenko) or build on fantasies of popular culture (Svarovsky). Both kinds of poem may strike the viewer as an abstraction or they may imprint a specific memory. These two forms of work—one meditative and philosophical, the other concrete—energize new possibilities for how poems reorganize temporalities. Most interesting are the poems that do both. One result of that doubled labor is that poems lacking the formal features that would make for easy memorization may nonetheless have an uncanny ability to linger in the mind's eye.

In several instances, the poems do this by circling around a psychoanalytic notion of the real, something that developmentally can predate our entry into the symbolic order or into language, and thus something especially well suited to representation by visual means. I have suggested a psychoanalytic context for that term, the real, and am inspired by Jacques Lacan's extensive work on elucidating the notion of the real.[12] But the real can also be useful in phenomenological terms.[13] Phenomenology, which I also draw on sparingly here, can help us recognize why the temporality of the present can remain so organizing, even when the work of photography seems to represent the past and be oriented toward an anticipated future moment of recollection and rediscovery. The real in this sense is also potentially political. As a concept meant to name that which is ineffable or even primordial, the real includes attitudes around gender, ethnicity, class, and nation that can feel so baked into experience as to require, if the poet seeks to really challenge them, that the poetry find ways to resist language's rules and hierarchies. In the examples that follow, the work of Lida Yusupova exemplifies a challenge around gender and sexuality, but Fyodor Svarovsky, Arkady Dragomoshchenko, and Anna Glazova also press poetic language into unfamiliar shapes meant to open a space for the reader to stare at unnamable visions of the real. I begin with Yusupova, the poet whose use of photography is perhaps the most unexpected.

Lida Yusupova, Materializing Inheritance

Lida Yusupova might seem an unlikely poet for a chapter on photography; her strong contributions as a feminist poet could make her a natural addition to chapter 1. Her orientation is not normally toward the image, photographic or otherwise. She is a leading exponent of the documentalist strategies well studied by Ilya Kukulin and in that sense preeminently a poet of the word.[14] Her best-known and most extensive work is based on found material: "Verdicts" ("Prigovory"), a poetic sequence begun in 2012, has now yielded a book of that title (2020).[15] These poems rearrange and reaccentuate the language of criminal trial verdicts, nearly all involving sex crimes and murders described coarsely and unsparingly. Yusupova renders the language of the court nearly as brutal as the crimes she chronicles, showing how the lived experience of a victim barely registers in a legal world bound by its own discourse and practices.[16] Yusupova often makes this fundamentally ethical point by means of repeated phrases, in one poem allowing the court's bloodless formulation to devolve into seemingly countless iterations of a single phrase: "the death of the victim" (smert' poterpevshei).[17] Yusupova can use distinctive formatting to accentuate these gestures of repetition, as when she puts this phrase on its own, at the top of a page, having the reader do the work of turning page after page to see the same words, again and again.[18]

Two texts, though, show us a different side of Yusupova. She used photographs in a poem related to the "Verdicts" cycle although not included in the book: "but Masha Sigova is silent" ("a Masha Sigova molchit").[19] There are two photographs alongside a text based on online posts. The two photographs feel forensic: they ask for assistance in finding Yulia Chistiakova, and the images stand in for the missing woman, not seen for two decades. The photographs do something of the same work, then, as the phrase "the death of the victim," urging readers to reflect on a woman's fate that can barely be imagined. The young woman is effectively objectified by the two photos, which partly match up to the description of the missing Chistiakova, but they look so unlike one another as to make readers suspect that someone with such different looks could not easily be found, particularly after so many years.

A quite different photograph appeared on the cover of Yusupova's 2016 book *Dead Dad*, an English-language title taken from the name of a sculpture by Ron Mueck. This photograph and the poem about it merit more detailed attention. The cover photo (figure 15) shows Mueck's sculpture *Dead Dad*. The sculpture that was used as the basis for the book cover is eerily realistic, an effect Mueck constantly seeks. He often works with dramatic enlargement, and his colossal figures can tower over visitors in a gallery.[20] But *Dead Dad* is a small sculpture, only three feet in length, as one can see from photographs of viewers alongside the artwork when it was on display in galleries.[21] The smaller size reads as a comment as potent as the title he gave to this artwork. Mueck diminishes the symbolically larger-than-life father and renders him weak and vulnerable in death. That gesture of reduction is not as exaggerated as his huge, hulking figures, but it has the same hyper-realism, the same creepy sense that some grotesque distortion belies the sculpture's placid mood. Calm is suggested by the barely splayed feet, the hands at rest, and the penis lying at its comfortable angle, but the position of the hands also suggests a corpse, confirmed by the sculpture's name. In *Dead Dad*, the small figure magnifies the vulnerability of the corpse, pitifully exposed for our inspection, and as photographed and reprinted on the cover of Yusupova's book, the sculpture is made to seem even more like a corpse lying on a concrete slab, rather than a piece of art on display in a gallery.

The dead body rests on the effaced boundary between artistic artifact and lived experience that Yusupova's poetry constantly retraces. The photographed object's alarming lifelikeness transposes the consistent aesthetic problem of Mueck's work—an overwhelming encounter with the body of another—into the zone of reading. The book *Dead Dad* itself ends up positioned at a juncture between materiality and verbal representation. And in the poem "Dead Dad," Yusupova replicates this disturbing encounter with another's body in a poem about the death of her own father.

FIGURE 15. Cover, Lida Yusupova, *Dead Dad* (2016)

At the very moment when her imagery is at its most material, Yusupova resorts to photography in "Dead Dad" as a point of comparison. The poem includes a remarkable passage about hair, prompted by the disclosure about Mueck's sculpture that he had used his own hair to make it.[22] She writes:

Ron Mueck gave dead dad his hair

It looks like the Chernobyl spider web
I read about in the *New York Times* yesterday

my hair came to me from my dad

the Chernobyl spiders weave jazzy webs

Ron Mueck gave dead dad his hair
dead dad gave me my hair

Рон Мьюек дал мертвому папе свои волосы

похоже на чернобыльскую паутину
о которой я вчера читала в Нью-Йорк Таймс

мои волосы дал мне папа

чернобыльские пауки плетут джазовые паутины

Рон Мьюек дал волосы метрвому папе
мертвый папа дал волосы мне[23]

The poetic logic seems straightforward: the poet sets up a parallel between a sculptor's artistic practice and her own family inheritance. There is something unnerving about his decision to affix strands of his own hair to a sculpture meant to replicate a corpse, and the poem taps into that weirdness. Hair, made up of dead cells even when growing from a live body, is grafted onto a sculpture of a father as if the artist were reversing the inheritance Yusupova claims for herself. And her own claim about her hair as something given to her by her father is similarly disturbed. The metaphors suggest that what he has given her is a set of damaged genes, like the disordered Chernobyl spider web described in the *New York Times*.[24]

The scientist featured in the article, Timothy Mousseau, took more than two hundred photographs of spider webs, to determine whether radiation exposure had altered the spiders' web-spinning ability. One photograph (by the article's author, Henry Fountain) was in the *Times* (figure 16). This is photography of a different sort from the picture of Ron Mueck's sculpture: it is embedded in a story about a scientist's work to archive changing natural phenomena in an irradiated environment, and it is a photograph published to illustrate a news story.

As an image meant to serve scientific and journalistic purposes, this photograph has a status more like that of the legal judgments Yusupova mined for her "Verdicts," or, if we wanted to think more broadly about her documentary practice, it resembles the television footage that gave rise to her poems "from Joel Waight's interview on channel five of Belizean TV" (iz interv'iu Dzhoelia Ueita piatomu kanalu belizskogo televideniia) and "murder suspected in death of Russian in King's Park" (the Russian text uses this English-language title).[25] In Yusupova's artistic world, rearranged and repeating phrases can expose the falsity or cruelty of public language, and the Chernobyl spider web has a comparable power to disrupt a fixed impression. The poem implicitly asks whether she resembles the dead father from whom she was estranged. What, after all, does the inherited hair signify?

This challenge is like the *punctum* in Barthes's theory of the photograph, as are the repeating phrases of the "Verdicts" cycle. For Barthes, the punctum is

FIGURE 16. Henry Fountain, spider web photograph, *New York Times* (May 5, 2014)

uncannily like the Lacanian real: the punctum is what he adds to the photograph, he says, but also, and here the emphatic typeface is his, "*what is nonetheless already there.*"[26] The metonymic links from nuclear catastrophe to irregular spider web to damaged genetic inheritance in spiders to her own family are what Yusupova adds, in effect, to the photograph, but the links, weblike, are already there. It becomes an eerie instance of self-portraiture, but without any actual description of what is portrayed—there is no ekphrasis, just the barest suggestion, by means of the spider web reference, that the hair itself might look like the disordered spider web. Yusupova has woven, excuse the pun, a masterful metonymy here, where the spider web is at once an example of how genetic flaws might be made material and an example of a fine texture of filaments that suggests wisps of human hair on the heads of the living and the dead.

Yusupova does not often refer to or describe her own appearance in her poetry, although there is a wry exception in "The Center for Gender Problems" ("Tsentr gendernykh problem," 2018), in which her makeup and ponytail give her an off-putting and jarring "heterosexual" look.[27] That moment is just barely funny, but in "Dead Dad," the hair is anything but humorous. It is associated with nuclear disaster, and it becomes a way to ask about damaged inheritance of an emotional as much as a physical kind. It sets out a scene of unconventional mourning. The passage just quoted leads to these two stark lines:

> I never saw my dad alive just like
>   I don't see myself

> я не видела живого папу так же
>   как не вижу себя[28]

What Yusupova slips into this poem is a disclosure of the difficulty of simply seeing oneself. Although she does not specify here that the barrier has to do with gender, a topic richly addressed in her other work, we can recognize a fundamental insight of feminist theory about women and the male gaze, the power of which creates innumerable obstacles to women's self-representation.

Yusupova's work overall, including in this poem, presents a challenge to an idea of poetry embracing the potential for freedom. The "Verdicts" cycle is her strongest statement about the broader social context of what can only be thought of as unfreedom: in writing poems based on court verdicts that almost uniformly travesty the very possibility of justice for victims of violent sex crimes, Yusupova pronounced her own stern verdict on a social order that was failing its citizens. That indictment of a broadly repressive social order stands in contrast to the poet's representations and celebrations of the possibility of personal freedoms, so that a poem like "The Center for Gender Problems," which ends with a celebration of sexual pleasure, becomes the opposite of the "Verdicts" poems.[29]

"Dead Dad" stands between these two poles. The poem enacts a liberation from the pieties of mourning a father whom the poet had in a deeper sense lost long ago, a father as small in significance as the Mueck sculpture is small (and the poem makes sure readers register the sculpture's scale, specifying that it was only 30 cm in length). But fathers—and thus the law of the father, as Lacan would say—retain a power that the small-sized sculpture belies. There is a several-page section of the poem, a second part, in fact, about a very different kind of father, one described by a student in Belize named Kenny Bennett. His father takes him to prostitutes and, on trips to the forest, dresses up as Tata Duende to act out the dangers of the world at night. Yusupova's poem "Dead Dad" thus includes other fathers and the lessons about pleasure and danger they pass on, but at the poem's center is her revelation that her father bequeathed her a complex inheritance made of his own flaws. The inheritance is as inescapable as a genetic code, and the horror of its meanings, rather than being narrated or spelled out in the poem, arrives through reference to a photographic image, although one not shown in the text. Yusupova exposes her own discovery of the real that cannot be spoken or even seen, and she constructs her poem, whose logic depends on a photograph on the book cover, so that an absent photograph of a damaged spider web is the point on which "Dead Dad" turns.

Fyodor Svarovsky and the Imprint of Time

Fyodor Svarovsky, photographer of the cat held aloft in figure 11, is a broadly popular and beloved poet.[30] His poems tell stories of cosmic adventure, time travel, spectral presences, dreamed loves or losses, and the adventures of remarkably insightful animals. Unlikely subjects for photography, all, and the poetic movement with which he was originally associated, the new epic (*novyi epos*), also suggests an orientation toward the verbal.[31] But the incompleteness that was a trademark of the new epic poetry opened a space for visual fantasies and for the kind of shadowy imagery and ambient allusions that privilege atmosphere over realist narrative. That is the space where photographs slip in. What Svarovsky does with photos is a bit unusual and nearly always ironic. The poems suggest a metaphysical or otherworldly context for the images that is never fully explicated, as incomplete as the narratives in the new epic poetry. Something beyond the poetic text is always about to be made manifest in the photographs.

Sometimes, though, Svarovsky's poems are in a clear relationship to photography. I offer several in quick succession, somewhat like a slide show meant to present the range of what this poet can do, including in poems not based in science fiction or robots, the work for which he is best known. We'll get to the science-fiction motifs in a minute, but first, the slide show of selected photography-related poems.

The most brutally ironic is "Antique Photographs" ("Antichnye fotografii," 2019). It rifles through some descriptions of old photographs impatiently, to land on one that lists the names of seven pajama-clad posing men defined by their place of work: an OGPU warehouse.[32] Their faces are no less ancient than the columns they stand before or the very photograph that contains them (both modified as "antichnyi"). The name OGPU may also seem an ancient, outmoded term for the state security services, but its recognizability is a reminder that its abuses never seem to go away.

In another poem, untitled, the state is a source less of surveillance than of potential assistance for its citizens, but the irony persists. It begins with a photograph as a way to identify a letter writer, but the letter (whose cadences reproduce spoken language) consists in nothing more than a request for translation assistance.[33] Another similarly dissolves into ironic self-commentary: "The Safari" ("Safari") shows tourists taking snapshots of a river, a chaffinch, crocodiles, and hippopotamuses, but then failing to send the photos off.[34] The poem compares the huge animal to two figures in a painting by Hieronymus Bosch, adverting to another prominent poetic logic in Svarovsky, the intersecting worlds of animals and persons. The hippopotamus takes offense, as if where he really belongs is not in a random tourist photograph but in a glorious canvas by Bosch. Photography is derided, but gently, almost optimistically.[35]

Animals also play a role in another photography-related poem, "Mama in the Wardrobe" ("Mama v shkafu"). Here, an idealized set of childhood memories is evoked nostalgically—"you loved this all so much / you hang photos all around" (vy tak eto liubite / vyveshivaete fotografii)—but vague dangers intrude. Giraffes amble into the parlor, and the dead are snuggling under the covers. The poem ends with the mother burrowing so deep into the wardrobe that she disappears and is never seen again.[36]

Each of these poems thematizes photography not to record for posterity a face or an experience, but as a failure to seize the moment. Photography is unable to ward off loss or to create connections between viewer and viewed. In Svarovsky's writings, each poem can create a wholly new imagined world, as these examples demonstrate. Each is replete with its own risks and rewards. Every poem is like a new microcosm, but Svarovsky is also interested in the cosmos in the largest possible terms. I now turn to that work, where the impulse to photograph is complicated by space travel and even time travel.

In "The Voyage" ("Puteshestvie"), a flight to the edge of the universe generates a desire to create an unarguable record of the journey, but not a desire to photograph. In fact the poem reverses the logic of photography, a reversal encoded in the poem's structure: it flies to its conclusion almost immediately. "The Voyage" begins in flight, then rushes to the moment "later" when the voyage is long over:

keep flying
to the very edge of the universe
know by taste the salty dust of the borders

later no one will be able to say
that we weren't there
we were there

we recorded
our presence
on the wild dust
with our magnetic boots

лети лети
до самого края вселенной
узнай солёный вкус окраинной пыли

после никто не скажет
что мы не были
мы там были

записали
присутствие
на дикой пыли
магнитными сапогами[37]

The poem continues for sixteen more lines, twelve of which list the things seen, but they are all impossible to capture in a photo.[38] They are themselves as if made of light—stars rising above them and descending, "strange things / floating in emptiness" (strannye veschi / plyvushchie v pustote), and thousands of ancient libraries yet to be decoded. These are images of the ungraspable, not just impossible to photograph but also impossible to turn into a keepsake. That logic of tactile elusiveness may explain why the poem ends with an otherwise odd refusal to let a nomad, the nomad's friends, and a bear onto the spacecraft as it is poised to leave.

What is seen and found must be left behind, and so, instead of light able to write its shapes onto photography paper, persons record—literally write down, inscribe (*zapisat'*)—their presence on the surface of this distant cosmic object. The work of photography has been transferred to the epithet for those boots: they are magnetic. Why magnetic? The poet invites us to imagine that they were engineered to help a cosmonaut stand firm on that distant surface in the absence of gravity, but the magnetic boots pick up some "wild dust" wherever they step. Proof of space travel has been picked up after all, and impossible photography has been transformed into an alternative form of imprinting.

These examples circle around a task that Svarovsky's poems take up more fully elsewhere—attempts to photograph imagined or impossible objects, to get at that Lacanian real that eludes one who has only language to work with. In fact, photography from its inception sought to catch fleeting visions of the ghostly and prove the reality of what was experienced at séances or in half-waking states. Peter Osborne has called this photography's theological origins, and he compares disputes within the history of photography, for example, Walter Benjamin's influential argument that photographs replaced the aura of the artwork with reproducibility, to the arguments within religious traditions about the representation of the divine.[39] As he puts it, the medium only seems to depend on the purely phenomenal.

There are many examples of modern photographs that probe at that dependence, some of them based as if on aesthetic error. Molly Blasing, for example, has written perceptively about how a striking photograph by Marina Tsvetaeva uses overexposure to ghostly effect—it connects "the architecture of space with the realm of the spirit."[40] And my late colleague Svetlana Boym created photographs with overexposure or printing errors that had the effect of capturing a ruinous history at the instant of its destruction.[41]

Svarovsky writes often in this spirit of error, including in his poems that track the collisions of space with spirit. He has rerouted photography into that project with a little help from his friends. Photographs play a key role in his second book of poems, *Time Travelers* (*Puteshestvenniki vo vremeni*, 2009).[42] There are forty-six photographs spread across the book, with datelines to suggest that these images were captured during experiences of time travel: the years look backward—1218, 1353, 1917, 1914, 2010, the 1930s—and far ahead: 2049, 2099, 2629, 3993. Each photograph has a caption, some elaborate. The photographs are not in chronological order. They do not tell separate, coherent stories, nor do they fully unify the poems of *Time Travelers*, but they do purport to give faces and bodies to two of the poems' heroes, who are in turn named as the photographers for other snapshots. The captions include accounts of how the image was obtained, some by drone or avatar or surveillance camera, some rescued from the trash bin of a film production studio.

These captions, as is obvious from the datelines and captions, are fictions, and from the copyright page of the book *Time Travelers*, we know that their striking visual presentation and perhaps sequencing was the work of Oleg Pashchenko, a poet highly regarded for his illustrations, photographic work, and book designs.[43] He would go on to write the introductory essay to Svarovsky's 2015 book *Glory to Heroes* (*Slava geroiam*), and their friendship is

documented in Svarovsky's social media posts.[44] The captions to the photo-
graphs in *Time Travelers* may be a collaboration, but the photographs are from
Svarovsky's personal archive. Some could be of his own family or even himself
younger; some are found photographs, like postcards.[45] Assembling these im-
ages feels like a labor comparable to assembling a book of poems, and it is
plausible that the labor was as much Pashchenko's, an experienced book de-
signer, as Svarovsky's.[46]

The captions become intriguing verbal complements to the poetic texts and
often read as slightly implausible accounts of what the photographs show. Two
heroes from the poems, Petr Kuznetsov and Aleksey Perakis, get a mini biog-
raphy as a result.[47] Both are said to have taken some of the pictures and are
themselves "photographed." Kuznetsov's photos, tagged as occurring across
several centuries, effectively document his time travel. Sometimes he is shown
in avatars. In one of the child photographs, he is said to be "localized" (361);
in another, dated 3993, he appears as a seventh grader named Sekko Matiushin,
pictured on a bench with a cat in his arms (400–401). Kuznetsov is not the
only character in *Time Travelers* who can morph into others: the book's final
photograph, dated 2629, shows someone named Elizaveta Gauk, said to be the
virtual double of Alexander Jenkins (408), mentioned elsewhere in the
photographs.[48]

What time travel enables, then, is not just the experience of other eras, as
is conventionally the goal of science-fiction narratives of time travel, but trans-
positions of identity as well. The borderlines between persons and things are
traversed when, for example, the photographer who caught that image of Eliza-
veta Gauk is identified as a robot (other pictures are attributed to robots,
too).[49] Elizaveta Gauk was photographed in what is said to be Lycis, New
Hellas—an evocative choice of place name: it brings into the twenty-seventh
century, when the image was said to be captured, two names associated with
the ancient world.

Which returns us to the other character shown in multiple photographs,
Perakis. His name is unmistakably Greek, echoing Elizaveta Gauk's journey to
a future version of the ancient world, and more generally exemplifying Sva-
rovsky's use of foreign-sounding names in his poetry (Dzhekson, Aiko, Bibi
Khlotros, to name a few).[50] Perakis's Greek name also makes him the kind of
time traveler with access to ancient culture, and it will fall to him to move not
just across eons and intergalactic spaces, but across the boundary between life
and death. The photographs establish for Perakis both a family identity and a
professional identity. He is introduced as a member of the large Perakis family,

with his grandmother Afrodita seen in two photographs (36–37, 42–43), and an ancestor seven generations back, Kostya (Konstantinos) Perakis, shown in another from 1970 but accessed only in 2125 by carefully detailed scientific means (152–53). We also see Perakis in a group of "space researchers" (prostranstvennye issledovateli) in Feodosia, Crimea, in 2049 (366–67). The setting of Crimea further links Perakis to Russia's colonization of Crimea beginning in the eighteenth century, and to the ancient world, given long-standing cultural associations of the region with ancient Greece.[51] Another photograph, which he is said to have taken, links him to a different site of antiquity, Egypt (men in elaborate military dress and shields before storming Khartoum, dateline 2099; 124–25).

The photographs and captions create a richer biography for Perakis than for anyone else pictured in *Time Travelers*, and one poem in the book also brings readers into Perakis's inner life: "part no. 0" (chast' no. 0). The poem appears in the book's last section, whose name also became the name of the volume, "Time Travelers." All the sections of the volume have expressive names, like "The Dead Speak" ("Pokoiniki govoriat"), "Deep Space" ("Glubokii kosmos"), "They're Already Here" ("Oni uzhe zdes'"), or "This Is the Future" ("Eto budushchee"). The final section heading, because it echoes the book's title, might seem to add the least affective charge, but that is misleading because of two tiny modifications. The subtitle reads "from the cycle *Time Travelers*" (iz tsikla *Puteshestvenniki vo vremeni*). It claims, then, that these ten texts come from a cycle that is only partially included in this book. The title presses readers to experience this already substantial volume of poems as a fragment of a larger whole, inviting a different kind of imaginative time travel—that this is a book with its own future.[52]

Svarovsky made good on that impression when he held back "The Death of Perakis" ("Smert' Perakisa," completed in 2009 when *Time Travelers* went to press). The poem did not appear in this book, but outside it, first in Svarovsky's LiveJournal blog in 2009, and then in the book *Glory to Heroes*.[53] Readers get to return to Perakis, to complete his story with both a future and a deeper past. On his deathbed, Perakis remembers a strange encounter with an eleven-year-old girl. When and where did all this happen? Rather than the highly specific captions of *Time Travelers*, this poem is pointedly vague about temporal location. He sees the girl in the year 39, which could be short for 1939, but the omission of the century makes the moment indeterminate. Time travel has become almost abstract to him. Dying, he realizes that he had thought travel would be forever. His own mortality comes as a shock that fills the poem's speaker with stuttering pity ("Perakisu / ochen' / zhal'," writes the poet).[54] With the last thought that he has missed out on what is most important, he dies, and again the poet reverts to radically foreshortened lines:

> with this last thought
> his soul
> quits
> his body

> с этой последней мыслью
> душа его
> покидает
> тело[55]

What could otherwise have been a banal thought in a lyric poem, that the body's death deprives its nonmaterial essence of any space for being, makes a different kind of sense in this poem because it speaks not as a first-person lyric utterance but through the experiences of a time traveler, Perakis.[56] He was as if materialized through photographs—not of him, but by him—and by the expressive captions that document that travel.

We know a bit more about Perakis from the poem that *was* included in *Time Travelers*, and now we should go back to "part no. 0." Such a strange title, as if the poem were the prehistory that anticipates the missing poem "The Death of Perakis." And such a strange text, in seven parts, the first of them devoted entirely to a broken hot water pipe on Prospekt Mira. It emits boiling water so hot that it scalds a repairman. Quite enough to make one want to leave, and Perakis does. He is about to fly to the United States, and the poem foretells an imagined future: marriage, a house on Long Island, big game hunting, disappearance, and transformation into a multiplicity of new dimensions and a new identity, Samomator Otmos. But for now, Perakis is stuck in a present as prosaic as the broken hot water pipe. His is the opposite of a heroic departure to distant climes: he's drunk, hiccuping in a taxi, called Lesha rather than Aleksei because, presumably, we're meant to know him all too up close and familiar. Svarovsky snaps one last quasi-photograph of Perakis at a moment when the future hasn't yet unfolded. And a blurry photograph it is, appropriate to his being already in motion in the taxi.

Photography becomes a near rhetorical device to help us understand Svarovsky's poetry, to show its recurrent fascination with representing the unseen or unseeable world. Perakis's future as Samomator Otmos puts him into

a multiplicity of spatial dimensions and temporalities, all experienced as if
at once:

> and around him are multitudes of times
> and his Earth is populated by countless tribes
> and in the sky are endless planets, stars
> and all at the same time it is summer, autumn, winter, spring
> and in every parallel stream
> are flowing streams of blood
> a destructive war is underway

> и вокруг—множественные времена
> и Землю его населяют неисчислимые племена
> и на небе—бесконечные планеты, звезды
> и одновременно—лето, осень, зима, весна
> а в каждом параллельном потоке
> льются потоки крови
> идет разрушительная война (398)

This hellish bit of time and space travel takes away the possibility of discerning
specificities of planetary object or season of the year. Every locus in the uni-
verse is flowing with the same river of blood. It's an apocalyptic rethinking of
what in the other poem is simply the death of Perakis, but here he's reborn into
an experience of what death means: there is no longer a way to have individu-
ated experiences, not of time or of place. That sense of loss is rewritten in the
poem's final lines as a form of wandering, from room to room, where behind
every unopened door the same experience happens.

Svarovsky brings back the logic of photography one last time to convey
what is so devastating about this endless wandering in an interior maze of
rooms. But, true to his tendency to pull back from the apocalyptic brink, he
also offers the reader an image of a consolatory, transformed keepsake:

> like motion from one room to another
> and every time he opens a door
> through which you can only take
> what will fit in the heart
> not what will fit in the pocket of a jacket or coat

> but it's as if what fits there
> is

practically

everything

как из комнаты в комнату
и каждый раз он открывает такую дверь
через которую можно вынести только то
что умещается в сердце
а не то, что можно положить в карман куртки или пальто

но, похоже, то, что в нем умещается
это
практически
всё (399)

Like the magnetized dust that replaces the missing photograph in "The Voyage," what is hidden in the heart compresses all that the rules of an alternative universe forbade. That essence is immaterial, and yet it is everything—the real.

Arkady Dragomoshchenko, Picturing Time and Space

I turn now to a poet who shares with Svarovsky a quest to find a material equivalent for an unknowable thing or idea. He is more likely to spin his poetic texts around that unknown entity in webs of visual metaphors. The visual poetics of his texts find a complement in Dragomoshchenko's photographs, often dreamy mixtures of specificity and abstraction like the hulking dumpster against its painterly backdrop seen at the start of this chapter (figure 13).

That provocation of thinking defines Dragomoshchenko's huge and varied body of work. An unyielding, relentless labor to find accounts of the mind's processes energizes his poems and his photographs. Both challenge us to reflect on how thoughts unfold, in effect becoming translations from the discourse of philosophy, which permeates Dragomoshchenko's creative work—one of his best-known poems, "Ludwig," is about Wittgenstein, perhaps the most significant philosopher for him. The poems and the photographs seize moments of incipient apprehension, challenging us to question what we think we see, or what we believe a poem is about.

Dragomoshchenko was born in Potsdam, grew up in Vynnitsia in Ukraine, and moved to Leningrad as a student (at the Institute for Theater, Music and Film). He participated in the poetry underground beginning in the late 1960s, although he stood apart from many of its ritualized gatherings.[57] His work is more readily defined by his connection to American poets, particularly to L=A=N=G=U=A=G=E poetry. His long relationship of mutual translation and rich conversation with Lyn Hejinian was one of the most interesting examples of American-Russian poetic cooperation in the late twentieth century.[58] His deep affinities with L=A=N=G=U=A=G=E poetry also define the philosophical ground on which his poems and photographs were made. Like the L=A=N=G=U=A=G=E poets, he rejects ideas of a unified, singular authorial voice; he resists rhyme and meter as poetic markers (and explores prose poetry); and he probes sensory experience and the workings of consciousness. Dragomoshchenko tests philosophies of mind and phenomenology in his poetry, alongside literary, cultural, and linguistic theories.[59]

His last book was *Tavtologiia*, which means *Tautology*; his previous book had been titled *Description* (*Opisanie*, 2000).[60] These rhetorical terms point to the roles of abstraction and of categorical thinking in Dragomoshchenko's poetry. For all the concreteness and specificity inherent in photography as an aesthetic practice, in his hands photography becomes a form of abstract thinking as well. Early in his long poem *To Xenia* (*Ksenii*, 1993), Dragomoshchenko wrote "poetry is not a confession of love / to language and the beloved / but an inquiry" (poeziia ne / priznan'e v liubvi 'iazyku i vozliublennoi', / no doznanie).[61] To say outright that poetry is not a confession of affection is to distance this poem, which is presented as direct address, from traditional love poetry. But to say that it is not a confession of love for language is to reject a poetic tradition, epitomized by Joseph Brodsky's proud if casual assertion, "we all work for a dictionary."[62] For Dragomoshchenko, poets have no such employer.[63] Poetry as inquiry is poetry as philosophy, practiced in intimate proximity to its objects.[64] My hypothesis is that it is an ontological inquiry, an inquiry into the nature of self and other, an inquiry into the place of the self in a world of otherness.

In emphasizing philosophy, I am following a trend in scholarship on Dragomoshchenko best exemplified in the work of Mikhail Iampolsky.[65] But unlike Iampolsky, I am interested in a particular strand of contemporary philosophy advanced by Stanley Cavell. He often described it as antiphilosophy. I follow Cavell into forms of contemplation with affinities to Emerson, Thoreau, and Wittgenstein. It is a kind of philosophy associated with skepticism. Cavell described the skeptic as "craving the emptiness of language, as ridding himself of the responsibilities of meaning, as being drawn to annihilate externality or otherness."[66] That "emptiness of language" is paradoxically the center of Dragomoshchenko's poetry, where it is often expressed by sudden changes of motif or theme, and thus by a kind of cognitive restlessness. Art, Cavell argues, shows us how to resist skepticism. The turn to art is thus ever a hopeful turn, and that intonation is also pervasive in Dragomoshchenko's work.[67] That paradox of hopeful skepticism was expressed well in an essay about Cavell by David Rodowick: it "opens the possibility of once again being present to self or acknowledging how we may again become present to ourselves."[68]

Dragomoshchenko searches out those moments when self-presence seems possible. He takes the task seriously, but he is not a systematic or consistent philosopher. He invokes philosophical terms and ideas, but not to build a system of truths. He circles around philosophical truths; he entertains them, lives with them long enough to write a poem, and then he writes another poem. Or revises one—his changeability in this regard is legendary. That unfinalizability of creative work, that sense that all is always in process, is more readily clear in the poetry than in the photography, but even there, Dragomoshchenko is often seeking what Neil Hertz called, in another context, "figures for the unrepresentable."[69] We have here another instance of the search for the Lacanian real that was also important to Yusupova and Svarovsky. In Dragomoshchenko's work, the challenge registers slightly differently: how to get that mass of sensation, impression, perception, and memory into visibility?[70]

In photography, Dragomoshchenko often explored texture, as seen in the safety pin and netting on the cover of his book *Tavtologiia* (figure 17). Its gently draped, off-kilter bit of netting takes what might otherwise be the suggestion of a grid, a repeating intersection of horizontal and vertical lines, and makes instead a pattern of tiny square demarcations that never seem to straighten out fully. The image is most marked by its small tear, an inverted V-shape that is copied in the shape of the safety pin piercing the net, open but hanging securely. The hole in the fabric is like the hole in time that can be opened in his literary texts by lapses in memory.[71] It is important that those holes gape, that they feel like abysses even when they are small, as in this image. The safety pin could emblematize repair, the work of reconnecting torn bits of fabric such as the hole seen next to the pin. But it is open, the gesture of repair refused, and we might read that detail as Dragomoshchenko's way of including, indeed praising, what he calls error. He writes in the poem "Accidia" that "everything begins in an error of vision" (vse nachinaetsia s oshibki zreniia).[72] The capacity to savor deviations and mistakes is consonant with the formalists' argument that poetic language is deformed language, and the photograph encourages such an argument in visual terms. The eye is drawn down the image toward the pin, and then still further, traveling to the two horizontal white stripes that seem to ground the image, stabilizing its thin, flimsy material nature.

FIGURE 17. Cover image, Arkady Dragomoshchenko, *Tavtologiia* (2011)

FIGURE 18. Arkady Dragomoshchenko, *Dry Snow*

One can especially appreciate the airiness and insubstantiality of the netting when it is compared to another beautifully textured image, one that Drago-moshchenko called *Dry Snow* (figure 18). What is most mysterious and beautiful about this image is its indeterminate solidity. The moist substances of the air are materialized and fastened over the leaves and stems caught on the icy pave-ment. The debris and leaves seem almost paused on a surface of foam.[73]

This spongy texture corresponds to the workings of the mind. Elaine Scarry has written memorably about the capacity of verbal instruction to elicit mental images in us, and she emphasizes flowers as having just the right texture and thinness for easy representation.[74] Anna Glazova's pictures of flowers provide uncannily precise examples of that process, and Dragomoshchenko is doing something similar but with material more resistant to imagination. When he gives us filmy surfaces, as in the next image, he complicates our reception of them by introducing something almost inappropriate. An insistence on the unexpected recurs in the poems, and in the photographs as well.

In a beautiful black tissue panel (figure 19), the allegory has less to do with the mind's work than with an aesthetic principle, of stopped time in photog-raphy. The image obscures but also doubles time's captured instant: the dim

FIGURE 19. Arkady Dragomoshchenko, *Goodbye Tissues*

circle of a watch face at the bottom of the image creates a sense of time's repeti-
tions.[75] Here is time plus textile, time crumpled as the surface of the filmy
blackness is crumpled, the differing shapes and designs of light caught at odd
angles suggesting process, movement rather than any arrest of chronology. The
image skirts the presence of human subjectivity—there is no one in the space
of the photograph, but it shows what is likely a pocket watch or a stopwatch,
thus an indexical sign of the person who would consult it. Nothing in the
photograph has anything to do with a specific time of day, so the labor of
counting the day's hours becomes an abstract concept rather than an
organizing specific.[76]

   Something similar happens in the filmy and reflective surfaces in a photo-
graph that separates textile from glass (figure 20), giving us two surfaces, one
rippling and one smooth. Both let us see through to the outside, but what
really holds our attention is the thin tissue of a dress or pinafore, a barely
bodily shape that again suggests an absent person. This photograph studies the
uncertain nature of surfaces, which are layered here, soft against hard, flowing
against flat, translucent, transparent, then the opaque materials of frame, wires,

FIGURE 20. Arkady Dragomoshchenko, *Dress / Window*

and buildings. Like the safety pin and netting, *Dress / Window* seems stabilized by the crossbars of the window frame, and of buildings at the bottom of the image and the wires above them. Those telephone wires are as if reshaped into the wire hanger above, a visual metonymy that surely pleased Drago-moshchenko. Water droplets on the window glass catch our attention if we look closely at the picture's bottom, but they are faintly seen. Similarly, the crossbar of the window, which should hold things firmly, is blurred at the center, softening its powers to stabilize. The dress itself, like the tissue surface over the watch, barely covers what is behind it, but it is held up to the light as a translucent shape of ruffle, bodice, skirt, ruffle. The vertical part of the crossbar is held by the fabric as if a ghost of the absent person whose dress this is.[77]

In our effort to conjure up the absent person, we are doing the work of imagination. Dragomoshchenko's photography, at least in these examples, defers the impulse to use photography to catch something that *is* (Roland Barthes's definition in *Camera Lucida*). As in his poems, he retreats from a documentary potential in favor of a kind of second-order representation, so that the photograph is the idea of the thing, the representation of our mind's work. Each photograph becomes a mind's assertion of a perceived reality, projecting a world of the imagination, a play of surfaces and textures, of haptic as much as visual power. Photography is doing ontological work for this poet, asserting the pleasures and the spaces of being.

Those spaces of being offer a new way to think about the poetry, to which I now turn. Many poems thematize photography, and it flickers as a topic in the poems I have chosen, but I mostly think more broadly about how the poems represent space and its freedoms. In Dragomoshchenko's poetic world, we rarely confront actual geographic space, exemplified especially well in his 2005 book *On the Shores of Unfounded River* (*Na beregakh iskliuchennoi reki*). One poem from that book begins with the assertion that there is no escaping the place where one is. That place is the place of the page and of the camera, which is to say there is no escaping who one is. In this poem, that means being a person who makes things hunched over a page, who pecks at letters, making poems, and who has "all sorts of photo cameras." Tellingly, nothing specifies the place of poems and cameras. Many signals of landscape description can be found in Dragomoshchenko's poetry, but here they are reduced to "shadows" and "green leaf."

And it's not like I can run off somewhere. First,
I'm poring over the page this is written on.
Second, all sorts of photo cameras, silver spoons, shadows.
Letters that are pecked out among shadows, various . . .
reflections even, just in case. Also I see
a window. And I have a headache. And I have more of a headache.
"Not like I can run off somewhere" becomes
a kind of opera singing. Why should I even need to

run off somewhere. Better my head split "in two."
To sing—better, without seeing anybody—something like "farewell"
then, it's faster and easier that way. And occasionally some wine
and a green leaf. To feel it in my hands,
                                    and then light up a cigarette.[78]

А мне и не убежать никуда. Во-первых,
рассматриваю страницу, на которой это написано.
Во-вторых, разные фотокамеры, серебряные ложки, тени.
Буквы, которые расклеваны между теней, разное . . .
даже и отражение на всякий случай. Я вижу еще—
окно. И у меня болит голова. И она болит сильнее.
"Не убежать никуда" становится
неким оперным пением. А мне и не нужно
никуда убегать. Лучше—чтобы голова "пополам."
И петь, а лучше никого не видеть, типа "прощай"
тогда,—быстрее и легче. А иногда вина
и зеленый лист. Подержать в руках,
                                    а потом зажечь сигарету.[79]

The poem invokes photography not through ekphrasis but by listing,
among other objects, "all sorts of photo cameras." To draw attention to the
machines that make pictures is to invoke the key aesthetic argument about
photography, whether it is art at all because it relies on the work of the
machine rather than the will of the artist.[80] Dragomoshchenko takes the
question of will in an unexpected direction. These cameras deny agency no
more than the implied keyboard that lets the poet peck out words. Neither
can be escaped; both compel the poet toward creation. The silver spoons
and shadows revive the possibility of ekphrasis, instructing us to imagine
two elements of a photograph that would gleam and darken before us, a
photograph that would in fact include "all sorts of photo cameras." The ob-
jects that make poems also make photographs: reflecting surfaces, more
shadows, a window. The window could open to an outside world, but the
poem closes off any escape, for the poet is locked inside his own head, a head
he knows by its pain.

When words from the first line repeat like a refrain in quotation marks, we
realize that the poet is having a conversation with himself. The head splitting
in two serves as an image for that internal conversation (and conversation and
letter writing abound in Dragomoshchenko's work), but here the chatter is

lonely, a wish to say farewell to someone unseen. The desired speech act is in fact a song, an opera song.[81] It could be any aria, but it could specifically be the famous aria that emphasizes that word "farewell" (proshchai)—Lensky's aria in *Eugene Onegin*.[82] For Dragomoshchenko, the specificity of the source is less important than the phenomenology of the event, an event of parting and of registering that gesture of farewell with a word that ends in an extended vowel sound.

Stanley Cavell offers an account of singing, especially of the aria, that is pertinent here: it conveys "the sense of being pressed or stretched between worlds."[83] That position between worlds, as between certainties that the poems call into question, is emblematic for Dragomoshchenko. Here, the poet fantasizes singing the perfect operatic word, farewell, as an act of valediction. We should resist the temptation to read this poem, published seven years before any sign of illness, as if Dragomoshchenko knew his readers would be mourning him, as they did deeply when he died in 2012. Pain and death hover, as they often do in his work.[84] Death, as one of his poems put it, is when one coincides with one's own limits.[85]

In the poem, the sung word is more than a distraction from an aching head, because its immediate force is to return the poet to himself, as if seen from afar. As we could have predicted from Cavell's argument about skepticism, the poet is brought to an apprehension of his own being. He says that the turn is quick and easy, but that is only because the idea of an aria has done its improbable work. Art, as Cavell predicted, has short-circuited the cognitive restlessness, brought the mind back to a point where it can fix on itself. The poet looks to his hands, to his wine and cigarettes, for which the hands seem about to reach.[86] The poet reminds himself of his own capacity for touch, the sensation that his photographs can conjure and the sensory capacity that his poetry most often imagines.[87]

There is a similarly introspective quality in a text entitled "Agora." It is presented as a work of prose, in that it is not lineated as poetry. But, as Alexander Skidan observed, the boundaries between prose and poetry are not firm in Dragomoshchenko's work, and his use of prose for what are essentially poems is another of the liberating formal traits that Dragomoshchenko bequeathed to subsequent poets, Skidan among them.[88] The aesthetics of the prose poems have the same density of figuration, quick-change mood and lexicon, refusal to meet expectations of narrative logic or syntactic lucidity, and tendency toward verbal formulations that give a shimmering quality to all entities, actions, qualities, and assertions.[89]

Agora

Railroad. The "object" of representation before us, having somewhat lost its fascination? Or else a phenomenon, whose boundaries are in no way defined. Station, airport, post office, nodes of another lymphatic nature. In a place that is not logically expressed although it is well enough known, a place between representation and ideation, an "other materiality" arises. I do not remember why, several years ago, a desire to "rewrite the trojan war" arose. Today, it seems like it was absolutely necessary, like any other random event, since "the shield of Achilles," almost like an effaced coin buried in sand, under water, lay on the sea floor of history. The bottom of imagination appears like a future reflection. The important thing here isn't that virtually everyone has undertaken the "description" of the shield, but rather that the shield has gradually taken on the features of the "tower of babel," of a transposition machine. Thus, instead of a sought-after photograph, a few lines that did not end up in the book *Distribution* owing to one's own carelessness and to the unfinished state of "the trojan war." I am interested not in the "*why*" of this change but rather in the "*from what*." However, they are easily interchangeable.[90]

Agora

Железная дорога. Несколько утративший очарование "предмет" представления? Либо явление, чьи границы ни в чем не определены. Вокзал, аэропорт, почтовая станция, узлы иной лимфатической природы. В не явственно выраженном, однако довольно известном месте между представлением и помышлением возникает "иная материальность." Не помню, почему несколько лет тому возникло желание заново "переписать троянскую войну." Сегодня кажется, это было необходимо, как и любая случайность, поскольку "дном истории" залегал "щит Ахилла" почти как затертая монета в песке под водой. У воображения дно предстает будущим отражением. Дело не в том, что едва ли не каждый брался за "описание" щита, а в том, что щит постепенно обретал черты "вавилонской башни," машины транспозиции. Затем вместо искомой фотографии несколько строк, не вошедших в книгу "Распределение," обязанной как собственному легкомыслию, так и незавершенности "троянской войны." Мне интересно не "*к чему,*" а "*из чего.*" Впрочем, это легко меняется местами.[91]

"Agora" is like other Dragomoshchenko texts in its evasions of topographical specificity, but with its title it makes a specific kind of place its main idea—cultural public space for conversation, for an exchange of ideas.[92] It describes more prosaic places, beginning with the railroad in its first utterance, and the various stations, all mentioned for their "lymphatic nature." That phrase can be understood as a trope for translation as well as transportation: the objects of representation mentioned in the text's second sentence are moved across undefined boundaries. Like the boundary between poetry and prose, it is the fact of a boundary that is notable, not the separation it might produce.

"Agora" reaches across time, and the term in its title takes readers back to the ancient world where philosophy was born. To the extent that this text is about place, it is a place or site where something happens to ideas, where an "other materiality" arises. That materiality is partly the stuff of culture: references to the Trojan War and to the shield of Achilles bring in a most familiar text, cited with a kind of boredom, Homer's *Iliad*. The shield is a great moment of ekphrasis in Homer, and thus a specific kind of translation, across aesthetic modes.[93] But here, this shield is as if effaced or buried, made into a coin, metonymically preserving the shield's raised metal surface, but rendering its image small and inscrutable. Dragomoshchenko makes the problem of the shield one of translatability, hence his comparison to the Tower of Babel.

The passage is about translation not across languages, which originated at Babel, but across aesthetic forms, and it concludes in a shrug at possible differences, blurring them as the poet's photographs blur substances and boundaries, or as a surface is blurred in the effaced coin of "Agora." The last lines in effect meditate on an open chain of substitutions, a chain that begins with a crumpled photograph for which lines of poetry substitute, like a photocopy. The text has become a meditation on Dragomoshchenko's writing practice, as is not uncommon in his work. We have references to the title of his published volume *Description*, and of a volume he did not complete, *Distribution*. Both are displaced by an absent photograph, itself replaced by what they would contain, lines of verse, creating a strong emblem of a second-order representation and an endless loop between the verbal and the visual, between the process of writing (or photographing) and the finished product, a book.

Dragomoshchenko's work presses us to create our own endless loop, and thus I return to photography. A landscape photograph (figure 21) models another feature of Dragomoshchenko's poetic practice: suggesting but not depicting a human subject. We recognize from his black and white photographs the fascination with a mottled, pebbled wet surface, but this is a color

FIGURE 21. Arkady Dragomoshchenko, untitled photograph

image, the drab gray tones bordered by a green of wet lushness, of rain just ended. Or perhaps still falling, thus the umbrella that covers the top of the photograph.

That umbrella changes what would otherwise be a richly Romantic landscape, its dead-center road narrowing into a near-triangle, into an image that is cut off at the top. The trees cluster in the distance in a way that perhaps brings the pathway to a halt, but the umbrella at the top really does the work of foreclosure. What it breaks into is the sky, blocking access to what might otherwise be a signifier of boundlessness, of eternity.[94] There is no transcendence here. Everything happens within the moment of the photograph, as is true of the poems, for all their references and allusions.[95] The poet is preoccupied with phenomena whose boundaries are not defined, as he says explicitly in "Agora," but not to contemplate their sublimity. There is nowhere to run off to, and no benefit to escape. The photograph snaps the moment when the road is apprehended, when one wonders how far it might lead. The photograph exclaims, but in a calmer tonality, what Dragomoshchenko wrote in a poem of the 1970s: "O, exultation of matter, pressed to the very limit of being!" (O, likovanie materii, dostigshei predela bytiia!).[96]

The umbrella plays one other important role in the photograph: it material-izes the subject, the one who presumably holds the camera and probably the umbrella as well. Other photographs by Dragomoshchenko can bring him into the image—as a reflection in a mirror, for instance. It's very like the forms of self-representation found in Andrei Tarkovsky's Polaroids, an uncannily apt comparison.[97] Not to Tarkovsky's cinematic practice (so rich in autobiograph-ical reference, something Dragomoshchenko eschews), but to a single mo-ment, near the end of his most autobiographical film, *The Mirror* (*Zerkalo*, 1974), when a man is lying in bed, dying. Only the arm is seen (portentously, as it leads to the man's hand opening, releasing a bird into flight, splitting open the film to let in Bach's gorgeous St. John Passion and the final shots of the movie). It is Tarkovsky's own arm, partially seen, all that the film will admit of the director's body.[98] That arm is like the absent subject in Dragomoshchen-ko's work: a metonymy for a self whose felt presence shapes the artful lines of both writing and photography.

Anna Glazova Imagines Flowers

Among Dragomoshchenko's most perceptive readers and great admirers is Anna Glazova, and he took a striking photograph of her that documented their friendship.[99] There are telling points of contact within their work. Across her six published volumes of poetry, the mental space of Glazova's poems is deeply attentive to subtle changes in what is before her, whether light, dark, or air it-self. Those changes can have metaphysical consequences, and Glazova's task as a poet is always to let language lead her toward revelations of perception.[100] Her engagement with the nature of the outside world and with the nature of language is thus a constant. This unflinching sense of investigation helps ac-count for the brevity of the poems, where a single sensory impression suffices to occupy the poem for its six or nine or thirteen lines.

My observation about brevity should be tempered, however, for Glazova can build quite specific cycles based around themes, like "Laws" ("Zakony," 2013), or around a mythological figure, as in "Hekate" ("Gekata," 2022).[101] Assembling poems into sequences lets Glazova link short texts through repeated images or sound patterns, creating Mandelstamian conversations across texts. Also, within them: Glazova is in constant dialogue with her readers, and her photographs also suggest a kind of conversation between the objects displayed.

These and other patterns, what the Structuralists call invariants—short form, reliance on free verse, preference for quick sketches rather than narratives, dense linguistic and rhetorical patterning—are enlivened by enormously subtle variability across the poems and across her books. I read that variability as its own gesture of freedom, Glazova's way of ensuring that the patterns of her poems do not become a set of rigid rules. In one poem from 2020, in fact, she linked freedom to dissimilarity, to difference.[102] From another perspective, we might say that her poems are like experiments or essays in the etymological sense of that word, and that each phase of the work sets a fresh version of a familiar hypothesis (for instance, probing the boundary between the subjectivities of humans and animals in *For the Shrew* [*Dlia zemleroiki*, 2013]).

That sense of a book or cycle as an investigation marks Glazova as a contemporary, twenty-first-century poet,[103] but her work has inherited some key elements of the Russian poetic tradition. I have consciously chosen Mandelstam as a point of reference in the last paragraphs: Glazova has written about him well, and she inherited from Acmeist poetics a will to bring the world's objects into her poems.[104] An exception to that orientation toward the tangible might be her book *Dream's Experience* (*Opyt sna*, 2014), but even there the leaves, wind, rivers, cold, and flames have a materiality that makes them feel embodied.[105] The poet's eye is trained on whatever is at hand, with intense and generous attention.

It is that capacious gaze that Glazova also brings to her photography, which almost always features flowers in a vase indoors. There is, though, a photograph of her, surrounded by flowers out of doors, in an image posted to her LiveJournal blog in the fall of 2012 (figure 22). It was taken by her friend Alena Geyser. Persons are entirely absent in Glazova's own photography work, and Geyser's snapshot invites us to shift our gaze from the poet to the bouquet she is assembling. She is surrounded by a beautiful scene, but she concentrates on the flowers she is holding. Something in the bouquet of fluffy white flowers needs adjusting, as if they are being arranged already with the photographer's eye. The poet is caught in the act of collecting material from which art might be made, assembling objects whose texture and color, whose capacity to reflect, contain, or to block out light will be the subjects of her photographs.

Glazova's photographs belong to the genre of the still life.[106] Unlike, say, news photography, or a quickly taken snapshot, the still-life photographer exercises immense control in composing an image, able to determine background, to alter a light source, and to create angles or patterns among objects shown. Many of Dragomoshchenko's photographs are still-life arrangements,

FIGURE 22. Alena Geyser, photograph of Anna Glazova (2012)

too, often featuring humanmade objects. But in Glazova's work, elements of the natural world take center stage, and the vases that hold the featured flowers are most often glass, valued for its shapes that complement the flowers or its capacity to nearly disappear. Most of the photographs are taken inside (the light-filled forest scene in figure 12 is an exception).[107] The elements of the natural world—flowers especially, and sometimes berries or mushrooms, sometimes bits of wood or debris—are selected and studiously arranged. Windows and window ledges are often present; like the window against which the empty dress hangs in Dragomoshchenko's photograph, Glazova's images often capture a glass pane through which light passes and a window's frame as well.[108] In her case, it is often the bottom of the window that we see, giving a ground of stability to the image. Similarly, many images show a table or floor serving the same function, with light coming from an unseen source and throwing shadows on a wall, or with a pattern of light reproducing the shape of a window.

Roland Barthes compared things in photographs to anesthetized, fastened-down butterflies, but his idea of stillness is one that photography can challenge.[109] Glazova, like other painters and photographers who have created still-life artwork, confronts absolute stillness by suggesting movement and change. She might include a petal or a leaf as if it has just fallen onto a surface, for example. Some of her photographs feature flowers in all their potential vivacity, clearly lit and as if radiant with that light, but more often we see faded, withering, broken flowers, lovely even as they prompt one to imagine demise and decay (figure 23). These fading roses, with their dropped petals carpeting the space at the bottom of the image, present the lingering beauty of flowers as they lose their vivacity. The pale petal colors are softened by the low lighting, made lower still by the panel of black on the left (a recessed wall surface, presumably, which does not catch the light). There is a softer intensification of shadow on the right. Light is drawn to the center, as in a triptych, but the way that the spent petals lie as if at the feet of the bouquet gives them the feeling of scattered light. What is being drained from the flowers is the play of color that light would otherwise catch (this is a color photograph, the colors extremely pale). This photograph shows Glazova as a photographer who can work with both darkness and light.

I begin with this rather romantic image because it suggests the multiple ways in which Glazova resists the notion of fixity associated with still-life photography, and because of the energetic diagonal lines and color patterns that accentuate a sense of visual energy. The dynamism of this image is paradoxical, its roses heavy with their own decaying petals. But decay is itself a form of change, one that Glazova writes about with great effectiveness in her poetry.[110] And heaviness is another of her great topics—perhaps she learned from Emily Dickinson, a favorite poet of hers, how to think in terms of heft, of estimating the weight of an object.[111]

FIGURE 23. Anna Glazova, untitled photograph

A photograph of a tulip images incipient decay that is romantic in a different way (figure 24). It focuses on a species of tulip that has a rosebud-like flower head, and it is angled out toward us in a way that enlarges it slightly. The drooping tulip is set off by a textured background of draped, very thin white fabric. The fabric filters the light and creates surfaces on which we can see several shadows. That play of fabric, light, and shadow is often present in Glazova's photography. This tulip blossom is an especially nice example of the curving surfaces of light and shadow that effect can create. The perfectly

FIGURE 24. Anna Glazova, untitled photograph

balanced angles of shadow boundaries and the tulip stem are also notable. They pose for us a question in spatial terms that the fading flower also suggests, a question of stillness and movement. And once again, heaviness is suggested by the photograph's lines, as if the blossom had mysteriously pulled the stem downward and slightly forward, toward the camera, with a kind of gravitational force. Heaviness and airiness are in strange sync, and lighting gives a near palpability to the air.[112]

In this image's white background, a darker diagonal line is seen, its angle the opposite of the tulip's stem, and an angle that is replicated downward in the image, adding further dynamism to the composition. Glazova often suggests movement with such angled lines, or with curved or slanted forms. This is a traditional way of energizing forms, as in the art of the Baroque, and in Glazova's work it has the familiar effect of gently prodding us to see a still image as if it were caught a split-second before movement or change. The precariousness of light and shadow intensifies that effect. Seen in this way, this photograph of a tulip could exemplify what has become an axiom of photography studies, the representation in a photograph of something that was but is no longer. The idea, like so much else, derives from Roland Barthes's *Camera Lucida* and is well expressed by Mary Price: "Photography is . . . a picture of that which is about to become a memory"; it is "a capturing of what, in the present is about to become the past, is to be remembered."[113] That incipient memory can be the source of mourning, as it is in *Camera Lucida*, but not so in Glazova's photographs. The tonality, as we shall see, is not melancholy. Rather, and this is true in her poetry as well, the objects found and arranged are offered to us in a spirit of generosity and attentiveness. We may sense that they are about to be gone, but their presence remains generous.

Glazova has several means to suggest this disappearing act, and one of them is to make a viewer less able to see the flowers. She can use thin draped fabric, very like the backdrop to the tulip, in front of a floral arrangement. The fabric is like a veil, dropped over some lovely face. It creates a barrier to clear vision and renders the floral arrangement in several senses spectral. In a lovely photograph of poppies (figure 25), the flowers are made blurry by a gray gauzy fabric. The iconography resembles the fading roses, in that the blossom placed on the table pulls some of the floral arrangement out of the vase. But there is no narrative here of flowers wilting or fading away. The gauzy fabric changes the story. Rendering the poppies slightly out of focus, the gauze makes them more like a thing of the imagination. The fabric acts like a scrim on a theater stage,

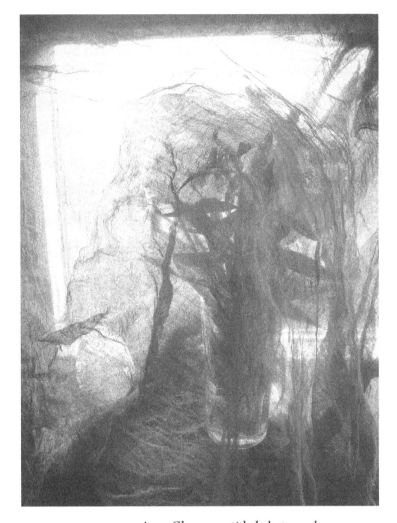

FIGURE 25. Anna Glazova, untitled photograph

posing a hazy barrier between audience and action that suggests the realm of dreams.

The gauzy fabric, whether in front of or behind the flowers, as in the image of the drooping tulip, puts a canvas-like substance into the photograph, reminding us that paintings are made on such fabric surfaces. The compositional work in this image was also linked to drawing by Glazova herself: when she posted this image on LiveJournal (June 18, 2012), an exchange with Gali-Dana Singer (whose nighttime acanthus photograph is shown in figure 14) took place. The fabric, Glazova explains, was a shawl that ripped the first time she wore it. So she began using it as prop, finding it indispensable in creating shading and texture (the word she uses here is "shtrikhovanie," meaning the pencil strokes of drawing). There has long been, in fact, a debate within photography theory as to whether painting is the origin of photography (also in Barthes's *Camera Lucida*). Glazova, with her deep knowledge of theory and philosophy, may well be referencing this debate.

Yet the fabric as a barrier to the floral arrangement could push us in a different direction, having to do more with vision itself. Let us compare another, ghostlier image, one that also uses an expressively textured scrim (figure 26). Glazova gave this image a title when she posted it on LiveJournal, unusually for her (the poems also rarely have titles): *Malva Specter* (*Prizrak mal'vy*). She has made the malva flower ghostly by draping a gauzy window curtain in front of it. The light from the window casts the flower's shadow on the fabric, making a double of what is already spectral, and Glazova adds a further shadow or double by including an additional vase, barely seen at the bottom of the image, to the right of the stem shadow's diagonal line. The second vase's more globular shape repeats the flower shape.

Glazova appended an explanatory sentence to this image when she posted it, as a kind of caption. These words entice us as a line of poetry might: "Fyodor and I were just talking about how a specter is different from a phantom" (Kak raz govorili s Fedorom o tom, chem prizrak otlichaetsia ot fantoma).[114] When asked about the difference between these terms, Glazova responded that a specter exists after death—"therefore the specter in a closet is one who lives in the closet, rather than a spectral closet. But the phantom is something you can't figure out: maybe it's an inhabitant, maybe it's the closet."[115]

Glazova leaves us to decide whether the malva is a specter (an image conjured as visible to the mind, as *seen*) or phantom (an image conjured as *unseeable* to the mind, as unreal). The difference between the two is a task that poetry takes up, with all the resources of language to hand. As one poem puts it, "how does the invisible see?" (a kak vidit nevidimyi?).[116] But the photograph has a different affordance: wordlessly, it can posit both the seeable and the unseeable, both specter and phantom. For the viewer of the photograph, a space of contemplation opens between these possibilities. What is at stake is not the difference between them, but the way a visual artifact could be both.

The photographed malva creates that space of contemplation in which two spectacles can be seen at the same moment—not the optical trick of

FIGURE 26. Anna Glazova, *Malva Specter*

goblet/profile, indeed not an optical illusion at all, but rather a spectacle of two abstractions. The rescued flower as photographed is a specter, a ghostly emblem of its own fading; the placement of the flower behind the gauzy curtain makes it more like a phantom, an apparition of a flower, a self-conscious rendering of an idea of a flower alongside the flower itself. It's the shadow of the flower that suggests the phantom. We stare at the shadow, trying to guess its size, since the shadow seems larger and longer than the flower. Studying the shadow, we pause at the thin column of glass, the vase that holds the flower, a repetition of the stem's shape. It seems for a moment as if the glass container could assure us of the reality of the flower. But the more we stare at the vase, the more we realize that its shadow has been cropped from the image—the shadow is all flower and stem. The other vase, however, is at the bottom of the image, rounder and fuller, more like the shape of the flower itself. And perhaps like another phantom. What is that second vase holding?

The impossibility of answering that question suggests how close Glazova's photography is to what Guy Davenport has called "the still life of philosophical meditation."[117] He notes that still-life painting "has always served as a contemplative form useful for working out ideas, color schemes, opinions." Remarkably, he adds a comparison to poetic expression: it has "the same relation to larger, more ambitious paintings as the sonnet to the long poem."[118] The tight focus in still life, I would argue, readies us for the way that Glazova's poems use small form. Attentiveness is intensified by the restricted nature of what is before us in image or in word. The resulting philosophical meditation can be profoundly inward, as a heightened awareness of sensory impressions that are themselves thematized in the poems, or it can constitute an outward gaze, toward the world where flowers have been gathered or glass vases and tissue-like fabrics produced.

Glazova delves further into that outer world in her poems than in the photographs. To some extent, that is an effect of her nearly always photographing flowers. Norman Bryson, writing about still-life painting, has emphasized the prominence of foodstuffs, and he makes much of the ideas of consumption, abundance, waste, and debris they encode.[119] Some striking photos by Glazova include mushrooms or pomegranates, but these images never do the symbolic work that interests Bryson—instead, they visually balance out the colors or shapes of flowers, and to the extent that they suggest a narrative, it is the same notion of gathering, collecting, or fading implied by the flowers. Glazova's flowers, then, even though they are still-life photographs, push the genre in a different direction.

Here we should return to Elaine Scarry's *Dreaming by the Book*, which was previewed in the discussion of Dragomoshchenko's photographic work. Scarry cites flowers as premier objects for mental representation. Flowers are just the right size for imagining: "It is as though the soft, self-illuminating petals are the tissue of the mental images themselves—not the thing pictured, but the surface on which the images will get made."[120] We are drawn to imagine flowers, Scarry says, because flowers have a physical substance like the mind itself. She describes gauzy fabrics as another such easy-to-daydream-about substance: "Phenomena in the actual physical world that have those same attributes of transparency or filminess (such as thin curtains, fog, and mist) can be more easily imitated in the mind than can thick or substantive phenomena. The gossamer quality of many flowers . . . the thinness and transparency of the petals . . . gives them a kinship with the filmy substancelessness of mental images."[121] Glazova, in my view, is thus draping her flowers with filmy fabrics for a further reason. She is interrogating the categories of mental vivacity in these pictures of textures, folds, shapes, and shadows—properties that belong to both the flowers and the fabrics. She uses these images of stem, petal, leaf, and scrim as emblems for the mental work of imagination.

Just as the photographs arrange the fading, decaying objects of the natural world into expressions of temporary aliveness, so her poetry explores mental states at the boundary zones of alertness, clarity, self-certainty, and self-knowledge. Glazova has said that she writes her poems in a state that is somewhere between being asleep and being awake.[122] That claim gives the poetic texts a kind of status—it is as if they come to her on their own, or well up from the unconscious—very unlike the meticulous work needed to compose still-life arrangements for a camera. But she reworks those lines she has noted down, as she went on to explain in that interview, and it is striking that a poet, Rostislav Amelin, without commenting on her photography, likens her poems to photographs.[123] For Amelin, the poem's images are as if three-dimensional: they rise off the page, looking as if they were placed into perspective. That eruption into perspective happens because of the way Glazova's language renews itself in the process of the poem's being written. Glazova has said something about Paul Celan and Friedrich Hölderlin, poets deeply important to her, that is also true of her own work: they wrote as if in every poem, language was created anew. The speaker in their poems becomes someone for whom language is not a home to be inhabited but pure space.[124] Glazova's poems are similarly estranged from their own words in a way that lets us meditate on their semantic, morphological, sonorous, and even typographical aspects, one word and one line at a time.

Consider this poem, then, from the collection *Loop, Unhalved* (*Petlia, nevpolovinu*, 2008). It offers a kind of exploded interior, and it mentions a flower as a crucial visual standard. The poem's conclusion also allegorizes her photography work when it reaches for imagery that can make light itself palpable.

we have so bent the wall
that all doors—are outside
and the sea—is inside

and all rivers flow down red carpets,
down which ships sail-step, like the truth.

all designs—are flowers
if you see through the stem.
we have so bent the see-through sea
that inside—is only night,
so we, in the dark and in the neon light,
can see air and light.[125]

мы так изогнули стену,
что все двери—снаружи,
а море—внутри,
и все реки текут по красным коврам,
по которым, как правда, идут корабельной ступнёй.

все узоры—цветы,
если видеть сквозь стебель.
мы так изогнули прозрачное море,
что внутри—только ночь,
чтобы и в темноте, и при свете неоновой лампы
видеть воздух и свет.[126]

This eloquent poem picks up on the flower imagery so important to the photographs, urging us to consider flowers as the measure of all visual design. The poem in a sense carries on where Scarry's work leaves off. Note the invitation to imagine the spaces of inside and outside as if interchangeable: the boundaries or walls can be bent and twisted. Just as flowers and vegetation may be brought inside to be photographed, so poems may bend the elements of nature and draw them into the mind for contemplation. Once brought in, these objects are as if seen in a photograph, studied for the light and air that surround them.

In its ending, the poem asks us to see what cannot be seen.[127] We have looped back to Glazova's ambition to see the unseeable, for how can one see "air and light"? Elaine Scarry has a ready answer to that question: we imagine it, and it is the work of this poem to ask its readers to try to picture a space created by so bending walls, so meshing interior with out of doors space, that the qualities of air and light would be different. Here, too, the photographs can help us, for amid all the flowers, they can track moments when rays of light seem to give shape and volume to air. Glazova's photograph of a vase with dried flowers (figure 27) is an image that beckons such imagination—the precarious

FIGURE 27. Anna Glazova, untitled photograph

placement of the vase pull our gaze off-center, and the image shows Glazova's exceptional sense of visual balance. The tiny triangle of ceiling slanting in the upper left corner is like a weird source of stabilization, setting up a cascade of diagonal lines that pour down toward the table itself. It's not a light source, but it acts as if it were. And how textured with light is the white space behind, creating depth in the whiteness that gently intensifies toward the bottom right. It is like the white space sculpted out of a page of poetry, no mere background but rather a space that defines what is layered over it.

Glazova can do the same thing with a floor, and several images project light onto a wood floor that seems almost to glow in responsiveness. The photograph of two vases with their flowers (figure 28) more warmly repeats the brown and white tones of the precariously placed vase with its dried flowers (figure 27). (Both of these images, in the color prints, rely on brown tones with touches of white.) The photograph of two vases, with their different oval shapes, includes plant life that seems chosen for its shapes—the shape of the lily and delphinium arching up, the lily itself catching further light, and the shape of the greenery in the vase on the right, which make for a shape on the floor that copies that of the lily. The light projected onto the floor is softened by lovely shadows, but it is recognizably the shape of a window, as a kind of metonymy that brings an idea of the architectural structure—our poem's bent wall—into the space of the picture, but without that structure being present. The window has a spectral presence, reminding us how often windows show up in Glazova's photographs. Whereas the poem ends with the desire to see air and light, the photographs show us pictures of light, and the imagery in which this is captured seems to change the quality of the air in the process. In this photograph, air feels warmed by sunlight and by the patterns that soften the light's outlines, giving a romantic glow to what is otherwise an austere image.

Austerity is a feature of Glazova's poetry, too, which has only intensified over the years, with poems growing shorter, tauter, so that even the lack of capitalization starts to feel like a mark of reticence. The counterweight for that pulling back is an ever-fiercer push cognitively, toward hard to grasp abstractions and sensory impressions so fleeting as to nearly escape attention. These traits are felt keenly in the volume *Earth Lies on the Earth* (*Zemlia lezhit na zemle*, 2017), from which the following untitled poem is drawn. We've already seen its final line, and the whole of it might now show what happens when we read Glazova's poems with her photography work in mind:

fur and hair
are closer in color to the earth
than variegated feathers and scales:

the more folds in the brain
the longer the road
leading from paradise's vivid brightness.

the more vividly one sees
the less good-looking the viewer:

FIGURE 28. Anna Glazova, untitled photograph

how does the invisible see?

шерсть и волосы
ближе цветом к земле
чем пёстрые перья и чешуя:

чем извилистей мозг
тем дольше дорога
от райской яркости.

чем ярче видит

тем невзрачней смотрящий:

а как видит невидимый?[128]

This gnomic little poem, with its references to the furry, feathery, and scaly surfaces of the animal world, has a lot in common with the two books that Glazova would write next—*For the Shrew*, with its steadier focus on the border zones where humans and animals exchange glances, and *Calculations of the Face* (*Litsevoe schislenie*, 2020), with its aphoristic abstractions and further compacting of language. But here Glazova is more intensely staying with the very idea of looking, a metaphor that controls the three final lines and that reverberates morphologically through its diction. I am reminded of the photographic work of Uta Barth, whose images can center on what has been called an "unintentional void." Barth makes that emptiness interesting by having it draw the viewer ever further into the experience of looking: "The question for me always is how I can make you aware of your own activity of looking, instead of losing your attention to thoughts about what it is you are looking at."[129] Glazova does not create a comparable void, particularly in her photographs, but her poems can dart between things to look at without ever resolving into the kind of clear image that she tells us, in the second stanza here, would be a kind of paradise from which we have fallen away. Still more challenging is the final line, in which the invisible itself is engaged in the act of seeing.

Just before that gnomic line, though, the third stanza explores multiple ways of seeing, and a whole vocabulary of seeing is established—this is a fine example of the way Glazova can estrange us from the words in a poem, get us to study them and see their ambiguities and paradoxes reverberate. That she does this with the diction of visibility makes this poem a kind of performance of our own ways of looking at her photographs. To see with a clarity that is almost angular is to become less beautiful. The epithet I translated as "less good-looking," a single word in Russian, *nevzrachnyi*, is notable. In modern Russian, it means unattractive, not so easy on the eyes, but without the slangy connotations of that phrase or of "good-looking" (my translation has only the virtue of preserving the etymological root). The language has a host of synonyms that all derive from roots related to seeing (*nevzornyi, nevidnyi, nevzgliadnyi*), and the one that Glazova chooses, *nevzrachnyi* (like *nevzornyi*), has a higher style. The root is *zret'*, an archaic equivalent of *videt'*, the common verb meaning "to see," and the source of one of the synonyms, *nevidnyi*. Glazova's choice is slightly elevated style because her poem moves toward philosophical abstractions, but she nicely brings it back from all lofty climes in the same line when she names the viewer *smotriashchii*: this participle acts as a noun that emphasizes the act of looking.[130] The noun denotes the person, but the only thing that matters is that act of looking. Glazova manifests a concern "with seeing rather than the seen," as she formulated it in describing a similar phenomenon in Dragomoshchenko.[131] Put another way, this is a kind of looking without an object, what Lucy Alford has called intransitive attention.[132]

Glazova thus advocates a kind of seeing more like that of Uta Barth, where looking itself is the interesting activity, where the folds and turns in the brain slow down the cognitive activity so much that the gaze turns back on itself. When that happens, a different phenomenon may be imagined, something that is unseeable, not merely spectral but also spiritual (the phrase "nevidimyi mir" also means the spiritual world). We direct our gaze toward this imagined phenomenon, this poem tells us, into the spaces where there is no light, where there is the darkness of the earth. That is where the poem in fact begins, with its preference not for colorful objects in the natural world, but for those that are the color of the earth.

The play of light and dark that defines Glazova's photography is also, then, a defining trait in the poetry. What is most striking is the movement from light to dark, and the will to see darkness for its mysterious potential. Glazova has had brilliant predecessors in this work of finding both dark and light in photography, among them Laura Letinsky, a still-life photographer Glazova admires.[133] Letinsky published a book, *After All*, in which the lighting in the photographs dims across the pages of the book, and she is an exemplary proponent of allowing the many shades of light and dark in a room to have equal weight. In American poet Mark Strand's foreword to Letinsky's book, he praises "the ravishing gloom of the darker images," and it is an oxymoronic phrase that feels appropriate to what Glazova can do in both image and poem.[134] Strand rightly finds a beauty in Letinsky's photographs that I also sense in Glazova's light-filled photographs, which feel most radiant in the spaces filled with air. Glazova, too, is careful to show us that darkness has its own heavier air (and heaviness, *tiazhest'*, is a suggestive term in her poetry: it carries meanings that range from significance to the force of gravity, *tiazhest'* being the Russian term in physics for gravity). She has a poem that begins:

humus births the sour air of respiration.

we
breathe this gloom,
rhythmically drinking into our own darkness

the quiet deaths
of seeds and plants.[135]

из перегноя рождается кислый дыхательный воздух.

мы
этой тьмой дышим,
мерно вбирая в свою темноту

тихую смерть
семян и растений.[136]

The darkness breathed in in this poem is associated with death. The paradoxical coupling of death and breath—as if Glazova, adept in English as well as her native Russian, hears the rhyme—is her own way of reattaching death to life itself, just as she attaches the poem's *we* to seeds and the plants they give life to. Seeing into darkness is thus like seeing into death, something we can detect in Glazova's photography, for instance, in her use of darkness and shadows. The fabrics have something of the shroud in them. What we are always moving toward, as Glazova's other poems and her scholarship suggest, is death, but in her poems, as in the flowers drooping toward decomposition, death is more a process, less an ending. It is what is most ineffable in the poetic and photographic worlds she creates, and what makes Glazova's work unlike elegy. She is not commemorating when she writes of death; she is observing, with an eye to all that is most alive. The poet Alla Gorbunova wrote that everything in a Glazova poem has the potential to die, to pass through the boundary between life and death—because, as Gorbunova put it, the potential to die is a requirement for any entity with which we can have a conversation.[137]

Glazova is ever in conversation, because to be in that conversation is to bring about the existence of a world.[138] She speaks with the shrews and trees and philosophical abstractions that appear in her poems, as with the tulips and vases and windows of her photography. I began with the images, promising that they would lead us to the poems in new ways, and the poems also lead us back to the photographs. In that back and forth, as with Yusupova, Svarovsky, and Dragomoshchenko, we find poets seeking alternative visual means to express the genealogies, ontologies, and perceptual equilibriums of their verbal texts. In each case, the turn to photography discloses new vistas on the poetic work. Glazova and Dragomoshchenko in particular seek to free the work from its materiality, whereas Svarovsky wants to free it from its temporal logics.

Whether working with their own photographs or with found materials, they push the aesthetic boundaries around poetry back just enough to reveal the complexities of their own creative processes, and the possibilities of admitting the insubstantial, the barely material into both image and text. The next chapter takes up poets who turn that quality of the insubstantial in a decidedly spiritual direction.

6

Freedoms of the Spirit

POEMS OF FAITH AFTER THE FALL

Magid • Shvarts • Kruglov • Khersonsky • Sedakova

THE PARADOXICAL freedom in Russia is at its most vexed when speech turns toward matters of religion. Religious institutions have their own strictures, and faith is an area of vast differences where people can feel strongly that their beliefs are an eternal truth. I well recall the dignified choice made by Andrei Sinyavsky, speaking to a large group of students at Amherst College many years ago: he refused to answer a question about his religious beliefs because faith, he said, is properly a private matter. To choose against speech can be a way of preserving privacy and authentic belief, but so is the urge to speak out in favor of toleration, or to speak against using religion as a wedge to drive people apart. Poets are not immune to that urge, and for some this topic descends on them, much like religious belief itself. They write first-person lyrics that ask the persistent questions of faith and doubt, and some have created heroes through whom to speak. They ask what a divinely ordered universe could feel like in fraught times, and in the poems that most interest me, they also push back against an idea that the language of religion is separate, safe from the language of daily life. Language itself is a subject of these poems, many of them written with great simplicity even when they are shot through with deep wisdom or deep passion.

Not all these poems are written within the framework of Russian Orthodoxy, although Orthodoxy is felt in an enormous cross section of poetry, often encountering other faiths or religious discourses, one of which, Judaism, has a long history on the territory of Russia.[1] Worldly power has always been a prominent feature of the Russian Orthodox Church's identity. As the philosopher Nikolai Berdyaev put it, "The Russian religious vocation, a particular and distinctive vocation, is linked with the power and transcendent majesty of the Russian State."[2] He wrote those words in 1946, his way to protest the atheism then reigning in the USSR. But in the twenty-first century, the Russian Orthodox Church (ROC) is walking in lockstep with authoritarian leaders. Perhaps the most vivid artistic exposure of that power is Andrei Zviagintsev's acclaimed film *Leviathan* (2014), and it is fair to say, given events in 2022, that the ROC's comfort level with endorsements of state violence has reached a new high. At such a moment, prophecy tastes sour in the mouth, and there is all the more reason to recoil from visionary speech, as Sinyavsky did in the 1980s. Poet prophets in post-Soviet Russia may appear not as Pushkin's prophet, called in 1827 to see and attend on all God's creations ("vizhd' i vnemli," as Pushkin wrote), but as Putin's prophet, called to warn listeners of the dangers that await dissenters.[3]

In such an atmosphere, the stakes for poetry that speaks of faith could not be higher. This is potentially dangerous speech, uttered in a heavily patrolled zone. One way to treat this poetry would be to study those who work at the borders of those limits, and in some of what follows, I do that. But I also want to think capaciously about where matters of faith and spirit might take the poet, particularly the poet who hopes to liberate listeners rather than modeling for them a life of subservience to doctrine or advocacy for a particular religious perspective. What is the contribution that poems of faith can offer to the work of creating freedom?

Here, I zero in on four poets: Elena Shvarts, Sergei Kruglov, Boris Khersonsky, and Olga Sedakova. Even when they write as visionaries, they use what they take as God's gifts to see the diversity of creation. When they offer cosmic visions of origin or end, they do so from a position of idiosyncratic humanity, even humility. They show themselves as what we might call a seeker, an errant believer, a chronicler of human history, and a rewriter of saints' lives. This is not a taxonomy, because these roles cut across their work, at times adopted in combination.

These poets have rejected intolerance and divisiveness to try to imagine the religious experience of the other—as holy fool, forgotten saint, strangely powerful monk, or Jew destined for diaspora. They are committed to a politics of free expression, and in their poetics of faith, the limits on autonomy brought by ritual, rules, and religious traditions are tested. These poets stand at the threshold between the secular and the sacred, creating visionary poems as ethical acts.[4] And their writings are discursively positioned between the languages of faith and the languages of everyday life.

To Start: Sergei Magid

Before treating each in some detail, I want to give a snapshot of one poet, Sergei Magid, who sets out some of the chapter's themes, but whose work is hard to categorize. He stands outside many modes of organizing contemporary Russian poetry and is less well known than Shvarts, Kruglov, Khersonsky, or Sedakova, yet very much their equal in stature (he might be one of the rare contemporary poets who in fact could compare to Sedakova in sheer erudition: he worked in the National Library of the Czech Republic for years and said that his every poem is constructed in conversation with other texts).[5] Magid's theology sits between Judaism and Christianity. That theology is beautifully exemplified in a poem that juxtaposes two wise elders: the Baal Shem Tov, who founded Hasidic Judaism, and Archbishop Sergius Korolev, leader of the Orthodox Church in Prague. True to Magid's scholarly inclinations, he includes the birth and death dates for each of them in his short poem, presenting first one, then the other, before a final stanza that meditates on all that divides and joins them:

> baal shem tov of berdichev (1700–1760)
> said
> all that happens around us
> all that we see
> all that we hear
> all this teaches us how to serve the God
> of abraham isaac and jacob
>
> archbishop sergius of prague (1881–1952)
> said
> the circumstances of our life
> are as wise elders
> who teach us
> how to follow in Christ
> the son of the God of abraham isaac and jacob
>
> I think about these two who are divided by everything
> time nation nationality confession

and united only by one thing
faith
that the beast may become cro-magnon
cro-magnon become a righteous man
the righteous man become a saint
and the saint finally become a man
created in the image and likeness of God.

баал шем тов бердичевский (1700–1760)
сказал
все что происходит вокруг нас
все что мы видим
все что мы слышим
все это учит нас как служить Богу
авраама исаака и иакова

епископ сергий пражский (1881–1952)
сказал
обстоятельства нашей жизни
нужно воспринимать в виде старцев
которые обучают нас
как следовать Христу
сыну Бога авраама исаака и иакова

я думаю об этих двоих которых разделяет все
время страна национальность конфессия
и только одно объединяет
вера
в то что зверь может стать кроманьонцем
кроманьонец праведником
праведник святым
и святой наконец-то человеком
созданным по образу и подобию Божию.[6]

Magid turns the poem on the word "faith," a pivot that first suggests to us that Archbishop Sergius and the Baal Shem Tov, so divided by time, geography, nationality, and confession, are united by a common faith in the God of Abraham, Isaac, and Jacob, whether taught to serve God directly or to follow in the paths laid out by Jesus. But "faith" turns out to be something else that these two men share, a faith in human progress and perfectibility. The poem's commitment to linear time is anchored in the datelines of birth and death, in the movement across deep time that makes for human physiological evolution but also human moral evolution, the highest point of which is not sainthood but humanity itself, so long as that human life sees itself as created in God's image. That secular timeline of species development becomes an eternal present of the human recognition that there is something larger and greater than the human. Archbishop Sergius and the Baal Shem Tov are joined in faith in that recognition, a faith that frees them from the differences that would keep them apart. The poem brings those two timelines and those two ways of thinking about the world together, what has been seen as the overall project of Magid's book of finding convergences between the secular and the religious.[7]

That point of intersection is itself a place of potential liberation, as the two modes of thinking push against each other's limits to create new openings unimaginable to either taken alone. Magid comes to that possibility from some hard-won struggles, and Sergei Stratanovsky finds in the poems of his 2003 book a tortured relationship with God.[8] The torture should not diminish the intensity of the relationship, however, and Magid's writings make clear his persistent search for a sense of the divine. In his diaries, for example, in a passage that charts several motifs of isolation and alienation, Magid adds, "I don't know God, but I feel Him. I feel Him by means of my sensation that He is. What I feel is not the result of knowledge, it is a fact of my naked skin. The sensation of a gaze. His gaze at my back."[9] It is a striking image, the feeling of being felt and seen by God, and it links Magid's work to the phenomenology of the flesh studied by theologians and literary scholars. Working from a Christian perspective (which he often does, although he was born Jewish and also writes from the perspective of a Jew), for Magid, the Word is made flesh in the coming of Christ.[10] Magid is writing about a sensory presence of the divine, of an experiential flash in which the flesh is made word.[11] The imagery in Magid's poetry can be remarkably physical, with a range from the exalted to the debased not unlike what we find in Elena Shvarts's poetry. That range is more familiar from Russian prose, and Magid wrote a poem comparing the soul to Gogol in his grave (silently nodding at the rumors of Gogol's having been buried alive).[12]

In a later poem, Magid can be seen working with material that is more immediate and less grotesque but still marked by extreme contrasts in discursive register and deeply based in the body. This is one of the texts that make up his book of one hundred four-line poems. A second volume of these poems has since appeared, making Magid also a practitioner of the serial creation of a short form, as studied in chapter 3. He's mentioned there, for his striking eight-line poems, but these four-line texts are greater in number (to date two hundred of them) and doubly compressed compared with his eight-line poems. The one I want to focus on has an afternote to describe its setting in the attic of a church building.[13]

> Sickness chatters indifferently like a magpie. It eats at a man for days
>   on end.
> He is exiled to his body innocently and without end. He expects no
>   liberation.
> But a diagnosis is expected. It will be approximate, rough, and the
>   doctors don't care.
> And a child's words are the only real remainder: warm, warmer,
>   warmest, burning hot . . .
>
> *[Written at 2:00 a.m. on Thursday, July 15, 2010, in the*
> *attic of the parish house of the Evangelical Church*
> *of Czech Brethren in Slavonice]*

> Болезнь болтливо-равнодушна как сорока. Ест человека сутки
>   напролет.
> Он сослан в тело без вины и срока. Освобождение не ждет.
> А ждет диагноз. Приблизительно-примерный, да равнодушие
>   врачей.
> И детские слова—единственный остаток верный: тепло, теплей,
>   еще теплее, горячей . . .
>
> *[Записано в 2 часа ночи в четверг 15 июля 2010 г. на*
> *чердаке приходского дома Евангелической Церкви*
> *Чешских братьев в Славонице]*[14]

Magid builds this poem on a familiar theological metaphor, that the body's sickness bespeaks the soul's pain, although the connection to religious thinking largely sits outside the four-line text, contained within the bracketed notation that locates the poem in a parish house attic. The building is affiliated with the main Reformation Church of the Czech lands, and although the old town of Slavonice, where this poem is set, boasts some remarkable feats of church architecture, Magid places his poem's speaker in a darkly squirreled away setting, writing in the middle of the night.

The sickness of its first word generates some sound echoes in its consonants (bolezn', boltlivo, priblizitel'no), and other parts of the poem are tied together by their sounds, like the magpie (soroka) and the length of a human life (srok); these two words also sit on top of each other in the middle of their respective lines.[15] The use of end rhyme (naprolet/zhdet, vrachei/goriachei) gives a formal feeling to the four lines, one loosened by the absence of regular meter or rhythm. The presence of rhyme means that this isn't fully free verse, but it is a form that Magid has found quite important, emphasizing its potential for a higher concentration of energy. He cites the opening of Allen Ginsberg's *Howl* (in Russian translation, but Magid's English is superb—his dissertation was on T. S. Eliot—and he'll know the original well). He argues with M. L. Gasparov and an unnamed samizdat editor by insisting that free verse is harder to write than lines in standard, "pre-given" (as he calls them) meters. Free verse is a minefield, where you have to "cross every centimeter without anywhere losing the tiniest bit of skin."[16] Note the intensely physical metaphor for the poetic risk Magid takes.

The sense of touch concretizes the physical logic of the poem, which begins almost as an abstraction of tactility. Disease eats at the body, we read, which elicits not so much the sense of taste as of a kind of physical pecking away at the flesh, as if the magpie chatter of the first sentence left a lingering avian presence in the second. The vagueness of the disease hovers even after the mention of a diagnosis, since the anticipated news from the doctors is to be merely approximate. I do not discount the possibility that the poet is writing about illness and its terrors, all the more so as he has recorded his own reactions to the body's ailments, for example, the heart attack he suffered in 1998.[17] But Magid is also diagnosing one of language's limitations, the way that its words approach or touch on meanings, rather than nailing them down. He switches the terms for who it is that uses language—magpies in l.1, doctors in l.3—to give us a children's guessing game. The child's words hold out the promise of some truth, as the guesses get closer and closer to the answer. Closeness is rendered as increasing warmth, which allows the tactile senses to return and to intensify. In another (not four-line) poem written about the same time, Magid similarly associates extreme heat with the literary word—he describes putting a book back on the shelf because of feeling overwhelmed by its Medusa-like impact, but even so, the book leaves a lingering sense of its hot flesh, and the fingers feel burned.[18] Magid worked in a library for decades, so this association of books with pain is shocking (and that poem ends with a bizarre imperative condemning the library to damnation). And yet it is another context for the affliction that opens our four-line poem: an allegorical reading that links malady to writing has its own compelling logic.

A logic, I would add, that further explains the parenthetical addition to this short poem: this is more than a byline, for it gives a location in which the poem was written. Magid's poems resist any easy identification of speaker with poet, as he adopts a range of positions from which to speak; in fact, most often, as in this poem, he has no first-person speaker at all. But the parenthetical description of where the poem was composed brings before the reader's eyes a sense of the writing poet, one who has been inspired to write in a place at once connected to religious institution and slightly apart from it—and at a time, the middle of the night, when that setting is rendered quieter and more private.

I said at the outset that Magid's theology crosses Judaism and Christianity, but this poem, although it was written in a building belonging to the Evangelical Church of Czech Brethren, displays no particular confessional orientation. Rather, it is proximate to such thinking, possibly inspired by that proximity, a position from which Magid often speaks and writes. Not to say that he does not engage directly with biblical texts and arguments about the church, or even incorporate into his diaries, for example, poems made out of bracingly eloquent prayer.[19] He can speak from multiple positions, including that of seeker, errant believer, and chronicler. He is proximate to others in the contemporary Russian tradition, but no one is really like him.

Elena Shvarts, the Seeker

Perhaps Sergei Magid crossed paths with Elena Shvarts before he left Petersburg, although I can find no trace of a meeting in their work. They share a curiosity about mysticism, but to differing degrees. There are streaks of mysticism in Magid's writings, and great swaths of it in hers; indeed it is not a stretch to say that Elena Shvarts was a visionary poet. She possessed an extravagant imagination for the consequences of divine visitations comparable to that of William Blake, but without Blake's will to create a system of prophecies. Her mysticism is most fully explored in the long cycle of Lavinia poems ("Trudy i dni Lavinii, monakhini iz ordena Obrezaniia Serdtsa," 1984), and it is felt throughout her work in visions that electrify the poet. Her visions are disruptive, not sustaining; they are transformative, but fleeting. Just as the rhythms and forms of her verse dynamically change within a single poem, so Shvarts's visions of the cosmos, of God's church on earth, of angels and demons and fools in Christ, are as if discovered anew in every poem. The advent of vision is like a blaze of first light, a point of origin that comes again and again, making her work exist not in the end time of the apocalypse but in the moment when the cosmos is created. Poetic creativity is allegorized in the making of the world, sometimes explicitly, as in her "Big Bang Rondo" ("Rondo Bol'shogo Vzryva," 2008). Here, a point of origin doubles as a vision of a glorious end, affirming that the universe will end in a reversal of the big bang, an implosion of all matter back into its tiny kernel-like beginning. Olga Sedakova rightly reads this poem as creating an exit strategy when all seems to be at an end—as Sedakova put it, this is the Creation as Exodus.[20] It is also affirmation by means of belief, not reason or science, that even an apparent ending is but a beginning.[21]

A less cosmic and more immediately somatic version of this originary vision and one that also mixes birth with demise is Shvarts's emblematic 1978 poem "Animal-Flower" ("Zver'-tsvetok"). She continued to feature this poem in her post-Soviet publications, and in 2008 used it to conclude her reading at the Akhmatova Museum in St. Petersburg, giving an animated performance as she brought the poem to physical life before her audience.[22]

Animal-Flower

> The tree of Judea blooms
> in lilac blossoms along its trunk.

A presentiment of life lives on till death.
A chilling fire burns along the bones—
When a bright shower passes over
On St. Peter's day at break of summer.
Scarlet blooms are just about to flower
On collarbones, on ribs, upon the head.
The cluster will be tagged *Elena arborea*—
Its habitat is freezing Hyperborea
In gardens made of brick, in grass of stone.
Eyes sprout dark carnations. I'm at once
A bush of roses and forget-me-nots
As if a savage gardener'd grafted on me
A virulent fluorescing leprosy.
I will be violet and red,
Crimson, yellow, black and gold,
Inside a perilous humming cloud
Of bees and wasps I'll be a sacred well.

And when my flowers fade, O Lord, O Lord,
What a bitten lump there'll be left over,
Grown cold and with its skin split wide,
A faded, half-dead Animal-Flower.[23]

Зверь-цветок

        Иудейское древо цветет
        вдоль ствола сиреневым цветом.

Предчувствие жизни до смерти живет.
Холодный огонь вдоль костей обожжет,
Когда светлый дождик пройдет
В день Петров на изломе лета.
Вот-вот цветы взойдут алея
На ребрах, у ключиц, на голове.
Напишут в травнике—Elena arborea—
Во льдистой водится она Гиперборее
В садах кирпичных, в каменной траве.
Из глаз полезли темные гвоздики,
Я—куст из роз и незабудок сразу,
Как будто мне привил садовник дикий
Тяжелую цветочную проказу.
Я буду фиолетовой и красной,
Багровой, желтой, черной, золотой,
Я буду в облаке жужжащем и опасном—
Шмелей и ос заветный водопой.
Когда ж я отцвету, о Боже, Боже,
Какой останется искусанный комок—
Остывшая и с лопнувшею кожей,
Отцветший, полумертвый зверь-цветок.[24]

"Animal-Flower" shows off all the riot of color and forms for which Shvarts is famous. The poet represents herself as neither beast nor blossom, neither flora nor fauna. As an entity of the natural world that defies the categories devised by human thinkers, she is a living testimony to the capaciousness of the divine imagination and to its embrace of flourishing beauty as well as death's decay. The body decomposing in a grave engenders flowers whose lurid colors and strange shapes defy the herbarium. From body to flower to the flower's hard seed (note the compression of mortal remains into a kernel of potential new life), Shvarts's imagery celebrates the changeability of matter and of the self. The poet regards the visible world with an eye to the invisible signs of being, discerning in the surfaces, the colors, and the textures a hidden cosmic order.

Compare a poem that stays with those botanical metaphors but images instead a cathedral and a forest. It is a poem of the soul rather than of the body, a poem in which the poet has a mystical vision. It is written about twenty years after "Animal-Flower," in 1996. It is thirty-two lines long, and I cite only its beginning:

Arboreous Cathedral

My soul entered the cathedral of night
Although the bolts were drawn
And walked through the congregation
Of oak, birch and rowan.
They stood unrooted
Quickened in a quiver
And bowed down all at once[25]

Арборейский собор

Душа моя вошла во храм
Ночной, презрев засов,
Она прошла через толпу
Рябин, берез, дубов.
Они стояли без корней
И трепетали в дрожь,
И наклонялись вместе враз[26]

Shvarts is building on a whole tradition of poems set in cathedral spaces, and Mandelstam's three cathedral poems, of which "Notre Dame" (1912) is the most famous, come quickest to mind.[27] In Shvarts's poem, both the space of prayer and the one who enters are transformed. This cathedral is not like a forest, it *is* a forest, made of trees standing and bowing in prayer. The poet does not enter the cathedral to stand before an icon in contemplation, but rather sends in her soul, its dematerialized substance able to penetrate the bolted doors and to behold this arboreal vision. At the end of the poem, the soul asks the smallest tree for an explanation—what are you doing here?—only to be told that there is an end to the natural order, to the cosmic rule of law ("Konets zakonu, vse vozmozhno"), permitting trees to walk, fish to speak. The poet offers us this vision of a forest at prayer, promising that even after the end of time, and even, perhaps, when humankind has no presence in the world, just as it has no presence in this poem, reverence for God endures.

That reverence persists in Shvarts's poetry even in the presence of blasphemy and evil—or leprosy and disease in "Animal-Flower." The blasphemy crashes around the end of her long poem "Kindergarten after Thirty Years" ("Detskii sad cherez tridtsat' let," 1986).[28] It dances around the edges of the Lavinia poems, where demons lie down next to nuns.[29] Where doubt that there is a God who listens to her poems appears, it is indirect, more a representation of God as a secretive child, playing hide-and-seek, as one critic put it.[30] For Shvarts, faith is something for which one pays with physical pain and searing doubt. That pain has been studied well by Dunja Popovic, who writes of the importance of the wounded or sacrificial body in Shvarts's poetry.[31] Psychic pain, as in the dozens of poems mourning her mother's 1998 death, can yield an outpouring of art.[32] Here Shvarts is doing something different from the connection between illness and writing seen in Magid, in part because she has in mind not just disease in general, but quite specifically bodily pain, which descends as if it were a message from on high.

For Shvarts, believing was not a choice, and thus she writes of falling in love with an icon, Our Lady of the Three Hands, unwillingly.[33] But it was also not given, or given easily. Believing lets one see, and it lets one see oneself as an implausible vessel for God's holiness. In a poem written when she was a teenager, Shvarts impishly appeals to demons and angels: "Is it for me, a rabble-rouser, to sing prayers to God?!" (mne l', khuliganke, / molitvy pet'?!; 1963).[34] Shvarts pervasively modeled herself on the itinerant wandering poet, the *nishchii, iurodivyi, kalika perekhozhaia, strannik.* She wrote a memorable long poem describing a procession of holy fools advancing on Kyiv ("Pokhod iurodivykh na Kiev," 1994),[35] and another on the holy fool Ksenia of Petersburg, who wore her dead husband's military greatcoat and insisted that she had become him as she walked the city's streets and uttered her blessings.[36]

I take Shvarts's model in the creation of these fools for Christ to be the poet Anna Barkova, who died in Moscow in 1986 and whom Shvarts likely never met. But she may have known the work. Barkova's poem "The Fool" ("Durochka," published 1922) picks up the simple speech melody of the itinerant poor. She wrote in part:

I sit by myself on the porch, on the porch,
And I try to chime out a song.
In my head a little man is running, twirling,
And a screw is turning, tightening.

Я сижу одна на крылечке, на крылечке,
И стараюсь песенку тинькать.
В голове бегает, кружится человечек
И какой-то поворачивает винтик.[37]

Barkova offered a distinctive and compelling prototype to Elena Shvarts, particularly as Shvarts tried to approach the divine. Barkova was fantastically contradictory, venomous, and likely she showed Shvarts a way to keep a hooligan image without sacrificing her visionary intensity, a way that was entirely different from the high-flown mysticism of the Symbolists, for example, or the piety and stiffness of others. Barkova, who could write poems fashioning herself as a criminal, an incendiary, a rebel who blows up churches, was ever the outsider.[38] Such a self-image is one way for poets to find a visionary impulse after the fall, and it may be the one that allows the strongest preservation of moments of religious doubt. Doubt is all over Shvarts's poetry, but so is faith. As Olga Sedakova has observed, the languages of the Bible and of Orthodox liturgy left strong traces on Barkova, whose early poems of rebellion are couched in an ethos of sin, repentance, the demonic, and the Last Judgment.[39] Shvarts, after major surgery in 2009, left a poem of prayer that recalls Magid's prayer, and it ends in a similar way, expressing gratitude to God for the strength to give thanks and to endure all tribulations.[40] It is a calmer text, written from a place of exhaustion, and it puts into sharp relief how salvation and grace are so hard won in her work. The critic Igor Gulin astutely recognized how the logic of salvation in her work moved across extremes, as if military action and tactical retreat were the way to deal with the challenges of belief. He compared this drama to a Baroque mystery play, played out on the body.[41]

Shvarts was thus also a poet of dramatic impersonations, which catalog many forms of seeing. Her persona poems as well as some of her shorter lyrics show vividly how she could represent not just what was seen—what she would call in her book of prose memoirs *The Visible Side of Life* (*Vidimaia storona zhizni*, 2003)—but also the lure of the invisible. Shvarts is unusual in largely not presenting her readers with some set of objects for contemplation. Her gaze rarely settles anywhere for long. She is rather a poet of dynamism, of changeability, of metamorphosis. She offers up visions of changing entities in the natural world, hence the rapid flowering and decay of "Animal-Flower." She is a scene creator, with the rhythmic pulse of her poetry constantly transforming (one of her metrical signatures, in fact, is a changing rhythmic pattern of lines held together by rhyme). We have now looped back to the place where we began, Shvarts's metamorphoses. One has the sense that she understood that creating poems changes not the world, but the poet herself. I want to end by connecting Shvarts's metamorphoses to her notion of the divine and to her sense of poetry itself.[42]

Here I draw on two poets' comments about her. First, Galina Rymbu. In an insightful short review, she singles out Shvarts for her serious investigations of poetic ecstasy—not old-fashioned inspiration, but a form of energy that could change the body and change the world.[43] To my mind, this energy resembles that of Sergei Magid, and as in his work, transformation is at the heart of the creative process. It was there from her very beginnings: we can find a diary notation from 1966 (Shvarts was seventeen years old), in which a very young poet prays that her poetic words will materialize with implausible intensity and lightness, becoming the flesh of fiery angels to populate the heavens.[44] It is as if the poet presciently knew that she would populate her creative universe with angels, demons, saints, and fools—and that her work, as she says in that same note, might burst open the heart and make the word into the poem's flesh (*plot' stikhotvoren'ia*).

The other poet I want to cite in this context is Alla Gorbunova, who writes that Shvarts was not really of her time, that she was not attuned to the vibrations of the contemporary world but instead was someone who came to her era already completely made, idiosyncratic and wild. And equally from the past and from the future, just not the present.[45] So, while other poets studied here take their cues from the stimulations of the immediate world around them, Shvarts in many ways liberates herself from that reality. She creates a cosmos in which to make her poems, and the creation of that cosmos is the event, in the phenomenological sense, of the texts. Gorbunova, earlier in her essay, finds here what she calls "a phenomenology of creative work." She pins down what that looks like: Shvarts, in her account, demonstrates that poetic inspiration—the impulse that lets the poet make poems—is a transformative event. It transforms the very embodiment of the poet. Gorbunova, like others writing on Shvarts and like the poet herself, resorts to the terms of alchemy to describe this transformation, and it is an appropriate metaphor for several reasons. Shvarts shared with the alchemists a fantasy of transformation that defied natural laws, and that risked competing with the gods she worshipped and communed with. The freedom created by Elena Shvarts and made manifest in her work comes about as close as one can, without crossing the line into blasphemy, to taking on God's power. Which is not to say that Shvarts wouldn't risk blasphemy—it's right there in her work. But its dangers are palpable. It's a reason freedom can be so fully associated with fear in her work: she knew what she was risking.[46]

She was, however, as everyone who knew her would attest, also fearless. A strong image of that fearlessness comes at the end of the long poem "The March of the Fools on Kyiv." Shvarts writes in the first person in the epilogue:

> I was out marking in charcoal
> A storm cloud—*leave me be*
> When I entered a fearful house
> And became a ghost unseen.
>
> But this ghostly me
> Whispered, made the sign of the cross.
> And for a good while
> My pale hand lit the darkness.
>
> My heart at once a stranger
> As if a blade had sliced it out
> In it Christ's own prayer
> Whispering to itself.[47]

> Я шла, чертила угольком
> По туче—что пристала?
> И в страшный заходила дом,
> Невидимою стала.
>
> Но и невидимая я
> Шептала и крестилась,
> И долго в темноте рука,
> Бледнея, всё светилась.
>
> Чужое сердце сразу стало,
> Как будто кто отрезал бритвой,
> И в нем сама себя шептала
> Исусова молитва.[48]

In a house of fear, the poet cloaks herself in invisibility. Shvarts is such a poet of the body that this moment of shedding all visible form is startling, and by the poem's end, it has the effect we might expect from Christian tradition. Denying the flesh enlarges the spirit, and the poet crosses herself and whispers the famous prayer to Jesus, asking as a sinner to be spared.

Invisibility has multiple meanings in this highly visual scene. The poem twice mentions it (in the admirable translation by Sasha Dugdale, there are two references to being ghostly; the Russian repeats "invisible" / "nevidimyi"). But becoming invisible offers the poet no protection. On the contrary, she experiences her heart as if it were someone else's ("chuzhoi") and as if it were cut out with a razor. Invisibility, it turns out, has not gotten rid of the body at all; in fact the pale hand with which she crosses herself seems to illuminate the frightening darkness. Having the heart cut out has the kind of violence Shvarts writes about often, and her great heroine Lavinia is a member of the Order of the Circumcision of the Heart.[49] Readers of Russian poetry cannot but associate this image with what Brodsky used to jokingly call open-heart surgery in Pushkin's poem "The Prophet" ("Prorok," 1826), and while it's possible that Shvarts had in mind Pushkin's source, Isaiah 6:1–3, her transformation of the biblical prophet into the model for a poet's terrifying moment of inspiration is also in conversation with Pushkin's. Shvarts, having created her long poem about the fools' march on Kyiv, retreats as from encroaching storm clouds into a house of terror and of prayer. The epilogue reprises her own transformation into one who could write that poem, a metamorphosis that made possible her every poem.

Sergei Kruglov, Stories of Faith

In turning to Sergei Kruglov, we encounter a figure with a more complex set of public roles than Shvarts's. He is an Orthodox priest, prolific poet, former radio host, and vivid online presence.[50] The number of poets who have commented on his work is striking. Elena Fanailova's remarks from 2008 are characteristic: "This poetry represents Christian life as it is, with no sense of the separateness of a priest from his flock, from the people [narod]. This may be the first fully adequate poetic testimony to that inseparability in contemporary Russia."[51] Grigory Dashevsky pinpointed the distinctive feature of that testimony when he emphasized that the poet never presumes to get at some deeper, experiential inner truth in the people he evokes, preferring instead to have us see them more fully by showing them in the light of the divine.[52]

Kruglov showers that light on his characters by telling their stories, and he has said that stories are what he most values in poetry.[53] The poetics of his writing make him a natural member of what Fyodor Svarovsky called new epic poetry (*novyi epos*), where Boris Khersonsky, our next poet, also belongs. But Kruglov is an allegorist—Dashevsky stressed the allegorical force of his stories—attuned to multiple sources: his poems respond to popular culture, music, politics, and many kinds of poetry. His poems' rich range of vocabularies and images seem able to render all manner of faith, errancy, failure, and love. Kruglov ceased writing poetry for a while, beginning in 1996.[54] He became a priest in 1999, and he resumed writing poems in 2003. He had published more than twenty books by the end of 2022.[55] Some are books of prose, including parables that read like lessons for congregants, but it is a very broad notion of the congregation. Kruglov dissociates himself from what has been called Orthodox poetry, and he has said flatly that literature is not divided by confession.[56] He has allied himself with the view of a poet arguing for islands or archipelagos of spiritual life that draw unto themselves creative energies.[57] His poetry writing, we might say, wanders among those islands, collecting stories. Not for nothing do his poems echo the intonations of the oldest creators of Russian spiritual poetry, the holy fools (*iurodivye*) and wandering beggars (*kaliki perekhozhie*), who from the peripheries of Orthodox practice sought a life in Christ and chanted the *byliny* and spiritual verses that began to be written down and collected in the modern period.[58] For many, these nearly mythic (because usually nameless) individuals and their poetry stand for a kind of authentic religious experience. This tradition is a reason that Shvarts wrote her long poem about a procession of holy fools to Kyiv and created her mad nun Lavinia as a similar outsider within the Orthodox Church.

Kruglov's ways of remixing these genres are especially interesting because of his vocation as a priest. He is drawing these peripheral figures toward the very heart of the church, claiming them as central to its mission. More important, his daily life includes the rituals of prayer and meditation, of consolation and advice to his parishioners.[59] In his poetry, the elevated lexicon of the Holy Scriptures or of liturgy mixes with down-to-earth conversational Russian. He can write poems to and about poets, priests, and mythological figures.[60] Yet his poems also retell the stories of the faithful and the fallen.[61] He has a poem that says that readers are not the same as parishioners, but Kruglov tells stories in his poems that feel as if they are meant to lead us to insight; his stories bring illumination by means of mystery and metaphor.[62] He is mostly a practitioner of free verse and a writer of prose poems and of prose. His poems can spread across several pages to tell stories and parables, and a patient unfolding of sometimes enigmatic detail gives the work a calm, unruffled tonality.

The absence of formal constraint does not prevent the poet from suggesting a disciplined, careful, and deeply self-doubting poetic persona. Self-doubting, but not one to take himself too seriously: Kruglov posed for a calendar of priests with their cats in 2016, and his sense of humor is often apparent in his poems and in the splendid drawings that accompany two of his books of poetry and often appear in his Telegram posts.[63] A love for the world's persons, animals, and objects suffuses his poems, even those whose gaze is trained on unsightly trivialities.[64] And there is a love and respect for the human body, a sense of what one critic called a sense of sacred eroticism if not of "religious materialism."[65] One poem focuses on a can of beer, passed from hand to hand during a time of ritual fasting; it is rejected by the ascetic men, who cast the beer into a trash heap. In the poem's last lines, Christ descends to walk among people and exhort them to prepare a feast, calling wistfully for that very humble can of beer.[66] The poem, "A Can of *Klinskoe*" ("Banochka 'Klinskogo'"), gives voice even to the can of beer, and it is at once a mock sentimental tale of animated detritus and a reminder that, as Shvarts was to say in her poem "A Gray Day" ("Seryi den'"), Christ is an emblem of humility as much as of glory.[67]

A similar change in tone marks a slightly earlier poem, "The Natural Views of Poetry According to Slavs" ("Prirodnye vozzreniia slavian na poeziiu," published 2003). The title playfully reverses the terms of Alexander Afanasyev's huge folklore study *The Poetic Views of Nature According to Slavs* (*Poeticheskie vozzreniia slavian na prirodu*, 1865–69). Kruglov asks whether poetry continues to do the work of transcending nature that Afanasyev saw as the core of myth. His poem is at once playful and tragic, as it was with the can of beer.[68]

The Natural Views of Poetry According to Slavs

Poetic creation is black gloom.
A blind alley, a dead end, a tunnel, a pothole.
An abandoned house, a deserted village,
a thicket on a starless night, an isolated well,
a bag over the head (and bang) a closet of mothballs (and
    witchy-woman,
bogeyman, black hand, it invisibly watches from the darkness).
Only oddballs are susceptible to it,

sick children, frightened children, worthless, blind children,
children whose legs are paralyzed, with congenital heart defects,
children who wet their beds,
children in whose room suddenly the night-light went on,
children who have grown up without a mother,
children cursed by childhood, the sun, light,
air, foliage, water, badminton, running,
laughter—to the gloom.

Nothing visible either before or behind. But someone
compels you to move through the gloom. You have to move
toward a hypothetical forward.
To find some analogy
with the torment, the agony of this impulse
a child will be able, only if it grows up,
lives, if—in the rare case—has children of his own
and—even farther along—grandchildren, and at the age of seventy,
on a sunny July day, sitting in a chair in the garden where
a grandson or granddaughter plays, laughs, catches bugs,
sweaty, they run to drink water, they slip out of your hands,
they run again, sun, light,—the black needle makes a sudden
puncture in the bright bubble,
and all the essence of the old child-poet
suddenly squeezes into hopelessness:
"Lord, my poor little boy! Don't let
him fall into the well, catch him, don't let him go!
Hold him in your hands, stay with him,
sing lullabies to him at night,
abide with him in his heart!"—
and the same thing, it seems, here comes time with the insipid,
    abundant
tears of an old man. But there are no tears, a look
petrifies, blinds him. He sees and doesn't see:
ghosts of whose voices—not familiar ones, not these,
but alien, still you have to move forward, catch the ghosts:
you feel the unevenness of the walls: what's on them?
cracks? doors? niches? epistles in bas-relief?
trifles where a delightful nightmare hides?

but not get there; and the child against his will,
susceptible to a mysterious feeling,
extends a hand in order to reach from top to bottom,
discover at the end of his fingers, grasp, squeeze;
and look as far as he can, blinded from the darkness, in order somehow
to get through in the gloom, to somewhere past the turning of the
    corridor,
and farther, in order to see the unseen road,
He tries to push himself into the gloom. This is
the writing of the text: to overcome the gloom by becoming it.
And nothing white—no butterfly, spectral horse, halftones,
moon, no phosphorescent wind—in the black, damned
river of poetry,
streaming toward an unknown, nonexistent light.[69]

Природные воззрения славян на поэзию

Поэтическое творчество—это черная тьма.
Глухой переулок, тупик, коридор, лаз.
Заброшенный дом, покинутая деревня,
лесная чаща в беззвездную ночь, колодец на окраине,
мешок на голове (и удар); шкаф с нафталином (и бабай, яга, бука,
черная рука, незримо следящее из темноты оно).
Ему подвержены только одинокие,
больные дети, боящиеся дети, неполноценные, слепые дети,
дети с отнявшимися ногами, с врожденным пороком сердца,
дети, мочащиеся в постель во сне,
дети, в комнате которых вдруг погас ночник,
дети, выросшие без матери,
дети, проклятые детством, солнцем, светом,
воздухом, листвой, водой, бадминтоном, бегом,
смехом,—на тьму.

Ничего не видно ни позади, ни впереди. Но кто-то
заставляет тебя двигаться во тьме. Надо двигаться
в гипотетический перёд.
Найти аналогию
мучительности, томительности этого посыла
ребенок сможет, только если вырастет,

выживет, если—в редком случае—заведет своих детей
и—далее—внуков, и в семьдесят лет,
солнечным июльским днем, сидя в кресле в саду,
когда внук или внучка играют, хохочут, ловят жука,
потные, подбегут попить воды, ускользнут от ладони,
снова бегут, солнце, свет,—черная игла делает внезапный
прокол в светлом пузыре,
и все существо старого ребенка-поэта
вдруг сжимается в безысходности:
"Господи, бедный мой, маленький! не дай
ему упасть в колодец, обними его, не отпускай!
положи ему на лоб руку, будь с ним,
спой ему на ночь нестрашную песню,
будь с ним в его сердце!.."—
и самое, вроде бы, время выступить старческим негустым,
обильным слезам. Но слез нет, взгляд
каменеет, становится незряч. Он видит и не видит:
призраки чьих-то голосов—не родных, не тех,
чужих,—но надо идти вперед, ловить призраки;
ты ощупываешь шероховатости стен: что на них?
трещины? двери? ниши? барельефы письмен?
пустоты, где таится сладостный ужас?
не дотянуться; и ребенок поневоле,
движимый неведомым чувством,
удлиняет руку, чтобы дотянуться ею до верха и низа,
нащупать, уцепиться, сжать;
и удлиняет взгляд, ослепший от тьмы, чтобы как-то
протиснуться во тьме, туда, за поворот коридора,
и дальше, чтобы увидеть невидимую дорогу.
Он пытается удлинить себя до тьмы. Это есть
написание текста: победить тьму, самому став ею.
И ничего белого—бабочки, призрачной лошади, полутóна,
луны, фосфорического ветра,—в черной, окаянной реке поэзии,
устремленной к незнаемому, несуществующему свету.[70]

The poem opens in darkness, as if beginning before God brought light into the world. It stays with that darkness for fifty-five lines, hoping that the river of its own poetry can carry the children it describes and all who read the poem toward an unrecognizable and nonexisting light. It is a debased darkness, sending forth a comical urban version of folklore in the images in a mothball-smelling closet.

Yet the darkness spreads a possibility of transcendence, of poetry. Susan Stewart has written about such endless black as mental deprivation, giving the mind "no object to limit the endless racing of its reflections."[71] Kruglov asks who could see in such darkness, and his account of vulnerable, suffering children leads his poem onto terrain familiar from Dostoevsky's fictions; in that urge to represent the sufferers, the abused, the lost, and in the urge to see into the dark, he also resembles Elena Shvarts, a poet for whom darkness never lost its fascinations. But Kruglov's poem insists that the seeing subject *becomes* the darkness, as if taking it into the surface of the body's skin; darkness is known through contact, not just through visual inspection. This is one of those saturated phenomena studied by Jean-Luc Marion in his book *In Excess*.[72] For Kruglov, the possibility of revelation is an experience of sensory and psychic saturation, and I take this as a reason for his poetry's extraordinary emphasis on the senses of sight, sound, and especially touch.

In this poem, what the poet sees in the dark is filled with promise and compassion, with vulnerability rather than anger, with prayer rather than invective. Here is another poem that leads to prayer across a quite different route—through music, which is one of Kruglov's great subterranean themes. He has explained in interviews that his wife is gifted musically and committed to bringing music into their lives, and he conjures up her musical spirit in a lovely poem dedicated to her, "Little Mother and Her Piano" ("Matushka i ee pianino").[73] Here is a shorter lyric, one that brings forth the voice of God from a piano's music:

Piano Keys

And Gershwin goes down them in the summer heat,
And Wagner goes back up in an icy current.
Life has ended but I am still alive.
No, I am not giving Your name to music—
I am calling You up from the sound, only You.

Love and pity will bring back freedom,
Which flies off in laughter, but comes back turned around,
And here—unheard, written over and above,
Your quiet voice, yet to come and indistinct.

Клавиши

И Гершвин опускает в летний зной,
И в ток ледяный Вагнер подымает.
Жизнь кончилась, но я ещё живой.
Нет, не зову я музыку Тобой—
Тебя, Тебя из звука вызываю.

Свободу, улетающую в смех,
Вернут любовь и жалость на попятный,
И здесь—неслышимый, записанный поверх,
Твой тихий голос, чаемый, невнятный.[74]

This nine-line poem conjures up multiple kinds of music, none of it the chanting we would associate with prayer, and decoding these references shows how tightly the poet has woven his themes here. We begin with Gershwin's "Summertime," that great lullaby heard several times in *Porgy and Bess*. The reference to Wagner is perhaps less obvious, most likely the rather obscure opera *Das Liebesverbot*, which contains both a reference to ice (unlike the dominant motif of fire in the Ring cycle) and the themes of love and freedom. The opera is based on Shakespeare's *Measure for Measure*, and thus, unusually for Wagner, has the kind of comic touch that would also explain the laughter in l.5 of Kruglov's poem.[75] There is another suggestion of lullaby in the poem's third line: it rephrases the first line of a 1953 Pasternak poem, "The Wind" ("Veter"), that ends in the hope of finding words to sing a lullaby.[76] That further hint prepares readers for the hushed quiet of the poem's final invocation of the voice of God.

The first two lines of the poem, where Wagner and Gershwin appear, hide a subtle grammatical trick: the verbs ("opuskat'" and "podymat'") are in a form that needs a direct object—they're transitive—but it looks like there is no object in that sentence. But surely the object is the piano keys of the title, so that the melody of Gershwin goes down the keyboard and rises back up toward the treble notes, when Wagner takes over. The noun meaning piano keys ("klavishi") can also denote keys on a typewriter or computer keyboard. Those lines beautifully evoke the image of the poet playing the poem's melodies in its words, setting up the comparison between music and poetic speech that will be likened, and contrasted, to the appeals to God that end both stanzas. The poem is thus formally unlike the loose, free-verse narratives for which Kruglov is better known and was well exemplified in "The

Natural Views of Poetry According to Slavs"—and not just because this poem is short: employing rhyme, the poem is written in iambic pentameter, with one line in hexameter (l.8). The slight unbalancing of line length (the extra iambic foot in l.8) is matched by the extra line in the first stanza, giving it five lines rather than four; the poem also boasts an extra rhyme word ("znoi," "zhivoi," "Toboi"). Attention is called to the extra third word, which refers to God, all the more so by this slightly unbalanced form: the weight of the poem is tipped toward the divine, named in the instrumental case ("Toboi"), and then pulled back in the next line, which shifts to the accusative ("Tebia," twice) to position God as called up by the music and, analogously, by the poem itself.

The second stanza opens with its own grammatical complexities because of the word order. The reversals don't work in English, so my translation has smoothed things out a bit, but the Russian shows us that we first get the direct object of the verb, freedom ("svoboda"), and only then the agent of its return, love and pity. The poet nicely includes the very idea of reversal by describing freedom as coming back in reverse ("na popiatnyi"). A reversal of what? Perhaps of the way that Gershwin and Wagner were moving up and down the keyboard in stanza one: now Wagner descends to the bass notes, and Gershwin rises toward higher treble notes, but what is written over them both is the quiet voice of God, barely heard, and as if still to come ("chaemyi"). That word comes from a higher stylistic register, and this is typical for what Kruglov will do at the lexical level—writing from a position of dailiness and down-to-earth lived experience, but with flickers of liturgical or biblical language that allow all of what is described to be imbued with divine meaning and value.[77]

A last thought on this short poem, on what constitutes its freedom. Here we need to return to the Wagner opera, and to Gershwin's "Summertime" from *Porgy and Bess*, which recounts the love between the title characters amid violence, drugs, and a hurricane. Wagner's opera is also a tale of love, comic in its overtones, with familiar Shakespearean disguises, prohibitions, and, in the end, liberation. Kruglov's poem ends in God's love, in effect, heard faintly and as if from on high, a transformation of the moment in the Bible when God says to the disciples, "This is my Son, whom I love. Listen to him" (Mark 9:7). There are of course many other references to love in both the Old and New Testament, but I hear this one because the poem suggests an act of listening into music, to hear its "yet to come and indistinct" instructions. Kruglov's poetry radiates forms of love, to be shared with generosity and forgiveness. We are called to love, and thus called to shun the divisiveness or hidden prejudices that might cast some kinds of love above others, or label them as permissible or forbidden.

This poem thus shows us, in terms of its imagery and grammar, what that love looks like on the page. Its recourse far outside the traditions of Russian Orthodoxy, toward the American Gershwin and the German Wagner, is not unusual for Kruglov. Elsewhere, he is open to what he calls the "syncopated faith" of Americans.[78] Kruglov also has dozens of poems that draw on Jewish wisdom, prophets, and traditions, including his cycle of poems about Nathan. Particularly striking is "Nathan and the Election of the Ruler" ("Natan i vybory pravitelia," 2008), with its interwoven extremes of theological and profane self-definition.[79]

In this long free-verse poem, people of different faiths contemplate their choices in an age of corrupt elections, which is to say our age. Each group—Orthodox, Buddhists, Seventh-Day Adventists, Muslims, and four last observant Jews—prays for a ruler of their own faith. The poem calls this a "battle of prayers" (bitva molitv). Father Nathan, though, is without prayer, feeling so sickly that he does not make the sign of the cross over his cup of tea. God is grateful that Nathan alone has not importuned Him, and the sympathy expressed toward Nathan is contrasted to the impatience toward a priest who is not supposed to be ill or to sin. The poem in turn sympathizes with God, burdened by the demands and confusions of these people, "real people" (Eto ved' real'nye liudi).[80]

> Thus He sits above Russia
> Holding His indescribable head in his hands,
> Looking straight ahead with a worn-out gaze.[81]

> Так и сидит над Россией,
> Подперев невыразимую голову руками,
> Смотрит перед собой измученным взором.[82]

Kruglov gives us a God who is exhausted and frustrated, transferring to the Lord a set of human qualities that his compassionate poems show toward the people he describes. It is the diversity of demands that wears out God, and perhaps that has worn out and sickened Father Nathan. We will come back to him in a moment, because the poet to whom I turn, Boris Khersonsky, has written some poems of his own about Father Nathan.

Boris Khersonsky: Between Orthodoxy and Judaism

With the explosion of war in Ukraine in 2022, Boris Khersonsky, long prolific and respected, has gained an even wider and more international audience. He is a Russian-language poet also able to work in Ukrainian and a strong supporter of Ukrainian sovereignty.[83] He has identified himself as a Ukrainian poet, an identity that is doubly important in the ongoing war. Increasingly, his work is available in multiple other languages, and a volume of translations into English by Ilya Kaminsky and Katie Farris, *A Country Where Everyone's Name Is Fear* (2022), is but one example.[84]

Khersonsky had been writing poems and working as a psychiatrist in Odesa for many years, and he had another advent of fame earlier, when he published *Family Archive* (*Semeinyi arkhiv*, 2006). He sustained that new readership with an extraordinarily prolific publication record, developing the themes and techniques of *Family Archive* and of his earlier books, which he ironically noted in the first section of his 2008 book *Square Under Construction* (*Ploshchad' pod zastroiku*), entitled "Still the Same Thing, the Same Way" ("Vse o tom zhe, vse tak zhe").[85] Khersonsky is adept at using a range of traditional religious forms, including psalms, Hasidic parables, the animal fables of the *Physiologus*, and prayers both Hebrew and Christian.[86] His formal range is considerable, from free verse and rhymed quatrains to deft incorporation of anaphora and rhythmic devices familiar from the Bible. He has written dozens of eight-line poems, a form I have treated in more detail in chapter 3; Khersonsky has even created wreathes of these eight-line poems, modeled after sonnet wreaths, in which a last line becomes the start of the next poem, and a final poem is made of all the repeating lines.[87]

One can see immediately why *Family Archive* brought such success: it is a mesmerizing cultural history of the Jews in and beyond Odesa. It evokes family photographs through its ekphrastic descriptions, and describes books, photographs, and Judaica artifacts left after the diaspora; there are poems that seek news of missing relatives, recount narrow escapes, and dream of release. Parents worry over children getting a secular education far from their family's safe embrace, and victims of marital betrayal turn to rabbis for enigmatic advice. The poet unfolds one story after another, bending the Russian language to accommodate Yiddish names, Hebrew prayers, and the diminished dreams and terrible losses of a people struggling to survive waves of violence and urgent escape.

Khersonsky's book is not the first to tell such stories, and one inevitably hears echoes of Isaac Babel's tales from earlier in the twentieth century. But there is little of the relief provided by Babel's extravagant metaphors or his exaggerated comic touches, and the characters are created with a more loving, generous touch. Arguably, Khersonsky paints a portrait of Jewish life that is from within its experience, even more so than is the case with Babel.[88] But he keeps to an unusually matter-of-fact tone, resisting sentimentalism or sensationalism. He anchors the stories in the objects that survive their owners, and he gives these objects a kind of strange unconscious by his use of dreams and fantasies. Webs of history are spun by place names and dates in some of the poem titles: Odesa, July 1954; Bessarabia, 1935; Brooklyn, 1994. People disperse along the familiar pathways of twentieth-century diaspora, and the recurring place names and first names juxtapose public history against the intimate revelations of family secrets.

The book punctuates these stories with five prayers, all given in italics. Most striking is Khersonsky's version of the Shehecheyanu prayer, the traditional Jewish praise of God for keeping us alive and allowing us to celebrate a happy event:

A PRAYER

Blessed art Thou, O Lord
Our God, Ruler of the Universe,
Who has kept us and protected us,
and sustained us to this day
a day it would be better we had never seen.

You have taken nothing from us:
neither despair nor dejection,
nor monotonous, dull hope.

You are ever the same, You who are One,
and we, the few, are also as we were.[89]

МОЛИТВА

Благословен Ты, Господь,
Бог наш, Царь Вселенной,
защищавший нас, поддержавший нас
и сохранивший нас до сего дня,—
лучше б нам не видеть его.

Ты ничего не отнял у нас:
ни уныния, ни отчаяния,
ни монотонной, тусклой надежды.

Ты все тот же, Единый.
И мы, немногие—те же.[90]

The first four lines reprise the familiar and beloved prayer, but the fifth line bespeaks a darker sentiment: the day one has lived to see is a source of pain and grief. Rather than expressing gratitude for God's generosity, the prayer bespeaks despair. For the gift of living to celebrate a *simcha*, Khersonsky substitutes the horror of living long enough to lose what one loves.

The book's final prayer and its final poem is similarly bleak:

A PRAYER

And Thou art faithful to Thy promise
to return the deceased to life.
Blessed art Thou, o Lord
our God, Ruler of the Universe,
who raises the dead.

(If only in our fragile memory.
If only now and then.)

МОЛИТВА

И верен Ты своему обещанию
вернуть к жизни усопших.
Благословен Ты, Господь,
Бог наш, Царь Вселенной,
воскрешающий мертвых.

(Хотя бы в непрочной памяти нашей.
Хоть изредка.)[91]

Khersonsky's God keeps faith with His people Israel, but their memories are weakening beneath His gaze. This is its own sort of fall, a fall from belief as tragic as it is understandable.[92]

These lost memories are allegorized in the book as the possessions of those who have perished. *Family Archive* offers recurring poems about auctions of Judaica, where a Torah crown, a mezuzah, a menorah, and other ritual objects are sold off one after another. Khersonsky emphasizes the spiritual value of these auction lots, for they are not just objects with monetary value. He thus begins one of the auction poems with the first words of another prayer, the

Sh'ma. For this prayer, he does not translate the familiar Hebrew words into Russian (as he did with the Shehecheyanu prayer), so there is not the same estranging effect of that linguistic substitution, but he disrupts the prayer in a different way, substituting a name of God, the familiar Hashem, for the holier name traditional to the prayer, Adonoi. The poem's narrative commences with words from the prayer that follows the Sh'ma in the daily service, and here too there is a disruption, where words are to be written not just on the gates of one's home, as the prayer has it, but on the Jewish body, as ordered by the Nazis. More vicious stereotypes follow, creating the narrative that motivates the crisis where this lot of Judaica is assembled for sale.

JUDAICA AUCTION

Lot 6: Mezuzah, Silver, Niello. Early twentieth century. Galicia

Sh'ma, Yisroel, Hashem Eloheinu. These words
shall be written everywhere. Upon the doorposts of your house
(upon your forehead, adds the Nazi). Capital
is the only God of the Jews,
asserted Mordechai, once he had turned into Karl
and swept across a third of the globe by means of
his beard, like a broom. For a long time thereafter
we had to comb out those fibers. There is another variant,
the one God of the Jews is life—*chaim*
("Hey, Hymie, begone!")—life, despite it all,
despite the nothingness: for the gates of Jewish cemeteries
are adorned with the inscription "Bet Chaim"—
that is, the "Dwelling Place of Life." Who else
could come up with such a thing? Witty,
don't you think? Actually, the One God
of the Jews is darkness and light,
and the One who divided them, and all
that happened then in the breach between white and black,
including the lines of black written on white
calf hide, on the smallest piece of it,
the prayer for mercy, rolled up like a snail
in its casket shell (Sh'ma Yisroel)
of blackened silver. In fact, it's this very object
that is exhibited for sale, most likely empty of its contents.

This is an auction of Judaica, nothing more, an auction of
Judaica. Do you hear the groaning
souls brought back to their dwellings now reduced to dust,
finding the loss of everything,
everything, even of themselves,
feeling their way, for there is only one
thing that cannot be known by touch—
the cross, on which You are crucified.

АУКЦИОН ИУДАИКИ

Лот 6. Мезуза. Серебро, чернь. Начало XX века. Галиция

Шма, Ишроэль, Хашем элехейну. Эти слова
нужно писать всюду. На косяке дверном
(на лбу—прибавит нацист). Капитал—
единственный Бог евреев,
утверждал Мардохей, обернувшийся Карлом
и прошедшийся своей бородой, что метлой,
по трети земного шара. Долго ж потом пришлось
вычесывать эту кудель. Есть иной вариант,
Единый Бог евреев—это жизнь, хаим
("Эй, Хаим, пошел!"), жизнь—несмотря ни на что,
ни на ничто, поскольку врата еврейских кладбищ
бывают украшены надписью "Бет-Хаим"—
то есть "Обиталище жизни." Ну кто же еще
может придумать такое,—забавно,
не правда ли? Впрочем, Единый Бог
евреев, наверное, это свет и мрак,
и Тот, кто их разделил, и все, что потом
случилось в разломе, между белым и черным,
в том числе и строки черным по белому
на небольшом кусочке телячьей кожи,
молитва-улитва, улиткой свернувшись
в раковину-футляр (шма, Ишроэль)
из черненого серебра. Собственно, именно он,
вероятно, пустой внутри, выставлен на продажу.
Это—аукцион иудаики, просто аукцион
иудаики. Слышишь стон

душ, вернувшихся на пепелище-жилище,

обнаружив пропажу всего,

в том числе и самих себя,

на ощупь, ведь есть только одна

вещь, недоступная осязанию—

крест, на котором Тебя распинают.[93]

Khersonsky here puns on the Hebrew word *chai* (life), the same syllable heard in the name Hyman (in turn, the source of a derogatory term for a Jew, "Hymie"). That name castigates and sends away the Jew, and then *chai* is heard as "Bet Chaim," the cemetery, and thus the house where the dead live on. Bet Chaim, the house of the living, is a common euphemistic name for cemeteries, and Khersonsky literalizes it to ask: What lives on when we are dead? One answer is ritual objects, but of what kind?[94]

In answering, the poem does something unusual. By its last lines, it trades Judaica for the supreme symbol of Christianity, the crucifix, but it is a different kind of object, one that cannot be known by touch. In one sense, the transformation is motivated by biography: a converted Orthodox Christian, Khersonsky turns the poet's gaze at the objects and stories of the Jews toward the enigmas of a suffering Christ. It is as if he proclaims not the Sh'ma—Hear, O Israel, God is one—but the miracle of Jesus's passion. It is a move toward Christian redemption and toward hope. The crucifix image takes the suffering of *Family Archive* to its logical extreme. In a sense, Khersonsky is asking: what is the point beyond which Jewish theology can no longer redeem suffering? Where does the belief system of Judaism yield to the possibility for grace afforded by Christianity?

Khersonsky's template of Judaism is the Old Testament, the foundation on which he builds the stories of a new set of truths about God from the perspective of Orthodoxy.[95] In his vast body of work, there are countless examples of poems based on Christian texts, rituals, and beliefs: the 2009 book *Spirituals* (*Spirichuels*) includes a large group of "Meditations," a series called "The Icon Shop" ("Ikonnaia lavka"), and another called "Holy Week" ("Strastnaia sedmitsa"). A great many poems have an exalted, hopeful intonation, and they lead away from error or failure toward salvation or resurrection. But the book *Spirituals* also has many poems about the world of Jewish life, lore, and liturgy, as do his other books. A distinctive feature of Khersonsky's work is free movement between the traditions of Orthodoxy and Judaism, in effect between the worlds of the New Testament and the Old.[96]

One of Judaism's reappearances will be my last example from his work, and here I return to the work of Sergei Kruglov, and to Father Nathan. In 2012, Khersonsky and Sergei Kruglov published a book together, one that is filled with heresies uttered by believers.[97] Each had written a cycle of poems featuring an invented hero. Khersonsky wrote of an aging priest, the Archbishop Gury; Kruglov's hero, as we know, is Nathan (Russian Natan), a convert to Orthodoxy who becomes a priest.[98] For this book, which includes those two cycles, Khersonsky and Kruglov also wrote poems about the other poet's hero, which were presented as poems written by that hero.[99] Kruglov wrote texts purporting to be by Archbishop Gury, Khersonsky doing the same with Nathan. This is like what Shvarts does in her persona poems, where she inhabits the imagination of another (writing, for instance, as if Cynthia, the beloved of Sextus Propertius).[100] But hers is a one-way move toward a distant and entirely unknowable figure. Khersonsky and Kruglov actively trade heroes who are like their contemporaries: Khersonsky writes as Nathan, ministering to congregants who despise the Jews, and Kruglov writes as Gury, lost in his own world. It is a book in which heroes misunderstand the world around them, but it is written by two poets whose capacity for the empathic embrace of the other is foundational to their ethical project.

Nathan is a convert from Judaism to Orthodoxy, which drenches the anti-Semitism of his congregants with irony, so that it will not be impersonal, not some historical truth that floats over individual lives and hurts. It is harder to assess what it means for this poetry that there remains some imprint of Khersonsky's own decision to convert.[101] But we do know that his conversion to Orthodoxy exists alongside a continuing allegiance to Judaism as historical experience and as religious practice. Kruglov's biography was also marked by conversion of a sort, from atheist to believer: he declared himself a member of the Orthodox faith in 1996, in advance of his entering the clergy in 1999. Kruglov's Orthodoxy also exists alongside a fascination with Judaism. His book *The Sabbath Queen* (*Tsaritsa Subbota*, 2016) collects his poems on Jewish themes. Its opening poem is dedicated to Khersonsky, and it is tempting to think about these two poets joined principally by their doubled allegiances toward Judaism and Orthodoxy, hardly the norm for Russian history.[102]

A swerve toward Judaism defines the last poem that Khersonsky wrote for Father Nathan. It supplies Father Nathan with eloquent words for Rosh Hashanah, asking God to inscribe him in the Book of Life for the coming year:

write me down in the book of life write
with a quill of fire from the cherub's wing
in the massive book bound at the seams
with cedar wood with stretched leather
with forged buckle closures in reddish bronze
write me down in the book of life write
in the book that is as heavy as life itself
which cannot be raised cannot be understood
on the page which cannot be turned
covered marks like a gradebook's grid
graduated to the next class
the next year
the next time
achievements attendance conduct
good for nothing unlikely to improve
have to call in the parents
the great grandparents
back to the seventh or eighth generation

write me down in the book's page
in drops of wax blood ink sperm
without which there is no life

a black angel flies with a shofar
flies and blows the horn in flight
I feel no fear truly I do not
write me down in the book of life
close the leather binding
snap the bronze fastenings
no matter I won't hear a thing

запиши меня в книгу жизни запиши
огненным пером из крыла керуба
в огромную книгу взятую в переплёт
из кедровых досок обтянутых кожей
с коваными застёжками из красной меди
запиши меня в книгу жизни запиши
в книгу тяжёлую как сама жизнь
которую не поднять не понять

на страницу которую не перевернуть
всю в пометках как школьный журнал
переведён в следующий класс
в следующий год
в следующий раз
успеваемость посещаемость поведение
никуда не годилось вряд ли исправится
нужно вызвать родителей
прародителей
до седьмого-восьмого колена

запиши меня в книгу страницы
в каплях воска крови чернил спермы
без чего не бывает жизни

чёрный ангел летит с шофаром
летит и трубит в полёте
мне не страшно честное слово
запиши меня в книгу жизни
захлопни кожаный переплёт
щёлкни бронзовыми застёжками
я всё равно не услышу[103]

This is as close as a Jew comes to the dream of confession and redemption, a theological practice at the center of Christianity. Jews are people of the book, and Jewish lore gives Khersonsky endless opportunity to recast the wisdom of the commentary, the beauty of Torah script, the arguments of the rabbis. But here, for Nathan, the only book is God's book, God's register of who shall live and who shall die. When the book slams shut, Nathan is left muttering his imprecations. Khersonsky's Nathan speaks uselessly and listens poorly, while Kruglov's Nathan, as we saw in his poem about the election, is at best absent-minded.

Both poets can put great moments of faith and celebration into their poetry. As they look out into the world, Khersonsky (until February 2022) in Odesa, Kruglov back in Minusinsk (in the Krasnoiarsk region), after having lived for several years in Moscow, what resonates are the stories of vision that at their best teach empathy and compassion. I now turn to a poet whose vision has no less compassion or empathy, and one with a keen sense of the political meanings of the fall after which all these poets write.

Olga Sedakova: Steps toward Freedom

Just as Khersonsky and Kruglov's connection helps us understand each of them better, so we should think initially about Elena Shvarts and Olga Seda-kova together. They had a complicated but enduring friendship.[104] They first stood out as two premier women poets in late Soviet unofficial poetry and as poets who could take up themes of faith and belief. One in Petersburg, the other in Moscow, they were inevitably compared. As with all such pairs, the differences are as striking as the similarities. The profusion of poems, images, colors, objects, and geographic spaces in Shvarts finds something of their op-posite in the restraint and control of Sedakova's work. Shvarts's poetic oeuvre might be described by the translated title of one of her volumes of poetry, *Wild Writing of the Recent Past* (*Dikopis' poslednego vremeni*, 2001), whereas Olga Sedakova tends toward less extravagant yet emotionally expressive book titles, like *Music* (*Muzyka*, 2006), *Chinese Journey* (*Kitaiskoe puteshestvie*, first pub-lished 1990), or *The Universe's Garden* (*Sad mirozdaniia*, 2014). Shvarts was idiosyncratically educated, fantastically imaginative, and not the most disci-plined thinker; Sedakova is a philologist in the etymological sense of that word, a translator drawing ably on many languages, and a trained scholar. She compiled a dictionary of Old Church Slavonic words whose meanings are different in current usage.[105] She has written dozens of essays on theological, literary, philosophical, and cultural topics; a book on the burial rituals of ancient Slavs; and extensive studies of Orthodox liturgy.[106] She was active in the international commemorations of the eight hundredth anniversary of the death of Dante in 2021, and long taught a seminar on Dante in Moscow.[107] She is unafraid of dense thought or abstract images, and she has also been unafraid to express her political views, including unflinching condemnation of Russia's invasion of Ukraine.[108] As of this writing, she lives in Moscow, so those con-demnations are not without risk.

Perhaps because of the ways in which she is a philosophical poet, some-thing about which Benjamin Paloff has written well, the interface between faith and freedom has a particularly expressive dynamic in her work.[109] The freedom that comes into her poetry is inner freedom, and it has the power to liberate its creators.[110] When her poems speak of freedom directly, it is usually in longer poems and in dreams, legends, and tales (*skazki*).[111] There are beau-tiful fantasies of mountainous landscapes, of monastic gardens, of journeys down Chinese rivers, and of embroidered textures or found treasures that de-light the eye. The poet who speaks in the lyrics interacts with abstractions as easily as with the objects of the natural world. And there are angels and saints, the prodigal son and King David the psalmist, dreamers and idlers forming a rich tapestry of poetic creation. Many poems, especially poems from the 1980s, are warm expressions of praise and celebration.[112]

A signature poem is again an apt way in to understanding Sedakova's poetics of the spirit. "The Wild Rose" ("Dikii shipovnik"), the first poem in the volume by that name (dated 1976–78, but not published in full until 2001), fits the bill nicely. But it has been fully explicated in a fascinating conversation among Robert Reid, the late Valentina Polukhina, and the poet herself when Sedakova was poet in residence at Keele University in the 1990s.[113] And the philosopher Vladimir Bibikhin has explicated the poem's metaphysical underpinnings.[114] So I begin instead with two poems from Sedakova's largest cycle, "Old Songs" ("Starye pesni," 1980–81). This cycle was created before the end of the USSR, showing yet again the continuities between unofficial poetry and post-Soviet creativity. Sedakova speaks of it as a favorite cycle, reciting it often.[115] It has an afterlife, too: "Old Songs" was first published in 1990, and the poet added three poems in 1991–92, demonstrating that the form continued to be productive for her.

It is, as I said, a large cycle, thirty-nine poems divided into three notebooks. The choice of "notebook" (*tetrad'*) to name the three groups is telling. A simple word, it suggests notetaking, a way to take dictation from the muse or, given the associations of this cycle with folk poetry, writing down the recitations of an oral performer as if in an ethnographer's notebook.[116] The word *tetrad'* also conjures up a child's pad of paper for schoolwork and thus the whole world of childhood. And "Old Songs," like Sedakova's ars poetica essay "In Praise of Poetry" ("Pokhvala poezii"), is bound up with the world of childhood.[117] Sedakova has explained that "Old Songs" is based on the folk poems recited to her by her grandmother, Daria Sedakova; the second notebook is dedicated to her, and the third to her memory. So, there is an echo behind the poems of a child encountering the world of folk poetry and encountering biblical stories and spiritual verses (*dukhovnye stikhi*). Several poems preserve elements of direct speech, something like how the muse would offer words of inspiration that have only one hearer, but the source here feels like an entity as biblical as it is mythological, and intimately familiar. In one of the old songs entitled "Childhood" ("Detstvo"), for instance, the closing lines include the poet's name: "Don't forget me, Olga" (Ty ne zabud' menia, Ol'ga).[118] All the poems in "Old Songs," even those with embedded allusions to literary and theological sources, preserve that quality of having been heard, and Sedakova has said that she likes to read them because "they are for the ear and for the sound."[119] So we need to listen into the simplicity of these poems, attending to their diction and to the rhythms of their lines, and to the movement within the poems between the poles of constraint and freedom. We should also listen for the poems' deft probing at the fundamental question of how mortal humans experience themselves in a divinely ordered universe. The poems in "Old Songs" are particularly vivid examples of how Sedakova can peel open an evocation of something tiny to reveal an apperception of a whole cosmos. (This is a capacity that her poems share with those of Elena Shvarts, a rare point of intersection in their poetics.)

"The Word" ("Slovo") concludes the first notebook in "Old Songs." In this poem, the word retains a feeling of mystery, but it is not obscure or abstruse. By the time we get to the third stanza, where the word is addressed directly, it feels like the word first uttered in the beginning of creation. The poem brings that word into contemporary use, displaying like fine apparel its immense powers of liberation and elevation.

The Word

He who loves will be loved in return.
He who serves shall be served—
if not now, then another time, later.

But the best reward comes of gratitude,
he shall walk forth, his work finished, and without Rachel
feel joyful, climbing green hills.

You, word, are the robes of Kings,
a dress of patience, both long and short,
more lofty than the sky, more joyous than the sun.

Our eyes will not see
your color—a color near to us, and dear,
no human ears shall hear the noise
of your swishing, broad pleats,

only the heart itself will say to itself:
"You are free, and you shall be free,
and you shall not answer to slaves."[120]

Слово

И кто любит, того полюбят.
Кто служит, тому послужат—
не теперь, так когда-нибудь после.

Но лучше тому, кто благодарен,
кто пойдет, послужив, без Рахили
веселый, по холмам зеленым.

Ты же, слово, царская одежда,
долгого, короткого терпенья платье,
выше неба, веселее солнца.

Наши глаза не увидят
цвета твоего родного,
шума складок твоих широких
не услышат уши человека,

только сердце само себе скажет:
—Вы свободны, и будете свободны,
и перед рабами не в ответе.[121]

The poem is in free verse, as are all but one poem in "Old Songs," a very rare choice for verse cycles.[122] Notice what Sedakova does with that formal freedom, shaping it into a compact and highly structured poem, using simple words but with syntactic parallelism and verbal repetition, suggesting an intonational resonance of folk religion. The poem also feels almost conversational, and ends with an act of speech, its culminating and defining gesture.

Before we get to those important final lines, consider the comparison of the word to a set of regal robes. It is a metaphor clothed like the apparel it mentions, wrapped in another rhetorical figure, apostrophe: the word is addressed directly, animated and treated as if it were a person, able to be dressed in these robes.[123] The Russian word for those robes, a quite ordinary word, *odezhda*, has another usage, as the fabric drapery that would cover an altar or a throne.[124] And Sedakova, with her deep knowledge of Russian semantics, echoes that alternative meaning to elevate this metaphor. In the fourth stanza, the poem evokes a person bearing this clothing, with its broad pleats, its swishing sounds. But there is something of a mismatch between the faculties of human persons and this glorious word. Its colors cannot be made out by human eyes; its swirling skirts cannot be heard with the ears. And in the third stanza, the word seems to come not from the surface of the earth, where mortals live, but from the realm of sky and sun, to whose heights and brightness the word is favorably compared. The rhetorical turns here leave undecidable whether the word is a human word—human because apostrophe always animates, because the clothing suggests a person—or a word emanating from the hills, sun, and sky, and thus from the cosmos, if not from a divine source.

This poem's figuration of the word, then, has a layered ambiguity, and it is left to the ending to reassemble the pieces of the poem's logic in a new way. In that brief final stanza, two things happen: first, the sentence that constitutes the previous stanza is finished. The sensory capacities of eye and ear had been doubted, as they found themselves in the presence of an object they could not fathom on their own. The final stanza adds a third faculty, that of speech, but it is a speech spoken by the heart. A very long digression could open here about the many ways in which the heart has been a figure or a substitute for the soul in the literary tradition, and a full explication of this history as it is felt in the Russian tradition would properly take us back to Elena Shvarts, whose Lavinia is a nun in the Order of the Circumcision of the Heart.[125] In Sedakova's poems, the image of the heart has manifold meanings, starting with the poem "The Wild Rose," which compares the rose in its first line to a "heart of suffering" (serdtse stradaniia) and ends with a wound hidden under the shirt that is surely a wound to the heart.[126] The heart appears as an image across her work, and it is often a kind of essence of being, connected to the soul—and not, as she has pointed out, in opposition to reason or the mind, as is conventional in some Romantic thinking.[127] Thus when the heart speaks at the end of "The Word," the speech is coming from an organ or faculty of authenticity and power. It is not God who speaks, but it is as if God has inspired the human body toward a kind of speech associated with divine truths.

One more thing to note: the heart speaks to itself. That reflexive formulation, "the heart itself will say to itself" (serdtse samo sebe skazhet), is one we find all over Sedakova's poetry.[128] It's the same structure in the great line that repeats in Sedakova's "Fifth Stanzas: De Arte Poetica" ("Piatye stansy: De Arte Poetica"): "A great thing is its own refuge" (Bol'shaia veshch' sama sebe priiut).[129] Here, in "The Word," Sedakova builds two grammatical layers, relying on two different rhetorical gestures: emphasis (the heart itself) and reflexivity (says to itself). English gives us no choice but to repeat "itself" in both these parts of the speech act, but Russian has two different pronouns available, sam and sebia (and we could note as well that the result is a powerfully alliterative line, four words beginning with s as if the very sounds create a feedback loop).

The grammar lets the speech act performed by the heart travel right back to the heart as its addressee, and the grammar also emphasizes that it is the heart, and not some other organ or faculty, that speaks and hears.

What is said is therefore presented to us in a way that emphasizes its source and its importance. It is a short statement, an epigrammatic prediction that has the force of a command. The statement is about freedom, and it has its own circular structure because the word of the free is not to be uttered to one who does not know what freedom means. The two lines read, "You are free, and you shall be free, / and you shall not answer to slaves." I take this pronouncement to mean that the word, itself a form of freedom, is reserved for uses that amplify its freedom—it is not for self-justifications before those who cannot know what freedom means. In Sedakova's usage, slavery is not the historical sin of holding persons in bondage, about which she would surely reflect in horror and revulsion, but an existential state of living without one's autonomy, of living consumed by fear.[130] To be free is to be free from that all-consuming fear.[131] Freedom thus relieves the word of obligations before those who eye it with suspicion or envy, those who cannot know God's love.

This is not, however, a kind of closed circuit, where speech never breaches the borders of those who already know what is to be said. Sedakova opens out that closed circle again by her figuration. The metaphor of the regal garments is distinctively of something outside the self. If the word is those robes, then it exists in the material world, outside of sensory perceptions of it. Sedakova creates a structure where the word has standing in both an external world—a world where there is clothing, sky, sun—and an interior world of the senses, where the capacities but also limits of eyes, ears and heart are measured. That engagement with an external world, a form of spiritual engagement, leads her to animate the world as she describes it, and leads to her remarkable habit of creating objects in a landscape—garden, tree, rain, rose, mountain—as if they were also dispersed elements of a self.[132] Just as she maintains shimmering ambiguities of meaning in her use of rhetorical figures, so Sedakova, as vibrantly as she creates that external world, also connects it at multiple points with the inner realities of the spirit and of subjectivity. The structure of representation in her poetry keeps shifting along the lines of this parallel between internal and external worlds. I am reminded of a sentence from a study of Plotinus that feels as if it could be written by Sedakova herself: "Although the spiritual world is within us, it is also outside us."[133]

That belief in the spiritual meanings to be uncovered in a seemingly material environment animates a second poem from "Old Songs." It comes in an addendum after the third notebook and gives the cycle its final word. The poem shows how Sedakova, even in her characteristic restraint, opens out moments of vision.

> The cold of the world—
> someone will warm.
>
> The deadened heart—
> someone will lift.
>
> These little monsters—
> someone will take them by the hand,
> like a naughty child, and say:
>
> "Come, I will show you something
> that you have never seen!"[134]

> Холод мира
> кто-нибудь согреет.
>
> Мертвое сердце
> кто-нибудь поднимет.
>
> Этих чудищ
> кто-нибудь возьмет за руку,
> как ошалевшего ребенка:
>
> —Пойдем, я покажу тебе такое,
> чего ты никогда не видел![135]

There is enormous confidence in that promise that someone ("kto-nibud'") will warm the cold world, will lift the sinking heart. The confidence is so great that the person need not be named, just invoked three times as in a folktale's magic charm. This could be a loved and trusted person, like the grandmother in whom so much of this cycle is wrapped up, and it could of course be God.

It is not unusual for Sedakova to create, as she does here, a sense of the divine universe without any direct reference to God, indeed, to create an intensely personal sense of that world by means of nothing more than pronouns and points of contact between persons—heart, hands.[136] The heart, as in our first poem, is an emblem of personhood at its most essential, here deadened to the world but able to be raised back up. This is a poem whose warmth radiates, believing that the sense of touch is an enduring source of wonder. We are again called to imagine ourselves as children in this universe, enchanted by its wonders. These are not the suffering children lying in the darkness of Kruglov's poem. Instead, we receive a promise of a vision, a vision of something never seen. It is an ending very much like that found in a later poem, "The Angel of Reims" ("Angel Reimsa"), a question radiant with the light of its own answer: "are you / ready / for unbelievable joy?" (ty / gotov / k neveroiatnomu schast'iu?).[137] The question is asked by the cathedral's famous angel, who acknowledges speaking to a world of hunger, fear, and fiery destruction, and whose own body, in the form of a statue, was damaged in a war. But the angel, like the voice that promises unimaginable vision in "The cold of the world," knows that the invitation to joy is falling on ears primed to hear it, for these are words not spoken to just anyone, but to you ("ved' ia govoriu ne komu-nibud', / a tebe").

The references to war and to suffering in "The Angel of Reims" are like the coldness and deadness in "The cold of the world," for the world can shower on its inhabitants both riches and deprivations. The loveliness of this poem, as in "The Angel of Reims," is its final speech act, a promise of renewal. That surprise, as Eve Sedgwick wrote in a very different context (the writings of Proust), is the "mark of reality," where reality is "what surrounds the subject, the weather of the world."[138] Sedakova's poem invokes that weather in its move from a chilling air temperature to promised warmth.

The beautiful intonations of Sedakova's poetry convey an unwavering belief that images of fullness and perfection can yet be brought into the world, even a world of suffering and pain. We should not underestimate how hard won is that hope, given Sedakova's extensive writings about ethical issues and her readiness to answer directly questions about good and evil, particularly in interviews since the 2010s.[139] She has made countless statements that spell out what is imaged in the poems as cold or harm or lack of sustenance. We may use the essays and interviews to fill in the picture of the poetry; essays, including extensive work in liturgical and poetic commentary, are at the center of Sedakova's writings now.[140] Her creative work has shifted decisively toward prose and toward translation over the last two decades. The rare poems written after the 1990s—we have just glimpsed one of them, "The Angel of Reims"—thus draw special attention, and each has the sense of a poem finely wrought in some newly found material. Most are printed centered on the page, rather than left justified. I take this change in layout as a way to draw our attention to balance in visual as well as verbal terms.

Here is an example, a poem dedicated to Pope John Paul II. Sedakova has written often of her admiration for Pope John Paul II, an admiration born from his connections to the Slavic world (he was known and loved as "the Polish Pope"), and from his having been, in her words, a poet, a theologian, and a philosopher.[141] She met him four times, beginning in 1995. In dedicating poems to him, or writing about him in any way, Sedakova was mindful of his teachings, particularly his hope to bridge gaps between Orthodoxy and Catholicism, and of his personal traits of humility, curiosity, learnedness, and openness.

I turn, then, to "Rain" ("Dozhd," published by 2001), more briefly than was the case with the fuller explication of "The cold of the world." The first of the three poems to the pope, "Rain" aims to speak for itself. Its lines are consoling, the rain falling calmly with all the tenderness of the snow that ends James Joyce's story "The Dead," for this rain, too, falls over all the living and all the dead. But that gentle intonation that is nearly pervasive in Sedakova's poetry is wrapped around an indictment, which is much more the tone found in her essays (collected in a volume named *Moralia*)—an indictment of changed times, and of superficial changes in those who encroach on the world of faith but cannot fathom its actual values. The way these lines are centered on the page can be read as an inscription of the poet's balancing act between faith in God and those who fail to fathom His teachings. And there is a further delicate balance in the poem between its very short lines and sweep of syntax that joins each stanza in a single complex thought.

RAIN

"It is raining,
and they say there's no God!"
so said an old woman from our village,
Nanny Varya.

The people who said there is no God
now light candles,
order special services,
are wary of people of other faiths.

Nanny Varya is lying in the graveyard,
and the rain comes down,
a magnificent, abundant, boundless rain,
comes down and down,
without knocking on anyone's door.[142]

ДОЖДЬ

—Дождь идет,
а говорят, что Бога нет!—
говорила старуха из наших мест,
няня Варя.

Те, кто говорили, что Бога нет,
ставят теперь свечи,
заказывают молебны.
остерегаются иноверных.

Няня Варя лежит на кладбище,
а дождь идет,
великий, обильный, неоглядный,
идет, идет,
ни к кому не стучится.[143]

In its three stanzas, which grow from four lines to five in the final stanza, we are once again oriented toward speech acts, like the promise that ends "The cold of the world" or the words spoken by the heart at the end of "The Word." But speech is our starting point in this poem, not its ending: first a quotation from those who would deny God's existence, then an explanation that these words are spoken by Nanny Varya. Unlike both the poems from "Old Songs," here the speaker has a name, an age (approximately, anyway—she is old, and we learn that she will be dead in the third stanza), and a location in a village that is shared with the poem's speaker (Nanny Varya is "from our parts"; iz nashikh mest). Nanny Varya speaks with the kind of folk wisdom and enduring values that Sedakova has said she wanted to capture in her "Old Songs," values contained in the traditional songs and prayers she heard from her grandmother. We would not be amiss in seeing Nanny Varya as another incarnation of that grandmother, even more so as Daria Sedakova is alive through the composition of the first two notebooks of "Old Songs," but the third notebook is dedicated to her memory. Nanny Varya lies in her grave in the third stanza of "Rain."

That third stanza gives way to the sound of the rain, the rhythm of which is heard in the penultimate line's echoing verbs ("comes down and down" in the English translation, with the knocking sound of "down"; the Russian requires only the repeating verb, "idet i idet," to get that knocking sound). The rain counters those who claim that God does not exist, we realize, remembering Nanny Varya's words from the poem's opening: welcome rain, pouring down from the heavens, recognized as the token of God's grace. Once again, Sedakova has found an entity in the external world—water, the source of life on earth, and rain that pours down even when one person's life has ended, in order that more life can be nurtured—to represent the inner experience of joy, that same "incredible joy" that ends "The Angel of Reims." Her answer to the question of where to seek vision is to look out into the rain, and to listen to it, to know the audibility of its sounds as an affirmation of God's grace. Sedakova's poems tap out that same rhythm, beckoning us to hear its regularity, to sense its balancing act.

In describing the intonation and diction of liturgical hymns, Sedakova has emphasized their orientation toward praise, and we might say the same of her poetry, beautifully evidenced in "Rain" and in the poem "December 26" ("26 dekabria," 2015). Where her poems are quite different is the diction: the poetics of liturgical hymns require an elevated diction—not, as she observed, the debris in which Akhmatova said that poems would grow.[144] But Sedakova's diction can seem plain, oriented toward the depth of meaning that can accrete in a single word, and often setting off reverberations of nearly lost etymological meanings as well. Sedakova has compared liturgical poetry's word-weaving around a single metaphor to the metaphysical conceits of Baroque poetry. A hymn can take a single metaphor or image (her example is the way that the Christmas *tropar'* is entirely and only about light) and prod it into multiple directions and meanings.[145] But where the comparison breaks down is in the premium Baroque poets, artists, and musicians placed on originality: in hymnography, by comparison, nothing was to be invented, no individual idea of genius was to be put on display. It was the traditional, known elements from which the hymn was to be built. When the hymn displayed the mind's capacities, it showed the value placed on wisdom, on a deeper knowledge or insight than is found in the wit of secular poetry, including the poetry of the Baroque. Those values also mark Sedakova's poetry, with its reliance on a constrained, limited poetic vocabulary, into which it burrows ever deeper.

One last poem, then, published by the poet on the day after her birthday in 2014, and then revised in this version, dated 2015. December 26 is Sedakova's birthday.

December 26

Where a point is speaking with a point,
a star is talking with a star,

where reason multiplies what is best by three,
and all else bespeaks gratitude,

above the frozen thickets,
above pastures darker than dark—
behold the burning, mind-altering
steps of a poem.

26 декабря

Где точка с точкой разговаривает,
звезда с звездою говорит,
где разум лучшее утраивает,
а прочее благодарит,

над замороженными чащами,
над пустырями, где ни зги—
горящие, сумасводящие
стихотворения шаги.[146]

Several elements are familiar here: the lines centered on the page; the sweep of a long sentence across short poetic lines (in this case, a single sentence over eight lines); the quick sketch of an external world's objects and attributes; the suggestion of light, then cold and dark, then light again; and verbs connoting talk and gratitude. The form of the poem, in eight lines, is one Sedakova has used before, in a group of "Eight Octaves" ("Vosem' vos'mistishii") in *The Wild Rose*, along with several other eight-line poems; and in a group of "Four Octaves" ("Chetyre vos'mistishiia") in *Evening Song* (*Vecherniaia pesnia*, 1996–2005).[147] It is clearly a productive form for the poet across her years of writing poetry (there are several in her juvenilia, too). The form is treated in more detail in chapter 3, and it has already come up again in this chapter, for Khersonsky is a prolific writer of *vos'mistishiia*. Sedakova's turn to the eight-line form offers a compact mode of expression with which she feels familiar. And like all her work, this poem conveys a tremendously natural intonational quality, a sense of ease layered over a poem whose syntax is actually quite intricately patterned. Six of the poem's eight lines create the setting for the steps of a poem, revealed only in the last line; line 7 describes the steps, using participles that have their own jolts of verbal energy.

The poem completes a fantastically long vertical journey over its eight lines, from the stars of l.2 down to the ground on which the steps of a poem might tread, with thickets and pastures flickering past during that journey down. There is a road along which the poem has traveled, a road the poem doesn't even have to mention as the echo of Mikhail Lermontov's poem "I come out alone onto the road" ("Vykhozhu odin ia na dorogu," 1841). It will reverberate instantly for readers of the poem, who will surely recognize the quotation from "I come out alone onto the road" in those stars talking back and forth in l.2: Sedakova cites Lermontov's line, "I zvezda s zvezdoiu govorit" with only the initial word (meaning "and") dropped.[148] Sedakova is also surely responding to the most famous recycling of Lermontov's line—a poem by Osip Mandelstam, "Concert in the Railroad Station" ("Kontsert na vokzale," 1921), where he notes gloomily that not a single star is speaking ("I ne odna zvezda ne govorit").[149] Sedakova casts off the gloom. Mandelstam's poem famously begins with a statement that it is impossible to breathe, but the purest oxygen wafts through every line of Sedakova's poem; his firmament seethes with worms, but she makes sure we sense the contrast by invoking the stars, which in her poem do talk, in the second line of the poem, just where Mandelstam had them silent. There may be a further conversation with Mandelstam in the very choice of the eight-line form, a model that, as seen in chapter 3, was crucial for Mikhail Eremin. And in that final word of the poem, "steps," Sedakova is no doubt again invoking Mandelstam, for whom walking and composing poetry were one.[150] Sedakova makes the poem's steps follow one after another with a natural sense of grace. The pun of those steps is wonderfully metonymic, the last word of the poem drawing our mental image of its depiction down toward a set of unseen feet, as if an alternative word for steps echoes across the borders of Indo-European languages so that we also hear *stopa*, the Russian word that can also denote poetic feet.

But the choice of "shagi" for steps has its own extraordinary resonance, taking us again to Mandelstam, to his "Essay on Dante" ("Razgovor o Dante," 1933). Early in that essay, he writes:

> *Inferno* and especially *Purgatorio* glorify the human gait, the measure and the rhythm of steps, the footstep and its form. The step, linked to breathing and saturated with thought, is understood by Dante as the beginning of prosody. To signify walking he uses a multitude of varied and charming turns of phrase.
>
> In Dante, philosophy and poetry are always on the move, always on their feet. Even a stop is a variation on accumulated movement: a platform for conversation created by Alpine exertions. A metrical foot—its intake of

breath, its exhalation—is a step. The step is conclusion-drawing, vigil-keeping, syllogism-forming.

"Inferno" и в особенности "Purgatorio" прославляет человеческую походку, размер и ритм шагов, ступню и ее форму. Шаг, сопряженный с дыханьем и насыщенный мыслью, Дант понимает как начало просодии. Для обозначения ходьбы он употребляет множество разнообразных и прелестных оборотов.

У Данта философия и поэзия всегда на ходу, всегда на ногах. Даже остановка—разновидность накопленного движения: площадка для разговора создается альпийскими усилиями. Стопа стихов— вдох и выдох—шаг. Шаг—умозаключающий, бодрствующий, силлогизирующий.[151]

Mandelstam makes the connection between the two words for steps, *stopa* and *shagi*, and he establishes the physical human step as the source of poetry's rhythms, its prosody. This lovely passage, so often quoted, may well have been the source of Sedakova's reliance on participles in her poem, and whereas Mandelstam has the step draw conclusions for the mind (his word is *umozakliuchaiushchii*), Sedakova creates a step that drives the mind right out of its own boundaries (*sumasvodiashchii*).[152]

Why end with this poem, beautiful as it is, and yet not directly speak to the concerns of faith and belief that have animated this chapter? In part because it is a chance to open out the topics of this chapter and of this book toward the running commentary about how poems get written in the contemporary world. To answer that question, we should recall the poem's Lermontov subtext: his poem ends with an affirmation that the sounds of poetry can yet waft over the landscape of the poem, caressing the poet's ears and singing sweet melodies of love. Sedakova's final image is less romantic, but no less inspiring, evoked in those participles of l.7, as bright as the fire of inspiration and so powerful as to be able to drive one quietly out of one's mind. Hers is not the perfect cosmic harmony created by Lermontov, but instead the invocation of a universe in which poems, against many odds, may yet be written.

The "yet" of that sentence might pertain to the time of this poem's writing, the very end of 2014, a turning point year in Russian political history, as it saw Russia's occupation of Crimea, and it certainly pertains to the moment of my writing these sentences, as Russia appears bent on destroying Ukraine if it cannot control it. The poets in this chapter are variously committed to writing alternative histories of faith, and to understanding the possibilities of tolerance and difference in a world that can all too often seek conformity. Some of their work insists that Judaism and Orthodoxy can speak each other's language, see with each other's eyes. For all of them, poetry's identification with marginal, forgotten individuals holds out possibilities for recuperation and recovery, and for sustaining faith itself. Each, in their own way, embodies what Sarah Pratt, writing about Sedakova, has called "the uncompromising insistence on the openness of art."[153] It is a marker of the community of contemporary poets traced in this book that this insistence on openness would extend to poems about faith, as if the poets themselves know that to cede this potentially most restrictive of topics would be to cede the very grounds on which freedom thrives.

Poetry and Freedom after February 24, 2022

NEVER HAS a preposition felt more freighted: after February 24, 2022, it seemed as if there would always only be a sense of *after*, of a world in which the destruction Russia was wreaking on Ukraine changed everything. For the rest of 2022, the horror only intensified, leading to attacks on civilians, mass graves and war crimes, and cities deprived of heat and light. The image of a young woman carrying a sign predicting that Russia will be free, featured in the introduction to this book, now looms up as if from some distant past, one whose confidence in future freedom feels unreal.

Like all hybrid wars, Russia's all-out assault on Ukraine has also been an assault on language, when even the word for war (*voina*) became illegal speech, and when accurate reporting about casualties or equipment failures were denounced as fake news, also potentially a criminal act. Russian speakers of conscience naturally want to wrest back ownership of their language. Whole communities of poets and readers, of citizens and activists, felt themselves in tatters, as repressions of free speech and free assembly were everywhere in evidence, particularly in cities. Holding up a sign protesting war or advocating for peace would have been entirely acceptable in Soviet parades, but it became an act of outsized bravado, epitomized by Marina Ovsyannikova's interruption of a Channel One news broadcast on March 14, 2022.[1] Her "no to war" (net voine) was already a slogan to protest Russia's invasion. Protesters are nothing if not resourceful, and a woman in Nizhny Novgorod arrested for holding a blank piece of paper was not the only person to go straight for the symbolism, without any words to get in the way.[2] That gesture spread, and an instance in Rostov-na-Donu was widely shared on Twitter (figure 29).[3] Other images of

FIGURE 29. Anastasia Nikolaeva, photographed in Rostov-na-Donu;
OVD-Info, Twitter (February 25, 2022)

this protest shared on social media feature the moment of arrest, which makes it an even more striking counterpart to the young woman whose sign announced "Russia Will Be Free." That both are women is a meaningful coincidence: the Feminist Antiwar Resistance (FAS) quickly became the best organized antiwar movement on the ground within Russia.

Is it deliriously optimistic to imagine that the prophecy of future freedom persists, that the will to live one's own life cannot be squelched? If the page is blank, the force of the protest is no less and may in fact be even more poetic. It is as if the blank page of the Futurist Vasilisk Gnedov's "Poem of the End" ("Poema kontsa," 1913) were transformed into a defiant gesture of protest. Wordless space can be maximally expressive, as the journal *Novoe literaturnoe obozrenie* proved in its three pages of blacked-out space at the start of the first issue to appear after February 24.[4] Those are the pages where the journal had been publishing new poems for many years under the heading "New Social Poetry" ("Novaia sotsial'naia poeziia"), and the black rectangular shapes suggested a raw, dark site of mourning and protest.

Large public protest gatherings became impossible in Russia after February 2022, and the aggressive arrests carried out by state security forces on the streets and the disproportionate criminal judgments within the courts had their effect. Hundreds of thousands of people who oppose the war—including many poets—fled Russia, fearful that the borders would close, and the mobilization in September 2022 produced another huge wave of departures. The last free media outlets were shut down, and people began to lock down social media accounts. As of late 2022, some accounts remained wiped clean or were confined to smaller groups of friends, but others slowly came back or moved to Telegram channels. The free news media has continued its work from the relative safety of locations outside Russia.[5] The persistence of individual voices of dissent, some safely abroad but a remarkably courageous few still speaking out within Russia, shows that the free speech created after the fall of the USSR has not been destroyed, even if persistence now comes at a very high price.

It was by no means obvious at first that poetry could continue to flourish, both because the social media crucial to sharing new work seemed under threat (especially Facebook, declared an extremist organization by the Russian state) and because of a widening sense of shame at the fact of being Russian and, for many, being a citizen of an authoritarian if not terrorist state. Immediately after February 24, the influential poet, translator, and editor Dmitry Kuz'min posted two eloquent statements, co-authored with Evgeny Nikitin.[6] Each was signed by nearly one hundred poets. The first statement addressed the people of Ukraine and ended by wishing them victory. The second, directed toward all readers of poetry and in a sense to all Russians, concluded by advising people to read Ukrainian poetry. As the statement put it, "Right on our doorstep, another nation at this very moment is demonstrating the kind of courage, fortitude, and unity of political leaders with poets, intellectuals, and the military, with public figures and the most ordinary of people—the very qualities that we can only dream of for our own nation."[7]

In effect, readers of Russian poetry were being told that if they wanted to learn about freedom, the place to look was in the poetry of Ukraine. Kuz'min has made good on that intention by regularly posting his own translations of Ukrainian poets, something he had long been doing in his publications and social media posts. Others have joined in that work of bringing ever more Ukrainian poetry into Russian. The Telegram channel Metazhurnal has published many translations from Ukrainian, with extensive work by Stanislav Belsky, who lives in Ukraine. To name only one other example, Olga Sedakova, who translates from many languages but not usually Ukrainian, took up the gut-wrenching poem Maxim Krivtsov wrote about the mass killings in Bucha, and her translation reached several thousand readers via Facebook within days.[8]

The sentiment that space should be cleared for Ukrainian voices persists within the ever-widening circles of those who oppose the war. And no one should underestimate just how much poetry is being written in Ukraine by Ukrainians during this war, poetry that is also being translated into English with fresh intensity.[9] Striking new work is also appearing at the border zones between languages, inspired perhaps by the surge of multilingual poetry but also by how the online environment makes it so easy to cross linguistic and geographic borders.[10]

It is too soon to know how this engagement will affect Russian poetry, and too soon to know what poetry will look like in the face of authoritarian crackdown at home and brutal, unthinkable war in Ukraine. At first, it was vexed question whether poetry-related events should go on, and there was no single uniform answer. One of *Colta*'s last publications, in March 2022, before it temporarily froze its web page was a survey asking whether poems, concerts, and events should continue and whether it mattered if they were explicitly antiwar.[11] The answers included assertions that being together as a community and hearing poems or listening to music was needed more than ever and equally emphatic claims that anything that looked like business as usual was tantamount to collaboration with the Russian state. The most interesting responses were somewhere in between, including Sedakova's two-sentence answer that she would not read her own work in public but very much wanted to hear others—this seemed the clearest demonstration that assembling as a community was still needed. Gali-Dana Singer, calling on her experience of living through wars in Israel when some soldiers carried volumes of Silver Age poetry with them, said that poetry in and of itself could be the strongest anti-war statement, no matter its topic. Evgenia Lavut's nuanced and empathetic response took a different direction: to assemble anthologies of poems or to gather people to read isn't a form of deluded self-comfort, she said, but a form of prayer. One of Lavut's own poems written in March 2022 was about as far from a prayerful intonation as one can get—it played directly off the inspiring moment on February 24, 2022, when Ukrainian border guards on Snake Island transmitted as their final communication that an encroaching Russian warship could go fuck itself.[12]

The ambivalence about events persisted, but Russian poets came to respond to repression at home and destruction in Ukraine in a flood of new work. Lavut's defiance, alongside intonations of prayer, lament, irony, anger, hope, indignation, determination, and compassion, is amply present in the enormous outpouring of poetry that came to define the year 2022. It may have been slow to start, but by the end of the year, the volume of new work was nearly overwhelming, and virtually every poet who had been stunned into silence at first and even those who urged silence on others found their voice. Ilya Kukulin, in the first assessment of this work, has compared the scale of new work to responses to the Second World War, and he argued that one reason for the sheer number of new poems was a desire to reclaim some sense of agency in the very act of speaking out.[13] In my terms, that amounts to an affirmation of free speech, to a demonstration of independent thinking and creative autonomy. These poems show poets as refusing to concede to the state's censorship or to its falsified narrative of the "special military operation."

Social media platforms have allowed this work to be widely shared, some of it on Facebook (which some in Russia continued to access via VPN), but even more on Telegram channels that have taken advantage of more secure encryption. It can be harder at first to find those Telegram channels unless you already know their names (a search of Telegram with the key word "poeziia" turns up none of them), yet page views prove that new work is reaching readers, if far fewer than had been the case with Facebook. But the readership may yet rise, and searches were eased when Metazhurnal asked which channels its readers relied on, and lists emerged. Reader comments are sparser than on Facebook, too, and the platform seems not to offer the same prompt for lively debate. The community's sense of being embattled may also have reduced the propensity for argument, although some sparks of disagreement have arisen, a good sign for things to come.

The work on Telegram channels, individual blogs, and other social media sites has begun to be aggregated. Linor Goralik created an online platform for poetry, prose, essays, and artwork produced by those opposing the war, *ROAR*, or *Resistance and Opposition Arts Review*.[14] By the end of 2022, it had posted five substantial issues in Russian, English, Japanese, and French versions, made possible by a worldwide team of volunteer translators and editors working behind the scenes. Also significant are five poetry anthologies that appeared in print in 2022.[15] Two of them were careful to foreground poets living in Ukraine or born there, tacitly following the recommendation in Kuz'min and Nikitin's statement. Taking a chronological approach allowed some anthologies to preserve for the future a kind of snapshot of the war's impact as if in real time. Because these books were rushed into print (understandably, and two were set up as fundraising projects), they are a place to start rather than anything definitive, and they largely reflect the first six months of 2022. None includes very much of the poetry from fall 2022, when the possibility that the war would continue for a long time began to set in. Rage at war crimes and atrocities was felt early on, as was the enduring hope for Ukrainian victory and Russian defeat. The poetry represented in these anthologies impressively captures the emotional as well as political responses of hundreds of poets, and absorbing this work will give future readers a way to comprehend the turning point that came to constitute the year 2022 for Russian poetry.

The most substantial anthology is *Poetry of the Recent Past* (*Poeziia poslednego vremeni*), which presented poems from March to July 2022 in the order in which they were written. Yuri Leving's in-depth introduction compared the volume to a minefield, a perhaps unfortunate metaphor since Russian forces were leaving mines in the Ukrainian territory they abandoned, but the metaphor aptly suggested that Leving knew that this project could be risky. It did engender intense and, in some cases, negative responses.[16] He also compared the project to an x-ray photograph, suggesting the diagnostic potential of what he had assembled. While he eschewed the poems written by triumphant pro-Russian poets, known as Z poets, there is something of the medical profession's neutrality in trying to lay out the situation of harm in all its particulars. The volume's range left it open to criticism on political grounds, but it makes the collection a more accurate snapshot of the war's impact.[17]

The metaphor of air, a marker of freedom and free speech in many of the poems treated in this book, can also be found in this anthology's texts. Leving's introduction cites lines from more than a dozen poems in which the dominant metaphor is atmospheric change, a sense that the air has thickened, become impossible to breathe.[18] The extended series of quotations shows that the metaphor of air has retained its salience at a moment when free speech has become riskier for some, extremely dangerous for others. The air brought not oxygen but menace, as in a poem by Alexandra Tsibulya: "Every scrap of air wants / to have power over me" (Kazhdyi klochok vozdukha khochet / imet' nado mnoi vlast').[19] Her expressive poem includes the sight of flags flying over a Petersburg bridge that produce the sensation of sand flying into the mouth. The flag as a symbol of the state's power is grotesquely suffocating, and air, rather than a medium on which words can sail, becomes a vehicle for pushing sand into the mouth and making speech impossible.

In a similar way, the air is turned into the earth's dirt and filth in a poem by Irina Kotova, posted to Facebook on November 7, 2022, and then circulated via Telegram. Kotova gave the poem the title "Air" ("Vozdukh"). It began:

> at night the air
> puts on its helmet of invisibility
> blown out to the horizon
>
> so as not to smell the war
> I walk out to the dark street
> but the war
> like a positive test for syphilis
> leaves its trace everywhere and always
>
> ночью воздух
> надевает шапку-невидимку
> прибитую к горизонту
>
> чтобы не чуять запахов войны
> я выхожу на улицу в темноте
> но война
> как положительная реакция на сифилис—
> остается везде и всегда[20]

Kotova, an endocrinologist and surgeon, knowledgeably pegs syphilis as a disease that can persist even after supposedly successful treatment.[21] Just as syphilis can disfigure the body, so the war's maiming injuries will produce the crowd of invalids in the poem's conclusion:

> is resurrection possible
> if now
> all the invalids
> from world wars
> gather in my bedroom
> uninvited
> replacing the air—
> with earth

> *November 7, 2022*

> возможно ли воскресение
> если теперь
> все калеки
> мировых войн
> без спроса
> собираются в моей спальне
> замещая воздух—
> землёй

> *07.11.2022*

Syphilis again seems a ghastly and appropriate choice, as the invasion of the intimate spaces of the poet's bedroom bring war's victims nightmarishly close. What was earlier in the poem cool night air is now unbreathable, thick with dirt.

I doubt that Kotova had in mind the poem by Grigory Dashevsky discussed in the introduction, "No self, no people," but comparing those two poems shows us where poetry has shifted in the nearly two decades between them (his poem appeared first in 2003, hers in 2022). The motif of invisibility connects them. Kotova's "helmet of invisibility" recalls magical fairy tales, but rather than having the poem's speaker put it on and observe the world unseen, Kotova makes the air itself invisible. In Dashevsky's poem, invisibility attaches to the gnats, felt as whining sounds and sawing actions. In both poems, invisible forces suggest an atmosphere thick with dread. His poem never drops down to specifics, staying with a metaphysical investigation of fear's deserted landscape; hers evokes public and intimate spaces, from street to bedroom, but also names all wars as a source of harm even as she responds to a specific, ongoing war in Ukraine. The innocents who suffer in Dashevsky's poem become maimed war veterans in Kotova's. We can sense her reaching for the metaphysical, abstract level of his poem in her metaphor of air, so many times in this book seen as the air of freedom, as in that huge sky suggested by Bulatov's poster, here clotted with choking particles of earth by poem's end. Any "helmet of invisibility" has lost its magic powers.

Kotova's poem reads as an intense lyric statement, but much of the poetry since February 24 grapples with the discomforts of first-person utterance and even more so with the sense of being part of a collective *we*. Among the most telling is a poem by Alexander Skidan that appeared in two of the new anthologies. It was first posted on March 1, 2022, and immediately translated into English, reaching a wide readership even before the anthologies further disseminated it.[22] It remains one of the most searing poems of a horror-filled year, and I cite it here in full. It transformed the shock of the preposition "after" into an adverb and filled it with the despair of realizing that all poems, whatever else they might achieve, will feel too "late." Belatedness was no longer the existential ennui of the modernists, but rather the rage-filled recognition of a generation that seems to have squandered its freedom. Formally, the poem demonstrates the continuing power of free verse and the ways in which anaphora and other repetitions create strong rhetorical patterns. The result is at once incantation and lament.

> too late to scroll through news and facebook too late to write on personal and collective guilt
>
> too late to read hannah arendt and carl schmitt both in love with schwarzwald too late to become provost of the state of emergency
>
> too late to stand on the troitsky bridge and gaze at the most beautiful city in the world too late to gaze at the ice of the most beautiful river in the world
>
> too late to go out on the ice of the most beautiful river in the world and write fuck war on it too late to raise and lower bridges
>
> too late to cry over bridges too late to build bridges too late to say too late to loved ones too late to embrace them

too late to rename the troitsky bridge as the trotsky bridge too late to say neither peace nor war

too late to say my grandma was born in poltava in 1909 too late to say her name was trepke von trepke

too late to say we are pissing our pants

too late to remember valery podoroga in 2001 after getting the bely prize in that café on leteiny and him saying who have we elected not only elected but with these very hands helped gleb pavlovsky and his media outlets

too late to say blockade patriotic war lydia ginzburg

too late to say i warned you in 2003 caution religion caution

too late to say genocide wwi turn the bayonets against imperialism as bakunin kropotkin taught and bruno schulz dreaming of maggots when he went down vinnytsia's streets to drink with arkady

too late to say dehumanization

mobile crematoria

special operation

it remains to be said
reread antigone give us back our dead

i want to mourn them

this precedes the polis precedes its violence and the law the law-as-violence this is sister this is brother becoming a bottomless grave and the promise of love

it's still maybe not too late to stop the mobile crematoria
to bury our children[23]

поздно листать новости и фейсбук поздно писать о личной и коллективной вине

поздно читать ханну арендт и карла шмитта влюбленных в шварцвальд поздно становиться ректором чрезвычайного положения поздно стоять на троицком мосту и смотреть на самый прекрасный город в мире поздно смотреть на лед самой прекрасной реки в мире

поздно выходить на лед самой прекрасной реки в мире и писать на нем хуй войне поздно поднимать и разводить мосты

поздно оплакивать мосты поздно строить мосты поздно говорить поздно любимым поздно их обнимать

поздно переименовывать троицкий мост в мост имени троцкого поздно говорить ни мира ни войны

поздно говорить моя бабушка родилась в полтаве в 1909 году поздно говорить ее фамилия была трепке фон трепке

поздно говорить что мы ссым

поздно вспоминать 2001 год валерия подорогу после вручения премии белого в кафе на литейном и его слова кого мы выбрали и не просто выбрали а вот этими вот руками и помогли глебу павловскому и его медиа

поздно говорить блокада отечественная война лидия гинзбург

поздно говорить я предупреждал в 2003 году осторожно религия осторожно

поздно говорить геноцид первая мировая обратим штыки против империализма как учили бакунин кропоткин и опарыши в снах бруно шульца когда он шел по улицам винницы чтобы выпить с аркадием

поздно говорить расчеловечивание

мобильные крематории

спецоперация

остается говорить
перечитай антигону верни нам наших мертвых

я хочу их оплакать

это раньше полиса раньше его насилия и закона закона-как-насилия это сестра это брат ставшие бездонной могилой и обещаньем любви вот это еще не поздно может быть остановить мобильные крематории

похоронить наших детей[24]

Skidan's poem ends in a place that pulls back from the rueful sense that it is too late to do anything with one's freedom, and it does that in its last seven lines that pose instead the possibility that there are things left to say. And left to do. His mythological model for that action is Antigone, the quintessential courageous sibling who refuses to comply with a king's orders and who insists on mourning the dead. Skidan is doing something not entirely unlike Elena Fanailova's Lysistrata poems (and she posted ever more anguished Lysistrata poems in 2022, some in Ukrainian and Russian). But his rhetoric is more broken, his emotions rawer. Rather than a heroine from antiquity whose resistance hopes to stop a war, and rather than a source, Aristophanes's comedy, that can mix jest and joy, Skidan goes straight for the tragedy that is Sophocles's *Antigone*, and for its tragic ending with the bodies of the dead piling up.

The poem also goes back to a moment before there is law, as it puts it, before there is even the polis in which free speech feels so urgent, goes back to an insistence on the humane impulse to mourn the dead as kin. If one could go back to that primal and humane impulse, the poem argues, then perhaps it would be possible to bury those already sacrificed, perhaps possible to prevent more deaths. It is a tiny hope, made smaller by the poem's magnitude. Skidan's work over the preceding several years had often yielded relatively short, wry texts.[25] But here he plays out the logic seen in chapter 3, where an interplay between long and short forms proves paradoxical: this long, repetitive text leads to the smallest scrap of hope.

One source of that hope is the way the poem finds its voice as first-person lyric, a process that seems impossible after the long litany of impersonal, flat statements of all the things that it is too late to do. But five lines from the end, Skidan writes, "i want to mourn them," a short utterance that pulls the singular voice of the poet out of the impersonal syntax and out of the collective *we* expected in war poetry. Other poets have pushed back against the undifferentiated mass of who "we" are at such a moment, including Kira Freger, whose poem from December, 2022 unites under one *we* all who oppose Russia's assault on Ukraine but then asks about the divisions between those of "us" who have fled Russia, and those who have stayed behind.[26] A similar rhetorical move is found in a short poem by Maria Stepanova that begins "while we slept, we bombed Kharkiv" (poka my spali, my bombili Khar'kov).[27] The "we" who sleep are as if at some distance from the "we" who drop bombs, but Stepanova's point is to close that distance. Skidan instead finds a way to speak in the first person, a rhetorical gesture that ought to come easily to a lyric poem but here is fraught with tension. Nor does Skidan perform the expected act of mourning, the gesture so desired by Antigone. For that, it is not too late, but too early. No elegy can yet be written, he says: now, one can but record the desire to mourn the dead.

Skidan's poem captures the temporality of Russian poetry in 2022 so perfectly—the sense that it is not yet possible to do many things, but that the groundwork for future freedoms can yet be laid—that I should probably end this afterword on his poem. But I want to add one more text, which is already able to show us concretely what that future will require. It is by the critic and writer Maria Boteva. It demonstrates in its very diction that Russians should know where to look for the lessons of the future: to Germany, a country whose reckoning with its Nazi past, as Kuz'min and Nikitin said of Ukraine, is marked by a courage that Russia has yet to muster. Boteva lets the German language do that work in her poem. It does nothing more than point the way forward, but that is quite a lot. Once again, I quote the poem in full.

> jeden Tag—says the German dictionary—
> every day read out these words:
> I
> don't want
> to conquer
> anyone
> I
> don't want
> to battle
> anyone
> jeden Tag jedes Mal
> every day every time
> open the dictionary
> and repeat
> head doesn't hurt
> from endless repetition
> that's how you learn this language of peace
> I
> don't want
> to battle
> anyone

I
don't want
to conquer
anyone
I
never
again

еден таг—говорит немецко-русский словарь—
каждый день читай эти слова:
я
никого
не хочу
победить
я
ни с кем
не хочу
воевать
еден таг едес маль
каждый день каждый раз
открывая словарь
повторяй
не болит голова
от бескрайнего повторения
так и выучишь этот язык мира
я
ни с кем
не хочу воевать
я
никого
не хочу
победить
я
никогда
больше[28]

Here the first-person pronoun is assured and repeated, heard almost from the start and five times given its own line. Boteva is writing against the same pressures as Skidan and Kotova but resisting them by emphatic assertions. That German-Russian dictionary (a wordbook, if we hear in our heads the German term for dictionary, *Worterbuch*) sets her on that path. Finding the confident equivalent of the phrase "jeden Tag" puts her poem in a different temporality as well: it's not too late, it's a repeating present, something like the everyday that marked poems treated in chapter 3 (by Daria Sukhovei or Ekaterina Simonova) or chapter 6 (by Sergei Kruglov and Olga Sedakova). Boteva takes up the hard work, the headache-producing work, of learning a new language, a language of peace.[29]

What Boteva's poem does by placing that work not in the future but in the everyday is to acknowledge how long and hard the work will be. She has pointed toward the German example by including German words, and by the poem's last two lines, the phrase "never / again." That is the familiar slogan from the Holocaust, the vow to resist genocide. Her resonant ending links Russia's war on Ukraine and genocide and suggests that the work to come may involve naming it as such. And it will surely require finding a whole new lexicon with which to forge, through repentance, genuine peace.

It is on that hopeful note that I want to end, fully realizing that the possibility for hope and for repentance is but a shadow flickering through Boteva's poem. The most striking poems of the months in late 2022 were filled with other, darker shadows, from the grotesquely dead soldiers of Daria Serenko's "The Bridegrooms" to Eugene Ostashevsky's English-language poem that calls Petersburg the "eater of Mariupol."[30] The tonalities of contemporary poetry in Russian cannot but reflect the horror of the war, but poets remain determined to use their talents and their inspiration to respond to the world in which they are living. Free speech is not happening widely in public in Russia as of this writing, but it is persisting, not least in Russian poetry. It will do what it can to ready its readers for the moment of their freedom.

NOTES

Preface

Source of epigraph: Aleksandra Tsibulia, "Rech' pri poluchenii Premii Arkadiia Drago-moshchenko," *NLO* 137 (no. 1, 2016): 275.

1. For a crisp statement of the principles of this legacy, see Aleksandr Skidan, "Katastro-ficheskoe stanovlenie bezumtsa N," *Nosorog* (undated publication, interview by Vladimir Korkunov dated May–June 2020), https://nosorog.media/interview/katastroficheskoe_stanovlenie_bezumca.

2. Il'ia Kukulin, "Proryv k nevozmozhnoi sviazi," *NLO* 50 (no. 4, 2001), 435–58, quotation on 436; the essay also appears in Kukulin's book *Proryv k nevozmozhnoi sviazi: Stat'i o russkoi poezii* (Kabinetnyi uchenyi, 2019), 285–316; see 287.

3. This notion of responsibility, sometimes translated as "answerability," was advanced by Mikhail Bakhtin, and its ethical potential is influentially explored in Michael Holquist, *Dialogism: Bakhtin and His World* (Routledge, 2002); and in Caryl Emerson, *The First Hundred Years of Mikhail Bakhtin* (Princeton University Press, 2018).

Introduction

1. Fanailova further changed the lead-in after Russia's full-scale invasion, adding that, for her guests, "the independence of Ukraine is their principle." She would also change the name of the podcast in 2024 to the *Babylon Station* (*Stantsiia Vavilon*). See the page on Radio Svoboda, https://www.svoboda.org/babylon, for links to all episodes.

2. The connection to Herzen was emphasized by human rights leader Ludmila Alekseyeva: see Dmitrii Ermol'tsev, "Za nashu i vashu svobodu," *Polit.ru*, August 25, 2008, https://polit.ru/article/2008/08/25/chehija/.

3. Polina Barskova, *Khoziain sada* (Knizhnye masterskie, 2015), 113–16, quotation from 116. The poem was first published online in the poet's LiveJournal feed in 2011. For a full translation, see Barskova, "The Battle," trans. Stephanie Sandler, *Fence*, Winter 2012–13, 97–100.

4. Barskova, *Besieged Leningrad: Aesthetic Responses to Urban Disaster* (Northern Illinois University Press, 2017); *Sed'maia shcheloch': Teksty i sud'by blokadnykh poetov* (Izdatel'stvo Ivana Limbakha, 2020).

5. By 2011, when this poem was written, the freedoms of an unfettered press were unnervingly balanced by the feared return of authoritarian rule in Russia, making Barskova's optimism all the more to be noted and prized.

6. An audio recording of the April 2011 performance is available: Barskova, "The Battle," 13:00, uploaded May 11, 2011, https://www.youtube.com/watch?v=gtcv3jnUqHw. Barskova also credits the English-language poet Eugene Ostashevsky, in the audience as well, in her opening remarks.

7. Aleksandr Genis, "Voina i iskusstvo: Khudozhnik Vitalii Komar o sots-arte bez kavychek," in *Vzgliad iz N'iu-Iorka*, podcast, November 14, 2022, repeated January 8, 2023, https://www.svoboda.org/a/32192465.html.

8. Poetry is not the only medium in which this turn to the present can be seen. For a persuasive account of something comparable in prose, see Varvara Bavitskaia, "Prikliuchenie uma," *Colta*, November 6, 2018, https://www.colta.ru/articles/literature/19654.

9. For two enthusiastic reviews, see Tim Adams, "The Road to Unfreedom by Timothy Snyder Review—Chilling and Unignorable," *Guardian*, April 15, 2018, https://www.theguardian.com/books/2018/apr/15/the-road-to-unfreedom-russia-europe-america-timothy-snyder-review-tim-adams; and Margaret MacMillan, "Are We Traveling the 'Road to Unfreedom'?," *New York Times*, May 8, 2018, https://www.nytimes.com/2018/05/09/books/review/road-to-unfreedom-timothy-snyder.html.

10. The dramatic difference between his perspective and mine is suggested by the two contrasting figures who launch our studies: I begin with the poet and scholar Polina Barskova, but Snyder focuses first on authoritarian philosopher Ivan Ilyin. See Timothy Snyder, *The Road to Unfreedom: Russia, Europe, America* (Tim Duggan Books, 2018), 15–22.

11. For a sharply worded and politically astute critique of Snyder's book, see Sophie Pinkham, "Zombie History," *Nation*, May 3, 2018, https://www.thenation.com/article/archive/timothy-snyder-zombie-history/.

12. As was influentially shown in Jochen Hellbeck, *Revolution on My Mind: Writing a Diary under Stalin* (Harvard University Press, 2006).

13. Sheila Fitzpatrick, *Tear Off the Masks!: Identity and Imposture in Twentieth-Century Russia* (Princeton University Press, 2005), 304.

14. Vsevolod Nekrasov, *I Live I See: Selected Poems*, trans. Ainsley Morse and Bela Shayevich (Ugly Duckling Presse, 2013), 59.

15. Vsevolod Nekrasov, *Stikhi 1956–1983*, ed. M. A. Sukhotin, G. B. Zykova, and E. N. Penskaia (Biblioteka Moskovskogo Kontseptualizma Germana Titova, 2012), 45.

16. Both positions are laid out in Igor' Gulin, "Zametki o poezii Vsevoloda Nekrasova," *Syg.ma*, October 19, 2020, https://syg.ma/@igor-gulin/zamietki-o-poezii-vsievoloda-niekrasova.

17. Nekrasov's poem remains inspiring. Vasily Borodin brilliantly riffed on it in "svoboda" (2011): see Borodin, *Tsirk "Veter"* (ARGO-RISK, 2012), 25.

18. In a three-minute clip, Nekrasov reads from his work in Bulatov's studio in 2003, with Bulatov at his side, listening: "Nekrasov_Bulatov_m1.mpg," February 22, 2003, video, 3:28, Vladislav Kulakov, June 7, 2010, https://www.youtube.com/watch?v=NJoziGnQB90.

19. Grids and sky-like blue space are frequent points of visual juxtaposition in Bulatov's work. See three untitled drawings for *The Sky behind the Grid* in Erik Bulatov, *Freiheit ist Freiheit / Freedom Is Freedom*, ed. Veit Görner, Caroline Käding, and Anne Prenzler (Kerber Verlag, 2006), 83.

20. Bulatov, *Freiheit ist Freiheit*, 21. In the same statement, Bulatov contrasts the terms "picture" and "painting," classifying his own work as painting (see 39).

21. There is another way to read the canvas's creation of three-dimensionality, as the art historian David Joselit pointed out to me: it features "the dramatic opening from a flat (and hence, conventionally modernist) composition to a highly exaggerated and even forced perspective—something that characterizes much of Bulatov's work. Given how fundamental perspective is to post-Renaissance Western painting, and how modernism is typically defined as its supersession, either through flatness, or literalness, or at least the fracturing of perspectival space (as in cubism or Suprematism), one could say that he is really allowing a 'suppressed' language to burst through a dominant one. And added to this, he does so by inverting the values of Western art history (from perspective to flatness rather than flatness to perspective). This is indeed a statement of freedom!" (email, September 25, 2020).

22. See Daphne Skillen, *Freedom of Speech in Russia: Politics and Media from Gorbachev to Putin* (Routledge, 2017), especially the first part, 1–112; quotation from 3. A more complex argument has been made about the changing role of journalism in this period, one that unmasks the appearance of speaking truth to power and tracks the rise of cynicism, particularly in the formative early 2000s. See Natalia Roudakova, *Losing Pravda: Ethics and the Press in Post-Truth Russia* (Cambridge University Press, 2017), esp. chapters 4, 5, and the conclusion, 157–224.

23. That slogan was also heard at a Moscow protest demanding that opposition candidates not be barred from city council elections. See, for example, "More than 1,000 Arrested at Moscow Election Protest: 'Russia Will Be Free!'" *CBS News*, July 27, 2019, https://www.cbsnews.com/news/moscow-protests-russian-police-arrest-hundreds-election-demonstration-today-2019-07-27-live-updates/.

24. The image was widely shared on social media. I saw it in Vlad Krasov, "Pod gimn RF nas vintil OMON, ili Kak strana otmetila Den' Rossii," *Babr24.com*, June 13, 2017, http://babr24.com/msk/?IDE=160882. A cropped version also became the emblem for a Facebook page bearing the name of her sign, *Rossiia budet svobodnoi*, which as of 2022, the date of its last post, had more than 19,000 followers.

25. Cited from "Russia: Shrinking Space for Free Expression," *Human Rights Watch*, January 12, 2017, https://www.hrw.org/news/2017/01/12/russia-shrinking-space-free-expression. Internet freedom has been closely monitored as well: in *Freedom of Speech in Russia*, Skillen cites a 2015 report by Freedom House that ranked Russia alongside Sudan and Ethiopia as not free (53). For a later report (2017) by Freedom House, see https://freedomhouse.org/sites/default/files/FOTN%202017_Russia_0.pdf.

26. A surprisingly extensive social resonance was seen in several sets of protests against election fraud and political corruption in the 2010s; periodic large-scale demonstrations were one of the defining elements of post-Soviet culture. Much less trumpeted events have become more broadly consequential. The summer of 2017 saw the controversial arrest of a teenager for reciting Hamlet's soliloquy in public: there were arguments about whether the child seemed neglected by his parents, but the preposterous police action to prevent the recitation of a Shakespeare text in public took on ominous cultural relevance and exuded paradoxes similar to those of Pussy Riot's cathedral performance.

27. For a brief account of the "Stroll with Writers" and an image, see Andrew Kahn, Mark Lipovetsky, Irina Reyfman, and Stephanie Sandler, *A History of Russian Literature* (Oxford University Press, 2018), 768–69. A similarly subtle instinct for how the state might be resisted occurred in summer 2014, when permits for performances and gatherings at the Moscow book

fair were revoked. That led to massive reconfigurations of planned events because writers wanted no part in the "permitted" gatherings.

28. Here and below, I am drawing on Svetlana Boym, *Another Freedom: The Alternative History of an Idea* (University of Chicago Press, 2010).

29. Boym, *Another Freedom*, 78.

30. Boym, *Another Freedom*, 81.

31. Boym, *Another Freedom*, 107. The discussion of Dostoevsky occupies chapter 3; for the reorientation in our thinking about his notion of freedom, see especially 105–7.

32. V. V. Bibikhin, *Dnevniki L'va Tolstogo* (Izdatel'stvo Ivana Limbakha, 2012); and *Grammatika poezii: Novoe russkoe slovo* (Izdatel'stvo Ivana Limbakha, 2009), 267–568 (not all of which is about Sedakova, but her work figures prominently). Their correspondence has also been published: *I slovu slovo otvechaet: Vladimir Bibikhin—Ol'ga Sedakova, Pis'ma 1992–2004 godov* (Izdatel'stvo Ivana Limbakha, 2019).

33. For a biography of Bibikhin, see the excellent website archiving his writings and translations: http://www.bibikhin.ru/biography. See also Sergei Khoruzhii and A. V. Akhutin, "Pamiati V. V. Bibikhina," *Voprosy filosofii* 4 (2005): 112–13.

34. It is available as "Khanna Arendt: Chto takoe svoboda?," Vladimir Bibikhin website, http://www.bibikhin.ru/chto_takoe_svoboda. See also "Khanna Arendt: O revoliutsii," first published in *Tochki* (2007), http://www.bibikhin.ru/o_revolutsii.

35. Boym, *Another Freedom*, 207.

36. Hannah Arendt, "What Is Freedom?" in *Between Past and Future: Eight Exercises in Political Thought* (Viking, 1973), 143–72, quoted from 146.

37. V. V. Bibikhin, *Slovo i sobytie: Pisatel' i literatura* (Universitet Dmitriia Pozharskogo, 2010), 3. Or, as he puts it slightly later in the volume, "The most meaningful discourse is that of the everyday" (33). Bibikhin's presence in Russian intellectual life has loomed larger since his death, with a number of posthumous publications and an active Facebook page that posts excerpts from his writings.

38. My formulation here is inspired by an exchange that appeared on *Gefter*. See Viktoriia Faibyshenko, "Kak (ne) poniat' Khaideggera," *Gefter*, June 1, 2018, http://gefter.ru/archive/25158, which is a response to Mikhail Bogatov, "Pochemu Bibikhin—ne Khaidegger," *Gefter*, May 18, 2018, http://gefter.ru/archive/24972.

39. Many others have emphasized this side of Cavell's work. For a short, strong statement written in the wake of his death, see Imani Perry, "Cavell's Passionate Utterance," *ASAP Journal*, July 26, 2018, http://asapjournal.com/cavells-passionate-utterance-imani-perry/.

40. The phrases come from Cavell, "Something Out of the Ordinary," *Proceedings and Addresses of the American Philosophical Association* 71, no. 2 (1997): 27–37; see 31.

41. The legacy of Bakhtin's thought is much richer than my brief account here suggests. A darker side is exposed in his wartime writings, which have shown the word as opening out toward freedom as much as toward violence. See the forum curated by Irina Denishchenko and Alex Spektor, "The Dark and Radiant Bakhtin: Wartime Notes," *SEEJ* 61, no. 2 (2017): 189–310.

42. See Caryl Emerson and Gary Saul Morson, "Penultimate Words," in *The Current in Criticism: Essays on the Present and Future of Literary Scholarship*, ed. Clayton Koelb and Vergil Lokke (Purdue University Press, 1987), 43–64.

43. Stanley Cavell, *Philosophy the Day after Tomorrow* (Belknap Press of Harvard University Press, 2005), 19. Cavell devotes much of chapters 1 and 7 in this book to elaborating on the notion of passionate utterance; see 7–27 and 155–91.

44. David Rodowick, "Ethics in Film Philosophy (Cavell, Deleuze, Levinas)," undated essay, https://www.academia.edu/36412056/Ethics_in_film_philosophy_Cavell_Deleuze _Levinas_, 3.

45. Cited from Rodowick, *What Philosophy Wants from Images* (University of Chicago Press, 2017), 37.

46. See Cavell's *Pursuits of Happiness: The Hollywood Comedy of Remarriage* (Harvard University Press, 1981) and the discussions of opera in his book *A Pitch of Philosophy: Autobiographical Exercises* (Harvard University Press, 1994).

47. It by no means excludes contemplation of a deity, and one chapter of this book treats poetry informed by faith or by a search for belief. But even those poems are down to earth as they reach for the heavens.

48. Boris Dubin, "Nartsissizm kak begstvo ot svobody," *Vedomosti*, August 27, 2014, https:// www.vedomosti.ru/opinion/articles/2014/08/27/narcissizm-kakbegstvo-ot-svobody.

49. Boym, *Another Freedom*, 26.

50. For an account of Dubin's thinking as it evolved, see Kirill Kobrin, "Geroi moderna," *Colta*, July 11, 2018, http://www.colta.ru/articles/society/18551; and the preface to Dubin, *O liudiakh i knigakh* (Izdatel'stvo Ivana Limbakha, 2018), 5–14.

51. Arseniev, a founding member of the Petersburg journal *[Translit]*, was arrested for reading a poem by Eduard Lukoianov, "Esli ia chto-to ne zabudu," which ends with an obscene word. See the brief reports in *OVD Info*, June 12, 2013, https://ovdinfo.org/express-news/2013/06/12 /v-peterburge-na-ne-mitinge-oppozicii-zaderzhan-poet-pavel-arsenev; and in *Colta*, June 12, 2013, http://archives.colta.ru/docs/24839.

52. For more on and by Arseniev, see his website, http://arsenev.trans-lit.info/?lang=ru_RU. The image of this slogan is widely available online, for example, as the announcement of a temporary exhibit of banners from the protest that appeared on *Colta*, February 20, 2012, http://os.colta.ru/news/details/34496/; and an announcement of a book about protest art in *Artgid*, October 22, 2014, http://artguide.com/posts/673.

53. Vladimir Markov, "O svobode v poezii," in *O svobode v poezii: Stat'i, esse, raznoe* (Izdatel'stvo Chernysheva, 1994), 27–46; for the reference to Kuzmin's poetry, see 44.

54. Kuz'min explained that the name change occurred because Grigory Dashevsky insistently requested it. See Vladimir Korkunov, "'Zumery, konechno, uzhe pishut stikhi'—Dmitrii Kuz'min: Bol'shoe interv'iu," *Colta*, June 22, 2020, https://www.colta.ru/articles/literature /24745-dmitriy-kuzmin-bolshoe-intervyu.

55. Osip Mandel'shtam, *Polnoe sobranie sochinenii i pisem*, 3 vols. (Progress-Pleiada, 2010), 2:350.

56. For an astute reflection on sources for the phrase, including an appropriately Mandelstamian speculation that the phrase was driven by sound associations, see Irina Surat, "Otkuda vorovannyi vozdukh," *Novyi mir* 8 (2016): 184–91, https://imwerden.de/pdf/surat_otkuda _vorovanny_vozdukh_2016.pdf. The phrase also gave the title to O. A. Lekmanov, *Osip Mandel'shtam: Vorovannyi vozdukh* (AST Redaktsiia Eleny Shubinoi, 2016); and to a remarkable

volume of translations by Christian Wiman, who worked with Ilya Kaminsky to produce *Stolen Air: Selected Poems of Osip Mandelstam* (Ecco, 2012).

57. Surat, "Otkuda vorovannyi vozdukh," 185.

58. Kira Freger, "ne veter a prosto vse glukhie govoriat na odnom iazyke," *NLO* 162 (no. 2, 2020): 9.

59. In the metaphor of air is also a decentering away from the human, for all living things rely on and absorb into their being the air that gives life. That decentering is not new—one thinks of Zabolotsky's poems or Platonov's prose for many examples of that expansion toward a larger concept of animacy. But it has intensified, particularly in the work of such poets as Maria Stepanova and Fyodor Svarovsky, and in Linor Goralik's prose and poetry. These writers and this argument form the basis of Maria Vassileva, "After the Seraph: The Nonhuman in Twenty-First Century Russian Literature" (PhD diss., Harvard University, 2019).

60. Tobias Menely, "Anthropocene Air," *Minnesota Review* 83 (2014): 93–101, quotation from 93. Menely's argument has to do with global warming, with the way that "air turns out to be the matter of history" (96) as we face the consequences of the billions of tons of carbon that have now been released into Earth's atmosphere. Galina Rymbu's book *Time of the Earth* (*Vremia zemli*, 2018), the very title of which refigures the metaphors of the term Anthropocene, takes up the challenge of facing those consequences.

61. To some extent, that shift is the consequence of some Conceptualist poetry, made famous by Dmitry Prigov, Lev Rubinshtein, Timur Kibirov, and others, which made such a mockery of the poetic tradition. But its effects are seen in poets with entirely different aesthetic orientations, including those whom Mikhail Epstein dubbed Metarealists: see Mikhail Epshtein, "Pokolenie, nashedshee sebia (o molodoi poezii 80-kh godov)," *Voprosy literatury* 5 (1986): 40–72; somewhat revised and with a new title, "Metamorfoza (o novykh techeniiakh v poezii 80-kh godov)," in Epshtein, *Paradoksy novizny: O literaturnom razvitii XIX–XX vekov* (Sovetskii pisatel', 1988), 139–76; translated as "New Currents in Russian Poetry: Conceptualism, Metarealism, and Presentism," in *After the Future: The Paradoxes of Postmodernism and Contemporary Russian Culture*, trans. Anesa Miller-Pogacar (University of Massachusetts Press, 1995), 19–50.

62. Mikhail Iampol'skii, *Iz khaosa (Dragomoshchenko: Poeziia, fotografiia, filosofiia)* (Seans, 2015), 16. He also sees such poetry as open to the world that is not literature ("neliteraturnyi mir," 10).

63. Epstein makes that observation at the end of his essay, coining the adjective "presentistic" (prezental'na) to describe it. See Epshtein, "Metamorfoza," 172–75; "New Currents in Russian Poetry," 48–50. Some of my ideas about a poetry of presence are also in consonance with Dennis Sobolev, "From Ideology to Ontology: An Existential Turn in the Russian-Israeli Poetry of the 1990s," paper presented in the symposium "Russian-Israeli Literature, a History," Bar-Ilan University, June 29, 2021, 1:39:07, video, posted on July 4, 2021, https://www.youtube.com/watch?v=PBirLEuNV24.

64. There is not the deep psychic investment in correcting or besting a precursor, as Harold Bloom found in English-language poetry. For a comparable argument about earlier Russian poetry, see David M. Bethea, *Realizing Metaphors: Alexander Pushkin and the Life of the Poet* (University of Wisconsin Press, 1998), 67–88.

65. Mikhail Iampol'skii, "Nam nado adaptirovat'sia k zhizni bez istorii," a conversation with Mikhail Nemtsev, *Gefter*, June 19, 2017, http://gefter.ru/archive/22583.

66. Jonathan Culler, *Theory of the Lyric* (Harvard University Press, 2017), 137 (a point made often and elsewhere in the book; the example of Sappho is on 15).

67. For a set of reflections on definitions and boundaries, see Amy Hungerford, "On the Period Formerly Known as the Contemporary," *American Literary History* 20, nos. 1–2 (2008): 410–19. She begins her essay with an analysis of why 1989 is an enticing boundary point, the start of "the age of multiculturalism, or, more negatively, sectarianism" (410). The flexibility of the term contemporary is also a tenet of Sophie Seita, *Provisional Avant-Gardes: Little Magazine Communities from Dada to Digital* (Stanford University Press, 2019), esp. chapter 5.

68. Assessing Brodsky's position also played an important role in the early issues of *Arion*, a poetry journal that began to appear in 1994 under the editorship of Aleksei Alekhin. See, for example, two essays by Igor' Shaitanov, "V zhanre epiloga," *Arion* 4 (1995), http://magazines.russ.ru/arion/1995/4/monolog1.html; and "Bez Brodskogo," *Arion* 1 (1996), http://magazines.russ.ru/arion/1996/1/arion_03.html.

69. *Vozdukh* marked the eve of its tenth anniversary with a comparable forum on Osip Mandelstam, as the 125th anniversary of Mandelstam's birth had just passed. See *Vozdukh* 3–4 (2015): 254–68.

70. See especially the chapter on Aronzon in Philip Redko, "Boundary Issues in Three Twentieth-Century Russian Poets (Mandelstam, Aronzon, Shvarts)" (Ph.D. diss., Harvard University, 2019), and the dissertation in progress on Aronzon and Brodsky by Julian Pokay, also Harvard University.

71. See Susan Stewart, *Poetry and the Fate of the Senses* (University of Chicago Press, 2002); and Charles Altieri, *The Particulars of Rapture: An Aesthetics of the Affects* (Cornell University Press, 2003). I also find much that is kindred in Brian M. Reed, *Phenomenal Reading: Essays on Modern and Contemporary Poetics* (University of Alabama Press, 2012).

72. Mariia Stepanova, *Odin, ne odin, ne ia* (Novoe izdatel'stvo, 2014), 226–30.

73. I echo here another book title, a small collection of Stepanova's poetry: *Lirika, golos* (Novoe izdatel'stvo, 2010).

74. Stepanova, "V neslykhannoi prostote," in *Odin, ne odin, ne ia*, 21–35; see esp. 32–33. This essay has been translated into English by Sibelan Forrester as "In Unheard-Of Simplicity," in Stepanova, *The Voice Over: Poems and Essays*, ed. Irina Shevelenko (Columbia University Press, 2021), 85–98.

75. Stepanova, "Peremeshchennoe litso," in *Odin, ne odin, ne ia*, 36–48, quoted from 36–37. For a translation into English by Sibelan Forrester as "Displaced Person," see Stepanova, *Voice Over*, 99–110.

76. Dashevskii, *Stikhotvoreniia i perevody* (Novoe izdatel'stvo, 2015), 83. The poem first appeared in *Znamia* 10 (2003), http://magazines.russ.ru/znamia/2003/10/dashev.html. A translation by Timmy Straw and Ainsley Morse has now appeared in "Translation Tuesday: Two Poems by Grigori Dashevsky," *Asymptote* (January 17, 2023), https://www.asymptotejournal.com/blog/2023/01/17/translation-tuesday-two-poems-by-grigori-dashevsky/.

77. Vladimir Dal', *Tolkovyi slovar' zhivogo velikorusskogo iazyka*, 4 vols. (Izdatel'stvo russkogo iazyka, 1978), 1:65. The appearance of this word in Dal' is among the many astute corrections made by an anonymous reader of this book in manuscript, for which I am grateful. As the reader pointed out, this epithet also occurs in the first line of a poem by Arseny Golenishev-Kutuzov,

"The Trepak," turned into a song by Modest Musorgsky in 1885. The desolation and ominous foreboding of "The Trepak" is felt in Dashevsky's poem, and it may be his source for the word.

78. Compare the formulation in a fine short reading of the poem by Mikhail Aizenberg, who says that the poem creates not persons (the villain, the innocent), but roles; not a place, but a space beyond boundaries, the space of law. His reading historicizes the poem, as written after no lessons were learned from Auschwitz. See his contribution to "Ko dniu rozhdeniia Grigoriia Dashevskogo," ed. Filipp Dziadko, *Arzamas Academy*, February 25, 2021, https://arzamas .academy/mag/935-dashevsky.

79. Dashevsky might have been reminded of Auden's poem in the early 2000s, when it was republished repeatedly after the September 11, 2001, attacks in the United States. See Peter Steinfels, "Beliefs; After September 11, a 62-Year-Old Poem by Auden Drew Attention. Not All of It Was Favorable," *New York Times*, December 1, 2001, http://www.nytimes.com/2001/12/01/us /beliefs-after-sept-11-62-year-old-poem-auden-drew-new-attention-not-all-it-was.html. Dashevsky translated one of Auden's poems, "O What Is That Sound," in Dashevskii, *Stikhotvoreniia i perevody*, 42–43.

80. The ominous overtones of that grating sound may owe something to Emily Dickinson's poem "I heard a Fly buzz—when I died." See *The Poems of Emily Dickinson*, ed. Thomas H. Johnson, 3 vols. (Belknap Press of Harvard University Press, 1979), 1:358.

81. Two anonymous readers of the manuscript heard Zabolotsky in this poem, pointing to different source texts: "Lodeinikov" (1946–1947), "Lodeinikov in the Garden" ("Lodeinikov v sadu," 1934–1936), and "The Creators of Roads" ("Tvortsy dorog," 1947). For the poems, see N. Zabolotskii, *Polnoe sobranie stikhotvorenii i poem* (Akademicheskii proekt, 2002), 188–92, 226–29, 340–41. If Dashevsky is channeling Zabolotsky's unnerving landscapes, he has stripped their narratives down and compressed their spaces. He writes in the minimalist aesthetic discussed in chapter 3.

82. Anna Glazova has written eloquently and briefly about this poem, calling its speaker a ventriloquist. The poem, she says, creates a new temporality, the impersonal present. See Glazova, "Sobstvennaia istoriia: O poezii Grigorii Dashevskogo," *Vozdukh* (nos. 1–2, 2009): 222–28.

83. That "phrase turned inside out" is also noted in Aleksandra Tsibulia, "'Nevidimka-pila,'" her fine review of Dashevskii, *Neskol'ko stikhotvorenii i perevodov*, in *NLO* 128 (no. 4, 2014): 285–89.

84. For the poem "Renunciation—is a piercing Virtue—," see *Poems of Emily Dickinson*, 2:568.

85. Dated from when the earliest poem was begun (May 1932) to the final changes made to several poems (July 1935). Some have datelines, including the one I cite, but not all; nine were written in November 1933.

86. There is a more literal version in Nancy Pollak, *Mandelstam the Reader* (Johns Hopkins University Press, 1995), 70. See also Mandelstam, *The Moscow Notebooks*, trans. Richard McKane and Elizabeth McKane (Bloodaxe, 1991), 77. Both give a different version of l.4, explained and corrected in O. Mandel'shtam, *Polnoe sobranie stikhotvorenii*, ed. A. G. Mets (Gumanitarnoe agenstvo "Akademicheskii proekt," 1995), 230.

87. Mandel'shtam, *Polnoe sobranie stikhotvorenii*, ed. A. G. Mets, 230. For a far-reaching account of resonances with Mandelstam's other work, see Pollak, *Mandelstam the Reader*, 70–84.

88. Mandelstam's commitment at the time he wrote "Octaves" was to a poetry that could establish itself "in a new, extraspatial field of activity" (vodvoriaetsia na novom, vneprostranstvennom, pole deistviia). Cited from "Razgovor o Dante," in Mandel'shtam, *Polnoe sobranie sochinenii i pisem*, 3 vols. (Progress-Pleiada, 2010), 2155. Nancy Pollak's comment in *Mandelstam the Reader* (39) drew my attention to this passage.

89. See Velimir Khlebnikov, *Sobranie sochinenii*, 6 vols. (IMLI RAN "Nasledie," 2000), 1:104; *Collected Works of Velimir Khlebnikov*, vol. 3, *Selected Poems*, trans. Paul Schmidt, ed. Ronald Vroon (Harvard University Press, 1997), 31.

90. The second poem in the cycle is "Mne ni k chemu odicheskie rati," which also uses "liudei" as a rhyme word, in its first stanza; the burdock (lopukh) appears in the second. See Anna Akhmatova, *"Ia—golos vash . . ."* (Izdatel'stvo "Knizhnaia palata," 1989), 162.

91. Anna Glazova, "Nartsiss," *Colta*, February 6, 2014, http://www.colta.ru/articles/literature /1954.

92. See Blaser, "The Recovery of the Public World," in *The Fire: Collected Essays of Robin Blaser*, ed. Miriam Nichols (University of California Press, 2006), 64–86. The phrase became the title of a book in his honor: *The Recovery of the Public World: Essays on Poetics in Honour of Robin Blaser*, ed. Charles Watts and Edward Byrne (Talonbooks, 1999). There are interesting intersections between the otherwise quite different poetic worlds of Blaser and Dashevsky, both committed, extensive translators, both advancing the work of creating an arena for free public discourse. Blaser is explicit in tracing that work to one of his most admired figures, Hannah Arendt; in this essay, she is in the company, by the last page, of Stanley Cavell.

93. See also a response to Aizenberg's assessment of one of his books in manuscript: Stanislav L'vovskii's interview in Linor Goralik, *Chastnye litsa: Chast' vtoraia* (Novoe izdatel'stvo, 2017), 58–104; see 100.

94. Translated from "Kak chitat' sovremennuiu poeziiu," in Dashevskii, *Stikhotvoreniia i perevody*, 143–56, quotation from 156. For the original publication of the essay, see *Open Space*, February 10, 2012, http://os.colta.ru/literature/events/details/34232/, based on an extemporaneous monologue delivered to Varvara Babitskaia, who recorded and published it.

95. This passage is often quoted. Compare its use in this stinging assertion of the poet's freedom: Oksana Vasiakina, "Bol'she nikakogo rok-n-rolla," *F-pis'mo*, November 29, 2019, https://syg.ma/@galina-1/oksana-vasiakina-bolshie-nikakogho-rok-n-rolla.

1. Writing Poems in a World of Harm

Sources of epigraphs: Mikhail Iampol'skii, "Po tu storonu ierarkhii," *NLO* 91 (no. 3, 2008), 310–12, quotation on 312; Galina Rymbu quoted in Francesca Ebel, "The Voice of Feminism: On *F Letter: New Russian Feminist Poetry*," *Los Angeles Review of Books*, December 6, 2020, https://lareviewofbooks.org/article/the-voice-of-feminism-on-f-letter-new-russian-feminist -poetry/.

1. Mark Lipovetsky catches this moment well at the start of "The Formal Is Political," *SEEJ* 60, no. 2 (2016): 185–204.

2. See Mark Lipovetskii, "Uzhas, no ne uzhas-uzhas: o poezii Igoria Kholina," *Gor'kii*, December 1, 2020, https://gorky.media/context/uzhas-no-ne-uzhas-uzhas-o-poezii-igorya-holina/, particularly its reading of Kholin's imagery as an example of Agamben's *zoe*, or bare life. He

draws on a quotation from contemporary poet Galina Rymbu to connect the dots from Kholin's "barracks poetry" to current work.

3. Michel Foucault, *Fearless Speech*, ed. Joseph Pearson (Semiotext(e), 2001). Foucault's term was invoked in a forum about Fanailova, which is also the source of this chapter's first epigraph: see Iampol'skii in "Po tu storonu ierarkhii."

4. The tireless work of Ivan Akhmet'ev should be singled out for his excavation of the full poetic legacies of nearly a dozen unofficial poets, and for his several anthologies, perhaps most significantly the volumes he and others edited, *Russkie stikhi 1950–2000 godov: Antologiia (pervoe priblizhenie)*, 2 vols. (Letnii sad, 2010). Akhmet'ev was awarded an Andrei Bely Prize for this work in 2013.

5. To most critics, this new wave has seemed a source of poetic energy and imagination, but for a dissenting view (that the "new social poetics" is a grandiose fake), see Aleksandr Zhitenev, "Megafon kak orudie proizvodstva," in *Emblemata amatoria: Stat'i i etiudy* (Nauka-Unipress, 2015), 161–64. As the critic and poet Evgenia Vezhlian noted, the lingering ambivalence about whether one ought to write politically engaged poetry is itself a sign that Russia is still post-Soviet. See her contributions to the roundtable "Konventsii, politiki pis'ma i 'obshchie mesta,'" October 25, 2020, video, 2:17:40, https://www.youtube.com/watch?v=cWniEklWxf4.

6. That name also identified the lead section of most issues of *Novoe literaturnoe obozrenie* when it began publishing poetry. The selection of poetry has been wide ranging, and the name has fluctuated, too, including "Iziashchnaia slovesnost'" and, in 2022, simply "Novaia poeziia."

7. For a good summary of this work and an account of its roots in the poetry of the earlier post-Soviet period, see Lev Oborin, "Russian Political Poetry in the Twenty-First Century," *Harriman*, Spring 2017, http://www.columbia.edu/cu/creative/epub/harriman/2017/spring/russian_political_poetry.pdf.

8. Seven of these poets are the subject of Marijeta Bozovic, *Avant-Garde Post–: Radical Poetics after the Soviet Union* (Harvard University Press, 2023), and see her essays on individual poets, noted below.

9. Kirill Korchagin, "'The Mask Is Ripped Off along with the Skin': Ways of Constructing the Subject in the Political Poetry of the 2010s," *Russian Studies in Literature* 54, nos. 1–3 (2018): 120–40, quotation from 124.

10. A searing poem, written in the wake of protests over the arrest of Aleksey Navalny, links war and sexual violence directly: Anna Golubkova, "kak na voine," part of "Stikhi protesta: My bez oruzhiia," assembled by Ekaterina Zakharkiv, *F-Pis'mo*, February 7, 2021, https://syg.ma/@ekaterina-zakharkiv/stikhi-protiesta-my-biez-oruzhiia.

11. In English, see Kirill Medvedev, *It's No Good*, ed. Keith Gessen (Ugly Duckling Presse, 2012), which includes a detailed introduction by Gessen and a wide range of translated texts. The Russian publications include *Vse plokho* (OGI, 2002), *Teksty, izdannye bez vedoma avtora* (NLO, 2005), and *Anti-fashizm dlia vsekh* (Svobodnoe marksistskoe izdatel'stvo, 2017). Many of his texts are found on his website, http://kirillmedvedev.narod.ru.

12. The new epic poets include Fyodor Svarovsky, Arkady Rovinsky, Leonid Schwab, and Sergei Kruglov, and to some extent Boris Khersonsky. The term was introduced by Svarovsky in 2008 in a lecture in Moscow, reported in Varvara Bavitskaia, "Chto takoe 'novyi epos,'" *Open-Space*, February 20, 2008, http://os.colta.ru/literature/events/details/1249/. Her definition remains apt: "texts that resemble fragments of a screenplay, drafts for a novel, bits of cinema dia-

logue, voice-over, synopsis." Where Medvedev differs is in not estranging the relationship of poet/storyteller to narrative.

13. For a rich analysis of the poetics and politics of Medvedev's poetry to 2005, see Aleksandr Skidan, "Konets peremiriia: Zametki o poezii Kirilla Medvedeva," in *Summa poetiki* (NLO, 2013), 101–10.

14. Medvedev, *It's No Good*, 42–44, translation modified.

15. Medvedev, *Vse plokho*, 59–61.

16. Lvovsky introduced this formal and intonational innovation in *Belyi shum* (ARGO-RISK, 1996) and *Camera rostrum* (NLO, 2008). Both poets learned from English-language poets, especially Charles Bukowski, whom each of them translated.

17. This subject position is not fixed across Medvedev's work and it changed in later poems: for example, a speaker declares that he is on his way to work (in "Mashiny idut po tret'emu kol'tsu"); another combines his job as a courier with writing poetry (in "Chelovek-zebra vkhodit v trolleibus"). For both poems, see Medvedev, *Pokhod na meriiu* (Svobodnoe marksistskoe izdatel'stvo / Translit, 2014), 29, 36–37.

18. Note the irony of Medvedev, a committed Marxist, eschewing any self-definition by means of labor. I discuss that element of the poem, Medvedev's political positions, and the consequences of the masculine position the poems often take in an essay from which this example has been taken. See "Kirill Medvedev and Elena Fanailova: Poetry, Ethics, Politics, and Philosophy," *Russian Literature* 87–89 (2017): 281–313.

19. The book appeared in the Kraft book series Medvedev edited. It contains only the title poem, with illustrations by Nikolai Oleinikov, who also figures in the poem. The Russian is also available online: *Zhit' dolgo umeret' molodym*, on the old *[Translit]* website, http://old.trans-lit .info/medvedev.pdf. Other poems where one can sense the aggressive potential of Medvedev's later work include "You are the mouthpiece of this society" ("Ty—usta etogo obshchestva"), in Medvedev, *Pokhod na meriiu*, 30.

20. For a perspective on what Marijeta Bozovic terms his "militant aesthetics," see Bozovic, "Poetry on the Front Line: Kirill Medvedev and a New Russian Poetic Avant-Garde," *Zeitschrift für Slavische Philologie* 70, no. 1 (2014): 89–118, esp. 92–95.

21. See Dmitrii Golynko, "Prikladnaia sotsial'naia poeziia: Izobretenie politicheskogo sub"ekta," *[Translit]* 10–11 (2012): 180–82. Most of his publications are as Golynko, but readers will find him as Golynko-Vol'fson as well; formal statements about him in Russian most often use that full name.

22. But Golynko's orientation toward Conceptualism and the visual arts allied him with Moscow more than Petersburg, as Vitaly Lekhtsier pointed out at a memorial gathering at Poriadok Slov Bookstore, August 11, 2023, video, 3:00:53, https://www.youtube.com/watch?v =qAN5mwqKtE8.

23. Kevin M. F. Platt, "Now Poet: Dmitry Golynko and the New Social Epic," *Jacket2*, August 8, 2014, https://jacket2.org/article/now-poet-dmitry-golynko-and-new-social-epic.

24. Or, as Ilya Kukulin called them, yuppie intellectuals. See Il'ia Kukulin, "Ischeznovenie spektaklia (traektoriia poeticheskogo soznaniia)," introduction to Dmitrii Golynko, *Betonnye golubki* (NLO, 2003), 5–20, quotation on 12.

25. Eugene Ostashevsky, introduction to Dmitry Golynko, *As It Turned Out*, trans. Eugene Ostashevsky and Rebecca Bella with Simona Schneider (Ugly Duckling Presse, 2008), ix–xiii,

where Ostashevsky explains that "the materialism of hip-hop English is just not as cynical as the materialism of the new Russia" (xiii).

26. In his introduction to the poem "Looking at the Around," *Common Knowledge* 22, no. 1 (2016): 147–53, citation on 148. His full claim is, "The poetic work of 2016 must be far more severe, embittered, and cruel than the work of 2010."

27. These comments are from his remarks at the symposium "Pointed Words: Poetry and Politics in the Global Present," Yale University, November 30—December 1, 2018.

28. Translated by Kevin Platt in "Looking at the Around."

29. Kevin Platt has emphasized that Golynko constantly widens the gap between any apparent, defined subject position and the utterances and views of the poems. See Platt, "Dmitry Golynko and the Weaponization of Discourse Poetry," *AZ: Essays in Honor of Alexander Zholkovsky*, ed. Dennis Ioffe et al. (Academic Studies Press, 2018), 419–32, esp. 420.

30. Golynko writes that applied social poetry arises "when the poet hands over his or her unique authorial voice to the oppressed, the masses with no rights. The contemporary cultural industry deprives them of the possibility of speaking for themselves" (translated from Golynko, "Prikladnaia sotsial'naia poeziia," 180).

31. A sense of what is to come, including the ongoing work of reassessing Golynko's place among his peers, can be gathered from the essays published in his memory in *NLO* 181 (no. 3, 2023): 279–308. Particularly interesting is the transcript of his 2018 conference paper "Novye depressivnye" (305–8), which explicates his understanding of the lyric subject in the age he calls capitalist realism.

32. Documentary impulses are significant in the work of Roman Osminkin, too. See his work, co-created with Anastasiia Vepreva, *Kommunalka na Petrogradke* (NLO, 2022). Vepreva and Osminkin discuss this book with Irina Prokhorova in the podcast *Za fasadom sovetskogo glamura*, November 29, 2022, https://nlo.media/catalog/podrazdel-antropologii/evolyutsiya -kommunalki-ot-sssr-i-do-nashikh-dney/. The conversation treats some of the paradoxes and fault lines in their anthropological experiment documenting life in a communal apartment.

33. I take up this kind of poetry made before readers' eyes more fully in the next chapter, on performance. For this poem in Russian and English, see Arseniev, *Reported Speech* (Cicada Press, 2018), 24–25; the video is found at "Prodaetsia Maiakovskii," video, 2:34, uploaded by chto delat, https://vimeo.com/16587369. For additional work by Arseniev, see his web page http://arsenev.trans-lit.info.

34. Arseniev, *Reported Speech*, 44–45.

35. Humor is also a feature of later work by Medvedev, as noted in the afterword to Medvedev, *Pokhod na meriiu*: Aleksandr Skidan, "Derzhat' distantsiiu, derzhat' udar," 46–50; see 49–50.

36. Dmitrii Strotsev, *Shag* (Novye Mekhi, 2015), 62.

37. Elena Fanailova, "Aborty i politika," Radio Svoboda, October 28, 2020, https://www .svoboda.org/a/30916726.html. A choice sentence later in the essay shows the combination of sarcasm and medical knowledge mobilized here. I translate: "Medicine did not develop its early fetal diagnostic practices for the last century in order for some cis-gender individual with macho tendencies who happens to be in power to deprive women of the right to make a personal and complicated choice." She is referring specifically to the attempt in Poland to exclude from allowable abortions those based on the nonviability or serious deformity of a fetus.

38. In 2009, Stanislav Lvovsky suggested that Fanailova found the outsized attention to the poem somewhat unfortunate; he does not explain. See Stanislav L'vovskii, "Elene Fanailovoi," *Vozdukh* (nos. 1–2, 2009): 5–6. But in 2020, Fanailova reposted the poem to Facebook and commented that sure, it was famous, but it was also prescient in looking ahead to the feminism and the Ukrainian crisis of the present ("ok, vot vam khit 2003 goda, perebiraiu arkhiv. tut i pro #mitu, i pro #krymnash i #namkrysh"); Fanailova, Facebook, June 17, 2020.

39. The poem appeared in *Znamia* 2 (2002), https://magazines.gorky.media/znamia/2002/1/oni-opyat-za-svoj-afganistan.html; then in Fanailova, *Transil'vaniia bespokoit* (OGI, 2002); and in a forum in *NLO* 62 (no. 4, 2003): 111–15, with the accompanying prose text. For a translation by Genya Turovskaya with facing original, see Fanailova, *The Russian Version*, trans. Genya Turovskaya and Stephanie Sandler, 2nd ed. (Ugly Duckling Presse, 2019), 49–50.

40. For the poems, see *Transil'vaniia bespokoit*, 55–60; of those three names, Marina Malich may need glossing—she was the wife of the writer Daniil Kharms, completing the cycle's trio of women married to famous men.

41. See Namwali Serpell and Maria Tumarkin, "Unethical Reading and the Limits of Empathy," *Yale Review*, Winter 2020, https://yalereview.yale.edu/unethical-reading-and-limits-empathy. Serpell was using the phrase to define and admire an aspect of Tumarkin's work.

42. See Mark N. Lipovetskii, "'Est' smerti dlia menia . . .': Politika sub"ektivnosti v poezii Eleny Fanailovoi," in *Imidzh, dialog, eksperiment: Polia sovremennoi russkoi poezii*, ed. Henrieke Stahl and Marion Rutz (Verlag Otto Sagner, 2013), 309–21; see 309–10. He cites several such reviews.

43. Fanailova made these remarks in the episode "Poeziia kak sobytie: Poeziia kak aktual'noe," on the television program *Vslukh: Poeziia segodnia*, June 13, 2013, hosted by Aleksandr Gavrilov (Telekanal Rossiia), http://tvkultura.ru/video/show/brand_id/20929/video_id/428523. She was agreeing with a view expressed by Kirill Medvedev, also a guest on the show, that the poet who is genuinely contemporary (aktual'nyi) reacts to those historical changes that happen only once every ten or twenty years. Fanailova agreed but added that the poet's task is to register those era-defining changes in language, and that the context for that language is culture, broadly construed (media, politics, myth, social structures, etc.)—what Akhmatova called rubbish. Later in the broadcast, she turns to a phrase from Mandelstam as if to define at last what it means to be contemporary: what the poet needs to do is to hear the noise of time (shum vremeni).

44. Fanailova, *Russian Version*, 57.

45. There were two Chechen wars. The first, 1994–96, ended in defeat for Russia. The Second Chechen War began in 1999 (thus the reference here to the two-year anniversary of its inception) and lasted nearly a decade. The fearless Anna Politkovskaya's reporting from Chechnya led to her murder in Moscow in 2006. See Politkovskaia, *Vtoraia Chechenskaia* (Zakharov, 2002), or, in English, *A Small Corner of Hell: Dispatches from Chechnya*, trans. Alexander Burry and Tatiana Tulchinsky (University of Chicago Press, 2003).

46. That polarity, the intimate and the civic ("intimna i grazhdanstvenna"), is one of several used by Alexander Ilichevsky to define Fanailova's perspective, which he calls the point from which she speaks ("tochka govoreniia"). See "Otzyvy," *Vozdukh* 1–2 (2009): 36. It was formulated by Linor Goralik as civic love poetry ("grazhdanskaia liubovnaia lirika"). See Goralik, "O 'Baltiiskom dnevnike' Eleny Fanailovoi," *OpenSpace*, July 10, 2008, http://www.litkarta.ru/dossier/goralik-o-fanailovoi/dossier_2050/.

47. As if to prove one aspect of the self-comparison to Kibirov's poetics, an essay by Iurii Leving about this poem exhaustively lists its subtexts. See Iurii Leving, "V dome durakov: Pesni nevinnosti, oni zhe—opyta," *NLO* 62 (no. 4, 2003): 114–28. Unlike the work of Mandelstam and the Acmeists, where subtext poetics were developed, the surface text in both Kibirov and Fanailova is rarely confounding: the intertexts add resonance and sometimes irony.

48. Fanailova, *Russian Version*, 59.

49. Fanailova, *Russian Version*, 54–55.

50. Her work is unexpectedly analogous to diary keeping, particularly in the terms Irina Paperno has laid out, emphasizing "the diary's special relationship to privacy, intimacy, and secrecy." See Irina Paperno, "What Can Be Done with Diaries?" *Russian Review* 63, no. 4 (2004): 561–73, quotation on 562.

51. Compare the far-reaching interview Fanailova gave to Linor Goralik, with extensive material from the poet's childhood and earliest adult years that shows her willingness to scrutinize her own experiences. See Linor Goralik, *Chastnye litsa: Biografii poetov, rasskazannye im samim* (Novoe izdatel'stvo, 2013), 339–71.

52. In that sense, Fanailova's work as a poet is not in tension with her journalism, in a way that aligns with the broad argument about poetry and the news in Jahan Ramazani, *Poetry and Its Others: News, Prayer, Song, and the Dialogue of Genres* (University of Chicago Press, 2014), 63–125. Many of Ramazani's examples show that poems can have surprising affinities with news reporting; those closest in spirit (although with quite different intonations) to Fanailova's project are by Irish poets (81–103), with their "textual index of the now" (92). But there is also much in common with William Carlos Williams's *Paterson*, with its "the precise incentive to epic poetry, the poetry of events" (107). Those are Williams's words, from an unpublished manuscript. Ramazani (in 253n100) gives the source as Mike Weaver, *William Carlos Williams: The American Background* (Cambridge University Press, 1971), 120.

53. The point is well made in Lipovetskii, "Est' smerti dlia menia . . . ," especially his concluding sentence (321).

54. See, for example, her stylized diary poems in the Bram Stoker cycle or, in a modified way, in an earlier poem about Frida Kahlo. For "Po kanve Brema Stokera," see Fanailova, *Lena i liudi* (Novoe izdatel'stvo, 2011), 101–9. For "Al'bom Fridy," see Fanailova, *S osobym tsinizmom* (NLO, 2000), 48–49.

55. I translated them as "Lena, or the Poet and the People" and "Lena and Lena" in *Russian Version*, 148–79. In what follows, I cite Fanailova's original Russian publications of these poems, and the translations sometimes modify those in *Russian Version*.

56. More poems mentioning Lena or Elena have appeared, and Fanailova has also used both poem titles, #ленаилюди and #ленаилена, as a Facebook hashtag for new poems.

57. Fanailova, *Lena i liudi*, 68–73, quoted from 68. The poem also appears in *NLO* 62 (no. 3, 2008): 306–9.

58. Fanailova, *Lena i liudi*, 73.

59. Mikhail Iampol'skii, in "Po tu storonu ierarkhii," 312 (see also his note 1).

60. I agree here with Boris Dubin, who was struck by the poem's renunciation of the "power of the Poet," the sense of being chosen. See Dubin, in "Po tu storonu ierarkhii," 317.

61. In "Lena and People," Fanailova also somewhat ironically cites a famous line, "you are your own highest judge" (ty sam svoi vysshii sud) from a different Pushkin poem: the sonnet "Poetu" ("To the Poet," 1830).

62. He also saw the poem as "socio-political poetry in its ethical dimension," in fact, as an "emotional-philosophical parable." Golynko sought to align this poem with the goals of the new social poetry. See Dmitrii Golynko-Vol'fson, in "Po tu storonu ierarkhii," 331.

63. Another way that democratizing gesture works in the poem is that the poet is shown to be in the same kind of commercial, economically driven relationship to her work as is the cashier who sells cigarettes and kefir: the poet must get involved in the distribution of her books because the publisher does so little. The commercial underside of this poem is well articulated in the *NLO* forum: see Aleksandr Skidan, in "Po tu storonu ierarkhii," 324.

64. For those poems, see Fanailova, *Lena i liudi* and *Chernye kostiumy* (Novoe izdatel'stvo, 2008). Some are included in translation in Fanailova, *Russian Version*.

65. In 2014, Fanailova published a poem that reads as a postscript to "Lena and Lena": untitled, it begins "Winter in Belgrade" ("Zima v Belgrade"). The poet writes that she can't "keep thinking about war all the time" (Ia bol'she ne mogu / Vse vremia dumat' o voine); the poem ends with the lines "We dress elegantly / When we go to the oncologist" (My elegantny, / Kogda idem k onkologu). See Fanailova, "Moia ukrainskaia sem'ia," *Vozdukh* 4 (2014): 132.

66. The references to bombing are presumably to the NATO air strikes against Belgrade during the Kosovo War in 1999. Compare Fanailova's two powerful poems about Sarajevo: "Saraevo porazhaet v samoe serdtse" and "Saraevo kak voronovo krylo," included in Fanailova, *Lena i liudi*, 117–19. She reads the former in the *OpenSpace* series Stikhi vzhivuiu, April 15, 2011, http://os.colta.ru/literature/projects/75/details/21834/?view_comments=all; the software no longer works for the recording, which is available here: "Fanaylova 1," video, 0:43, https://drive.google.com/file/d/1XgXW7aeJ9DUM1WktSTE97zrH5m5P_4DY/view.

67. Here and below, all references are to Fanailova, "Lena i Lena," *Zerkalo* 35 (2010), https://magazines.gorky.media/zerkalo/2010/35/lena-i-lena.html.

68. Fanailova, *Lena i liudi*, 69. We might also read the reference to "fucking" as "an instrument of cognition" to be a version of knowing the self through the encounter with the other in Levinasian terms, which are explored more in the poem "Lena and People."

69. That observation about Akhmatova's poetry was famously made in Osip Mandelstam's "Pis'mo o russkoi poezii" (1922), in Mandel'shtam, *Polnoe sobranie sochinenii i pisem*, 3 vols. (Progress-Pleiada, 2010), 2:55–59; see 57–58. This approach to Akhmatova was developed in Viktor Zhirmunskii, *Tvorchestvo Anny Akhmatovoi* (Izdatel'stvo "Nauka," Leningradskoe otdelenie, 1973); he saw her as continuing the traditions of Russian realism (25).

70. Fanailova, "Stikhi dlia Sashi Kabanova," Facebook, July 28, 2014.

71. On Savchenko's later treatment in Russia and her hunger strike, see Masha Gessen, "Nadiya Savchenko Gives Russia the Finger," *New Yorker*, March 10, 2016, https://www.newyorker.com/news/news-desk/nadiya-savchenko-gives-russia-the-finger. Savchenko survived the hunger strike and was later returned to Ukraine during a prisoner swap.

72. Fanailova, "Sineet plamen', ugasaet led," Facebook, June 2, 2015.

73. Fanailova, writing a comment related to her poem "Liubila koroleva generala," Facebook, November 9, 2018.

74. The publication includes two poems on elections in Donetsk in 2014 and in Voronezh in 2002, contrasting a populace mobilized for war with one urged to cast ballots.

75. Translation by Eugene Ostashevsky, from Fanailova, "Two New Poems," *White Review*, January 2016, http://www.thewhitereview.org/poetry/poem-for-zhadan-my-ukrainian -grandmother/.

76. Fanailova, "Moia ukrainskaia sem'ia," 138.

77. Translation by Eugene Ostashevsky, from Fanailova, "Two New Poems."

78. Fanailova, "Moia ukrainskaia sem'ia," 141.

79. Fanailova, "Moia ukrainskaia sem'ia," 142.

80. As the Russia-Ukraine War escalated, Ukrainians have made clearer their resentment of Russians' penchant for talking about their Ukrainian relatives, and Fanailova, whose sensitivity to Ukrainian reactions to the war is acute, might now see these poems as more fraught.

81. See Fanailova's statement about rape as a tool of war in Belarus: "Telo kak ulika: Elena Fanailova—o proteste i iznasilovanii," Radio Svoboda, December 19, 2020, https://www .svoboda.org/a/31007317.html.

82. *Colta* flourished until it was shut down in March 2022, but it promised even then not to disappear for good. It announced in September 2022 on Telegram and Facebook a partial return through the *Syg.ma* platform, and it has continued to offer periodic special reports. For the first installment, see Polina Patimova's conversation with sociologist Ella Paneiakh, "Chut' nizhe radarov," September 15, 2022, *Vokrug gorizontali*, https://syg.ma/@sygma/vokrugh-ghorizontali -chut-nizhie-radarov.

83. A fine selection of these essays is gathered in Stepanova, *Odin, ne odin, ne ia* (Novoe izdatel'stvo, 2014) and *Tri stat'i po povodu* (Novoe izdatel'stvo, 2015).

84. Stepanova, *Pamiati pamiati: Romans* (Novoe izdatel'stvo, 2017), 303.

85. The book made some readers feel as if they were reading about their own lives. See the comments by Evgenia Vezhlian cited in Ol'ga Balla, "Osoznat' i uvidet'," *NLO* 151 (no. 3, 2018): 313–17. See also "Poema bez geroia? Proshloe na styke vekov: 'Pamiati pamiati' Marii Stepanovoi," *Gefter*, February 26, 2018, http://gefter.ru/archive/24137.

86. She draws on Marianne Hirsch, *Family Frames: Photography, Narrative, and Postmemory* (Harvard University Press, 1997).

87. For the poem, see Stepanova, *Fiziologiia i malaia istoriia* (FNI Pragmatika kul'tury, 2005), 37–42. For a translation into English by Sibelan Forrester, with facing Russian, see Catherine Ciepiela, ed., *Relocations: 3 Contemporary Russian Women Poets* (Zephyr, 2013), 156–63.

88. See Stepanova, *Sviashchennaia Zima 20/21* (Novoe izdatel'stvo, 2021), which has been translated into English by Sasha Dugdale as *Holy Winter* (New Directions, 2024), as well as the as yet unpublished poems of "Bez yka" (2024).

89. The poem is "Est' tselomudrennye chary" (1909), in Mandel'shtam, *Polnoe sobranie sochinenii i pisem*, 1:45.

90. The poem is translated into a more poetic English version by Sasha Dugdale in Stepanova, *War of the Beasts and the Animals* (Bloodaxe, 2021), 21–44, and in Stepanova, *The Voice Over: Poems and Essays*, ed. Irina Shevelenko (Columbia University Press, 2021), 113–38.

91. Stepanova, *Spolia* (Novoe izdatel'stvo, 2015), 31. The irony is intensified because a passage very similar to this is at the very start of the poem: "esli sobrat' v kuchu / bylo skazano vot

chto—// ona ne sposobna govorit' za sebia, / potomu v ee stikhakh obiazatel'ny rifmy // i fal'sifitsiruiutsia otzhivshie formy" (9).

92. Stepanova reformulates the opening of the Igor Tale, quoting its first words, in fact, about a third of the way into the poem. For the Russian text of the poem, see Stepanova, *Spolia*, 35–58. It was first published in *Zerkalo* 45 (2015), https://magazines.gorky.media/zerkalo/2015/45 /vojna-zverej-i-zhivotnyh.html, and generated immediate lively commentary, beginning with Mikhail Iampol'skii, "Smert' i soobshchestvo: O poeme Marii Stepanovoi 'Voina zverei i zhivotnykh,'" *Gefter*, July 7, 2015, http://gefter.ru/archive/15613. There is a splendid reading of the poem's cultural antecedents in Maria Vassileva, "After the Seraph: The Nonhuman in Twenty-First Century Russian Literature" (PhD diss., Harvard University, 2019), 79–87.

93. In 2008, Stepanova tersely observed in an interview that family stories were a source of pain and guilt. Her words were meant to explain why she avoided these stories, but one can also see why work on *In Memory of Memory* was, for Stepanova, so extensive and important. For the interview, conducted by Linor Goralik, see *Vozdukh* 4 (2008): 17–21, esp. 18–19.

94. Heaney is writing about poets' ways of establishing a connection to Englishness, but this is one of several formulations in this essay that feel keenly appropriate to Stepanova. See his "Englands of the Mind," in *Preoccupations: Selected Prose 1968–1978* (Farrar, Straus and Giroux, 1980), 150–69, quoted from 151.

95. Another way to draw on the past appears in the section that begins "on June 22" ("dvadtsat' vtorogo iunia"). That day commemorates Ukrainian victims in the Second World War.

96. This connection between language and resistance was inspired by a presentation by Gasan Guseinov, "Echolalia, or a Flight from the Cloaca Tongue," at the online symposium "Poetry as Resistance: In Twentieth-Century Eastern Europe and Beyond," Uppsala University, August 31–September 2, 2020; Guseinov's examples are from earlier periods. A recording is available: "Poetry as Resistance Symposium—Session 4 and 5," video, 4:23:16, posted by Zakhar Ishov on September 3, 2020, https://www.youtube.com/watch?v=qHGA5jZ3Q30.

97. Heaney, "Englands of the Mind," 150.

98. Stepanova, *Spolia*, 51. Compare the expressive version by Sasha Dugdale, which departs from the text significantly and opens out its very tight layout, in Stepanova, *Voice Over*, 155–56. As Ilya Kukulin pointed out to me, the Russian lines, beginning "my ne nem tsy," allude to a text designed to teach literacy to adults in the 1920s, which reads "My ne ra by" (meaning, we are not slaves, with the two-syllable Russian word for "slaves" spelled out in syllables).

99. Iampol'skii, "Smert' i soobshchestvo."

100. Sergei El'kin, "Mariia Stepanova: 'Stikhi vyravniaiut dykhanie.' Razgovor s poetom o tom, kak rozhdaetsia poeziia," *Minsk-Chikago: Blog Sergeia El'kina*, March 1, 2017, http:// sergeyelkin.blogspot.com/2017/03/blog-post.html.

101. But it does that as well: a 2015 program at Svoboda Radio hosted by Fanailova on poetry during the Ukraine war featured Stepanova's "War of the Beasts and the Animals": see "Stikhi o gibridnoi voine," October 25, 2015, https://www.svoboda.org/a/27324155.html.

102. Aleksandr Markov, "Svoboda o sebe, zabota ne o sebe: O 'Spolia' Marii Stepanovoi," *Gefter*, June 30, 2014, http://gefter.ru/archive/12654.

103. Mikhail Iampol'skii, Facebook, June 14, 2014.

104. For the passage, see Stepanova, *Spolia*, 23–26.

105. Stepanova, *Spolia*, 40. Compare Dugdale's translation in Stepanova, *Voice Over*, 144.

106. Mikhail Iampol'skii, "Podzemnyi patefon (Ob odnom motive v poezii Marii Stepanovoi)," *NLO* 130 (no. 6, 2014): 231–68. Possibly his work with the technology of the gramophone for this study alerted Iampolsky to the philosophical implications of photography as technology in "Spolia," but his extensive writing on Dragomoshchenko (see chapter 5) surely also played its role.

107. I stand by the assertion that this commitment deepens in the 2010s, but unsentimental celebration of women's bodies is in Stepanova's work as early as "The Women's Changing Room at Planet Fitness" ("Zhenskaia razdevalka kluba 'Planeta Fitnes'"), translated by Sibelan Forrester in Ciepiela, *Relocations*, 164–67 (with facing Russian). The poem first appeared in *Fiziologiia i malaia istoriia*, 27–30.

108. For the poem, see Stepanova, *Staryi mir. Pochinka zhizni* (Novoe izdatel'stvo, 2020), 45–54. The poem first appeared in 2019 on Stepanova's Facebook page.

109. "Telo vozvrashchaetsia," a complex and compelling text that deserves its own essay, does many things with its reverse-alphabetical structure, but one way to read it is as the imagination of a woman's body deep in the earth as the source of language. The underground has been a source of provocative thinking within and about Stepanova. See especially Iampol'skii, "Podzemnyi patefon." To my mind, that image recalls Elena Shvarts's "Zver'-tsvetok," although Stepanova's "Telo" is explicitly in conversation with the work of Inger Christensen, Marjorie Pickthall, and Anne Carson. For Shvarts's poem, see *Izbrannye stikhotvoreniia* (Vita Nova, 2013), 37. For "Telo vozvrashchaetsia," see Stepanova, *Staryi mir*, 5–24. The first publication of "Telo vozvrashchaetsia" was in *Vozdukh* 37 (2018): 187–98.

110. See "Poeticheskie itogi Galiny Rymbu: Chast' 2," *God literatury*, December 31, 2019, https://godliteratury.ru/public-post/poyeticheskie-itogi-galiny-rymbu-chast-2. Lev Oborin finds Stepanova in conversation with women poets throughout *Staryi mir*. See his review in "Avtor umer, avtor proros: Poeticheskie novinki dekabria," *Gor'kii*, January 8, 2020, https://gorky.media/context/avtor-umer-avtor-proros/.

111. Stepanova, *Staryi mir*, 47.

112. Stepanova, *Staryi mir*, 48. Fifteen is also the age of the speaker in Galina Rymbu's poem "Ee paren' rabotaet vyshibaloi," which contrasts the uncertainties of a girl's understanding of sexuality with a brutal world of prostitution, pimp enforcers, and the possible solidarity of women. The poem appeared in *Colta*, March 3, 2020, https://www.colta.ru/articles/literature/23723-ee-paren-rabotaet-vyshibaloy-novye-stihi-galiny-rymbu.

113. Stepanova meditates on the force of that word *vsegda* in public discourse. She comments on phrases that are, to her mind, telltale signs of a worldview that believes there is no tomorrow. See her essay "Posle mertvoi vody" in Stepanova, *Tri stat'i po povodu*, 27–37; see 36. A translation of that essay by Maria Vassileva appears in Stepanova, *Voice Over*, 171–78.

114. This is not to say that the layers of cultural memory are gone; rather they are displaced into a different register. Here, that register is rhetorical. As has been pointed out, the poet speaks as if having been silenced, precisely the rhetorical structure at the heart of Osip Mandelstam's great poem "Stikhi o neizvestnom soldate": See Igor' Gulin, "Mariia Stepanova. Staryi mir. Pochinka zhizni," *Kommersant" Weekend*, January 31, 2020, https://www.kommersant.ru/doc/4227793.

115. An exemplary feminist reading of a Keats poem that exposes the harassment hidden in seductions is Karen Swann, "Harassing the Muse," in *Romanticism and Feminism*, ed. Anne K. Mellor (Indiana University Press, 1988), 81–92.

116. Stepanova, *Staryi mir*, 47.

117. Stepanova, *Staryi mir*, 48.

118. As specified on the main page of the Andrei Bely Prize, http://belyprize.ru/?pid =469&bmk=0&ppar=0. The award committee's statement about *F Letter* was written by Dmitry Kuz'min: "F-Pis'mo proekt," Premiia Andreia Belogo, http://belyprize.ru/index.php?id=640.

119. For a compact statement about the new feminist poets, see Rymbu's introduction to *F Letter: New Russian Feminist Poetry*, ed. Galina Rymbu, Eugene Ostashevsky, and Ainsley Morse (Isolarii Press, 2020), 11–30.

120. I treat the poets of *F Letter* in more detail in "The Body Returns: Recent Poems by Russian Women," in *Poetics and Politics by Women in the Post-Soviet Space, Internationale Zeitschrift für Kulturkomparatistik* 6 (2022): 261–300.

121. Stepanova showed her respect through *Colta*, publishing interviews and reviews of their work. Also, and quite unusual for *Colta*, which rarely featured poetry, there was the important publication of Vasiakina's poem "chto ia znaiu o nasilii," included in "Dva teksta o nasilii," *Colta*, November 3, 2017, http://www.colta.ru/articles/literature/16480. Among pertinent texts by Fanailova, see "'Pochti vse o Eve'—Elena Fanailova o novoi knige Oksany Vasiakinoi," *Diskurs*, May 21, 2019, https://discours.io/articles/chapters/pochti-vs-o-eve-elena-fanaylova-o-novoy -knige-oksany-vasyakinoy. And see Rymbu's praise for Fanailova's political poetry: "Poeziia v internete: Aprel'," *God literary*, May 2, 2019, https://godliteratury.ru/articles/2019/05/02 /poyeziya-v-internete-aprel.

122. Serenko's *Devochki i institutsii* (No Kidding Press, 2021) is the place to start in reading her work. To put her poetics alongside those of Rymbu, see the publication by Maria Bobyleva of their texts, with commentary by each of them on poetic lexicon: "(Ne)korrektnye stikhi," *Takie dela* 5 (May 27, 2020), https://takiedela.ru/2020/05/nekorrektnye-stikhi/.

123. Among interesting attempts to categorize this vast body of work, see Anna Golubkova, "K voprosu o klassifikatsii sovremennoi zhenskoi russkoiazychnoi poezii," *Artikuliatsiia* 14 (March 2021), http://articulationproject.net/10316.

124. I trace some of that history in "On Russian Poems, Poets, and Prizes, Late into 2020," *Russian Review* 80, no. 2 (2021): 497–505.

125. Rymbu also wrote bluntly about the ways in which the community of poets epitomized in the selection committee had not lived up to the standard of gender equity that the award would seem to value. For the statements, see Mariia Bikbulatova, "F-Pis'mo otkazyvaetsia ot Premii Andreia Belogo," *F-Pis'mo*, December 3, 2020, https://syg.ma/@mariia-bikbulatova/f -pismo-otkazyvaietsia-ot-priemii-bielogho.

126. See Rymbu, "Introduction: Grains of Transformation," in *F Letter*, 11–33

127. Comments made during a reading to celebrate the publication of *F Letter*, "F-Letter: New Feminist Poetry in Russian—A Conversation with Poets, Translators and Editors," November 4, 2020, video, 1:59:16, GlobusBooks SF, https://www.youtube.com/watch?v=K1Ea _GR_EMM. See Rymbu, "Introduction: Grains of Transformation," 12, for the comment about Al'chuk and Temkina.

128. On Al'chuk, see the introduction by Mikhail Ryklin to Al'chuk, *Sobranie stikhotvorenii* (NLO, 2011), 5–20. There is a fine analysis of her poetry in Dar'ia Sukhovei, "Poetika Anny Al'chuk," *Deti Ra* 9–10, nos. 35–36 (2007), http://www.litkarta.ru/dossier/suhovei-ob-alchuk /dossier_814/. Al'chuk was an organizer of the 2003 *Ostorozhno, religiia!* exhibit, vandalized by

offended viewers. She was tried for inciting religious hostility. For a rich sense of her life and work, see Ryklin, *Pristan' Dionisa* (Izdatel'stvo "Logos," 2003).

129. I write about this side of her work in "Marina Temkina and Marginally Jewish Russian Poetry," in *New Studies in Russian Literature: Essays in Honor of Stanley J. Rabinowitz*, ed. Catherine Ciepiela and Lazar Fleishman, Stanford Slavic Studies, vols. 45–46 (Berkeley Slavic Specialties, 2014), 46:338–50.

130. Temkina, *Kalancha: Gendernaia lirika* (Slovo-Word, 1995), 24–31. Temkina emigrated in the late Soviet period and developed within the art world and in feminist circles in and around New York and Paris, publishing largely in the West. Her importance in Russian poetry was reaffirmed with two major Moscow publications: *Canto immigrant* (NLO, 2005) and *Nenagliadnye posobiia* (NLO, 2019). Fanailova provided an introduction for the latter (5–8), Prigov for the former (5–7). For a good, small selection of her recent work, with an excerpt of Fanailova's introduction, see "Marina Temkina: Deviat' rechitativov dlia zhenskogo golosa," *F-Letter*, September 5, 2019, https://syg.ma/@ekaterina-zakharkiv/marina-tiomkina-dieviat-riechitativov-dlia-zhienskogho-gholosa.

131. For the poem in Russian, with an English translation by Kevin M. F. Platt, see *F Letter*, 220–43.

132. "Velikaia russkaia literatura," Facebook, July 3, 2020.

133. Tsvetkova's website *The Vagina Monologues* prompted a criminal investigation of local authorities in Komsomolsk-on-Amur, leading to months of house arrest and subsequent additional charges. She was found innocent in July 2022, and after prosecutorial appeals, fully cleared only on November 21, 2022, as reported in multiple news sites (including the BBC, "Khudozhnitsu Iuliiu Tsvetkovu, kotoruiu sudili za risunki vul'v, okonchatel'no opravdali," November 22, 2022, https://www.bbc.com/russian/news-63714614). For a study of Rymbu's poem, see Josephine von Zitzewitz, "Case Study: Galina Rymbu, 'Moia vagina' 2020," in *Poetics and Politics by Women in the Post-Soviet Space*, 187–210.

134. She posted the poem to Facebook and prefaced it with a statement of solidarity with those protesting in Russia (Rymbu lives in Ukraine). See Rymbu, "Zakon ne obladaet zdes' sily i konstitutsiia ne spaset ot boli i nenavisti," Facebook, May 27, 2020, reposted January 31, 2021.

135. Rymbu, Facebook, May 27, 2020.

136. I cite both English and Russian from *F Letter*, 220–21 and 242–43; the translation is by Kevin M. F. Platt. The poem first appeared on Rymbu's post to Facebook, June 27, 2020. On February 9, 2021, Rymbu posted the surprised announcement that the post had been taken down by Facebook.

137. Translated from an interview with Anastasia Osipova and Marijeta Bozovic, "Depressiia i melankholiia—eto sposob znaniia," *Colta*, October 11, 2019, https://www.colta.ru/articles/literature/22622-galina-rymbu-bolshoe-intervyu. In the interview, Rymbu continues: "At a certain point, it became obvious to me that for me personally two types of political poetry ceased to work: that which imitates direct speech, direct utterance or that absorbs the speech of others (either seriously or ironically), or that which is built on 'mobilizing' images, those to which it's easy to attach affects and that produce a kind of vaporization: they guarantee the tension of the poetry, but this isn't the same thing as intensity of meaning. I tried all of this, but it often seemed to me that something important was just beyond my grasp" (my translation).

138. Translated from Rymbu's commentary to her poem "Stikhi s novymi slovami," in Bob-yleva, "(Ne)korrektnye stikhi."

139. For a striking and explicit instance, see a poem addressed to her young son, "Ty—budushchee," when she writes, describing their family life, "eto prazdnik vnutri katastrofy." For the poem, see Natal'ia Beskhlebnaia, "'Mne doch' ne skazhet slovo papa': Monologi trekh po-etov o roditel'iakh i detiakh," *Afisha Daily*, January 15, 2021, https://daily.afisha.ru/brain/18445-mne-doch-ne-skazhet-slova-papa-monologi-treh-poetov-o-roditelyah-i-detyah/. In the com-ments attached to this publication of the poem, Rymbu notes that people often complain that there is not enough utopia in art or in politics. She has given a lot of thought, she says, to what kind of utopia there could be during a global ecological catastrophe, during a time when there are no solutions to social inequality or capitalism, but in this poem, she finds a utopia in her son.

140. In writing of her own identifications, Rymbu has said, "I see myself as queer, but with a woman's experience, the experience of motherhood, of being socialized as a woman. These are experiences I in no way renounce." Translated from "Depressiia i melankholiia."

141. In the poem "Ia perekhozhu na stantsiiu Trubnaia i vizhu," in Rymbu, *Peredvizhnoe prostranstvo perevorota* (Knizhnoe obozrenie ARGO-RISK, 2014), 54–61, quotation on 54.

142. See "Elections," trans. Eugene Ostashevsky, *Asymptote*, June 12, 2017, http://www.asymptotejournal.com/poetry/elena-fanailova-elections/.

143. A particularly vivid example appears in her poem "Oskorblenie vlasti," which she spoke about when reading the poem in London in 2020. For the reading, which includes translation into English by Helena Kernan, see "'Disrespecting the State' Poetry Reading by Galina Rymbu," Pushkin House, March 13, 2020, video, 19:41, posted June 25, 2020, https://www.youtube.com/watch?v=pGaezb4_aQI. The poem is included in Rymbu, "Ee paren' rabotaet vyshibaloi."

144. That phantom connection to Whitman was prompted by Jacques Rancière, *Aisthesis: Scenes from the Aesthetic Regime of Art*, trans. Zakir Paul (Verso, 2013), the chapter on the "Poet of the New World," 55–74.

145. Rymbu, *Zhizn' v prostranstve*, 75.

146. I write about this poem in detail in "The Body Returns." It was called an ars poetica in Tiffany Troy, "Readings and Conversation about the Stylistic Multitudes in Galina Rymbu's Poetry and *Life in Space*," *Columbia Journal*, November 2, 2020, https://www.columbiajournal.org/articles/2020-readings-and-conversation-about-the-stylistic-multitudes-in-galina-rymbus-poetry-and-life-in-space.

147. *The Poems of John Keats*, ed. Jack Stillinger (Belknap Press of Harvard University Press, 1978), 476–77.

148. For the poem, see Heaney, *Selected Poems 1966–1987* (Farrar, Straus and Giroux, 1990), 7. The poem appeared in Heaney's first book of poems, *Death of a Naturalist* (Faber and Faber, 1966).

149. The translation is by Valzhyna Mort, from *F Letter*, 205.

150. Cited from Rymbu, "Leto: Vorota tela," *F-Letter*, June 25, 2019, https://syg.ma/@ekat-erina-zakharkiv/galina-rymbu-lieto-vorota-tiela. The Russian text is also in *F Letter*, which is bilingual (see 204 for this passage).

151. Readers may sense a fairy-tale world here. The poet as a child played at being a witch in the bathhouse with her grandmother; their dog was named Till Eulenspiegel.

152. Here and below, the translation is by Eugene Ostashevsky: Rymbu, "Poem for Food," included in the bilingual anthology *This Is Us Losing Count* (Two Lines Press, 2022), 55–77. I cite from the Russian version there. The Russian text first appeared on *Syg.ma, Life in Space*, November 13, 2020, https://syg.ma/@galina-1/stikhi-dlia-iedy.

153. In Rymbu's poetry, abstract or philosophical terms like *materiia, forma, vremia, organizatsiia*, and *znak* are mixed into poetic lines about a grimy street, a light-dappled field, a body speckled with wounds or mud. That admixture is one way her concrete images take on such philosophical force.

154. See "Belyi khleb," in Rymbu, *Ty—budushchee* (Tsentr Voznesenskogo, 2020), 90–92. The poem is also in *Zhizn' v prostranstve*, 84–85.

155. Rymbu, *Ty—budushchee*, 63.

156. Rymbu, *Ty—budushchee*, 68.

157. Rymbu, *Ty—budushchee*, 69.

158. Rymbu, Facebook, February 2, 2021.

159. Lipovetsky, "Formal Is Political," 199.

160. Living through the Ukraine war in Lviv has recast Rymbu's rhetoric for writing politics into something at once mournful and clear headed, determined. See her long text "Sledy," posted in November 2022 via Facebook: "Sledy_ves' tsikl," https://docs.google.com/document/d/1UFmQjWjbOYewLMJ6LRQeeZ58qqxcXPeX/edit. She published part of this long text earlier: "okazavshis' na samom kraiu skorbi," *Soloneba*, July 20, 2022, http://soloneba.com/galina-rymbu.

161. "Interv'iu" by Linor Goralik, *Vozdukh* (no. 1, 2016): 22–28.

162. See Rancière, "Rimbaud: Voices and Bodies," in *The Flesh of Words*, trans. Charlotte Mandell (Stanford University Press, 2004), 41–67. There is an uncannily apt formulation of Rymbu's achievement in a phrase on which Rancière's chapter ends: Rimbaud "made the song of obscure misfortune resound in the logical revolt of his poems and his prose" (67).

163. The sound similarity is noted in Niall McDevitt, "Another Rimbaud," *International Times*, November 24, 2016, http://internationaltimes.it/another-rimbaud/.

164. This is a cornerstone of his argument about poetry, most fully worked out in *The Flesh of Words*. It is fruit for another essay to consider how important Russian material has been to his theorizing—see, for example, the chapter on Mandelstam in *The Flesh of Words*, 9–40, or the discussion of Dziga Vertov's film work in *Aisthesis*, 225–43. Or the chapter on *War and Peace* in *The Politics of Literature*, trans. Julie Rose (Polity, 2011), 72–79.

2. Performing Poetry in the Age of the Internet

1. See Walter Benjamin, "The Work of Art in the Age of Its Technological Reproducibility: Second Version," in *Selected Writings*, vol. 3, *1935–1938*, trans. Edmund Jephcott et al., ed. Howard Eiland and Michael W. Jennings (Belknap Press of Harvard University Press, 2002), 101–33.

2. Many years ago, my linguistics professor, Edward Stankiewicz, developed for us the notion of what he called the "paucal" to account for how the dual left its trace on Russia's grammar of counting. There are not two ways to think about number (singular and plural), but three: sin-

gular; two, three, or four of something; and plural. It's the two-three-four group that Professor Stankiewicz called the "paucal."

3. A. S. Pushkin, *Polnoe sobranie sochinenii v desiati tomakh*, 4th ed., vol. 3 (Izdatel'stvo "Nauka," Leningradskoe otdelenie, 1977), 246–48. There is a lovely translation in Pushkin, *Selected Poetry*, trans. Antony Wood (Penguin Random House UK, 2020), 64–67.

4. Galina Rymbu, "Ee paren' rabotaet vyshibaloi," *Colta* (March 3, 2020), https://www.colta.ru/articles/literature/23723-ee-paren-rabotaet-vyshibaloy-novye-stihi-galiny-rymbu.

5. For example, on November 1, 2020, Fanailova posted a poem with several hashtags, including one that mentions Lysistrata. The poem is based on a story, "A Second Autumn," by Bruno Schulz, which uses evocative museum settings to occasion ekphrastic accounts of pictures, as Fanailova does in the poem (the images mix erotic encounters with military display). The poem also refers to the dreams of friends (whom she tags); its postscript, couched as a prayer, recalls the labor of caring for a dying mother. See "Vse istonchaetsia. Zoloto osypaetsia kak ne u nas ne barokko," Facebook, November 1, 2020. The hashtags are in Cyrillic. Although I normally transliterate inserted words in the main body of this text, I stay with Cyrillic for hashtags, to aid readers who want to do their own searching and to show clearly when Fanailova uses a Ukrainian hashtag. They include #лисистрата, #лисистратапишет, #лисистратапишеттайныеписьма, #лисистратаидругие, #лисистраевропоп, among others, which could translate roughly as #lysistrata, #lysistratawrites, #lysistratawritessecretletters, #lysistrataandothers, #lysistrataeuropop.

6. The number is approximate, and it is an undercount. While I have looked carefully through Facebook posts since 2014, with the superb research assistance of Maria Vassileva to comb through the posts as well, it is possible that we missed poems, and some might not have appeared on Facebook at all. We used November 1, 2020, as a stopping point, and more poems have appeared since. For readers who want to do their own digging, go to Elena Fanailova's Facebook page: https://www.facebook.com/fanailovae.

7. For example, a new poem appeared in March 2021, with the heading "#лисистратапишет опять" (#Lysistratawrites again). See Fanailova, "Mir prichiniaet vred," Facebook, March 24, 2021.

8. See, for example, the poem labeled "Lisistrata opiat' za svoe," which begins "Pristreli menia, kapitan," in *Artikuliatsiia* 3 (December 2018), http://articulationproject.net/1409; and the poem with four hashtags instead of a title, "Taaak, zakhodim s pedali, medlennoi klavishi, partitury ne pomnim," in *Tsirk Olimp + TV* 30, no. 63 (2019), https://www.cirkolimp-tv.ru/articles/848/kholodnaya-voina.

9. See her comments with a link to a new publication of Lysistrata poems, Facebook, March 15, 2021.

10. It has also been argued that the erotic vision of this play, unlike other work by Aristophanes and much else in antiquity, is one of "caring, loving ritual, and mutual pleasure." That intonation is consonant with Fanailova's representations of sexuality. See Bernard Freydberg, *Philosophy and Comedy* (Indiana University Press, 2008), 162–63.

11. That last point is important, as Fanailova, like the modernists, sees Russia as a part of European culture and history, even when it most resists Western norms.

12. The drive to include Ukrainian intensified in 2020 and then redoubled in 2022. See, for example, a poem that has among its hashtags, in Ukrainian, a claim that "Lysistrata writes in two

languages" (#Лісістратапишенадвімови): "Every time, remembering your beauty" ("Kazh-dyi raz, vspominaia tvoiu krasotu," Facebook, October 17, 2020). This forty-one-line poem in Russian appeared with a Ukrainian version following; Fanailova said that it was her translation.

13. The poems also are marked by the frequent use of direct address, what might be called a remnant of the old vocative. That, too, connects Fanailova's poems to the Homeric texts, particularly the *Iliad*, where direct address is prominent. In Fanailova's Lysistrata poems, imperatives are common, even in scenic and descriptive segments. See, for example, "Pristreli menia, kapitan."

14. Fanailova, "Den' nezavisimosti (Troia vs Lisistrata)," *Snob*, June 12, 2017, https://snob.ru/selected/entry/125462/.

15. My thinking about how women poets write war is indelibly shaped by Jorie Graham's *Overlord*, particularly the three poems entitled "Spoken from the Hedgerows": see Graham, *Overlord* (Ecco, 2005), 34–42. See also chapter 1's discussion of Stepanova.

16. See the three-part poem "#Lisistrata tri pis'ma delovomu partneru," as well as "#Lisistrataidrugie 14 marta 2018," both included in Fanailova, "Dnevnik za 2018 (Troia vs. Lisistrata)," *Snob*, May 9, 2018, https://snob.ru/entry/160590/.

17. The comment comes in the first of a two-poem cycle dedicated to Zhadan, in "Moia ukrainskaia sem'ia," *Vozdukh* 4 (2014): 138. For the second poem to Zhadan, a fine translation exists: see "Two New Poems," trans. Eugene Ostashevsky, *White Review* (January 2016), http://www.thewhitereview.org/poetry/poem-for-zhadan-my-ukrainian-grandmother/.

18. Fanailova's interest in Zhadan is not new. For her first published translations, see "Sergei Zhadan v perevodakh Eleny Fanailovoi," *Znamia* (no. 9, 2008), http://znamlit.ru/publication.php?id=3680. Other translations include "Po kanve Sergeia Zhadana 'Ognestrel'nye i nozhevye," *Znamia* (no. 4, 2015), https://magazines.gorky.media/znamia/2015/4/po-kanve-sergeya-zhadana-ognestrelnye-i-nozhevye.html. See also Rymbu, "Poeziia v internete."

19. Bob Holman, foreword to Serhiy Zhadan, *What We Live For, What We Die For*, trans. Virlana Tkacz and Wanda Phipps (Yale University Press, 2019), ix–xiv, quotation on xiii.

20. C. D. Wright, *One Big Self: An Investigation* (Copper Canyon Press, 2007), xiv.

21. Fanailova made these remarks in "Avgust: Marina Tsvetaeva," *Belyi shum*, hosted by Tatiana Tolstaya and Ksenia Burzhskaya, August 27, 2020, video, 1:31:58, :https://www.youtube.com/watch?v=q2VquBYweUg&feature=youtu.be. The conversation also included Irina Shevelenko and Valery Shubinsky.

22. The word for death is often given as "sm-rt'," as if reifying the blockage between event and naming. I believe that more than one death is involved here, but Fanailova has written that the loss of designer, photographer, and artist Alexander Belosludtsev in 2004 hit her very hard. See her comments on Facebook, October 23, 2020. As was true for Akhmatova, multiple deaths haunt Fanailova, and the Lysistrata poems refer to other losses, including that of her parents.

23. Fanailova's poetry, combining the theme of love, which she reiterates constantly, with that of public life, military conflict, and political repression might retrospectively also offer a way to see Akhmatova's legacy as a coherent unity, rather than split in two, the love poet distinct from the poet of "Requiem."

24. Here I would include myself. I once wrote: "Akhmatova built her early poetic reputation on a self-presentation as the woman men loved to leave." She is "seduced, abandoned, abused,

ignored," I added. See Stephanie Sandler, *Commemorating Pushkin: Russia's Myth of a National Poet* (Stanford University Press, 2004), 205. A far more interesting approach, which emphasizes the way Akhmatova turns "the archetypal misogynic, ethno-exclusive perspective upside-down," has been advanced in Alexander Averbuch, "The Theurgy of Impurity: Fin-de-Race and Feminine Sin in Russian and Ukrainian Modernisms," *Russian Review* 78 (July 2019): 459–85; quotation from 462.

25. The pronouns and their sequence can change in a line of poetry, for example, "they it she" (oni ono ona) in the poem that begins "The Cold War" ("Kholodnaia voina"). This is the title poem in a group of Lysistrata poems published in *Tsirk Olimp + TV* 30, no. 63 (2019), https://www.cirkolimp-tv.ru/articles/848/kholodnaya-voina.

26. An obsolete form, *one*, marks a feminine plural, which can still turn up in poetry through the Silver Age.

27. Among the most striking is a poem labeled #Онаонаони vs #ТрояЛисистрата with the title "fragment o devushkakh bitvy, moikh partnershakh," Facebook, August 27, 2018, and reposted one year later.

28. See Fanailova's comments on "ia vstrechaius' so svoim dvoinikom," Facebook, August 22, 2018, reposted May 14, 2020, for example.

29. Fanailova, Facebook, August 22, 2018. The poem has two hashtags, one of them #Онаонаони.

30. Fanailova, Facebook, August 22, 2018.

31. See Seamus Heaney, *Anything Can Happen: A Poem and Essay* (Town-House, 2004), 14. Heaney's essay, written to accompany a poem, "Horace and the Thunder," that responds to the September 11, 2001, attacks, says that art, including poetry, is meant to wake us from dreams imbued by violence and fear, "to bring us to our senses" (14). Fanailova, by comparison, is committed to exploring the dreams.

32. Fanailova said, for example, that Russia is stuck on the notion of its own exclusivity, and that no serious conversation about the gulag in art or in society is possible so long as the May 9 parades feature portraits of Stalin. See Fanailova, "Seichas pisat' stikhi dlia rodiny amoral'no," interview by Elena Rybakova, *Moskovskie novosti* 110 (September 2, 2011), http://www.litkarta.ru/dossier/seichas-dlia-rodiny-pisat-stikhi/dossier_2050/.

33. I am paraphrasing and reorienting here a line by the poet Elena Kostyleva: "Tell us, children: how did violence become an essential condition of your existence?" Translated as Kostyleva, "The Language of Violence," trans. Bela Shayevich, *n+1* 26 (Fall 2016): 118–23; quotation on 119. For the Russian, see Kostyleva, "Iazyk nasiliia," *Village*, July 23, 2014, https://www.the-village.ru/city/situation/160853-stihotvorenie.

34. Fanailova, "Moia ukrainskaia sem'ia," 138.

35. Fanailova, "#лисистрата и демократия," Facebook, March 19, 2018; the poem begins "Ne nado boiat'sia."

36. The work of Charles Altieri on poetry and affect has inspired my thinking here. See Charles Altieri, "Reading for Affect in the Lyric: From Modern to the Contemporary," *Poetry and Pedagogy: The Challenge of the Contemporary*, ed. Joan Retallack and Juliana Spahr (Palgrave Macmillan, 2006), 39–62.

37. Here and below, the material about *OpenSpace*'s *Live Poetry* series draws on an essay I published earlier: "*Live Poetry*: Doubled Performances on *OpenSpace*," for *Russian Performances:*

Word, Object, Action, ed. Julie Buckler, Julie Cassiday, and Boris Wolfson (University of Wisconsin Press, 2018), 114–22.

38. For the poem, see Dmitrii Kuz'min, "Dva mal'chika i devochka s pervogo kursa zhurfaka," *Kreshchatik*, no. 3 (2005), https://magazines.gorky.media/kreschatik/2005/3/141163.html. The erotic triangle of Bertolucci's film is refigured in the poem, with the vectors of attraction rearranged toward same-sex desire. The entire *Live Poetry* series is archived on *OpenSpace*, http://os .colta.ru/literature/projects/75/. But as of 2021, the videos were not playable because Adobe Flash no longer functioned. The videos were recoded by Anna Ivanov and linked on a Google spreadsheet; individual links to poets' performances are given below.

39. For a study of his verse forms, see Iurii Orlitskii, "Svobodnyi stikh Dmitriia Kuz'mina," in *Svobodnyi stikh Dmitriia Kuz'mina*, ed. Stanislav L'vovskii and Il'ia Kukulin (SapereAude, 2018), 57–74.

40. Her readings are available on her website, http://www.olgasedakova.com/878/page/s .php?f=chtr and in a 2014 video, "Ol'ga Sedakova, 'Kitaiskoe puteshestvie' (1986)," February 20, 2014, video, 18:18, posted by ocahsat on March 22, 2014, https://www.youtube.com/watch?v =1UWCBj2RQyM. Compare also her quiet, deeply meditative contribution to *Live Poetry*, discussed below.

41. Olga Sedakova, "The Chinese Journey," trans. Andrew Wachtel, *Conjunctions*, no. 23 (1994): 9–20; quoted from 16–17, translation modified.

42. Ol'ga Sedakova, *Stikhi* (Universitet Dmitriia Pozharskogo, 2010), 342.

43. In this readiness to embody the poems read or recited, Russian poets differ from the image described for contemporary American poets in Mike Chasar, "Orality, Literacy, and the Memorized Poem," *Poetry*, January 2015, 371–92; see especially 379, where Chasar emphasizes the reading poet as one disengaged from the act of creating poetry. I suggest here the exact opposite.

44. The serendipity of these acts of choice has been cultivated in other ways as well. Compare *McSweeney's Book of Poets Picking Poets*, ed. Dominic Luxford (McSweeney's, 2007), where the editor selected one poem each by ten poets, then asked these ten poets to add a poem and pick a poem by someone else. That chosen poet in turn repeated the process to produce a book with ten chains of poems, five poets each, two poems per poet. Remarkably, the McSweeney poets do not repeat (that is, no two poets picked the same poet), which may suggest some editorial control. Not so at *OpenSpace*, where the repetitions and intersections are fascinating and revealing. Another instance of paired poets is the *New Yorker Poetry* podcast, where poets are invited to look through the journal's archive and pick out a poem for reading and discussion; one of the poet's own poems, recently published in the journal, is also read and discussed. Episodes are archived at https://www.newyorker.com/podcast/poetry.

45. Christopher Grobe, "The Breath of the Poem: Confessional Print / Performance circa 1959," *PMLA* 127, no. 2 (2012): 215–30. Grobe's superb analysis of Plath, Sexton, Lowell, and Ginsberg turns on a tension between poetry as printed and poetry as delivered orally: he sees confessional poets resisting that kind of opposition.

46. Other examples include Oleg Iur'ev, creator of dramatic experiments with choral passages, and Sergei Zav'ialov, who has drawn on ancient dramatic forms for his poetic texts. See Iur'ev, *Izbrannye stikhi i khory* (NLO, 2004) and "Stikhi o russkikh p'esakh," *NLO* 128 (no. 4, 2014): 10–11; Zav'ialov, *Melika: Vtoraia kniga stikhotvorenii* (ARGO-RISK, 1998).

47. Philip Auslander, *Liveness: Performance in a Mediatized Culture*, 2nd ed. (Routledge, 2008). For Auslander, the differences between live and "mediatized" performances are no longer so stark; neither has ontological priority, and both are culturally and historically contingent. The material I work with here effaces that boundary still further. Because the technologies of the internet change rapidly, uploaded recordings can have a terminal life—or can flicker off into inaccessibility until someone comes along to figure out how to change the technology and make them spring back to life (as happened with *Live Poetry*). Thus, recorded performances can become as ephemeral as a live performance that survives only in the audience's memory.

48. See Charles Bernstein, "Hearing Voices," in *The Sound of Poetry / The Poetry of Sound*, ed Marjorie Perloff and Craig Dworkin (University of Chicago Press, 2009), 142–48, esp. 142–43, where he fantasizes on the invigorating possibilities in re-accentuated, idiosyncratic performances by Harold Bloom and William Shatner.

49. The University of Pennsylvania's *PennSound*, https://writing.upenn.edu/pennsound/, includes an immense video and audio archive; all the material there, or in the encyclopedic site for contemporary Russian poetry, the *New Map of Russian Literature* (*Novaia karta russkoi literatury*, known as *Litkarta*, www.litkarta.ru), has this potential for the uncanny. *Litkarta* was created by Dmitry Kuz'min.

50. The statement appeared multiple times, including on the page where Andrei Rodionov reads, *OpenSpace*, May 23, 2008, http://os.colta.ru/literature/projects/75/details/960/.

51. *Vse srazu* (Novoe izdatel'stvo, 2008), with poems by Rovinsky, Svarovsky, and Leonid Schwab.

52. Two poets chosen multiple times are Mikhail Aizenberg and Sergei Gandlevsky, both important representatives of the late Soviet group Moscow Time (Moskovskoe vremia). Poets who choose them or their contemporary, Olga Sedakova, suggest the lasting influence of these poets.

53. Immediate responses to Dashevsky's death were vivid and intense. See, for example, Sergei Kozlov, "Pamiati Grigoriia Dashevskogo," *Gefter*, December 18, 2013, http://gefter.ru /archive/10856; Mariia Stepanova, "Nashe solntse," *Kommersant* 234 (December 19, 2013), https://www.kommersant.ru/doc/2371268.

54. The same might be said of a few other poets' choices, most vividly Sedakova's solemn reading of a poem by Elena Shvarts, discussed below.

55. As translated by Sasha Spektor, Daniil Cherkassky, and Anton Tenser in Brooklyn Rail's journal *InTranslation*, January 2011; the link was not working in late 2023, but the page, "Four Contemporary Russian Poets: Grigori Dashevsky, Leonid Schwab, Semyon Khanin, and Oleg Yuriev," is findable at https://web.archive.org/web/20230316140430/https://intranslation .brooklynrail.org/russian/four-contemporary-russian-poets-grigori-dashevsky-leonid-schwab -semyon-khanin-and-oleg-yuriev/.

56. Dashevskii, "Tikhii chas," *Duma Ivan-chaia: Stikhi 1983–1999* (NLO, 2001), 87. This poem is featured on the poet's web page as his "calling card" at *Litkarta*: http://www.litkarta.ru/russia /moscow/persons/dashevsky-g/.

57. For example, from the same volume of poetry, "Cheremushki" and "Bliznetsy." See *Duma Ivan-chaia*, 76, 88.

58. The poem's Sapphic stanzas (three lines of eleven syllables, one of five) bears a relationship to Catullus 51, also in Sapphics and itself based on Sappho 31. How such poems are and are

not translations is one of several topics addressed in Mariia Stepanova, "O smerti i nemnogo do," in *Protiv neliubvi* (Izdatel'stvo AST, 2019), 187–225.

59. For an astute reflection on this new world by a poet writing from an audience perspective, see Caroline Clark, "Zoom's the Ticket," *PN Review* 258 (47, no. 4, 2021): 10–11.

60. Other pandemic-era online reading series of Russian poetry were curated by the Tsve-taeva Museum in Moscow and the Poriadok Slov Bookstore in St. Petersburg. For samples of these performances, see the Dom-muzei Tsvetaevoi channel on YouTube, https://www.youtube .com/channel/UCk26GIPUBExOmY8X2PXSguA; and the Poriadok Slov channel, https:// www.youtube.com/user/vPoryadkeSlov/videos.

61. For example, Lida Yusupova, who published both a Russian-language book, *Prigovory* (NLO, 2020), and her first bilingual Russian-English collection, *The Scar We Know*, ed. Ainsley Morse (Cicada, 2021), read from her work with translators on January 25, 2021: "Lida Yusupova's New Book Launch," Globus Books, https://www.globusbooks.com/pages/events/28/lida -yusupovas-new-book-launch. Galina Rymbu's first bilingual Russian-English collection, *Life in Space*, ed. Joan Brooks (Ugly Duckling Presse, 2020), was featured on October 17, 2020: "Life in Space: Translation of a Poetry Book by Galina Rymbu," Globus Books, https://www .globusbooks.com/pages/events/14/life-in-space-translation-of-a-poetry-book-by. All Globus Books events are archived on the GlobusBooks SF YouTube channel, https://www.youtube .com/channel/UCogNzhgTorWuUGb0MWIUg0w.

62. The readings are archived at "Events at the Amherst Center for Russian Culture," Am-herst College, https://www.amherst.edu/academiclife/departments/russian/acrc/events.

63. Glazova has sometimes projected her Russian poems as she reads them, so that the audi-ence can see the lineation, for example, at a reading at Harvard University (March 5, 2020).

64. For the main page of the project, see *Zhenskaia poeziia: Prostranstvo i vremia*, Biblioteka im. V. G. Belinskogo, https://belinkaex.wixsite.com/womens-poetry.

65. The cutoff was loosened in practice to include poems of the early 1920s and was explained in the website project description: "The temporal frame of the project was determined by the fact that in the spring of 1917, women in Russia for the first time in history received the right to vote and became subjects in politics and in social life in the broad sense of that term." Translated from *Zhenskaia poeziia: Prostranstvo i vremia*, Biblioteka im. V. G. Belinskogo (initiated 2021), https://belinkaex.wixsite.com/womens-poetry/опроекте.

66. Ekaterina Simonova, Facebook, March 20, 2021.

67. The hoax eventually led to a duel, which showed how much this was an affair between men. The story has been told by multiple memoirists and scholars. For a summary, see Kristi Groberg and Catriona Kelly, "De Gabriak, Cherubina," *Dictionary of Russian Women Writers*, ed. Marina Ledkovsky, Charlotte Rosenthal, and Mary Zirin (Greenwood, 1994), 144–46.

68. On the theme of doubling in her poetry and on the way that a split within Dmitrieva was exploited by Voloshin, see Olga Peters Hasty, *How Women Must Write: Inventing the Russian Woman Poet* (Northwestern University Press, 2020), 86–90. The poem "The Double" has its own twin in her work, a second poem about doubling: "I slepye nochi novolun'e," as explained in the commentary to *Sub rosa: Adelaida Gertsyk, Sofiia Parnok, Poliksena Solov'eva, Cherubina de Gabriak* (Ellis-Lak, 1999), 677–78; for the poem, see 481–82.

69. Dmitrieva's roots in Spanish mysticism make the *Vertigo* connection uncannily apt, given the film's Carlotta Valdes subplot and fateful scenes at Mission San Juan Bautista: Dmitrieva's

first publication under her own name was Spanish religious poetry. Her connections to anthroposophy likely caused her arrest and exile to Tashkent in 1927.

70. Mikhail Gronas, *Cognitive Poetics and Cultural Memory: Russian Literary Mnemonics* (Routledge, 2011), 143n2.

71. For Sedakova's recitations of *Old Songs* in Russian, see her website: http://www .olgasedakova.com/878.

72. For the poem, see *Vozdukh* (no. 4, 2007): 59. The version differs slightly from the one he recites. Gronas dedicated his second book of poems to the memory of Grigory Dashevsky, and this poem appears there as well, as the second of a three-part poem, dedicated to G. D.: *Kratkaia istoriia vnimaniia* (Novoe izdatel'stvo, 2019), 9–10. For the recitation, see "Gronas 1," video, 0:30, https://drive.google.com/file/d/1iTlYJl1QZsnJcJL6SrI-DqANrtRveayl/view. This choice is another instance of poets drawing strong lines of affiliations in the Live Poetry series: Dashevsky reads a poem by Gronas in his turn, "Budil'nik ostyvshii, ty—cherep v rukakh," published in Gronas, *Dorogie siroty,* (OGI, 2002), 36; for the recording, see "Dashevskiy 2," video, 0:52, https://drive.google.com/file/d/1_mGs0YYAkUYlXk9XdDcfIasxU2nN236d /view.

73. He rarely performs to live gatherings, and very few recordings are available. For audio recordings made in 2002, see his page on *Litkarta*, http://www.litkarta.ru/world/usa/persons /gronas-m/. During the pandemic, he participated in the reading series set up by the Moscow Tsvetaeva Museum, "'Poeticheskaia sreda': Mikhail Gronas," December 23, 2020, video, 30:01, https://www.youtube.com/watch?v=SC_dwt7mJaQ&t=3s. I write about Gronas's reading style in "On Russian Poems, Poets, and Prizes, Late into 2020," *Russian Review* 80, no. 2 (July 2021): 497–505.

74. Gronas resembles the image suggested, unlikely as it may be, by the very popular American poet Billy Collins: "an echo of the Orphic singer, the embodiment of the ancient lyric impulse." Collins, "Prologue: Poems in the Page," in *The Spoken Word Revolution: Slam, Hip Hop and the Poetry of a New Generation*, ed. Mark Eleveld (Sourcebooks MediaFusion, 2003), 4.

75. For the poem: Elena Shvarts, *Solo na raskalennoi trube* (Pushkinskii fond, 1998), 7. For Sedakova's recitation, see "Sedakova 2," video, 1:16, https://drive.google.com/file/d /1ioIy4VYqlVkwDFzg5wbUGwKpkwCLQU-0/view. I have written about Shvarts's poems of mourning in "On Grief and Reason, on Poems and Films: Joseph Brodsky, Andrei Tarkovsky, Elena Shvarts," *Russian Review* 66 (October 2007): 647–70.

76. Sedakova's admiration and affection for Shvarts are well attested. See, for example, Sedakova, "L'antica fiamma," in Shvarts, *Pereletnaia ptitsa: Poslednie stikhi 2007–2010* (Pushkinskii fond, 2011), 41–51, as well as the memorial essay she published on the one-year anniversary of Shvarts's death: "Elena Shvarts: Pervaia godovshchina," *OpenSpace*, March 11, 2011, http://os .colta.ru/literature/events/details/21037/.

77. Diana Taylor, *The Archive and the Repertoire: Performing Cultural Memory in the Americas* (Duke University Press, 2003), 20.

78. These thoughts on doubling are inspired by a superb essay written at the intersection of theology and philosophy: Rebecca Schneider, "'Judith Butler' in My Hands," in *Bodily Citations: Religion and Judith Butler*, ed. Ellen T. Armour and Susan M. St. Ville (Columbia University Press, 2006), 225–51.

79. For an excellent study of performance styles and the history of a poetic tradition, see Aleksandra Kremer, *The Sound of Modern Polish Poetry: Performance and Recording after World War II* (Harvard University Press, 2021).

80. On performance and embodiment, see Peggy Phelan, "The Ontology of Performance: Representation without Reproduction," in *Unmarked: The Politics of Performance* (Routledge, 1993), 146–66.

81. With the exception of one site for translations, inactive since 2013, Skandiaka deleted all her websites shortly after February 24, 2022. When I cite Skandiaka's poetry, it is from published versions.

82. Kuz'min triumphantly reported, however, on meeting the Irish poet Trevor Joyce in California: "He has one essential advantage over all of us: he has SEEN Nika Skandiaka." See Kuz'min, Facebook, May 27, 2020. Joyce is among the poets Skandiaka has translated; Kuz'min published some of those translations in *Vozdukh* (no. 3, 2006): 139–45.

83. *Osvobozhdennyi Uliss: Sovremennaia russkaia poeziia za predelami Rossii*, ed. Dmitrii Kuz'min (NLO, 2004), 990; for the poems by Skandiaka, see 97–107. The same biographical information appears in *Deviat' izmerenii: Antologiia noveishei russkoi poezii* (NLO, 2004), 403.

84. Skandiaka set up two separate websites for translations, the contents now deleted in one of them; her only remaining blog is an older one, also all translations, http://skandiaka.blogspot.de. Some pages can be viewed through the Wayback Machine, for example, "sistema mashinal'nogo dialoga's journal" (translations of Kari Edwards), https://web.archive.org/web/20191011205829/https://999999.livejournal.com/. I have written about Skandiaka's translations as a pathway to understanding her poems (and challenged the boundary between translations and one's "own" poems in her case) in "Nika Skandiaka and the Poetry of Translation," *Translation—Transition—Transformation: Forms of Interaction in Contemporary Poetry*, ed. Maria Khotimsky et al. (Academic Studies Press, 2024), 61–77.

85. The amoeba appears in "dobroe slovo i koshke priiatno" (note that this poem has a cat's reaction to language and an assertion that fish feel despair). The ivy is in "k goloi stene." Both those poems appear in *Reflect . . . KUADUSESHSHCHT* 12 (2002), https://polutona.ru/?show=reflect&number=12&id=119. For the bird call (which starts in Cyrillic and switches to the Latin alphabet: "тиуу-wick! wick! wick!"), see Skandiaka, "mart na dvore, vetrishe i vzapravdu," *Deviat' izmerenii*, 320.

86. For the poem of that title, see the selection of her poetry in *Reflect . . . KUADUSESH-SHCHT* 18 (2005), https://polutona.ru/?show=reflect&id=151.

87. "Sistema mashinal'nogo dialoga" was the owner name of a now deleted translation blog.

88. There are other points of connection between her work and L=A=N=G=U=A=G=E poets, however. See Anna Rodionova, "Language School i poeziia Niki Skandiaki: Vliianiia i transformatsii," *Paradigmy perekhodnosti i obrazy fantasticheskogo mira v khudozhestvennom prostranstve XIX-XXI vv.* (Natsional'nyi issledovatel'skii Nizhegorodskii gosudarstvennyi universitet im. N. I. Lobachevskogo, 2019), 342–49. Rodionova chose Leslie Scalapino and Robert Grenier as her examples, which make for interesting choices, particularly Grenier, whose work in later years became intensely visual and tactile.

89. Skandiaka's publishing began on screen as well. The earliest publications are in the online journal *Reflect . . . KUADUSESHSHCHT*, created by the late Raphael Levchin. An early print publication concludes with a poem that reflects on the comparative pleasures of reaching readers

on screen as opposed to on the page; the poet says that she is opting for the page, so that a reader can take the page of poetry out into an apple orchard and have it warmed by the sun. See *Vavilon* 10, no. 26 (2003): 54–57, http://www.vavilon.ru/metatext/vavilon10/skandiaka.html (this hard-to-find print publication is archived online; thus the poem is now ironically read on screen).

90. Helen Vendler, "Indigo, Cyanine, Beryl," *London Review of Books* 25, no. 3 (2003), https://www.lrb.co.uk/the-paper/v25/n02/helen-vendler/indigo-cyanine-beryl.

91. Helen Vendler, "Married to Hurry and Grim Song: Jorie Graham's *The End of Beauty*," in *Soul Says: On Recent Poetry* (Harvard University Press, 1995), 235–43; quotations on 237 and 241.

92. See Mariia A. Tarasova, "Bilingvalizm v original'noi i perevodnoi poezii N. Skandiaki," *Kritika i semiotika*, no. 1 (2015): 340–49; and Anna Rodionova, "Sovremennaia poeziia kak informatsionnaia praktika: K tekstam Niki Skandiaki," *NLO* 167 (no. 1, 2021): 223–34; see 230–31. Rodionova's argument, as the essay title suggests, is more broadly focused on poetry as a kind of information practice; she takes Skandiaka as her chief example.

93. See Il'ia Kukulin, "'Sozdat' cheloveka, poka ty ne chelovek': Zametki k russkoi poezii 2000-kh," in Kukulin, *Proryv k nevozmozhnoi sviazi: Stat'i o russkoi poezii* (Kabinetnyi uchenyi, 2019), 457–78, esp. 464–65. Rodionova, in "Sovremennaia poeziia," also comments on fragmentary dispersal in Skandiaka's work.

94. A number of these graphic devices are noted in Artemii Magun, "Novye imena sovremennoi poezii: Nika Skandiaka," *NLO* 82 (no. 6, 2006): 400–405.

95. Skandiaka, *[12 / 4 / 2007]* (NLO, 2007), 48.

96. Excellent criticism on poetic practice shaped by computers includes Ekaterina Zakharkiv, "Sovremenaia poeziia v epokhu tsifrovykh tekhnologii: Novaia funktsiia pragmaticheskikh markerov," *NLO* 167 (no. 1, 2021): 211–22. This essay appears in a group of articles, "Poeziia v tekhnokognitivnom landshafte," edited by Evgeniia Samostienko (Suslova), whose introduction is also very helpful (207–10). See also, on Skandiaka as a cyborg, Anna Ivanov's 2022 ASEEES paper, "The Blurred Boundaries of the HTML Box: Nika Skandiaka's Post-Humanism"; Ivanov is at work on a dissertation, "Network(ed) Russian Literature: 1820s–2020s," which includes a chapter on Skandiaka.

97. Parshchikov wrote an essay that became the introduction to Skandiaka's published volume of poetry: see "Vozvrashchenie aury?," in Skandiaka, *[12 / 4 / 2007]*, 5–19.

98. Parshchikov, "Vozvrashchenie aury?," 18.

99. Skandiaka, "Stikhi," *Reflect . . . KUADUSESHSHCHT* 18 (2005), https://polutona.ru/?show=reflect&id=151.

100. This is the same 2003 poem mentioned above in note 89; it begins "esli ran'she schitala—ne stoit pytat'sia" and is the final poem in that published grouping.

101. Il'ia Kukulin, "Ot redaktora," *NLO* 82 (no. 6, 2006): 379–80; this short statement introduces a group of articles about Skandiaka where Parshchikov's essay first appeared. Another critic used the term "ecstatic" to describe the state reached for in Skandiaka's texts. See Oleg Dark, "Vozbuzhdenie [ot] teksta," *Russkii zhurnal*, September 10, 2007, http://www.litkarta.ru/dossier/vozbuzhdenie-ot-teksta/dossier_6135/.

102. For Skandiaka's text, see *Reflect . . . KUADUSESHSHCHT* 18 (2005), https://polutona.ru/?show=reflect&id=151.

103. In one extensive interview, David Naimon asked Graham about her writing practice (did she read her poems aloud to herself?), and he quoted her former students, who said that

her voice was a crucial part of their experience reading her work. See his *Between the Covers* podcast episode "Jorie Graham: Runaway," April 2021, https://tinhouse.com/podcast/jorie -graham-runaway/.

104. Dark, "Vozbuzhdenie [ot] teksta."

105. See Steven Owen, "What Is World Poetry?" *New Republic*, November 19, 1990, 28–32. He refined these views and responded to critics (many listed in a footnote) in "Stepping Forward and Back: Issues and Possibilities for 'World' Poetry," *Modern Philology* 100, no. 4 (2003): 532–48.

106. Sabena Khengsen, "Poeticheskii performans: Pis'mo i golos," in *Nekanonicheskii klassik: Dmitrii Aleksandrovich Prigov (1940–2007)*, ed. Evgenii Dobrenko, Il'ia Kukulin, Mark Lipovetskii, and Mariia Maiofis (NLO, 2010), 451–68; and Ilya Kukulin and Mark Lipovetsky, "'The Art of Penultimate Truth': Dmitrii Prigov's Aesthetic Principles," *Russian Review* 75 (April 2016): 186–208, which includes an especially fine discussion of Prigov's performances of theory and of performativity in the work more generally. There are also some pertinent observations in Mark Lipovetskii, "'Ia ne poet, ia deiatel' kul'tury': Desiat' let bez Dmitriia Aleksandrovicha Prigova," ed. Evgeniia Ofitserova, *Gor'kii*, July 17, 2017, https://gorky.media/context /ya-ne-poet-ya-deyatel-kultury-desyat-let-bez-dmitriya-aleksandrovicha-prigova/.

107. A list of the series of photographs had been on the website of the Moscow Museum of Contemporary Art (2006), https://mmoma.ru/col/view?id=115, but that link is broken. One image, the same one discussed here, is posted: https://mmoma.ru/en/know/collection /favourites/artworks/115.

108. Prigov, *Sobranie sochinenii v piati tomakh*, 5 vols. (NLO, 2013–2019).

109. For an account of Prigov's life and work that opens out these questions in broader terms, see Il'ia Kukulin and Mark Lipovetskii, *Partizanskii logos: Proekt Dmitriia Aleksandrovicha Prigova* (NLO, 2022).

110. For a study of those works, see Catherine Ciepiela and Stephanie Sandler, "Telo u Prigova," trans. E. Kanishcheva, *Nekanonicheskii klassik*, 513–39.

111. This was a collective project with Mikhail Razuvaev and Anna Razuvaeva. The GIFs appeared in the archived selection on the Prigov website, http://prigov.ru/action/goglus.php, which was not functioning in late 2023 but was included as a link on the new Prigov site, http:// www.prigov.org/ru/biblio#Видеоперформансы (but without the material).

112. As reported in Elena Fanailova's podcast, then called *Vavilon-Moskva*, December 18, 2022, https://www.svoboda.org/a/non-fiction-literatura-na-fone-spetsoperatsii-/32180313.html. For an example of an earlier "Kubok Kikimory" competition, see the report on the 2019 Moscow Book Fair, Aleksandr Solov'ev, "Prigovskii 'krik Kikimory' snova zazvuchal," *God literatury*, December 12, 2019, https://godliteratury.ru/articles/2019/12/12/prigovskiy-krik-kikimory -snova-zaz.

3. On Magnitude: Poetry in Large and Small Forms

1. On the bounty and variety of fixed forms in the tradition, see Irina Reyfman, "Verse Forms," in *Oxford Handbook of Russian Poetry*, ed. Catherine Ciepiela, Luba Golburt, and Stephanie Sandler (Oxford University Press, forthcoming).

2. For the poem, see Rybakova, *Gnedich* (Vremia, 2011). There is an English translation by Elena Dimov (Glagoslav, 2015).

3. Caroline Levine, *Forms: Whole, Rhythm, Hierarchy, Network* (Princeton University Press, 2015), 19, and elsewhere in the book.

4. For a different version, see *Everburning Pilot*, trans. Alexander Spektor, Anton Tenser, Sibelan Forrester, and others (Cicada, 2022), 81.

5. Leonid Shvab, *Vash Nikolai* (NLO, 2015), 91.

6. Dmitrii Kuz'min, *Russkii monostikh: Ocherk istorii i teorii* (NLO, 2016).

7. For a striking selection, see Ivan Akhmet'ev, "Monostikhi," *Vozdukh* (no. 1, 2014): 146–47.

8. Marina Temkina, "Monostikhi," *Vozdukh* 40 (2020), issue online only, http://www.litkarta .ru/projects/vozdukh/issues/2020-40/temkina/. Temkina's one-line poems feature her signature irony and humor, both also common in one-line poems.

9. Monostich with rhyme is singled out in a comprehensive account of the form that predated Kuz'min's book: Evgenii Stepanov, "Sovremennyi russkii monistikh i odnostrochnaia poeziia," *Deti Ra* (no. 9, 2009), https://magazines.gorky.media/ra/2009/9/sovremennyj -russkij-monostih-i-odnostrochnaya-poeziya.html.

10. There are some later poems as well. The latest poem in the huge volume that appeared in 2015 was dated 2008. See Rubinshtein, "Rodoslovnaia," in *Bol'shaia kartoteka* (Novoe izdatel'stvo, 2015), 596–602. The books of prose include Rubinshtein, *Znaki vnimaniia* (Astrel', 2012) and *Kladbishche s vaifaem* (NLO, 2020).

11. As noted in Mark Lipovetskii, "Delo v shliape, ili Realnost' Rubinshteina," in Rubinshtein, *Pogonia za shliapoi i drugie teksty* (NLO, 2004), 7–26; see 16 and 26.

12. See Rubinstein's web page, http://rubinstein.vavilon.ru, for texts from 1976 to 1995. Facsimile editions also exist in English translation: Rubinstein, *Unnamed Events*, trans. Philip Metres and Tatiana Tulchinsky (Poems-for-all, 2005), a set of cards in a tiny manila envelope. See also their larger translation of Rubinstein, *Compleat Catalogue of Comedic Novelties* (Ugly Duckling Presse, 2014). A middle ground was established by the translations in Rubinstein, *Here I Am*, trans. Joanne Turnbull, *Glas New Russian Writing* 27 (Glas, 2001), where the book's pages reproduce a stack of cards, three to a page, using a font that mimics that of manual typing.

13. See his 1975 statement of his poetics, as cited in Gerald Janecek, *Everything Has Already Been Written: Moscow Conceptualist Poetry and Performance* (Northwestern University Press, 2019), 87.

14. For an account of a very different performance (Rubinstein distributed cards to audience members and had them read aloud; one card disclosed that the author was present), see Natal'ia Azarova, Kirill Korchagin, and Dmitrii Kuz'min, *Poeziia: Uchebnik* (OGI, 2016), 667.

15. The audio could be clearer, but a range of Rubinstein's performance styles, with readings from both cards and books, can be heard at "April' v FT: Lev Rubinshtein—'Stikhi na kartoch-kakh,'" Fanernyi teatr v BDT, April 26, 2019, video, 1:01:42, https://www.youtube.com/watch?v =89yG_L77VlQ. Two shorter recordings have better sound quality. He reads from the 2006 text "Lestnitsa sushchestv" in "Tvorcheskii vecher L'va Rubinshteina proidet v Novosibirske posle spektaklia po ego tekstam," *Taiga.info*, January 11, 2016, https://tayga.info/125064. Rubinstein reads the full text of his 1996 poem "Eto ia" at the Nekrasov Library in honor of an exhibit of his library card poems, October 5, 2017, video, 13:03, https://www.youtube.com/watch?v =QORdXEycKj4.

16. Mikhail Epstein, "New Currents in Russian Poetry: Conceptualism, Metarealism, and Presentism," in *After the Future: The Paradoxes of Postmodernism in Contemporary Russian Culture*, trans. Anesa Miller-Pogacar (University of Massachusetts Press, 1995), 19–50, quoted from 34. For details about the Russian original, see note 61 to my introduction.

17. Just because Rubinstein would surely love this book, I refer readers to Charles Simic, *Dime-Store Alchemy: The Art of Joseph Cornell* (NYRB, 1992).

18. Quoted in Janecek, *Everything Has Already Been Written*, 99.

19. For example, see the several sequences of couplets that structure "Malen'kaia nochnaia serenada" (1986), well discussed in Gerald Janecek, "Lev Rubinstein's Conceptualism: Theory and Practice," *Canadian-American Slavic Studies* 35, no. 4 (Winter 2002): 435–45.

20. One of the texts most extensively analyzed in terms of its quotations is "Shestikrylyi serafim," in Gerald Janecek, "Citationality in Lev Rubinštejn's 'Šestikrylyi serafim,'" *Russian Literature* 66 (2009): 37–50; and, briefly, in Mark Lipovetskii, "'Tsitatnyi' sub"ekt: Neoakmeizm, kontseptualizm, post-kontseptualizm," in *Sub"ekt v noveishei russkoiazychnoi poezii—teoriia i praktika*, ed. Henrieke Stahl and Ekaterina Evgrashkina (Peter Lang, 2018), 397–414; see 405–6.

21. Rubinshtein, "Eto ia," in *Bol'shaia kartoteka*, 568–85; quotations from 579 and 577, respectively.

22. Janecek, "Lev Rubinstein's Conceptualism," 443.

23. Rubinshtein, *Bol'shaia kartoteka*, 276–90, quoted from 277. Compare a discerning comment by Alexander Ulanov about Rubinstein's poems: "the fragments of discursive practices" in the poems draw us in largely "by means of the air around them, the air in which they can grow out meanings that are barely indicated in the fragments." Translated from Aleksandr Ulanov, "Dogovarivat'? O knige L'va Rubinshteina *Pogonia za shliapoi i drugie teksty*," April 29, 2008, http://www.litkarta.ru/dossier/ulanov-o-rubinsheine/dossier_3169/. Ulanov claims that in the prose writings, the fragmentary or unsaid elements of the poems get spelled out. I do not entirely share that view, as explained below.

24. For the "Sluchai," see Kharms, *Polnoe sobranie sochinenii*, 3 vols. (Akademicheskii proekt, 1999), 2:330–61. Many are included in the excellent translations of *Today I Wrote Nothing: The Selected Writings of Daniil Kharms*, trans. Matvei Yankelevich (Ardis, 2009).

25. Rubinshtein, *Bol'shaia kartoteka*, 281–82.

26. As is especially well observed in Lipovetskii, "Delo v shliape," 15ff. Although written as an introduction to the prose, this short essay is a superb account of his poetics more generally.

27. To stay with this prestigious prize as a measure, one could note that Tsvetkov (2007), Kruglov (2008), Zav'ialov (2015), and Medvedev (2014) would all go on to win. The prize has not been without its controversies (see chapter 1).

28. Elena Fanailova, "Rech' o Mikhaile Gronase," Premiia Andreia Belogo (2002), http://belyprize.ru/index.php?id=161.

29. Gronas uses the comma in the title to signal that the words are an act of address. I cannot help but wonder if Vasily Borodin's splendid poem about a comma was inspired by Gronas's: see "zapiataia chitala medlenno," in Vasilii Borodin, *Losinyi ostrov* (NLO, 2015), 21.

30. Mikhail Gronas, *Dorogie siroty,* (OGI, 2002), 64.

31. The added expressiveness comes in l.6, where there is an extra syllable/word at the start of the line, the word for "and" (*i*). It means that there is a slight violation of the metrical scheme,

corrected in the repetition of l.5 in l.6, but without the added *i*. The poem's effects hinge on this kind of minuscule shift in formal or other expectations.

32. All words here are common, save one: the term for "pastures" (*pazhiti*). The presence of this archaic, poetic word in a poem with otherwise utterly mundane lexicon intensifies the irony of comparing a grave to the greening pastures of pastoral poetry.

33. As Glazova says about another poem in the same book, "the words are all simple, but one meaning makes a deception of another, as if trying it on for size, but the word remains the same." Translated from Anna Glazova, "Vyrazhenie slov: O stikhakh Mikhaila Gronasa," *TextOnly* 29 (2009), http://www.litkarta.ru/dossier/expressionofwords/dossier_1970/.

34. A minimalist poet who can also use repetition very expressively is Vasily Borodin; the repetitions can have the same effect of radically limiting the lexical field of a poem, and can deepen a sense of every repeating word. See, for example, "svet unizhen'ia valis' na sneg," in Borodin, *Luch: Parus* (ARGO-RISK, 2008), 10. For a splendid reading of this poem, and of Borodin's early poetics generally, see Anna Glazova, "Urok sopostavleniia," *NLO* 94 (no. 6, 2008): 235–37.

35. Good examples include "chto nazhito—sgorelo," "ne liubi ne liubi," the refrain in "na svetlykh plastinakh nebes," "dolgo li korotko li," and "kogda ia plakal kogda ia plakal kogda ia plakal poslednii raz?." See also the two-part poem that begins "On v telefonnoi budke," where the vowels are stretched out; Gronas, *Dorogie siroty,*, 5, 29, 33, 61, 66, 68–69. The rhetoric of repetition is most pronounced in this book, but the second book has some spectacular examples, including "vot znachit kak vot znachit kak vot znachit," in Gronas, *Kratkaia istoriia vnimaniia* (Novoe izdatel'stvo, 2019), 65.

36. Dmitrii Kuz'min, "'Zabyvshie, chto my brat'ia . . .'" *NLO* 54 (no. 2, 2002): 288–90. The sense of freedom in the work was also observed by Polina Barskova in "Pochti nichego nigde: Pokhvala otritsaniiu," *TextOnly*, January 13, 2008, http://www.litkarta.ru/dossier/barskova-o -gronase/dossier_1970/.

37. See Lev Oborin, "Cherneiut orud'ia i merznut nogi," *Gor'kii*, October 29, 2019, https:// gorky.media/reviews/cherneyut-orudya-i-merznut-nogi/.

38. Igor' Gulin, "Do smerti i obratno," *Kommersant" Weekend* 35 (October 18, 2019), https:// www.kommersant.ru/doc/4119908. Despite that comment, his review is a fine introduction to Gronas's work, and his formulation of the poems as hovering between the rhetoric of prayer and lullaby is quite apt.

39. See Jakobson, "Shifters, Verbal Categories, and the Russian Verb," in *Russian and Slavic Grammar: Studies 1931–1981*, ed. Linda R. Waugh and Morris Halle (Mouton, 1964), 41–58. A splendid example of Gronas's play with pronouns is "Geopolitika Sodad," in *Dorogie siroty,*, 57. For "Ia zdes'," see Rubinshtein, *Bol'shaia kartoteka*, 554–67; in English, "Here I Am," *Compleat Catalogue of Comedic Novelties*, 372–83.

40. Gronas, *Dorogie siroty,*, 7.

41. Gronas, *Kratkaia istoriia vnimaniia*, 36.

42. Such writing was perfectly characterized by Mikhail Gasparov (the example he gives is the work of Maria Shkapskaya) as "mnimaia proza." He emphasized how rhythm delineates such texts into word groups and other patterns. The connection to Gasparov's observations about Shkapskaya is made in Kuz'min, "Zabyvshie, chto my brat'ia . . . ," 290. For Gasparov's comments, see his *Russkie stikhi 1890-kh—1925-go godov v kommentariiakh* (Vysshaia shkola, 1993), 17–18.

43. See, for example, his synoptic account of economic criticism in "Vstupitel'naia zametka: O novoi ekonomicheskoi kritike," *NLO* 58 (no. 6, 2002): 3–24, as well as in his study of Amazon ratings as a measurement of literary taste. He applied for a patent for this research, which was reported in multiple places, including in Lia Miller, "Amazon Ratings Count After All," *New York Times*, January 24, 2005, https://www.nytimes.com/2005/01/24/technology/amazons-ratings-count-after-all.html.

44. The pun is on the prefix *za*, which can mark the inception of an action, as if the word for "to forget" (zabyt') were split into prefix and root and meant "to start to live." For the poem, see "chto nazhito sgorelo: ugli," in Gronas, *Dorogie siroty,*, 5. Morphological variations are another method through which Gronas's short poems can build intense effects out of sparse semantic and phonic material. A particularly fine example is his three-part poem in memory of Grigory Dashevsky. It begins "Khodit' khodit' vykhazhivat'"; see Gronas, *Kratkaia istoriia vnimaniia*, 9. For the scholarship on memory, see Gronas, *Cognitive Poetics and Cultural Memory: Russian Literary Mnemonics* (Routledge, 2011).

45. See the essays in Myung Mi Kim and Cristanne Miller, eds., *Poetics and Precarity* (SUNY Press, 2018), particularly Sarah Dowling's contribution, "Supine, Prone, Precarious," 145–60. She is writing about a very different mode of textuality, the maximalism of Bhanu Kapil's *Ban en Banlieue* (2015), but I have found quite instructive the way Dowling historicizes and pinpoints a physicalized experience, that of lying down, for a subjectivity that "undercuts the mastery and singularity associated with a flaneur-type commentator, who might curate and select the city's sights and sites for readerly consumption" (156).

46. Dowling, "Supine, Prone, Precarious," 156.

47. "Nu-ka otvechai, rodnaia rech'! / Vechno otvechai, avtootvetchik" in "My stoiali v ocheredi za" and "skvoznaia dyra / no iz etoi dyry / soznan'e gliaditsia / v pustye miry" in "zakryty glaza"; see Gronas, *Kratkaia istoriia vnimaniia*, 12, 16.

48. These lines are in "v den' kogda golova pusta," Gronas, *Kratkaia istoriia vnimaniia*, 20.

49. Susan Stewart, *On Longing: Narratives of the Miniature, the Gigantic, the Souvenir, the Collection* (Duke University Press, 1993), 44.

50. In his scholarship, Gronas also writes about tip-of-the-tongue phenomena, which is in some ways analogous, particularly given the metaphysical potential of his prime example, the work of Osip Mandelstam. See Gronas, *Cognitive Poetics and Cultural Memory*, 97–129.

51. See Gronas's poem "Ia ves' den' prolezhal na ladoni u snegopada," in *Kratkaia istoriia vnimaniia*, 45.

52. Anna Glazova, who has written extensively about Celan, pinpoints this element of Gronas's poetry and its philosophical implications. See the last paragraph of Glazova, "Vyrazhenie slov," where she also refers to "Ia ves' den' prolezhal."

53. Anna Glazova, *Dlia zemleroiki* (NLO, 2013), 13. English translation from Glazova, *For the Shrew*, trans. Alex Niemi (Zephyr, 2022), 13. For a different version, see the translation by Anna Khasin in Ciepiela, *Relocations*, 63. I write about this poem in "Mandelstam among Contemporary Poets: Zhdanov, Eremin, Glazova," in *Living through Literature: Essays in Memory of Omry Ronen*, ed. Julie Hansen, Karen Evans-Romaine, and Herbert Eagle, Uppsala Studies on Eastern Europe (Uppsala University Acta Upsaliensis, 2019), 121–40. Much of the writing here about Eremin is adapted and condensed from this essay.

54. Lev Losev, "Zhizn' kak metafora," in *Filologicheskaia shkola: Teksty. Vospominaniia. Bibliografiia*, ed. Viktor Kulle and Vladimir Ufliand (Letnii sad, 2006), 472–82; the comparison to riding an escalator is on 476.

55. The *vos'mistishiia* began by 1955; the three poems in other forms are all dated 1958. For the latter, see Kulle and Ufliand, *Filologicheskaia shkola*, 37, 39, 40.

56. One example of the form's enduring appeal in Russian showed up in a Facebook post by Valery Shubinsky, July 25, 2018: two *vos'mistishiia*, one by Konstantin Sluchevsky, one by Innokenty Annensky, elicited quick and enthusiastic approval from readers.

57. Mikhail Aizenberg, "Neskol'ko slov o Mikhaile Eremine," *NLO* 14 (1995): 263–64.

58. For the poems, see O. Mandel'shtam, *Polnoe sobranie stikhotvorenii*, ed. A. G. Mets (Gumanitarnoe agentstvo "Akademicheskii proekt," 1995), 227–30; for the comment about the poems as failed larger work, see 595. As is noted there, the poet did not want them collected into a cycle, and no definitive order exists.

59. Andrew Kahn, *Mandelstam's Worlds* (Oxford University Press, 2020), 252. Other exemplary readings of individual *vos'mistishiia* include Nancy Pollak's analysis of the final poem, "I ia vykhozhu iz prostranstva," in *Mandelstam the Reader* (Johns Hopkins University Press, 1995), 70–83.

60. These are literal translations of individual lines from the poems. For a translation of all eleven poems, see "Octets" in Mandelstam, *Moscow Notebooks*, 74–77; and "Octaves" in Kahn, *Mandelstam's Worlds*, 255–57.

61. For the poems, see Andrei Rodionov, "Nit'," *Vozdukh* (no. 2, 2016): 10–35; and his book *Poeticheskii dnevnik, nachatyi v den' smerti Iuriia Mamleeva 25 oktiabria 2015* (NLO, 2018); Sergei Magid, "Vos'mistishiia 14-go goda," in *Stikhi 2011–2019 gg.* (Vodolei, 2020), 113–34; and Natal'ia Gorbanevskaia, "Odinnatsat' tsiklov vos'mistishii 1992–2013 godov," in *Izbrannye stikhotvoreniia* (Izdatel'stvo Ivana Limbakha, 2015), 219–74. An important statement about Rodionov's eight-line poems and the heritage of the form is included in Il'ia Kukulin, "Ob"iasnenie v liubvi: Andreiu Rodionovu," *Vozdukh* 2 (2016): 5–9, where he lists other poets who have worked productively in the form.

62. For the poems, see Aleksei Parshchikov, "Som," "Poet i muza," "O sad moikh druzei," "Statui," "Pustynia," "Gorbun," "Svobodnye stikhi," "Real'naia stena," "Vse tak i est'," "Narkoz," "Pliazhnye kreposti," "Derevo na kraiu sportivnoi ploshchadi," "Rynok, uragan," and "V stepi: Na pamiat'," in *Dirizhabli* (Vremia, 2014), 19, 21, 42, 61, 124, 127, 128, 154, 173, 175, 176, 215; and Ol'ga Sedakova, "Vosem' vos'mistishii" and "Chetyre vos'mistishiia," in *Stikhi*, 92–96, 362–65. Also of interest are Boris Khersonskii, "Vos'mistishiia," in *Spirichuels* (NLO, 2009), 282–96, as well as other examples noted in chapter 6; and Lev Oborin, "Iz tsikla '50 vos'mistishii,'" *Homo Legens* 1 (2013), http://magazines.russ.ru/homo_legens/2013/1/iz-cikla-50-vosmistishij.html. See also the work of Leonid Schwab, for whom the eight-line form is not a signature because he as easily might write poems slightly shorter or longer, but poems this size are important in his work: see *Shvab, Vash Nikolai*. This is meant not to be a complete list, but to show how the form has been immensely productive for contemporary poets.

63. The forgotten word as an image in Eremin is also linked to Mandelstam in Dmitrii Bak, *Sto poetov nachala stoletiia* (Vremia, 2015), 192.

64. Il'ia Kukulin, "Podryvnoi epos: Ezra Paund i Mikhail Eremin," in *Poryv k nevozmozhnoi sviazi: Stat'i o russkoi poezii* (Kabinetnyi uchenyi, 2019), 158–72. A different way to see Eremin as Mandelstam's successor would place the poet in a succession of poet-philosophers that started in the eighteenth century: Derzhavin, Tiutchev, Khlebnikov, late Mandelstam, then Eremin. See Igor' Gulin, "Vse tainoi stanoviatsia odoi," *Kommersant" Weekend* 25 (July 23, 2021), https://www.kommersant.ru/doc/4897702.

65. Some other poets are also pertinent. For a productive account of the dialogue with Pasternak in several poems, see Iuliia Valieva, "Prozhit' v otechestve," in Eremin, *Stikhotvoreniia* (NLO, 2021), 424–46.

66. When asked in 2014 how many poems he had written, Eremin said "more than 300": see "Mikhail Eremin: 'Mne tiazhelo, chto ia deistvitel'no ostalsia odin,'" interviewed by Dar'ia Sukhovei, *Colta*, January 15, 2014, https://www.colta.ru/articles/literature/1689-mihail-eremin-mne-tyazhelo-ottogo-chto-ya-deystvitelno-ostalsya-odin. Eremin's poems have appeared in seven volumes published by Pushkinskii fond, plus the collected volume *Stikhotvoreniiia*, on which I based my count. A volume of Eremin's poems was assembled in 1991 and pulped, as reported in Oleg Rogov, "Tainopis', tom chetvertyi," *Chastnyi korrespondent*, December 2, 2009, http://www.litkarta.ru/dossier/rogov-o-eremine/dossier_940/, and I do not know that all those poems have found their way to publication. Some posthumously published poems are starting to appear: Eremin, "Iz neopublikovannogo," *Kvarta* 8, no. 2 (2023), http://quarta-poetry.ru/eryomin/.

67. Eremin insisted that the foundation is iambic, sometimes with paeons in the second and fourth lines. See Natal'ia Babenko, "Vecher Mikhaila Eremina," *St. Petersburg News*, March 14, 2008, http://www.litkarta.ru/russia/spb/news/2008-03-13-eremin/. Scholars and critics have hazarded other descriptions, most of them hovering around the category of free verse. Aizenberg said that the lines seem to remember earlier rhythmic foundations in "Neskol'ko slov o Mikhaile Eremine." Roman Leibov and Roman Voitekhovich call it the illusion of free verse in "O stikhotvorenii M. Eremina 'Schitat' li proiskami zaastral'nykh sil . . . ,'" *NLO* 62 (no. 4, 2003): 154–57. Dar'ia Sukhovei has written about the way the lines reorient toward their beginnings, not their endings, about the unusual enjambments, and about his rhythms as an evolution toward greater freedom in "Sed'maia kniga vos'mykh stikhov," *NLO* 108 (no. 2, 2011): 299–304.

68. There is one exception to the eight-line rule: Eremin also translated poetry, often guided by the form of the original. Those translations make up all but thirteen pages of *Stikhotvoreniia, kn. 6* (Pushkinskii fond, 2016). The translated poets are T. S. Eliot, Muqamal Iqbal, W. B. Yeats, Khushal Khattak, and Hart Crane. Eremin entered the Soviet Writers' Union as a translator. He pointedly observed that this was not the alienated labor some poets complained of, nor did he work with interlinears: he studied the needed languages and found translation to be an education in versification. See Mikhail Eremin, "Mne tiazhelo."

69. Sergei Zav'ialov, "Otrazhenie v zerkal'nykh vodoemakh mertsaiushchikh nad nami zvezd," in Eremin, *Stikhotvoreniia* (2021), 5–15; see 11–12.

70. Aizenberg's "Neskol'ko slov" makes this point, but he, too, adds that some poems are remarkably open.

71. For example, the poem chosen as Eremin's calling card on the *Litkarta* website, http://www.litkarta.ru/russia/spb/persons/eryomin-m/, begins "Rangout okna—sozertsat' zastekliannye vody." The poem appears in *Stikhotvoreniia* (Pushkinskii fond, 1998), 57.

72. See Anne Ferry, *The Title to the Poem* (Stanford University Press, 1996), 246–51; "withholding" is mentioned on 248, and "evasions of the title space" is a chapter title (246–77). Ferry sees generic labels as a comparable kind of evasion (252–54); Eremin's decision to call all his books *Stikhotvoreniia* invokes such a label. In semiotic terms, for Eremin, the title becomes a minus device, noticeable by its consistent absence, especially because other paratextual elements are deployed liberally.

73. The poem is "Top'—zyb'. Tverd'—ziab'. Mel'–," in Eremin, *Stikhotvoreniia* (Hermitage, 1986), 94. I discuss this poem as an ars poetica on translation in "Mikhail Eremin pishet stikhotvorenie 'Perevod,'" trans. E. Kanishcheva, *Vtoraia kul'tura: Neofitsial'naia poeziia Leningrada v 1970-e-1980-e gody*, ed. Jean-Philippe Jaccard (Rostok, 2013), 217–23.

74. Eremin, *Stikhotvoreniia: Kn. 2* (Pushkinskii fond, 2002), 48.

75. Compare Kirill Korchagin, "V poiskakh predskazannogo vremeni," *Novyi mir* (no. 6, 2014), http://www.nm1925.ru/Archive/Journal6_2014_7/Content/Publication6_1178/Default.aspx. He reads Eremin's timelessness as a defining feature of late Soviet and unofficial poetry.

76. Eremin, *Stikhotvoreniia: Kn. 3* (Pushkinskii fond, 2005).

77. As of volume 4 of these books, he included only new work. See Eremin, *Stikhotvoreniia: Kn. 4* (Pushkinskii fond, 2009).

78. Delayed reception is familiar to Russian readers who experienced Mandelstam, Tsvetaeva, Khlebnikov, and other Silver Age figures as significant poets in the 1970s, or when the poets of OBERIU were prominently published in the late 1990s. Several poets who were known only in unofficial circles similarly enjoyed belated new attention in post-Soviet culture: the poets of SMOG and Lianozovo, for example, or Leonid Aronzon and Roal'd Mandel'shtam, both of whom became much more extensively available.

79. Translated from the conversation recorded by Aleksandr Genis, "Homo ludens zhiv," Radio Svoboda, April 15, 2003, https://www.svoboda.org/a/24200093.html.

80. As noted in Rogov, "Tainopis', tom chetvertyi."

81. Eremin, *Stikhotvoreniia: Kn. 4*, 5. A few examples of other poems that are in some sense about world formation: "Iz nedr poliskorii, svalki tozh, dobyv," in *Stikhotvoreniia: Kn. 4*, 39; "Vyprastivaetsia li veshenka" and "Poka pytlivyi um prirodu obdiral do genov," in *Stikhotvoreniia: Kn. 3*, 30, 35; "Granit, almaz, ravno i neolity, kak to," in *Stikhotvoreniia: Kn. 6*, 14; "Ne byt' li zamirennym nabliudatelem," in *Stikhotvoreniia: Kn. 7* (Pushkinskii fond, 2017), 5.

82. Aleksandr Zhitenev notes that the poems open themselves out temporally as well, suggesting a prolonged reaction to an event through multiple discourses and vocabularies. See Zhitenev, *Poeziia neomodernizma* (Inapress, 2012), 371. Zhitenev treats what he calls doubled referentiality, focusing on Eremin's 1998 volume of poems (371–82). He traces this doubled referentiality to avant-garde techniques advanced by Khlebnikov, Bely, and others.

83. Mikhail Eremin, *Stikhotvoreniia: Kn. 2*, 8. When Eremin republished the poem in the 2021 collected volume, he adjusted the final line typographically: "Вознёсся лáвровый привой." See *Stikhotvoreniia* (2021), 30.

84. For the earlier version, also dated 1972, see Eremin, *Stikhotvoreniia* (Hermitage, 1986), 66, and *Sixty Years—Stikhotvoreniia: Selected Poems of Mikhail Yeryomin, 1957–2017*, trans. J. Kates (Black Widow, 2022,) 44–45, where it is also translated into English. It appeared as well in *Mitin zhurnal* 54 (Winter 1997), http://www.vavilon.ru/metatext/mj54/eremin.html. Both versions

are thus easily available to readers; this doubling, which is unusual in Eremin's work (but not in Mandelstam's, including the two versions of a poem within his eleven *vos'mistishiia*), is another way in which the poem's boundaries are porous. For other translations of Eremin into English, see J. Kates, ed., *In the Grip of Strange Thoughts: Russian Poetry in a New Era* (Zephyr, 1999), 189–201; "From 'Poems,'" trans. Alex Cigale, *Words without Borders*, April 2017, https://www.wordswithoutborders.org/article/april-2017-russian-from-poems -mikhail-eremin-alexander-cigale; and "From *Poems: Book 5*," trans. Alex Cigale, *Asymptote*, July 2016, https://www.asymptotejournal.com/poetry/mikhail-eremin-poems-5/. Several excellent translations are embedded in David MacFadyen, "Where to Find the Russian Language: The Poetry of Mikhail Yeryomin," *World Literature Today* 72, no. 1 (Winter 1998): 27–32.

85. Some locutions in my version are from a forthcoming translation by Alex Cigale, used with his permission.

86. Eremin, *Stikhotvoreniia* (1998), 71.

87. A reader at the least stumbles metrically over the chemical formula, uncertain how to pronounce $Cu_2(OH)_2CO_3$ in a line of poetry. According to Yulia Valieva, when Eremin read this poem in her presence, he read it as a chemical formula, not as "malakhit." Conversation in Cambridge, MA, October 2011.

88. "Paris Quadrifolia," Kew Botanical Gardens, http://powo.science.kew.org/taxon /urn:lsid:ipni.org:names:539724-1. The plant is also called herb Paris.

89. For the interview, see Eremin, "Mne tiazhelo." Her reviews of his work include "Sed'maia kniga vos'mykh stikhov."

90. She has also written dozens of short poetry book reviews in *Vozdukh*. For links to those reviews, as well as further details about her publications and other activities, see her page on *Litkarta*, http://www.litkarta.ru/russia/spb/persons/sukhovey-d/.

91. For the poems, see Sukhovei, *48 vos'mistishii* (Avtokhton, 2015) and *Potoma ne budet* (Svoe izdatel'stvo, 2016), 45–59. The last three *vos'mistishiia* in the latter book are part of a separate cycle, "antiflarf."

92. As Sukhovei explained, her goal was to draw not on pop culture or internet searches, which was a guiding principle of the early twenty-first-century flarf movement, but on classical poetry, so that her own language by comparison would sound "crustier and more complex"; translated from Sukhovei, *Potoma ne budet*, 56. She made her quotations from poets like Tiutchev and Khlebnikov look as if they were hyperlinks, simply by underlining them, another way of mimicking the aesthetics of flarf.

93. See Sukhovei's conference paper "Kniga 'Deti v sadu' Genrikha Sapgira kak povorotnyi moment v istorii poetiki poluslova," November 18, 2004, http://levin.rinet.ru/FRIENDS /SUHOVEI/Articles/article2.html. See also her contribution on Nekrasov to "Pamiati ushed-shikh," *Vozdukh* (no. 3–4, 2009): 240–41.

94. Compare the reduction enacted by Sergei Magid, also a creator of admirable eight-line poems. He subsequently published two books, each including one hundred four-line poems: *Pervaia sotnitsa* (Vodolei, 2013) and *Vtoraia sotnitsa: Ob oskorblenii dushi* (Vodolei, 2016).

95. Sukhovei, Facebook, October 23, 2020.

96. *Princeton Encyclopedia of Poetry and Poetics*, 4th ed. (Princeton University Press, 2012), 1297.

97. Sukhovei has one poem that plays wildly on this expectation: "(odin katren pro med)," in Sukhovei, *Po sushchestvu* (NLO, 2018), 53.

98. In Russian, by comparison, the crown of sonnets has thrived, beloved of Viacheslav Ivanov and picked up by Maximilian Voloshin, Valery Briusov, Viktor Sosnora, and Inna Lisnianskaia, among others.

99. In that critical engagement, Sukhovei is building on her philological education. Her dissertation was on the visual in contemporary Russian poetry.

100. For the poem, see Sukhovei, *Po sushchestvu*, 45. Sukhovei sends up the expectation that her poems catalog the useless and the uninteresting in "malyi svet (14–15 stikhotvorenii o nenuzhnom, 2014–2015)," *Polutona*, May 3, 2015, https://polutona.ru/?show=0503164347; and it was the source of the title of her first book, *Katalog sluchainykh zapisei* (ARGO-RISK, 2001).

101. Sukhovei, "Shestistishiia-vtorzheniia" *TextOnly* 48 (no. 1, 2019), http://textonly.ru/self/?issue=48&article=39102.

102. See Vsevolod Nekrasov, *Izbrannye stikhotvoreniia*, ed. Ivan Akhmet'ev (1998), http://www.vavilon.ru/texts/prim/nekrasov1-3.html. For the English, see Nekrasov, *I Live I See: Selected Poems*, tr. Ainsley Morse and Bela Shayevich (Ugly Duckling Presse, 2013), 155.

103. Several of Sukhovei's poems register as visual poetry, for example, by putting letters in bold type to spell out a midline acrostic, as in "togda eshche vspot**el i s ty-**." Another use of visuality occurs when the elements of the poetic text call attention to themselves, as in a poem that contrasts two Cyrillic letter: "d povliial na t potomu chto d"; for the poems, see Sukhovei, *Po sushchestvu*, 111 and 100.

104. The observation that her lineage derives from both Symbolists and Acmeists belongs to the poet Mariia Malinovskaia, in "Ekaterina Simonova: Pereopredelenie liubvi," *Vozdukh* 39 (2019), 5–12; see 5–6.

105. "Mir pronzitel'nykh melochei," interview conducted by Galina Rymbu, *God literatury*, November 20, 2019, https://godliteratury.ru/public-post/mir-pronzitelnykh-melochey. The book is Iu. S. Podlubnova and E. Simonova, eds., *Kul'tura puteshestvii v Serebrianom Veke: Issledovaniia i retseptsii* (Kabinetnyi uchenyi, 2019).

106. Simonova, *Gerbarii* (Ailuros, 2011). An imagined persona, Adel' S., opens this volume with supposed memoirs from Paris, 1955; she recurs as a figure in some poems and as a poet whose work is cited (see 11–12, 67, for example).

107. Ol'ga Sedakova, "Novaia kniga," introduction to Simonova, *Elena: Iabloko i ruka* (Ailuros, 2015), 7–9, quoted from 8.

108. Simonova, *Elena*, 53. The point of reference would be one of Sedakova's most famous early poems, the title poem of her first volume of poetry, *Dikii shipovnik*. For the poem, see Sedakova, *Stikhi*, 59. Another orientation for Simonova's poem is Anna Akhmatova's poem "The Wild Rose Blooms" ("Shipovnik tsvetet," 1946–64), an inspiration for Sedakova's poem as well, and some of Simonova's images come directly from Akhmatova (dust and odors, for instance). Simonova has an earlier and quite different poem with a wild rose image, part of the cycle "Khor," in Simonova, *Vremia* (Slosvet, 2012), 65.

109. Compare the poems she published as miniatures, not particularly short but quite compressed: Simonova, "Miniatiury," *Homo Legens* 3 (2013), https://magazines.gorky.media/homo_legens/2013/3/miniatyury-23.html. The most minimalist of her poems might be those in the

cycle "Pripravy i pravda," where poems in short lines are preceded by recipes. See, for example, "Poka gliadish'," Simonova, *Vremia*, 120–21.

110. These references to Christian symbolism are well investigated in Olga Sedakova, Valentina Polukhina, and Robert Reid, "Collective Analysis of Olga Sedakova's 'The Wild Rose,'" *Essays in Poetics* 22 (1997): 237–57. I date the poem to 1976 according to Sedakova's accounting here of its composition (239).

111. Ol'ga Sedakova, *Poetika obriada: pogrebal'naia obriadnost' vostochnykh i iuzhnykh slavian* (Indrik, 2004).

112. Simonova, "Mir pronzitel'nykh melochei."

113. The poems first appeared in a journal publication, "Uekhavshie, vyslannye, kanushchie, i pogibshie," *Volga* 7 (2018), https://magazines.gorky.media/volga/2018/7-8/uehavshie-vyslannye-kanuvshie-i-pogibshie.html; and are included in Simonova, *Dva ee edinstvennykh plat'ia* (NLO, 2020), 148–77.

114. Simonova, *Dva ee edinstvennykh plat'ia*, 156.

115. Amid these historical figures, Adel' S., invented for Simonova's 2011 book *Gerbarii*, makes an appearance, as a figure in the erotic life of Alexander Vertinsky; see poem 12, *Dva ee edinstvennykh plat'ia*, 172–74.

116. Simonova, *Dva ee edinstvennykh plat'ia*, 162, 156.

117. The poet has acknowledged her grumpy fascination with him. See the interview conducted by Linor Goralik, *Vozdukh* 39 (2019): 48–53. Polina Barskova suggested that Simonova is like Kuzmin reincarnated, both the vocabulary and the poetic orientation. See Barskova, "S tekh por ia nauchilas' lgat'," introduction to Simonova, *Dva ee edinstvennykh plat'ia*, 5–10; see 6–7.

118. Shvarts would have admired the mystification of Anna Arno, "Rakovina, ostavlennaia ulitkoi," *Literratura*, August 16, 2016, http://literratura.org/poetry/1858-anna-arno-rakovina-ostavlennaya-ulitkoy.html.

119. Simonova, *Dva ee edinstvennykh plat'ia*, 70. That move between the domestic and the cosmic also recalls Shvarts's aesthetic orientation.

120. For a splendid example, see Simonova, "Devochki," which appeared in *Literratura*, July 30, 2018, but has been taken down. An account of the poem with many quoted excerpts gives a good sense of it: Iuliia Podlubnova, "O tsikle 'Devochki' Ekateriny Simonovoi," *Artikuliatsiia* 5 (May 2019), https://articulationproject.net/2314.

121. Simonova has affirmed her sense of herself as a feminist (in "Mir pronzitel'nykh melochei"), and the anthology *F Letter* included her work. See *F Letter: New Russian Feminist Poetry*, ed. Galina Rymbu, Eugene Ostashevsky, and Ainsley Morse (Isolarii, 2020), 166–75.

122. In addition to the 2016 poems, see Arno, "Rakovina." See also Anna Arno, "Siiaiushchaia, kak bulavka v trave," *Artikuliatsiia* 12 (October 2020), with an introduction by Iuliia Podlubnova, http://articulationproject.net/8270. The mystification was treated briefly and insightfully in Mariia Malinovskaia, "Pereopredelenie liubvi," *Vozdukh* 39 (2019): 5–12.

123. The honors include the 2013 Razlichie Prize, but she has occasioned discomfort with her quarrelsome comments on Facebook, leading some to ban her from their pages. Grimberg elicited an uncharacteristically gentle response from the hosts of *Shkola zloslovia* (in a preinterview chat, Tatiana Tolstaya and Avdotia Smirnova warned their audience not to expect their usual banter and edginess); see "*Shkola zloslovia*: Faina Grimberg," February 9, 2009, video, 44:14, posted by Apollinarium on May 19, 2020, https://www.youtube.com/watch?v

=5MPwDxHe4Zc. Grimberg also utterly confounded the clever host of *Za obedom*, Vladimir Raevsky, November 15, 2013, video, 13:34, http://www.m24.ru/videos/33962.

124. For her own account of her gradual success in publishing her work, see Faina Grimberg (Gavrilina), "'Ia vsegda khotela byt' samymi raznymi liud'mi, kotorykh ia sama pridumaiu . . . ,'" *Znamia* 5 (2000), https://magazines.gorky.media/znamia/2000/5/ya-vsegda-hotela-byt -samymi-raznymi-lyudmi-kotoryh-ya-sama-pridumayu.html.

125. To name a few of the authorial mystifications: Iakob Lang, *Nalozhnitsa faraona* (1994) and *Taina magicheskogo znaniia* (1994); Sof'ia Grigorova-Alieva and Sabakhatdina-Bora Eter- giun, *Sud'ba turchanki, ili bremena imperii: Trilogiia* (1992–94); Mirianna Benlaid, *Demony pustyni* (1994). Grimberg has also translated extensively from Bulgarian, Greek, English, German, Finnish, Czech, and Swedish.

126. Grimberg also comments frequently on Facebook, typically in all caps.

127. Grimberg, "Chetyrekhlistnik dlia moego ottsa," in *Chetyrekhlistnik dlia moego ottsa* (NLO, 2012), 257–348.

128. The cycle ". . . Esli by Viion byl evreem . . ." is included in *Faina Grimberg: Stat'i i mate- rialy* (ARGO-RISK, 2014), 130–43.

129. As a student, Grimberg specialized in Balkan history. Southeastern Europe (including her beloved Greece), with its tangled history of cultures and its claim to be a point of origin for Slavic cultures, exerts an enduring fascination for Grimberg.

130. In "'Ia vsegda khotela byt' samymi raznymi liud'mi,'" Grimberg gives 1997 as the first date, but I find her *Liubovnaia Andreeva khrestomatiia* (ARGO-RISK, 2002) as the earliest text that includes it; the book is also available at *Vavilon*, http://www.vavilon.ru/texts/prim /grimberg1.html.

131. As E. A. Balashova notes, there are references to three-year, five-year, and seven-year wars, but those names suggest multiple possibilities rather than naming particular events. See Balashova, "'Andrei Ivanovich vozvrashchaetsia domoi' Fainy Grimberg: K voprosu o sinkreticheskom soznanii v individualisticheskuiu epokhu," in "Russkaia filologiia" series, *Vest- nik Moskovskogo gosudarstvennogo oblastnogo universiteta* 3 (2020): 66–70; see 67.

132. When Andrei Ivanovich is said to be a huge pine tree with branches that resemble his arms, he is also likened to something in rotation, in circulation, a "krugovorot." That circularity is rendered as if it is nature's law, science's law: "I eto nazyvaetsia v prirode i v nauke: / krugovo- rot"; see Grimberg, "Andrei Ivanovich vozvrashchaetsia domoi," in *Chetyrekhlistnik dlia moego ottsa*, 23. And the two women who look for him are locked in a terrible circle of friendship: "Poidem iskat' ego," says the speaker to Marina Markovna, "poidem, moia podruga / Ty teper' / moia podruga. / V tosklivom serdtse zamknutogo kruga—/ ty moia podruga" (23).

133. Grimberg, *Chetyrekhlistnik dlia moego ottsa*, 17.

134. It is of great symbolic importance that the poem comes to rest on this image of a child. Grimberg's poetry strikes a position that we might call childlike, and she inherits OBERIU's poetics of foolishness. For a reading of the powerful cultural role played by the childlike aes- thetic, focusing on OBERIU and on Russia's unofficial poets of the 1960s as their heirs, see Ainsley Morse, *Word Play: Experimental Poetry and Soviet Children's Literature* (Northwestern University Press, 2021).

135. Galina Rymbu, "Sobytie-sobranie: K poetike Fainy Grimberg," in *Faina Grimberg: Stat'i i materialy*, 6–10; see esp. 7.

136. Stanislav L'vovskii, "Faina Grimberg protiv istorii: k postanovke problemy," in *Faina Grimberg: Stat'i i materialy*, 20–50; see 36–41.

137. The topic of connectivity (visually, formally, phonetically, and thematically) is taken up well in Svetlana Bochaver, "Sviaznost' v poezii Fainy Grimberg," in *Faina Grimberg: Stat'i i materialy*, 67–78.

4. The Music of the Present

1. Two standard accounts of the tradition are James Winn, *Unsuspected Eloquence: A History of the Relations between Poetry and Music* (Yale University Press, 1981); and Lawrence Kramer, *Music and Poetry: The Nineteenth Century and After* (University of California Press, 1984).

2. Keats writes, "Heard melodies are sweet, but those unheard / Are sweeter: therefore, Ye soft pipes, play on; / [. . .] Pipe to the spirit ditties of no tone" (ll.11–12, 14); quoted from *The Poems of John Keats*, ed. Jack Stillinger (Belknap Press of Harvard University Press, 1978), 372.

3. In Russian poetry, Andrei Bely and Valery Briusov exemplify this valorization of music; their aesthetic choices as Symbolists lingered in the works of later poets, particularly Boris Pasternak, a serious student of music. This productive turn to music has been well studied. For compelling readings and a useful bibliography, with special attention to the work of Velimir Khlebnikov, see L. L. Gerver, *Muzyka i muzykal'naia mifologiia v tvorchestve russkikh poetov: Pervye desiatiletiia XX veka* (Indrik, 2001). Boris Kats has also done extensive work on this topic. See especially his jointly authored book with Roman Timenchik, *Anna Akhmatova i muzyka: Issledovatel'skie ocherki* (Sovetskii kompozitor, 1989).

4. Elena Shvarts, "Elegiia na rentgenovskii snimok moego cherepa," in *Sochineniia*, 5 vols. (Pushkinskii fond, 2002–2014), 1:28.

5. I refer to Sianne Ngai, *Ugly Feelings* (Harvard University Press, 2005).

6. For a brilliant study of intermedial poetry, where a musical layer creates a new environment for poetic material, see Ilya Kukulin, "Contemporary Russian Poetry and the Musical Avant-Garde: Performative Intersections," *Internationale Zeitschrift für Kulturkomparatistik* 2 (2021): 171–94. His analysis is relevant to my accounts of Chukhrov and Borodin, although his chief examples are Dina Gatina and Stanislav Lvovsky. I draw here on his distinction between musical performances that amplify the expressive qualities of a poetic text versus those that undermine its mood, and I develop the role of poetic mood in the discussion of Borodin.

7. Brodsky also dedicated poems to his pianist friends (Elisabeth Leonskaja and Alfred Brendel), and it is particularly interesting to consider his poems about the piano. One study found motifs of flight associated with the open lid of the grand piano: see Boris Kats, "K genezisu poeticheskogo obraza roialia u Iosifa Brodskogo," in *Iosif Brodskii: Tvorchestvo, lichnost', sud'ba* (Zvezda, 1998), 66–72.

8. In conversation, June 24, 2009, Bass Harbor, Maine. Among his writings on Brodsky, see G. S. Smith, "Going Back (Mainly on Brodskii)," *Canadian-American Slavic Studies* 33, nos. 2–4 (1999): 335–51; and "Joseph Brodsky: Summing Up," *Literary Imagination* 7, no. 3 (Fall 2005): 399–410.

9. Translated from an unpublished 1995 interview, cited in Elena Petrushanskaia, "'Remember Her': 'Didona i Enei' Persella v pamiati i tvorchestve poeta," in *Iosif Brodskii: Tvorchestvo, lichnost', sud'ba*, 75.

10. Joseph Brodsky, *Collected Poems in English*, ed. Ann Kjellberg (Farrar, Straus and Giroux, 2000), 530.

11. This radio program was a singularly important source of knowledge about jazz for many Russians, including Brodsky. See Elena Petrushanskaia, "'Muzyka sredy' v zerkale poezii," in *Mir Iosifa Brodskogo: Putevoditel'*, ed. Iakov Gordin and I. A. Murav'eva (Zvezda, 2003), 89–117; and Petrushanskaia, "'Uslyshu i otzovus': o 'muzykal'nykh tsitatakh' u Brodskogo," *Russian Literature* 15 (1999): 103–19; see esp. 118n11, where his early poem "P'esa s dvumia pauzami dlia saks-baritona" (1961) is offered as evidence of Brodsky's listening to the late-hour program.

12. B. L. Pasternak, *Stikhotvoreniia i poemy*, ed. Vadim Baevskii and E. B. Pasternak, 2 vols. (Sovetskii pisatel', 1990), 1:133–34.

13. The formal features of jazz have had a visible impact on American poetry, as has blues music. For specifics on both jazz and the blues, see Erik Redling, "The Musicalization of Poetry," in *Handbook of Intermediality*, ed. Gabriele Rippl (DeGruyter, 2015), 494–511.

14. Brodsky, *Collected Poems in English*, 450. Dateline as published.

15. Brodskii, *Stikhotvoreniia i poemy*, 2 vols. (Izdatel'stvo Pushkinskogo Doma / Izdatel'stvo "Vita Nova," 2011), 2:185.

16. The association of music with (body) temperature is also felt in terms of heat: compare the tango scene in "1867" from Brodsky's "Mexican Divertimento," in *Collected Poems in English*, 89.

17. On related matters, see Joost Van Baak, "Brodsky and the North," *Neo-Formalist Papers*, ed. Robert Reid and Joe Andrew (Rodopi, 1998), 248–68.

18. *Glenn Gould's Solitude Trilogy*, 3 discs (CBC Records / Les Disques SRC, 1992). In the opening of part 1, "Idea of North," from December 1967, Gould creates a sound montage of overlapping voices, each later expanded to demonstrate that sense of community.

19. Brodsky, *Collected Poems in English*, 289–94. For the Russian, see *Stikhotvoreniia i poemy*, 2:72–76. The date is as given in the latter; the translation first appeared in 1982, per *Collected Poems in English*, 522.

20. Brodsky, *Collected Poems in English*, 292; *Stikhotvoreniia i poemy*, 2:74. Compare the earlier lines: "A bitter, brittle / cold represents, as it were, a message / to the body of its final temperature // or—the earth itself" (289); "Sil'nyi moroz sut' otkroven'e telu / O ego griadushchei temperature // libo—vzdokh Zemli" (2:72).

21. Brodsky, *Collected Poems in English*, 291; *Stikhotvoreniia i poemy*, 2:73.

22. On Brodsky's self-translations, see Alexandra Berlina, *Brodsky Translating Brodsky: Poetry in Self-Translation* (Bloomsbury, 2014). The importance of rhyme to the poet is well-established and a frequent point of reference in Natasha Rulyova, *Joseph Brodsky and Collaborative Self-Translation* (Bloomsbury, 2020).

23. The famous quotation comes from a letter Thomas Wentworth Higginson wrote to his wife, about his August 1870 encounter with Dickinson: *The Letters of Emily Dickinson*, 3 vols., ed. Thomas H. Johnson (Belknap Press of Harvard University Press, 1958), 2:473–74

24. The title poem in Elena Shvarts, *Solo na raskalennoi trube* (Pushkinskii fond, 1998), 14.

25. Keith Gessen, "The Gift," *New Yorker*, May 16, 2011, https://www.newyorker.com /magazine/2011/05/23/the-gift-keith-gessen.

26. The less showy nature of the poetic form could have something to do with the poem's memorial gesture, not unlike the stern hexameter in his 1989 poem in memory of Anna Akhmatova: "Na stoletie Anny Akhmatovoi," *Stikhotvoreniia i poemy*, 2:129.

27. Gessen, "Gift."

28. The quotation is from Jean-François Augoyard and Henry Torgue, eds., *Sonic Experience: A Guide to Everyday Sounds*, trans. Andra McCartney and David Paquette (McGill-Queen's University Press, 2005), 4; the authors find associations of the city with a musical instrument as early as the seventeenth century (153n4).

29. For more of Malanova's work in Russian and for the sparse published commentary on her writings, see her page on *Litkarta*, http://www.litkarta.ru/russia/moscow/persons/malanova-m/. Translations into English include four poems, trans. Nika Skandiaka, in Daniel Weissbort and Valentina Polukhina, eds., *An Anthology of Contemporary Russian Women Poets*, (University of Iowa Press, 2005), 112–14; four poems, trans. Stephanie Sandler, *St. Petersburg Review*, no. 4–5 (2012): 325–30; nine poems, trans. Stephanie Sandler, *Jacket* 36 (2008), http://jacketmagazine.com/36/rus-malanova-trb-sandler.shtml. She has written somewhat longer prose, and her poetry books include some prose poems. Malanova has written a lot but published little since her two books. For a new poem that takes urban auditory phenomena in a different direction, see "Slukhovaia galliutsinatsiia," posted by Olga Sedakova to Facebook, November 20, 2022.

30. For an eloquent account of Tudor's performance, see Kay Larson, *Where the Heart Beats: John Cage, Zen Buddhism, and the Inner Life of Artists* (Penguin, 2012), 273–76; some later performances are described as well (278).

31. Mara Malanova, *Prostorechie* (ARGO-RISK, 2006), 46.

32. His philosophy was described aptly as a form of mystical pragmatism in Marjorie Perloff and Charles Junkerman, eds., *John Cage: Composed in America* (University of Chicago Press, 1994), 2. A fine meditation on Cage's engagement with Zen is found in Larson, *Where the Heart Beats*.

33. Could such a performance even exist on the radio? There are reports of radio performances of Cage's *4′33″*. For reference to a 2004 BBC performance, see Kyle Gann, *No Such Thing as Silence: John Cage's 4′33″* (Yale University Press, 2010), 14–15. William Marx can be seen giving a fussy performance in Palm Beach in 2010: "John Cage's 4'33'," video, 7:44, posted by Joel Hochberg, December 15, 2010, https://www.youtube.com/watch?v=JTEFKFiXSx4 (it opens with a slide featuring a quotation from Cage: "Everything we do is music").

34. The poem appeared in Krivulin, *Obrashchenie* (Sovetskii pisatel', 1990), 46–47.

35. On Krivulin's poem, see Sergei Zav'ialov, "Tishina i gospodstvo bessmertiia," *NLO* 52 (no. 6, 2001): 249–52.

36. Larson, *Where the Heart Beats*, 277.

37. Larson, *Where the Heart Beats*, 277.

38. In an exchange with me about this poem, Malanova insisted that it was in fact very slight, based on a memory of a teacher who demonstrated window washing using newspapers; it was the "harsh everyday of Soviet schools." Email exchange, July 31, 2014.

39. Cited in Eugene Ostashevsky, introduction to Alexander Vvedensky, *An Invitation for Me to Think*, ed. and trans. Eugene Ostashevsky (NYRB, 2013), xix; Ostashevsky is translating from Leonid Lipavskii, *Issledovanie uzhasa*, ed. Valerii Sazhin (Ad Marginem, 2005), 323.

40. See Branislav Jakovljevic, *Daniil Kharms: Writing and the Event* (Northwestern University Press, 2009); Jakovljevic, "Daniil Kharms, the Hunger Artist: Toward Eden, and the Other Way Around," *Theatre Journal* 57, no. 2 (2005): 167–89; Ostashevsky, introduction to Vvedensky,

An Invitation for Me to Think; "Eugene Ostashevsky on Alexander Vvedensky's 'Snow Lies' and the Meanings of Its Form," Poetry Society of America, https://www.poetrysociety.org/psa/poetry/crossroads/own_words/Eugene_Ostashevsky/; and L. F. Katsis, "Prolegomeny k teologii OBERIU: Daniil Kharms i Aleksandr Vvedenskii v konteksta Zaveta Sv. Dukha," *Literaturnoe obozrenie*, nos. 3–4 (1994): 94–101. A foundational work on philosophical approaches to Kharms's writings is Mikhail Iampol'skii, *Bespamiatstvo kak istok: Chitaia Kharmsa* (NLO, 1998).

41. Victor Pelevin, introduction to Daniil Kharms, "A Man Came Outside," trans. Susan Brownsberger, *Grand Street* 15, no. 60 (1997), http://www.grandstreet.com/gsissues/gs60/gs60k.html.

42. Cage, preface to "Lecture on the Weather," quoted in Gerald L. Bruns, "Poethics: John Cage and Stanley Cavell at the Crossroads of Ethical Theory," in Perloff and Junkerman, *John Cage*, 206–25, quoted on 206.

43. Bruns, "Poethics," 212.

44. Mara Malanova, *Ekspress* (Zhurnal ITAKA, Zhurnal Kommentarii, 2002), 97–99 (the line recurs three times across those three pages).

45. Malanova, *Ekspress*, 98.

46. Malanova, *Ekspress*, 25.

47. Malanova, *Ekspress*, 25.

48. Julia Trubikhina-Kunina, introduction to Vladimir Aristov, *What We Saw from This Mountain: Selected Poems 1976–2014*, trans. Julia Trubikhina-Kunina and Betsy Hulick (Ugly Duckling Presse, 2017), xi. On Metarealism, see the influential essay by Mikhail Epshtein, "Tema i variiatsiia metamorfoza (o novykh tendentsiiakh v poezii 80-kh godov)," in *Paradoksy novizny: O literaturnom razvitii XIX i XX vekov* (Sovetskii pisatel', 1988), 139–76, esp. 159–68. Aristov has written on Metarealism as well: "Zametki o 'meta,'" *Arion* 4 (1997), http://magazines.russ.ru/arion/1997/4/48.html.

49. For a fuller list of Aristov's publications and links to many writings and some reviews, see his page on *Litkarta*, http://www.litkarta.ru/russia/moscow/persons/aristov-v/. The play is *Teatr odnogo filosofa (proekt i ustava): Dokumental'naia drama v odnom deistvii s videniiami-kartinami* (Progress-Pleiada, 2013).

50. I note also the underground setting for Olga Sedakova's poem "V metro: Moskva"; for the poem, see Sedakova, *Stikhi* (Universitet Dmitriia Pozharskogo, 2010), 409. Both poets are alert to the background noise of daily commutes; Sedakova's short poem insists on an almost improbable joy, and Aristov's ends in a sensation of aesthetic pleasure.

51. See Carolyn Abbate, "Music—Drastic or Gnostic?" *Critical Inquiry* 30 (Spring 2004): 505–36; and Abbate, *Unsung Voices: Opera and Musical Narrative in the Nineteenth Century* (Princeton University Press, 1991).

52. Vladimir Aristov, *Mestorozhdenie* (ARGO-RISK, 2008), 6–7. This poem opens the book.

53. The gusli appears in several fairy tales, and the Library of Russian Folklore includes one entitled "Gusli-samogudy": see *Biblioteka russkogo fol'klora: Skazki, kniga 2* (Sovetskaia Rossiia, 1989), 151–52.

54. Aristov, "Zametki o 'meta.'" A few sentences earlier, Aristov writes about the task of poetry as he and his peers experienced it starting in the late 1970s, recording and making possible an "ontology of oneness" (ontologiia edinichnosti).

55. Timothy Morton, "Sublime Objects," *Speculations* 2 (2011): 207–27; here and below, quotation from 208.

56. Zakhoder, "Pesenki Vinni-Pukh," Akademiia Podarka, http://www.acapod.ru/3763. html; Ludwig Wittgenstein, *Tractatus Logico-Philosophicus* (Harcourt Brace, 1922), 35–36 (text has facing German and English).

57. Aristov has written a short treatise linking the languages of description that define poetry and physics: "Sviaz' opisaniia v iazykakh fiziki i poezii," in *Iazyk nauki—iazyk iskusstva: Sbornik nauchnykh trudov* (Progress, 2000), 295–301. He argues that the structure of the mathematical equation and the structure of metaphorical equivalence create a significant zone of contact between the two seemingly disparate intellectual activities.

58. Quotations from Vladimir Aristov, *Izbrannye stikhi i poemy* (Inapress, 2008), 6–7; Aristov opens the volume with this poem, just as "Predmetnaia muzyka" opens *Mestorozhdenie*. The poem is translated with facing Russian text in Aristov, *What We Saw from This Mountain*, 2–5.

59. The poet's firm claim that the sea has no name has not stopped its naming by others. The scene is decisively placed in the Kola Peninsula in Nataliia Chernykh, "Zrenie i slukh: O stikhakh Vladimira Aristova," *Znamia* 9 (2009), http://www.litkarta.ru/dossier/chernyh-ob -aristove/dossier_824/.

60. Vladimir Aristov, "Verlibr kak perevod s neizvestnogo iazyka," *Kommentarii* 15 (1998): 111–15.

61. For the translations, see a large group of texts he prepared, translating with others, and interviewing Palmer himself: Maikl Palmer, "Stikhi, esse, interv'iu, zapisnye knizhki," *Inostrannaia literatura* (no. 3, 2013), http://magazines.russ.ru/inostran/2013/3/p9.html (interview), http://magazines.russ.ru/inostran/2013/3/p11.html (one of the translations).

62. A comprehensive account of Aygi's life and work has been created by his principal translator into English, Peter France. See France, "Gennadii Aigi," in *Russian Poets of the Soviet Era, Dictionary of Literary Biography* 359 (Gale Cengage Learning, 2011), 3–20.

63. Aygi also produced a highly regarded volume of Chuvash translations of French poetry, and he saw translation work as very significant for his own poetic practice.

64. Aigi, *Zdes': Izbrannye stikhotvoreniia 1954–1988* (Sovremennik, 1991). It has an unfortunate introduction by Yevgeny Yevtushenko that makes Aygi out to be an elitist poet, as noted by Victor Krivulin in a perceptive review: see Krivulin, "O prostote, svobode, i pochve," in *Aigi: Materialy, issledovaniia, esse*, ed. Iurii Orlitskii, Natal'ia Azarova, and Dmitrii Derepa (Vest-Konsalting, 2006), 1:170–75. Krivulin asserts the great significance of Aygi's work for 1960s and 1970s unofficial poets.

65. Sergei Zav'ialov, "Poeziia Aigi: Razgovor s russkim chitatelem," *NLO* 79 (no. 3, 2006): 205–12.

66. Sedakova, "Aigi: Ot"ezd," *NLO* 79 (no. 3, 2006): 205–12. Sedakova's and Zav'ialov's statements appear in a small memorial section about Aygi in *NLO*, the only journal, to my knowledge, to publish a posthumous tribute (compare the many statements that appeared after the deaths of Elena Shvarts in 2011 and Dmitry Prigov in 2007). But attention to Aygi did slowly increase subsequently in Russia, including the publication of new collections of his work, some cited below.

67. Michael Wachtel, "Aigi, Gennadii Nikolaevich," in *Encyclopedia of Contemporary Russian Culture*, ed. Tatiana Smorodinskaya, Karen Evans-Romaine, and Helena Goscilo (Routledge, 2007), 9–10, quotation on 10.

68. French has also been seen as a bridging "super-language" for Aygi as he thought his way between Chuvash and Russian. See Natal'ia Azarova, "Mnogoiazychie Aigi i iazyki-posredniki," *Russian Literature* 79–80 (2016): 29–44.

69. They include Malevich, Khlebnikov, Kruchenykh, Leskov, Platonov, Shalamov, and Pasternak (reviled in the post–Nobel Prize fiasco, when Aygi knew him). Aygi granted many interviews, a good source for understanding his creative evolution. See, for example, "Poeziia, kak sneg, sushchestvuet vsegda . . . ," *NLO* 62 (no. 4, 2003): 202–9; Vitalii Amurskii, "Byla, krome 'Vekh,' i smena atmosfer," *Deti Ra* (no. 11, 2006), https://magazines.gorky.media/ra/2006/11/gennadij-ajgi-byla-krome-veh-i-smena-atmosfer.html (which highlights the importance of Malevich); "Poet—eto nesostoavshiisia sviatoi: Beseda Viktora Kulle s Gennadiem Aigi," in *Aigi: Materialy*, 1:213–21 (which ends with Celan and Kafka); and "U nas byli svoi nepisanye 'manifesty' (Razgovor s pol'skim drugom)," in Aigi, *Razgovor na rasstoianii* (Limbus, 2001), 16–27. The last volume includes several other interviews (250–93). Of these relationships, the most fully studied is Aygi's connection to Pasternak. It is central to the keen analysis in O. V. Sokolova, "Neoavangardnaia poeziia G. Aigi i V. Sosnory: Esteticheskoe samoopredelenie i poetika," (PhD diss., Tomsk State University, 2007), 80–144; see also 53–69 on Aygi and Malevich.

70. Music plays a further role in Aygi's poetry in his adaptations of Chuvash, Tartar, Mari, and Udmurtian folk songs. He created dozens of four-line poems based on this material. See Aigi, *Poklon peniiu: Sto variatsii na temy narodnykh pesen Povolozh'ia* (OGI, 2001).

71. Aygi makes this observation in *Gennadii Aigi*, dir. Marina Razbezhkina, 2001. I thank Jeffrey Yang for sending me this film several years ago, which is now available on YouTube: "Fil'm 'Gennadii Aigi,'" video, 51:39, posted on April 21, 2013 by Muzei Organicheskoi Kul'tury, https://www.youtube.com/watch?v=Ob0_YnPpjcU. He also generously shared some footage of Aygi by an unnamed videographer in a ten-minute film shot in 1998 (as referenced below).

72. The freedom is not like, say, the polymetric poetry of Elena Shvarts or the visual poetries of Ry Nikonova, Sergei Sigei, and Elizaveta Mnatsakanova. The formal variety of Aygi's work is exceptional. While he did write apparent signature poems—with limited lexicon, uneven line length, unusual punctuation, and rhythms shaped by the white space around the text, numerically these poems are not in the majority. There is a great deal else.

73. A summary of their mutual admiration appears in the commentary to his 1977 poem to her in Aigi, *Provintsiia zhivykh*, ed. A. Mirzaev (Pal'mira, 2020), 283–84. Aygi's connections to Gubaidulina are more fully documented than his friendships with others, including Volkonsky, to whom he was closer. See Michael Kurtz, *Sofia Gubaidulina: A Biography*, trans. Malcolm Hamrick Brown (Indiana University Press, 2007), esp. 98–100. Gubaidulina's use of silences and her having set several Aygi poems to music are discussed in Sarah Valentine, "Music, Silence, and Spirituality in the Poetry of Gennady Aigi," *SEEJ* 51, no. 4 (2007): 675–92.

74. Russian text from Aigi, *Razgovor na rasstoianii*, 40. Compare the version by Peter France, presented as lineated poetry, in Gennady Aigi, *Child-and-Rose* (New Directions, 2003), 102.

75. Slightly different line breaks can be seen, for instance, in Aigi, *Provintsiia zhivykh*, 146. Prose poems are uncommon in his work, but this is not an isolated instance. See, for example, "Rodina-Limb" (1977) in Aigi, *Polia-dvoiniki* (OGI, 2006), 121.

76. Cited from Don Michael Randel, ed., *Harvard Dictionary of Music*, 4th ed. (Belknap Press of Harvard University Press, 2003), 151–52.

77. Poet and scholar Larisa Berezovchuk studied Aigi's use of verbs in poems of 1967–70. Her findings suggest that this poem with no verbs is quite unusual. See Berezovchuk, "Ogon' odet v tragediiu glagola (Popytka aspektologicheskogo analiza knigi Gennadiia Aigi 'Odezhda ognia')," in *Aigi: Materialy*, 1:33–57.

78. For a detailed study of the markings, see Gerald Janecek, "The Poetics of Punctuation in Gennady Aygi's Free Verse," *Sight and Sound Entwined: Studies of the New Russian Poetry* (Berghahn, 2000), 91–108.

79. Cited from Aigi, *Polia-dvoiniki*, 184; note on 226. The dedication is to the Lithuanian poet Balys Sruoga, and the poem comes from a group of texts associated with Aigi's trip to Lithuania; see Aigi, *Zdes'*, 258.

80. The poem is in Aigi, *Teper' vsegda snega: Stikhi raznykh let, 1955–1989* (Sovetskii pisatel', 1992), 276–77.

81. Aigi, *Razgovor na rasstoianii*, 73.

82. Once in Vienna, Mnatsakanova began self-publishing her work as Elisabeth Netzkowa or Elisabeth Netzkowa (Mnatsakanjan). A detailed chronology of her life and works appears in *Arcadia: Izbrannye raboty 1972–2002* (Izdatel'stvo R. Elinina, 2004), on unnumbered pages at the end of the volume, beginning after 188. It is updated in *Novaia Arkadiia* (NLO, 2018), 341–48.

83. Mnatsakanova's international and Russian reputation grew after 2000. In 2004, Harvard University hosted a symposium and year-long exhibit dedicated to her work. In Petersburg, an exhibit curated by Mikhail Shemiakin opened to great acclaim in 2008, culminating in a performance of her work by the actor Leonid Mozgovoi. Shemiakin's interest in Mnatsakanova dates to her first publications in the West: his drawing accompanied her "Osen' v lazarete nevin-nykh sester: Rekviem v semi chastiakh" in the journal *Apollon-77*, and his artwork adorns the cover of *Novaia Arkadiia*.

84. A group of essays appeared in honor of the hundredth anniversary of her birth in *NLO* 177 (no. 5, 2022): 255–316.

85. On visual aspects of the work, see Tatiana Nazarenko, "Words Abandoned: Pictograms and Ideograms in Contemporary Russian Visual Poetry," *Canadian-American Slavic Studies* 36, no. 4 (2002): 447–69; and Nazarenko, "Re-thinking the Value of the Linguistic and Non-Linguistic Sign: Russian Visual Poetry Without Verbal Components," *SEEJ* 47, no. 3 (2003): 393–421.

86. Gerald Janecek, "Elizaveta Mnatsakanova," *Russian Women Writers*, ed. Christine D. Tomei, 2 vols. (Garland, 1999), 2:1381–82. Mnatsakanova gave "Das Hohelied" a German name, adding the Russian equivalent, *Pesn' pesnei* (*Song of Songs*). For the poem, see Elisabeth Netzkowa (Mnatsakanjan), *Das Buch Sabeth* (1988), 129–52.

87. First published in Paris in *Apollon-77* (Michel Chemiakine, 1977), 173–83. For a slightly revised version, see *NLO* 62 (no. 4, 2003): 253–71.

88. I focus on *Das Buch Sabeth* in "Visual Poetry after Modernism: Elizaveta Mnatsakanova," *Slavic Review* 67, no. 3 (Fall 2008): 610–41.

89. Readers can also read an excerpt from *Metamorphosen* in *Novaia Arkadiia*, 285–300, although all visual ornamentation is omitted there.

90. Edward W. Said, *Music at the Limits* (Columbia University Press, 2008), 161.

91. In *Novaia Arkadiia*, the subtitle is given as "20 prevrashchenii odnoi piatistrochnoi strofy, prolog i final," an error not repeated in the table of contents, which has "chetyrekhstrochnoi stofy," the correct translation of Mnatsakanova's German subtitle. A translation error, I assume, and a curiously revealing one: there is no four- or even five-line strophe that initiates the cycle at all; the prologue, or "motto," begins with a six-line strophe.

92. My report on Mnatsakanova's views of her work is based on multiple conversations with the poet in Vienna in 2004 and 2008, as well as correspondence (email letters, June 30, 2009; July 18, 2009; July 20, 2009; and subsequently), and telephone conversations (July 19, 2009, and subsequently). I also draw on two notebooks of handwritten commentary and a marked-up copy of *Metamorphosen* she kindly sent to me in 2009.

93. On mourning and melancholy in Strauss's *Metamorphosen*, see Michael Steinberg, "Metamorphosen for 23 Solo Strings (1944–45)," concert notes for the American Symphony Orchestra performance in Avery Fisher Hall, April 30, 1995, https://americansymphony.org/concert-notes/metamorphosen-for-23-solo-strings/.

94. I suspect that Mnatsakanova also found Gould's image intriguing: he was described by Edward Said as seeking to "create a terrain entirely his own—anomalous, eccentric, unmistakable"; see Said, "The Music Itself: Glenn Gould's Contrapuntal Vision" in *Music at the Limits*, 3–10, quotation on 4. Gould famously admired Richard Strauss. Gould likely also appealed because of the intense mental work in each performance. One sensed always "a mind at work, not just a fleet pair of hands": Said, "Remembrances of Things Played: Presence and Memory in the Pianist's Art," in *Music at the Limits*, 11–22, quotation on 14.

95. Mnatsakanova, in describing the project of the poem in her 2009 notes to me, from which I translate, wrote that the spontaneity of these notes should help one to understand the text's own sense of "endless movement." She believed she had succeeded in creating a feeling of "open, endless movement in the text—it 'flows' like a river."

96. Elisabeth Netzkowa, *Metamorphosen* (1988), 1.

97. In addition to the well-known requiem "Autumn in the Lazaretto of Innocent Sisters," Mnatsakanova wrote a "Little Requiem" ("Malen'kii Rekviem: Pamiati doktora Anny N.," 1977–93, revised 2014), included in *Novaia Arkadiia*, 93–105. She also created a large text with the German title *Beim Tode Zugast* (*A Guest of Death's*). A words-only version is included in her *Shagi i vzdokhi: Chetyre knigi stikhov*, which appeared as *Wiener Slawistischer Almanach* 9 (1982) with the dateline Moscow 1972. She used texts from this cycle to create a calligraphy and visual album, *U smerti v gostiakh Beim Tode Zugast* (1986).

98. Netzkowa, *Metamorphosen*, 16. In my copy of the book, the poet wrote in the margin of these lines: "the final dreams!" (poslednie sny!). In other inserted notes to the volume, she called this a requiem to herself ("Vot kak ia sebia 'otpevaiu—otpela!'").

99. I am drawing on the notebook that Mnatsakanova prepared for me here. She mistakenly wrote Dresden opera house in those notes, substituting a powerful symbol of the Second World War's fiery destructive force.

100. The poem also includes a long excerpt from a Leipzig newspaper article about a performance of a Bach oratorio.

101. Harold Bloom, *The Anxiety of Influence* (Oxford University Press, 1973).

102. Mnatsakanova embedded other musical terms in her texts. Part 1 of *Das Buch Sabeth, Laudes,* for example, includes several motets and a *choral mit dem tenore ostinato.* The motets are for three voices and are laid out in vertical columns that suggest three sets of words resounding at once. See Netzkowa (Mnatsakanjan), *Das Buch Sabeth,* 17, 25, and, for the "choral," 23.

103. Bach scholars agree on the orientation of the suites toward dance, as indicated by the names for their parts. See Leslie Gerber's liner notes for Glenn Gould's recording of the *English Suites* (Columbia Recordings, 1977), http://www.lesliegerber.net/writing/progam-notes/bach-english-suites/.

104. John Eliot Gardiner, *Bach: Music in the Castle of Heaven* (Random House, 2013), xxix.

105. Christoph Wolff, *Johann Sebastian Bach: The Learned Musician* (Norton, 2000), 170–71. Wolff quotes Forkel as translated in *The New Bach Reader: A Life of Johann Sebastian Bach in Letters and Documents,* ed. Hans T. David and Arthur Mendel, revised and expanded by Christoph Wolff (Norton, 1998), 441–42. My earlier phrase, "musical thinking," comes from a chapter of Wolff's book: "'Musical Thinking': The Making of a Composer," 169–74.

106. Wolff, *Johann Sebastian Bach,* 171.

107. Netzkowa, *Metamorphosen,* 20.

108. Netzkowa, *Metamorphosen,* 20–21.

109. As one can hear in her 2004 CD, *E. Netskova (Mnatsakan'ian) chitaet iz svoikh knig.*

110. For an interview that explores her orientation toward the feminism of Judith Butler, see "Filosof Keti Chukhrov: Gender pokazyvaet shatkost' sushchestvovaniia," *Theory and Practice,* undated, https://theoryandpractice.ru/posts/6160-filosof-keti-chukhrov-gender-pokazyvaet-shatkost-sushchestvovaniya. This link ceased working in 2024, but the interview was also uploaded to VKontakte by Milada Yarceva on April 3, 2020, https://vk.com/@takizhivemgim-ranazhdem-filosof-keti-chuhrov-gender-pokazyvaet-shatkost-suschestvova and to Live Journal by Elis Wolf on January 13, 2015, https://fun-and-games.livejournal.com/43135.html. She connects her writing and performance practices to theory, philosophy, and politics in a PennSound interview with Kevin Platt, Marijeta Bozovic, and me, February 27, 2015, audio, 37:25, https://media.sas.upenn.edu/pennsound/groups/Your-Language-My-Ear/Your-Language-My-Ear_Conversation_Wexler-Studio_2-27-15.mp3.

111. See Keti Chukhrov, "O poiskakh immanentnogo smysla (o sbornike *ne BU*)," in Anna Al'chuk, *Sobranie stikhotvorenii* (NLO, 2011), 336–41; see 337. In the passage I refer to, she adds that post-Conceptualist poets have not given up on a search for truth, or as she writes it, Truth (Istina).

112. The Russian text is in Chukhrov, *Prosto liudi* (Kraft, 2010), 52–67, which also includes "El'pida i 'Greki'" and "Medik-Madona" (18–29). Of these, one is available in English: *Communion,* trans. Julia Bloch et al., *Common Knowledge* 24, no. 1 (2018): 130–48.

113. In writing about several of Chukhrov's texts, Marijeta Bozovic has aptly linked this emphasis on multiplicity to the centrifugal politics of Gilles Deleuze, a thinker important to Chukhrov. See Bozovic, "The Voices of Keti Chukhrov: Radical Poetics after the Soviet Union," *Modern Language Quarterly* 84, no. 4 (2019): 453–78, esp. 459.

114. A constant in Chukhrov's highly varied work is this critique of all forms of abstract language, perhaps most pleasurably in "Global Congress of Post-Prostitution" ("Vsemirnyi kongress post-prostitutsii," 2019). This text was staged in English (translation by Ainsley Morse) by

Guram Mnatskhonashvili for the Graz festival Steirischer Herbst. For a video with extensive excerpts in English and discussion including Chukhrov, see "Keti Chukhrov: Global Congress of Post-Prostitution," [*Translit*], http://www.trans-lit.info/video/global-congress-of-post-prostitution. In introducing the performance, Chukhrov describes the text as a carnivalesque distortion of theoretical discourses, a good way to think about much of her work.

115. Chukhrov, "The 'Afghan' Market: Kuzminki," *N + 1* 26 (Fall 2016): 132–46, quotation from 134 (translation amended); *Prosto liudi*, 40. Within a few minutes Galina retells some more of the plot, and its suicidal contemplations are the same mix of the elevated and the debased. For example, "he's trying to decide how to kick the bucket" (on reshaet, kak emu okochurit'sia), 135, 41.

116. "Ot tepla narrativa k kholodu ritma," *Zhenshchina i novatorstvo v Rossii*, ed. Anna Al'chuk, September 9, 2009, http://www.owl.ru/avangard/otteplanarrativa.html.

117. Chukhrov also used the subtitle "radio-oratorii" for her audio CD, *Istina i Konstantin* (kraft-audio, 2013) of three dramas: "Aelita grud'," "Istina i Konstantin," and "El'pida i 'greki.'" The disk is described on the [*Translit*] site: http://www.trans-lit.info/knigi/kraft_audio/keti-chuhrov-istina-i-konstantin.

118. The video of that performance at Smolny (2008) has been taken down.

119. There are two recorded versions of the September 25, 2011, performance at Teatr.doc, one with only one interpolation of visual material, "Keti Chukhrov: 'Afgan—Kuz'minki,' Chelovecheskaia oratoriia," video, 27:40, posted by chto delat on September 26, 2011, https://vimeo.com/29630925; and another, with multiple interpolations, "'Afgan—Kuz'minki,' Chelovecheskaia oratoriia," video, 1:01:49, posted by chto delat on October 25, 2011, https://vimeo.com/31101019. Those insertions of video and of actors holding enlarged photographs and other visual material were designed by Ksenia Petrukhina and Andrei Parshikov. There was also a performance in Kyiv, for voice and piano only, June 19, 2012.

120. As reported by Pavel Rudnev in *New Drama*, June 19, 2012, after the Kyiv performance: "'Afgan-Kuz'minki' Keti Chukhrov v Kieve," https://newdrama.livejournal.com/2715095.html.

121. Peter Szendy, *Listen: A History of Our Ears*, trans. Charlotte Mandell (Fordham University Press, 2008), 3. His comments on intentional borrowings in musical compositions (21–22) also feel pertinent to Chukhrov's process.

122. That performance, organized to mark the start of the Kraft book series in St. Petersburg on April 11, 2010, was recorded: "Keti Chukhrov i Aleksandr Skidan chitaiut 'Afgan—Kuz'minki,'" video, 19:12, posted by chto delat on April 13, 2010, https://vimeo.com/10891733. Chukhrov begins to sing the lines of the Tsvetaeva poem at 17:00. In the Teatr.doc performance ("Keti Chukhrov," https://vimeo.com/29630925), this moment occurs at 23:45.

123. Chukhrov, *Prosto liudi*, 48; this passage is omitted in the English translation.

124. Strikingly, the first two extracts correspond closely to published versions (although with some remarkable errors, including "oni" rather than "ochi" in "Akhmatovoi"—perhaps Chukhrov is showing the television performer's vulgarity), but in the third case, from "Poem of the End," Chukhrov excerpts Tsvetaeva's lines without some of Tsvetaeva's trademark punctuation. For the texts, see Tsvetaeva, *Sobranie sochinenii v semi tomakh* (Ellis-Lak, 1994), 1:309 ("Akhmatovoi"); 2:337–41 ("Stikhi sirote"); and 3:41–42 ("Poema Kontsa").

125. Chukhrov, *Prosto liudi*, 50; for a fuller English translation of this passage, see *Selected Poems of Marina Tsvetaeva*, trans. Elaine Feinstein (Oxford University Press, 1981), 60–61.

126. The political elements of the text have been emphasized in other readings. See Irina Solomatina, "Keti Chukhrukidze i Keti Chukhrov," *Gendernye issledovaniia* 19 (2009), http:// kcgs.net.ua/gurnal/19/; and Bozovic, "Voices of Keti Chukhrov," 460–67. Bozovic reads the turn to Tsvetaeva as political, seeing her as "another nomad, another woman, with politics re-sistant to appropriation by either Soviet or anti-Soviet literary historians" (466).

127. "Mladshee poeticheskoe pokolenie—o sebe," *Vozdukh* (nos. 1–2, 2012): 195–213.

128. Many statements were tagged with his name and can be found on his Facebook page, which continues to draw posts connected to his legacy. Several short essays of remembrance and reassessment appeared quickly as well, for example, Lev Oborin, "Est tol'ko odushevlen-nost'," *Colta*, June 11, 2021, https://www.colta.ru/articles/literature/27549-lev-oborin-pamyati -vasiliya-borodina-poeziya; and Sergei Sdobnov and Rostislav Amelin, "Pamiati Vasiliia Boro-dina (1982–2021)," *Colta*, June 11, 2021, https://www.colta.ru/articles/literature/27539-sergey -sdobnov-rostislav-amelin-pamyati-vasiliya-borodina. There were gatherings in Moscow and Petersburg in his memory, including "Vecher pamiati poeta Vasiliia Borodina," Tsentr Vozne-senskogo, July 2, 2021, video, 39:21, https://www.facebook.com/voznesenskycenter/videos /189357576463066, and others noted below.

129. Igor' Gulin, "Svet bolit i poet," *Kommersant" Weekend* 20 (June 18, 2021), https://www .kommersant.ru/doc/4849917.

130. As Ol'ga Devsh noted, the title of this book is a musical reference (to George Harrison's 1987 album *Cloud Nine*). See her contribution to "In Memoriam Vasilii Borodin," *Litteratura* 185 (2021), https://literatura.org/actual/4579-in-memoriam-vasiliy-borodin.html. *Cloud Nine* was the last album Harrison released, as this book was the last Borodin would see published. A ninth volume containing short works of prose was assembled by the poet and appeared in 2021: *Kho-chetsia tol'ko spat'* (Izdatel'stvo Iaromira Khladeka). More is to come: NLO will publish as com-plete a collection as can be assembled, and Gulin notes in "Svet bolit i poet" that the book publications are but a part of all that he wrote. Reassessments are also likely to confirm that Borodin was less of a loner intellectually than his social isolation would suggest: the web page devoted to Borodin on *Litkarta* has links to his many contributions to forums and his reviews of others' books, http://www.litkarta.ru/russia/moscow/persons/borodin-v/.

131. The term *audiable* is from Lawrence Kramer, *The Hum of the World: A Philosophy of Listening* (University of California Press, 2018), 4–6. The similarity to Aygi was also noted by Alina Dadaeva: for both poets, silence is filled with yet unheard sounds. She refers to a striking poem by Borodin about the absence of music, "goloe derevtse": see her contribution to "In Memoriam Vasilii Borodin."

132. See her comments in an interview, Anton Azarenkov, "V nyneshnykh dvadtsatiletnikh est' vozmozhnost' novoi ser'eznosti," *Uchitel'skaia gazeta* 27 (July 6, 2021), https://ug.ru/olga -sedakova-v-nyneshnih-dvadczatiletnih-est-vozmozhnost-novoj-sereznosti/.

133. As noted by Ivan Beletsky at "Vecher pamiati Vasiliia Borodina," Poriadok Slov Book-store, June 17, 2021, video, 1:37:15, https://www.youtube.com/watch?v=nG4nFc6-Xwo, starting at 1:29:50.

134. His poetry practice included translation, specifically of songs. The work of Vashti Bun-yan particularly attracted him; four of her songs are featured in Vasilii Borodin, "Novye stikhi," *Polutona*, May 25, 2015, https://polutona.ru/?show=0525191916. A famous song by Violeta

˲, Gracias a la vida," appears as well, and its title encapsulates the gratitude and grace felt across Borodin's poetry.

135. Borodin, "Stikhotvoreniia; Illiustratsiia avtora," *Netslova* (2011), https://www.netslova .ru/borodin_v/stihi.html.

136. Borodin is in good company in this chapter in his recourse to the childlike: it is important in the writings of Mnatsakanova, Malanova, and Aygi as well. In that association of musicality with the simplicity of childhood, they point us back to the Futurist Elena Guro; for Borodin, she was a model for the constellation of music, drawing, watercolors, and poetry. On the childlike in Guro, see Kahn et al., *History of Russian Literature*, 618–19.

137. The images were posted by Veronika Pavlenko to Facebook on news of his death, June 10, 2021. I have presented the poem in lineated form according to the images (one image / one poetic line), although it is entirely likely, if this poem appears in the planned posthumous collection of Borodin's work, that there will be a different version, splitting what is now the long line 3 into two lines. But the logic of the drawing makes the words a single poetic line, in a sense, although the words are spread out over the page (as on other pages).

138. Note the strange likeness established by means of shape between bread, with its nourishing solidity, and air, with its inherent lightness. Air, as is true of so many poets studied here, wafts through Borodin's poetry. In an insightful essay about the 2015 volume *Losinyi ostrov*, Sergei Sdobnov noted that the book is distinguished by its feeling of changing atmospheres, as if layers of air were in constantly shifting touch with one another. See Sdobnov, "Usloviia osveshcheniia Losinogo ostrova," *Colta*, June 3, 2015, https://www.colta.ru/articles/literature/7526-usloviya -osvescheniya-losinogo-ostrova.

139. Alice Oswald, *Woods etc.* (Faber and Faber, 2003), 3. The role of hymns and blessing in Oswald, well exemplified in this book, also connects her work to Borodin's, again in an uncanny way because it is improbable that Borodin knew Oswald's poetry.

140. Borodin, *Losinyi ostrov* (NLO, 2015), 92.

141. Borodin, "Stikhotvoreniia; Illiustratsiia avtora."

142. She has made this observation often, including in a conversation with Marta Werner, "Transcription and Transgression," in Mike Kelly et al., *The Networked Recluse: The Connected World of Emily Dickinson* (Amherst College Press, 2017), 123–38; see 128.

143. A memorable example appears in the poem that begins with an imperative to draw—no object is given—and within six short lines offers up song as redemption. See "porisui," in Borodin, *Losinyi ostrov*, 28.

144. Kramer, *Hum of the World*, 96; on Rembrandt, see 98–99, eloquently read as "a picture of the need for sound" (99).

145. Translated from Gulin, "Svet bolit i poet."

146. It is a striking feature of Borodin's poetry that he is a poet of the individual word—not the line, not the sentence, not the stanza. In this he is again very like Olga Sedakova. A fine example of this orientation, one which in fact bares the device, as the formalists would say, is his poem "u 'rany' 'moroz,'" *Klaud nain*, 39.

147. Borodin, *Tsirk "Veter,"* 27.

148. Susan Stewart, "What Praise Poems Are For," *PMLA* 120, no. 1 (2005): 235–45, cited from 236.

149. Following the logic of Susan Stewart's other writing about praise, we could say that theremin, icon, and sneakers equally merit praise because they are made by humans, not by the gods. See Stewart, *The Poet's Freedom: A Notebook on Making* (University of Chicago Press, 2011), 30.

150. These comments were inspired by the performances and text of Jonathan Biss, *Unquiet: My Life with Beethoven* (Audible Originals, 2020), where he speaks about "performing conviction."

151. Susanne Langer's observation of what she called assimilation remains important in musicological study of song and in the encounters between philosophy and music. See Langer, "The Principle of Assimilation," in *Feeling and Form* (Scribner, 1953), 149–58. Hers is one of the models for songs laid out in Kofi Agawu, "Theory and Practice in the Analysis of the Nineteenth-Century 'Lied,'" *Music Analysis* 2, no. 2 (1993): 3–36.

152. On complementarity, see Walter Bernhardt, "What Can Music Do to a Poem? New Intermedial Perspectives of Literary Studies," *Lectures in English: Priorities of Research*, ed. Wolfgang Zach and Michael Kenneally (Stauffenberg Verlag, 2008), 41–46.

153. For example, a performance in an unnamed art gallery space, February 16, 2017, starting at 44:00: "Vasilii Borodin," video, 48:40, posted by Tat'iana Neshumova on February 17, 2017, https://www.youtube.com/watch?v=wPekfyJmqEU.

154. There are some especially lovely examples in footage shot by Mikhail Il'in in Borodin's apartment, March 28, 2021, video, 28:39, uploaded by kosmonastya, https://www.youtube.com/watch?v=z3hcS1oMEas. At the 10:00 mark, you can hear him frustrated that he's messed something up, and he restarts twice, leading to some three minutes of extended guitar work. Il'in gave Borodin the guitar he plays for most of that 2021 recording, and in an earlier performance, Borodin spoke about the guitar at length, personifying it as someone whom he is just getting to know: "Vasilii Borodin v kontserte v Zverevskom tsentre," June 21, 2018, video, 43:55, uploaded by kosmonastya, https://www.youtube.com/watch?v=p64YnJpa8Zc. Borodin also mixed sung and spoken poems in recorded concert a year earlier; it ends with a lovely guitar flourish: "Vasilii Borodin v Zverevskom tsentre," October 19, 2017, video, 44:16, uploaded by kosmonastya, https://www.youtube.com/watch?v=HTE1dOS7hZs.

155. Stewart, *Poet's Freedom*, 84.

156. There are good examples from 2018 in "Vasilii Borodin v kontserte v Zverevskom tsentre."

157. Charles Altieri, *The Particulars of Rapture: An Aesthetics of the Affects* (Cornell University Press, 2003), 55.

158. One such performance in the Zverev Center in 2017 had the title "Identical Elegies: The Songs of Vasily Borodin." The link to that performance leaves out the title, but Borodin gave it in an interview with Vladimir Korkunov: "Summarnyi opyt koshki," *Ex Libris NG*, October 20, 2017, http://www.litkarta.ru/dossier/summarny-opyt-koshki/dossier_5461/. The title *Identical Elegies* (*Odinakovye elegii*) is also the name Borodin gave to an album, available at Band Camp, https://vassilyborodin.bandcamp.com/album/--2, with a note that it was recorded in the summer and fall of 2017 in Moscow. This page includes the song lyrics in full.

159. In reviewing Borodin's first poetry book, *Luch: Parus* (ARGO-RISK, 2008), Anna Glazova began by noting the solitary mood suggested by the title; see Glazova, "Urok sopostavleniia," *NLO* 94 (no. 6, 2008): 235–37. Borodin did not normally use these terms about his work,

but in accepting the 2015 Andrei Bely Prize, he speaks of the award as offering rare relief from loneliness ("chuvstvuiu redko sluchaiushcheesia *neodinochestvo*"); Borodin, "Pis'mo komitetu premii Andreia Belogo," http://belyprize.ru/index.php?id=121.

160. Good examples are in the compelling recording in which Borodin reads alone to a video camera in the series "Poeticheskaia sreda," hosted by the Tsvetaeva Museum in Moscow, March 17, 2021, video, 23:45, https://www.youtube.com/watch?v=vE-ib2t-Ar4.

161. The distance between Borodin's poetic and musical practice is not as far from opera as one might think, given how much he drew on other traditions. He wrote a chamber opera, as he subtitled it, which became the title poem of the volume *Mashen'ka: Stikhi i opera 2013–2018 gg.* (Literature Without Borders, 2019), 35–51. The piece emphasizes its orientation toward musical performance by specifying, for example, tenor, baritone, and bass lines for its two choral groups.

162. The work of Stanley Cavell, particularly his attention to what he (after Wittgenstein and Austin) calls the voice of the everyday, has inspired my thinking about Borodin. See "Counter-Philosophy and the Pawn of Voice," in *Pitch of Philosophy*, 53–128. Elsewhere in this volume, Cavell also writes about opera, of its ability to bring one closer to "a grander world" (145). That, too, is pertinent to Borodin, as to Chukhrov.

163. I draw further here on Kramer, *Hum of the World*; see 147–63 for a discussion of how literary language opens access to the "inaudiable." Kramer's orientation toward a future is uncannily like the temporality in Susan Stewart's account of rhythm in *Poet's Freedom*: rhythm makes us "alert to something in the circumstances of the present without quite knowing what will happen next" (58).

5. Poems and Photographs: Materializing the Ineffable

1. For a reading of Singer's poetics in terms of her photographic work, suggesting that both poems and photos seek the "hidden side of reality," see A. A. Zhitenev, *Poetika neomodernizma* (Inapress, 2012), 195–97, quotation from 197. Zhitenev treats poems from her book *Khozhdenie za naznachennuiu chertu* (2009) that thematize photography and the visual. Still to be analyzed are projects by Singer that combine word and image, for example, in her book *Tochki skhoda, tochka ischeznoveniia* (NLO, 2013), 147–82.

2. Roland Barthes, *Camera Lucida: Reflections on Photography*, trans. Richard Howard (Noonday, 1981), 82.

3. Malcolm Bowie, *Lacan* (Harvard University Press, 1991), 94.

4. The real was perhaps the most complex term in Lacan's famous triad of the real, the symbolic, and the imaginary, or R.S.I., as he called them. Lacan's insights into the real are scattered all over his work; for his extended reflections, see Seminar 22, *R.S.I. 1974–1975*, for example, https://esource.dbs.ie/items/33050538-9564-4574-a4a1-2a8d27c3a9e4 . This text was fully available at Lacanian Works, but the site was subject to attack and is being rebuilt at https://lacanianworks.org. For a usefully compact account of the real, see Bruce Fink, *The Lacanian Subject: Between Language and Jouissance* (Princeton University Press, 1995), 24–28.

5. Penelope Lively, *Life in the Garden* (Viking, 2017), 38.

6. Charles Sanders Peirce, "What Is a Sign?" in *The Essential Peirce: Selected Philosophical Writings (1893–1913)* (Indiana University Press, 1998), 4–10, quotation on 5–6.

7. That digital applications can alter the image should not unduly distract us from the truth value implicit in photographs, even when altered: we can ask about enhancements, as about any activity in which the photographer performs what Lively calls interpretation or expansion.

8. Aleksandr Markov, "Poeziia kak fotografiia: Ot mgnovennogo soobshcheniia k mgno-vennoi chuvstvennosti," *Vozdukh* 1 (2016): 212–16.

9. For an insightful study of the problematic relationship to a ruined past in the poetry of Galina Rymbu and the photographs of Anastasia Tsayder, see Nadezhda Vikulina, "Arcadian Ruins: Remains of the Past in Contemporary Russian Art" (master's thesis, University of Oregon, 2020).

10. See Oksana Sarkisova and Olga Shevchenko, "Soviet Past in Domestic Photography: Events, Evidence, Erasure," *Double Exposure: Memory and Photography*, ed. Olga Shevchenko (Transaction, 2014), 147–74. Family photography has received rich treatment by theorists, well summarized in Allan Sekula, "The Body and the Archive," *October* 39 (Winter 1986): 3–64; see 6–10. Family photography recurs in work by Fyodor Svarovsky, discussed later in this chapter.

11. Stanley Cavell, *The World Viewed*, enlarged ed. (Harvard University Press, 1979), 23.

12. I give several sources on Lacan above. I am following the example of one of Lacan's interpreters, Jane Gallop, aiming for "psychoanalysis with a light touch": see Gallop, *Living with His Camera* (Duke University Press, 2003), 46.

13. There is also considerable ontological impact from the orientation of poetry toward photography, as is suggested in Yves Bonnefoy, *Poetry and Photography*, trans. Chris Turner (Seagull, 2017).

14. Ilya Kukulin, "Documentalist Strategies in Contemporary Russian Poetry," *Russian Review* 69 (October 2010): 585–614. It was Ilya Kukulin who first urged me to read Lida Yusupova, well before she was writing the work that brought her wide attention.

15. The cycle continues to fascinate the poet. See her poems published after the appearance of *Prigovory* (NLO, 2020): "Ona byla krasivoi devushkoi," *Russkii pioner* 102 (May–June 2021), http://ruspioner.ru/project/m/single/57/single_job/36813.

16. I write about these poems with an emphasis on the representations of sexual violence in "The Body Returns: Recent Poems by Russian Women," *Internationale Zeitschrift für Kulturkomparatistik* 2 (2022), 261–300, see 277–83.

17. For the poem, see *Prigovory*, 17–35; and the bilingual volume *The Scar We Know*, ed. Ainsley Morse (Cicada, 2021), 132–73. The translation is by Madeline Kinkel.

18. A more direct command to look and scrutinize occurs in a poem that features several words in Inuit, beginning with the title: "saxifrage ᐃᓪᓗᓂᖅᐸᒃ" (kamnelomki ᐃᓪᓗᓂᖅᐸᒃ), which appeared in *Ritual C-4* (ARGO-RISK, 2013), 5–10, and is included in *Scar We Know* (20–33) in my translation.

19. Iusupova, "Zimniaia kost'," *Literratura*, June 12, 2017, https://literratura.org/poetry/2318-lida-yusupova-zimnyaya-kost.html.

20. Multiple examples are included in Alan Taylor, "The Hyperrealistic Sculptures of Ron Mueck," *Atlantic*, October 9, 2013, https://www.theatlantic.com/photo/2013/10/the-hyperrealistic-sculptures-of-ron-mueck/100606/.

21. For gallery shots, see Philip Pocock, "With Reference to Death," May 26, 2015, http://withreferencetodeath.philippocock.net/blog/mueck-ron-dead-dad-1996/.

22. As noted in Pocock, "With Reference to Death," who adds that this is the only case in Mueck's sculptural practice where he used his own hair.

23. Quoted from Iusupova, *Dead Dad* (Kolonna, 2016), 8; English translation by Ainsley Morse and Bela Shayevich (slightly modified) from *Scar We Know*, 55.

24. Henry Fountain, "At Chernobyl, Hints of Nature's Adaptation," *New York Times*, May 5, 2014, http://www.nytimes.com/2014/05/06/science/nature-adapts-to-chernobyl.html.

25. Both poems are in *Scar We Know* in Russian and English (translation by Hilah Kohen), 42–49; and in Iusupova, *Ritual C-4*, in Russian, 34–37.

26. Barthes, *Camera Lucida*, 55.

27. The poem is included in *Scar We Know* (translation by Hilah Kohen), 256–75. The Russian original first appeared in *F-pis'mo* on the platform *Syg.ma*, January 15, 2019, https://syg.ma/@galina-1/lida-iusupova-tsientr-ghiendiernykh-probliem.

28. Yusupova, *Scar We Know*, 54–55; Iusupova, *Dead Dad*, 8.

29. This opposition is obviously schematic, and some of the poet's most interesting work rests between these two poles, also where I am situating "Dead Dad." Another particularly compelling poem in that middle ground is "saxifrage Δᷟᴗᴄᴜᷟᡆᵇ."

30. A striking testimony to his popularity was heard in an interview with Ekaterina Belinkina on Elena Fanailova's podcast then named *Vavilon-Moskva*, May 30, 2022, https://www.svoboda.org/a/31860443.html. Her brother had been arrested in a protest, and she wanted to send poems by their favorite poet: Svarovsky.

31. Svarovsky co-wrote (with Arseny Rovinsky) its manifesto in "Neskol'ko slov o 'novom epose,'" *Zhurnal RETs* 44 (June 2007): 3–6. Three poets who exemplified the trend (Leonid Schwab, Rovinsky, and Svarovsky) brought their poems together in a signal publication, *Vse srazu* (Novoe izdatel'stvo, 2008). Another poet associated with the new epic, Maria Stepanova, wrote the foreword: "Predislovie," *Vse srazu*, 5–6.

32. Svarovsky, "Antichnye fotografii," Facebook, July 18, 2019.

33. The poem, "—Pishet Zukhra," appears in "Nikakikh ugnetaemykh ili neslyshnykh golosov net," interview conducted by Sergei Sdobnov, *Colta*, October 25, 2015, http://www.colta.ru/articles/literature/8917.

34. For the poem, see Svarovskii, "Iaponskie blatnye pesni," *Vozdukh* 1–2 (2015): 60–71; see 63.

35. Stanislav Lvovsky observed that optimism is exuded by the texts in *Time Travelers* (*Puteshestvenniki vo vremeni* [NLO, 2009]) precisely because there always seems to be a way to slip out of danger. See Stanislav L'vovskii, "O skitaniiakh vechnykh i o zemle," *OpenSpace*, June 23, 2009, http://www.litkarta.ru/dossier/o-skit-vech/dossier_2336/.

36. "'Ryba s risom i ovoshchami' ili 'Predlagaem uslugi': Stikhotvoreniia 2016–17 gg.," *Post(non)fiction*, undated, https://postnonfiction.org/narratives/fswr. This selection has another slightly creepy photograph poem, "Oborotni v kholodil'nikakh."

37. Svarovskii, *Slava geroiam* (NLO, 2015), 86.

38. Elsewhere in the same volume, the photograph simply misses its mark: see "Ne letaiut," in *Slava geroiam*, 143.

39. Peter Osborne, *Photography and the Contemporary Cultural Tradition: Commemorating the Present* (Routledge, 2019), 81, and see chapter 4 (79–94) more generally.

40. The photograph shows Nikolai Gronsky's apartment shortly after his death. See Molly Thomasy Blasing, *Snapshots of the Soul: Photo-Poetic Encounters in Russian Modernism* (Cornell University Press, 2021), 113–27, quotation on 127.

41. Several images from her Ruined Prints series, including *Leaving Sarajevo*, are included in Boym, "The Off-Modern Mirror," *e-flux* 19 (October 2010), https://www.e-flux.com/journal/19/67475/the-off-modern-mirror/. See also Cristina Vatulescu, "Afterimages: Svetlana Boym's Irrepressible Cocreations," *Diacritics* 43, no. 3 (2015): 98–109.

42. It followed *Vse khotiat byt' robotami* (2007), which brought him great attention. I cite poems above from the third book, *Slava geroiam* (2015). A fourth and long-awaited book has also appeared: *Besporiadok v savanne: Stikhi 2019–2020* (Izdatel'stvo magazina "Babel'," 2021). Svarovsky published since 2009 extensively on his website and through social media, first on LiveJournal (as ry_ichi) and since 2014 on Facebook.

43. Pashchenko collaborated with Yanina Vishnevskaya on *Iskusstvo ukhoda za mertvetsami* (2009). For a study of Pashchenko's poetry as a form of intermedial experiment, see Maksim Lepekhin (Konstantin Chadov), "Intermedial'nye eksperimenty i sovremennyi religioznyi opyt v sbornike 'Iskusstvo ukhoda za mertvetsami,'" *NLO* 171 (no. 5, 2020): 232–49. An astute account of Pashchenko's earlier poems appears in Il'ia Kukulin, "Aktual'nyi russkii poet kak voskresshie Alenushka i Ivanushka: O russkoi poezii 90-kh godov," *NLO* 53 (no. 1, 2002): 273–97.

44. Pashchenko was also an important friend for the poet Stanislav Lvovsky: see Linor Goralik, *Chastnye litsa: Chast' vtoraia* (Novoe izdatel'stvo, 2017), 58–104, esp. 80, 94.

45. Curiously, Svarovsky recalls finding letters and photographs between the pages of books he was reading in a church library when he was living in Denmark. He kept some of the photos, he says, and one wonders whether they didn't end up in this book, too. See Linor Goralik, *Chastnye litsa: Biografii poetov, rasskazannye im samim* (Novoe izdatel'stvo, 2013), 266.

46. Their artistic practices in any case converge here, and both *Puteshestvenniki vo vremeni* and Pashchenko's book *Iskusstvo ukhoda za mertvetsami* appeared in 2009, further suggesting a time of mutual influence.

47. Kuznetsov is shown as a child in the 1930s, in a "bohemian group" in Moscow in 1987, and shortly before and during his arrest in the year 2060. He is also the photographer of multiple images, for example, a regiment taking Mars-6, the "Cossack restorers" on horseback (dateline Jan. 16, 2112); five people posing at a table, in what looks to be a café (but is called a "conspiratorial apartment" in the caption), representatives of the "Balkan" wing of the Romei restoration (dateline Munich 2539); three leaders of the movement to liberate Mars-6, shown in Georgian military dress (dateline Delaliia Plateau, November 2159). For the images and captions, see Svarovskii, *Puteshestvenniki vo vremeni*, 46–47, 238–39, 100–101, 108–9, 126–27, 376–77, 110–11. The last image has an intriguing background: you can see two figures setting up a tripod to do some photography work. Several of the book's images, whether supposedly taken by Kuznetsov or someone or something else, are meta-photographs. Subsequent quotations from this volume are given as parenthetical page numbers.

48. Jenkins can be identified via another photograph, taken by him (80–81). Gauk is not the only instance of a kind of body double: there is an image of an artist-researcher in a child's body, dateline 1997 (308). This photograph is said to have been taken by a robot.

49. The permeability of subjectivities among persons, animals, and things in Svarovsky's poetry is well studied in chapter 2 of Vassileva, "After the Seraph."

50. They appear in Svarovskii, *Vse khotiat byt' robotami* (ARGO-RISK, 2007), 13–14, 32–41, 45–50.

51. The most famous instantiation of that association was during the Silver Age, perhaps most eloquently in Osip Mandelstam's poems in his second volume, *Tristia* (1922). But the Russia-Ukraine War has made it impossible to think of Russia's proprietary view of Crimea as mere cultural history. For a clear-headed assessment of how the image of Crimea is changing, see Polina Barskova, "The Peninsula of Utopias: Reactions to the Annexation of Crimea in Contemporary Russophone Poetry," *East European Jewish Affairs* 51, nos. 2–3 (2021): 282–96. Svarovsky wrote his poems in and before 2009 and thus is not referring to the Russia-Ukraine war, but he may well have the longer history of imperial conquest in mind.

52. The book is more than four hundred pages, in fact, as compared with *Vse khotiat byt' robotami*, only seventy-seven pages. In thanking Ilya Kukulin, who edited the book, Svarovsky noted as if with embarrassment that he writes a lot: comment on LiveJournal, May 16, 2009.

53. Svarovsky, LiveJournal, March 27, 2009. "Smert' Perakisa" was published in book form six years later in *Slava geroiam*, 53–55.

54. Svarovskii, *Slava geroiam*, 55.

55. Svarovskii, *Slava geroiam*, 55.

56. This channeling of experiences and emotions through his characters is Svarovsky's signature as a poet, as frequently noted and best studied in Il'ia Kukulin, "Ot Svarovskogo k Zhukovskomu i obratno: O tom, kak metod issledovaniia konstruiruet literaturnyi kanon," in Kukulin, *Proryv k nevozmozhnoi sviazi: Stat'i o russkoi poezii* (Kabinetnyi uchenyi, 2019), 599–614. This influential essay first appeared in *NLO* 89 (2008): 228–40.

57. Dragomoshchenko's name turns up in histories of the famous Leningrad Café Saigon, and his work appeared in the well-known samizdat journal *Chasy*. But he was more associated with the theory-oriented journal *Kommentarii* and with *Mitin zhurnal* and its editor, Dmitrii Volchek. He won the first Andrei Bely Prize (1978), an extravagantly marginal event created by underground poets. He won in the category of prose, for his novel *The Disposition of Buildings and Trees* (*Raspolozhenie domov i derev'ev*), circulated in carbon-copied typescript as an "addendum" to *Chasy*.

58. Their connection informs two chapters of Jacob Edmond, *A Common Strangeness: Contemporary Poetry, Cross-Cultural Encounter, Comparative Literature* (Fordham University Press, 2012). See also Edmond, "'A Meaning Alliance': Arkady Dragomoshchenko and Lyn Hejinian's Poetics of Translation," *SEEJ* 46, no. 3 (2002): 551–63. I have written about it from a different perspective in "Arkadii Dragomoshchenko, Lyn Hejinian, and the Persistence of Romanticism," *Contemporary Literature* 46, no. 1 (Spring 2005): 18–45.

59. Many L=A=N=G=U=A=G=E poets were engaged with issues of political critique and social justice; Dragomoshchenko rarely followed suit, but he did evince a concern for matters of power and hierarchy, often via his layering of linguistic registers and by the quasi-characters fleetingly created in his work. The political substrata in his work repay careful excavation. For a fine example, focusing on the poem "Politiku," see Evgeny Pavlov, "Resisting the Weather: Dragomoshchenko's Revolutions," *Russian Literature* 87–89 (2017): 261–79.

60. *Description* was also the title chosen by Lyn Hejinian and Elena Balashova for their translated volume of his poetry (Sun and Moon, 1990). For the Russian books, see *Tavtologiia: Stikhotvoreniia, esse* (NLO, 2011); and *Opisanie* (Gumanitarnaia akademiia, 2000).

61. Dragomoshchenko, *To Xenia*, trans. Lyn Hejinian and Elena Balashova (Sun and Moon, 1994), 11; Dragomoshchenko, *Opisanie*, 150.

62. In Brodsky, "The Condition We Call Exile," *On Grief and Reason: Essays* (Farrar, Straus and Giroux, 1995), 33.

63. Thus, in a poem from *Ksenii*, "To speak of poetry is to speak of nothing" (govorit' o poezii oznachaet govorit' o nichto), *To Xenia*, 28; Dragomoshchenko, *Opisanie*, 162.

64. Compare an expressive phrase in Alexander Skidan's review of *Opisanie*: "a penetratingly intimate form of muttering" (pronzitel'naia intimnost' bormotaniia). The review, which first appeared in *Novaia russkaia kniga* in 2000, is reprinted in Skidan, *Syr bukv mel* (Jaromír Hladík, 2019), 87–105; see 93. A stronger statement about the consequences of that intimacy for genre appears in an essay by Catherine Ciepiela: "his poetry is suffused with the intimacy—and eroticism—of the traditional lyric poem," but she adds that he "erases the lyric poem . . . in order to let it appear again, almost unrecognizable." See Ciepiela, "The Legacy of the Underground Poets," in *Russian Literature Since 1991*, ed. Evgeny Dobrenko and Mark Lipovetsky (Cambridge University Press, 2015), 207–25, quotation on 223–24.

65. Mikhail Iampol'skii, "Poeziia kasaniia (Dragomoshchenko)," in *O blizkom* (NLO, 2001), 210–33. His work has been extended by that of Skidan, Pavlov, and others.

66. Stanley Cavell, "Benjamin and Wittgenstein: Signals and Affinities," *Critical Inquiry* 25, no. 3 (Winter 1999): 235–46, quoted from 237.

67. Elena Fanailova had this quality in mind when she wrote, in response to Dragomoshchenko's death, that he was a peerless educator ("kak prosvetitel' ne imeet ravnykh"). See Fanailova, "Velichie smerti i ee zhe nichtozhnost'," *Colta*, September 13, 2012, http://www.colta.ru/docs/5611.

68. Rodowick, "Ethics in Film Philosophy," 3.

69. Neil Hertz, "Some Words in George Eliot: Nullify, Neutral, Numb, Number," in *George Eliot's Pulse* (Stanford University Press, 2003), 284. Molly Thomasy Blasing also zeroes in on this side of Dragomoshchenko's creative impulse in her stimulating account of what she calls his "photographic unconscious." See Blasing, *Snapshots of the Soul*, 220–28.

70. A different approach to the poet's resistance to representation was posited by Michael Molnar in an early assessment of his poetics: "this is a poetry of relationships, not essences." See Molnar, "The Vagaries of Description: The Poetry of Arkadii Dragomoshchenko," *Essays in Poetics* 14, no. 1 (1989): 76–98, quotation on 84.

71. In writing about such a hole in time, Skidan has given the salient example of a young boy walking to school who incomprehensibly finds himself in a railroad station in *Chinese Sun* (*Kitaiskoe solntse*, 1997); see "Slepoe piatno," in Skidan, *Syr bukv mel*, 10–21; see 11, 18–19.

72. Dragomoshchenko, *Description*, 83. The citation comes from the poem "Accidia," dedicated to Hejinian. Dragomoshchenko published this version only in the almanac *25 Tverskoi Bul'var: Golosa molodykh* (Sovetskii pisatel', 1990), 216–21. A shorter revised text without the dedication appears in Dragomoshchenko, *Tavtologiia*, 149.

73. My thinking about textures in photography is inspired by Robin Kelsey, *Photography and the Art of Chance* (Harvard University Press, 2015), especially the chapter on Alfred Stieglitz, 149–79.

74. See Elaine Scarry, *Dreaming by the Book* (Farrar, Straus and Giroux, 1999).

75. Dennis Ioffe treats a different photograph of a pocket watch paired with a wedding ring in "Arkady Dragomoshchenko's Photography: A New Visuality and a Poetics of Metaphysical Inebriation," *SEEJ* 55, no. 4 (Winter 2011): 586–613. He reads the image as illustrating "the poet's vision of the idea of Eternity confronted with the omnipotent image of Chronos" (592).

76. In a sense, the presence of the watch face without any further context reverses the concerns of Christian Marclay's remarkable twenty-four-hour film *The Clock* (2010), with its splicing together of film footage featuring clocks telling the precise time at which a viewer is meant to be watching the film.

77. Persons appear often in Dragomoshchenko's photographs, both friends, acquaintances, and substitute persons, like masks or mannequins.

78. Translated by Eugene Ostashevsky in Dragomoshchenko, *Endarkenment: Selected Poems* (Wesleyan University Press, 2014), 37.

79. Dragomoshchenko, *Tavtologiia*, 262.

80. That original argument, by Roger Scruton in 1981 and Kendall Walton in 1984, is compactly presented and challenged in Diarmuid Costello and Margaret Iverson, "Introduction: Photography between Art History and Philosophy," *Critical Inquiry* 38, no. 4 (Summer 2012): 679–94.

81. That operatic performance shows Dragomoshchenko doing something else that is typical of his poetry, enacting a transposition between art forms, here moving from conversation to a singing register. Note that the poet does not drift into the praise of song as beautiful—it is the transposition that matters.

82. As suggested to me by Julie Buckler, which I note with gratitude.

83. Cavell, *Pitch of Philosophy*, 144.

84. The poem "Dreams Photographers Appear To" ("Sny, kotorye vidiat fotografov"), for example, begins with the short sentence "'We are dying'" ("Umiraem"): Dragomoshchenko, *Tavtologiia*, 236.

85. The poem is part of "Ksenii," and the line reads "Smert', eto kogda sovpadaesh' s sobstvennymi predelami" (*Opisanie*, 185). The line is mentioned in Mikhail Iampol'skii's moving tribute to the poet on his death, "Smert' i pamiat' (Opyt neestiticheskoi poezii Arkadiia Dragomoshchenko)," *NLO* 121 (no. 3, 2013): 253–57, reprinted in Iampol'skii, *Iz khaosa*, 269–78, quotation on 270. Revealing comments about the pervasiveness of death in his poetry appear in the conversation Lev Oborin had with poet and photographer Gleb Simonov about the poem "The Weakening of an Indication" ("Oslablenie priznaka") on the podcast *Mezhdu strok*, October 29, 2021, https://mezhdu-strok.simplecast.com/episodes/ep-19.

86. The wine and cigarettes are typical signs of the writing life, appearing often in the photographs. Dennis Ioffe reads the wine as "in intimate companion of human existence"; see Ioffe, "Arkady Dragomoshchenko's Photography," 598.

87. On Dragomoshchenko's poetics of touch, see Iampol'skii, "Poeziia kasaniia (Dragomoshchenko)."

88. This suggestion of a lineage might be disputed by Mikhail Iampol'skii, who writes that Dragomoshchenko had neither teachers nor followers. See Iampol'skii, "Smert' i pamiat'." But the turn to prose-like formats for texts that read as metaphysical descriptions was something Dragomoshchenko modeled for others, Shamshad Abdullaev and Aleksei Parshchikov among them.

89. Skidan, "Otstuplenie k istokam vyskazavaniia," in *Syl bukv mel*, 22–29; see 22.

90. A modified version of my translation that first appeared in "New Translations," *Jacket2*, August 8, 2014, https://jacket2.org/poems/new-translations.

91. Dragomoshchenko, *Tavtologiia*, 58.

92. Compare the spatial evasions of "Dreams Photographers Appear To," located in a place of transit, a Casablanca of the movies but also of the mind.

93. The shield also names one of W. H. Auden's best-known poems, which compares the benighted modern world to distant ancient glories. The poem first appeared in Auden, *The Shield of Achilles* (Norton, 1955), 35–37. Brodsky's love of this poem may have been known to Dragomoshchenko, so his revisionist transformation of its central image may also contain a subtle gesture of polemic.

94. The sky in Dragomoshchenko's earlier work was well described by Shamshad Abdullaev as "a measured flow of pure abstractions, of invisible connections." See Abdullaev, "Priblizhenie k A. D.," in *Dvoinoi polden'* (Borei-Art, 2000), 183–88.

95. That point has been made by many and is especially well put in Shamshad Abdullaev, "O Dragomoshchenko," *NLO* 121 (no. 3, 2013): 240–41.

96. Dragomoshchenko, *Pocherk* (Limbus, 2016), 54.

97. See Andrei Tarkovsky, *Instant Light: Tarkovsky Polaroids* (Thames and Hudson, 2006).

98. Many critics have commented on the director's inclusion of his own hand, including Robert Bird, *Elements of Cinema* (Reaktion, 2008), 85, who notes that a shot of Tarkovsky's face was cut from the scene.

99. Zinaida Dragomoshchenko, Facebook, April 2, 2019; on seeing it, Glazova commented that it was from 2010 or 2011.

100. That notion of language as moving beyond itself, as an entity with its own desires, is one that Glazova would have studied with Werner Hamacher. As he put it in his "95 Theses on Philology" (#16), the language of knowledge and the language of longing are the two incompatible regions in which philology lives. He said that poetry is *prima philologia*." See Werner Hamacher, "From '95 Theses on Philology,'" trans. Catherine Diehl, *PMLA* 125 (no. 4, 2010): 994–1001, quotations on 995. Glazova translated "95 Theses on Philology" into Russian. For a selection with her brief introduction, see Glazova, "Verner Khamaker i neobkhodimost' radikal'nogo obnovleniia filologicheskikh praktik," and Khamaker, "95 tezisov o filologii (fragment)," trans. Anna Glazova, *NLO* 156 (no. 2, 2019): 15–25.

101. Those are dates of publication (Glazova almost never adds datelines to her texts). For "Zakony," see *Dlia zemleroiki*, 17–20. "Gekata" has appeared on the poet's website, https://3roga.mynetgear.com/?page_id=594. In English, see *Hekate*, trans. Alex Niemi (Toad Press, 2023).

102. Glazova, *Litsevoe schislenie*, 33.

103. Glazova described the "Hekate" poems as an unfinished project, in fact, in posting them to Facebook, June 29, 2022.

104. Glazova's writings about Mandelstam include "Poetry of Bringing about Presence: Paul Celan Translates Osip Mandelstam," *Modern Language Notes* 124 (2009): 1108–26, as well as her PhD dissertation, "Counter-Quotation: The Defiance of Tradition in Celan and Mandelstam" (Northwestern University, 2008). See also Sandler, "Mandelstam among Contemporary Poets: Zhdanov, Eremin, Glazova," *Living through Literature: Essays in Memory of Omry Ronen*, ed. Julie

Hansen, Karen Evans-Romaine, and Herbert Eagle (Eastern Europe Series, Uppsala University's Acta Upsaliensis, 2019), 121–40.

105. That tangibility is one reason that many critics write of the theme of the body in Glazova's work. See, for example, Sergei Sdobnov, contributing to "Otzyvy," *Vozdukh* (no. 1, 2014): 25.

106. She has created a website for her work, https://3roga.mynetgear.com, in addition to the images shared on her LiveJournal site until 2015 (user name aagg) and later on Facebook.

107. Another exception is a series of ice and snow crystal close-ups from 2012 posted to her LiveJournal site.

108. A photographer whose work surely inspired Glazova's and whose use of the window views from his studio are renowned is Josef Sudek. See, for example, Sudek, *The Window of My Studio* (Torst, 2007) and *Still Lifes* (Torst, 2008).

109. Barthes, *Camera Lucida*, 57.

110. The poetry in her books *Dlia zemleroiki* and *Zemlia lezhit na zemle* (MRP, 2017) is particularly rich in images of decay, dirt, decomposition. A fine example is the poem "humus births the sour air of respiration" ("iz peregnoia rozhdaetsia kislyi dykhatel'nyi vozdukh"), discussed below. Also very expressive are "ribbons of lesser acidity" ("lenty malen'koi kisloty") and "in the deepest burrow" ("v samoi glubokoi nore") from *Zemlia lezhit na zemle*, 61, 77.

111. In one of Dickinson's most famous poems, "There's a certain Slant of light," in fact, the word "heft" appears in the first stanza—in the phrase "the Heft / of Cathedral Tunes." It's a prime example of how weight and light come to be associated, and there is a variant reading for "Heft": weight. For the poem and the variant, see *The Poems of Emily Dickinson*, ed. Thomas H. Johnson, 3 vols. (Belknap Press of Harvard University Press, 1979), 1:185.

112. For an astute observation on the way that airiness and heaviness can coexist in Glazova's early poetry, linking both properties to Mandelstam, see Dmitrii Golynko-Vol'fson, "Legche vody, tiazhelee slov: O stikhakh Anny Glazovoi," a review of *Pust' i voda*, NLO, no. 62 (no. 4, 2003): 462–64.

113. Mary Price, *The Photograph: A Strange Confined Space* (Stanford University Press, 1994), 163. See also Barthes, *Camera Lucida*, for an important refinement: "The Photograph does not necessarily say *what is no longer*, but only and for certain *what has been*" (85).

114. Posted to LiveJournal, August 2, 2012, no longer accessible. Fyodor is Glazova's son.

115. In the comments, we also learn that the flower was "rescued" (making it another about-to-be-lost material object) and that the photograph was composed by placing the flower and vase behind a curtain.

116. Glazova, *Zemlia lezhit na zemle*, 78.

117. Guy Davenport, *Objects on a Table: Harmonious Disarray in Art and Literature* (Counterpoint, 1998), 86.

118. Davenport, *Objects on a Table*, 9. Davenport's comments about painting feel suitable to photography's still-life images, and he notes in passing that the first daguerreotype (in 1837) was a still life (17–18).

119. Norman Bryson, *Looking at the Overlooked: Four Essays on Still Life Painting* (Reaktion, 1990). See the last chapter, "Still Life and 'Feminine' Space" (136–78), which treats the lingering associations of "waste and filth" with the genre. The contemporary American photographer Laura Letinsky has taken up that aspect of still-life photography brilliantly; her work is briefly discussed below.

120. Elaine Scarry, *Dreaming by the Book* (Farrar, Straus and Giroux, 1999), 48.

121. Scarry, *Dreaming by the Book*, 59–60.

122. She said that on waking fully, she can look at the lines she has noted down, having forgotten them during the time of waking. Then she edits what she wrote down. See the conversation with Ol'ga Livshin, "Relocations: Peremeshchenie poezii," *Colta*, April 22, 2014, http://www.colta.ru/articles/literature/2981?part=2.

123. Rostislav Amelin, contribution to "Otzyvy," *Vozdukh* (no. 1, 2014), 25.

124. "Sposob sushchestvovaniia," an interview with Dmitrii Deich, *Booknik*, December 16, 2008, https://booknik.ru/today/all/sposob-sushchestvovaniya/. A different gloss was provided by the poet Alla Gorbunova, who compared Glazova's language to an interlinear translation from a nonexisting language. See her contribution to "Otzyvy," *Vozdukh* (no. 1, 2014), 23–24.

125. See also the excellent translation in Glazova, *Twice Under the Sun*, trans. Anna Khasin (Shearsman, 2008), 37.

126. Glazova, *Petlia, nevpolovinu* (NLO, 2008), 63.

127. In that wish to represent what cannot be visualized, Glazova expresses a desire she has also found in the work of Arkady Dragomoshchenko. See Glazova, "The Fluid Image in Arkady Dragomoshchenko's Poetics," *SEEJ* 55, no. 4 (Winter 2011): 572–82.

128. Glazova, *Zemlia lezhit na zemle*, 78.

129. Camilla Brown, "Looking at the Overlooked," in *Stilled: Contemporary Still Life Photography by Women*, ed. Kate Newton and Christine Rolph (Ffotogallery Wales, 2006), 72–75, quotations on 72. Brown is citing Barth's comments from Pamela Lee, *Uta Barth* (Phaidon, 2004), 12.

130. An emphasis pointed out to me by Anna Vichkitova, whose insights into Glazova's poetry have inspired me. See her unpublished essay, "The Poetry of Anna Glazova: Address to a Non-Communicative Reader Is Possible."

131. Glazova, "Fluid Image," 578.

132. Lucy Alford, *Forms of Poetic Attention* (Columbia University Press, 2020), 151–66.

133. See Glazova, "Chto ostaetsia, kogda vse ushli?: Gorizont soznaniia," a review of Laura Letinsky, *Untitled #64*, screenshot from *Russkii Zhurnal*, https://3roga.mynetgear.com/wp-content/uploads/2019/09/Screenshot-from-2019-09-04-11_48_39.pdf. I suspect that Glazova was drawn to the ways in which gravity and precarious balance work in the photographs. For discerning comments on that aspect of Letinsky's work, see Anthony Elms's afterword to Letinsky, *III Form and Void Full* (Radius, 2014), 111.

134. Laura Letinsky, *After All* (Damiani, 2010); for Strand's foreword, see 5. He also notes that the most important element of these photographs is the evocative power of light, which surely drew Glazova to them.

135. The translation is Alex Niemi's, from Glazova, *For the Shrew* (Zephyr, 2022), 45, period added at the end of l.1.

136. Glazova, *Dlia zemleroiki*, 46. The poem is discussed briefly in Luba Golburt, "The Ethics of Grammar in Anna Glazova's Nature Lyric," *Subjekt und Liminität in der Gegenwartsliteratur*, vol. 2, *Schwellezteit—Gattungstransitionen—Grenzerfahrungen*, ed. Matthias Fechner and Henrieke Stahl (Peter Lang, 2020), 267–90; see 286–87.

137. Gorbunova, contribution to "Otzyvy," *Vozdukh* (no. 1, 2014), 24.

138. I quote Glazova here: "As long as the conversation continues, the world exists." Cited from her essay "Katataksis: Kommentarii k odnomu predlozheniiu," *Rets* 46 (August 2007), http://www.litkarta.ru/dossier/katataxis/dossier_6135/.

6. Freedoms of Spirit: Poems of Faith after the Fall

1. Also increasingly important are poems infused by the tenets of Islam and Buddhism. Much of this poetry presses toward broader philosophical ends, as Arkady Dragomoshchenko drew on Buddhism. The poems of the 2021 recipient of the Dragomoshchenko Prize, Dordzhy Dzhal'zhireev, continue that trend. On his work, see "Dordzhy Dzhal'zhireev," Premiia Arkadiia Dragomoshchenko, https://atd-premia.ru/2021/08/19/dordzhi-dzhaldzhireev-rossiya-elista/; and Anna Glazova's introduction to his book *Opyty i namereniia* (Poriadok slov, 2022), 4–8.

2. Nicolai Berdyaev, *The Russian Idea*, trans. R. M. French (Geoffrey Bles / Centenary, 1947), 9.

3. Patriarch Kirill, current primate of the ROC, has called the advocacy of human rights a heresy: see Anna Dolgov, "Russia's Patriarch Kirill: Some Human Rights Are 'Heresy,'" *Moscow Times*, March 21, 2016, https://www.themoscowtimes.com/2016/03/21/russias-patriarch-kirill-some-human-rights-are-heresy-a52213. He has loudly supported Russia's invasion of Ukraine, beginning in his speech on the eve of the invasion, February 23, 2022, "V Den' zashchitnika Otechestva Sviateishii Patriarkh Kirill vozlozhil venok k mogile Neizvestnogo soldata u Kremlevskoi steny," Russkaia Provoslavnaia Tserkov', http://www.patriarchia.ru/db/text/5903402.html.

4. My account is thus narrowly focused. For a survey of the poetry of Orthodoxy, see Irina Rodnianskaia, "Novoe svidetel'stvo: Dukhovnaia poeziia. Rossiia. Konets XX—nachalo XXI vekov," *Novyi mir* 3 and 4 (2011), https://magazines.gorky.media/novyi_mi/2011/3/novoe-svidetelstvo.html and https://magazines.gorky.media/novyi_mi/2011/4/novoe-svidetelstvo-2.html.

5. In conversation with Dmitrii Volchek, "Mezhdu stellazhami," Radio Svoboda, October 20, 2010, http://www.litkarta.ru/dossier/mezhdu-stellazhami/dossier_2013/. The conversation ends with the poet talking about his isolation. That emotion is amply documented in his published diary writings: *Za gran'iu etogo peizazha: Dnevniki 1997–2001* (Vodolei, 2011). In some poems it is associated with Jewish identity, for instance, "byt' zhidom odinokim prezrennym nichtozhnym," in Sergei Magid, *Zona sluzhen'ia: Izbrannye stikhotvoreniia* (NLO, 2003), 18–19; or, in the same book, "Doroga tianetsia. Obochiny begut," which ends "evrei—chudesnyi, strannyi zver' . . ." (47–48).

6. Sergei Magid, *V doline Elakh* (Vodolei, 2010), 182.

7. Stanislav L'vovskii, "Sergei Magid. V doline Elakh," *OpenSpace*, August 31, 2010, http://www.litkarta.ru/dossier/lvovsky-magid/dossier_2013/.

8. Sergei Stratanovskii, "Odinokii golos cheloveka," introduction to Magid, *Zona sluzheniia*, 5–10.

9. Translated from Magid, *Za gran'iu etogo peizazha*, 11. This entry (April 22, 1998) sets out Magid's religious credo: the sense of God's gaze at his back; the impossibility of deceiving God; and the certitude of God's pastoral guidance. Note the physicality in two of these three premises.

10. As he explains in *Za gran'iu etogo peizazha*, 87–88.

11. My insight into Magid's writings is here inspired by a formulation in Richard Viladesau, "Revelation and Inspiration among Theologians and Poets," in *Poetic Revelations: Word Made Flesh Made Word—The Power of the Word III*, ed. Mark S. Burrows, Jean Ward, and Małgorzata Grzegorzewska (Routledge, 2017), 89–97; see 90, as well as the subtitle to the volume, "Word Made Flesh Made Word."

12. For the poem, see Magid, *Zona sluzheniia*, 16.

13. In using a range of paratextual expansions, Magid adopts a practice used authoritatively by Mikhai Eremin in his eight-line poems, as detailed in chapter 3. But unlike Eremin, Magid writes in multiple formats, including quite extensive work in prose. See, for example, Magid, *Staraia proza* (Vodolei, 2015); and the diaries of *Za gran'iu etogo peizazha*.

14. Magid, *Pervaia sotnitsa* (Vodolei, 2013), 90. This is poem 58 of 100.

15. The poet has chosen the magpie (soroka) for those sounds, which point in several directions. Russian speakers will hear the same consonants as in the word for the number forty (sorok). As in English, that number resonates with biblical connotations, a limit number that the Russian etymology retains (from *srok*). But the magpie is also an apt choice because of the chatter—among birds, magpies have remarkable abilities to imitate human speech. And in Russian there is a superstition that a magpie landing on the house is a sign of recuperation from illness ("Soroka skachet na domu bol'nogo—k vyzdorovlen'iu"); see Vladimir Dal', *Tolkovyi slovar' zhivogo velikorusskogo iazyka*, 4 vols. (1882; Russkii iazyk, 1980), 4:274.

16. Magid, *Pervaia sotnitsa*, 21–24, quoted from 23.

17. See Magid, *Za gran'iu etogo peizazha*, esp. 69–80, where the poet includes frank accounts of the sense that he was dying.

18. The poem is "liubuiu knigu s polki snimesh'," in Magid, *Angulus Opticus: Tret'a kniga stikhotvorenii 2009–2011 gg.* (Vodolei, 2012), 157.

19. For a striking example of the latter, see the 2010 poem "Nochnaia molitva" in Magid, *Angulus Opticus*, 104.

20. Ol'ga Sedakova, "L'Antica Fiamma (Vmesto poslesloviia)," in Shvarts, *Pereletnaia ptitsa* (Pushkinskii fond, 2011), 41–51; see 50.

21. For a sustained reading of "Big Bang Rondo," see Andrew Kahn et al., *History of Russian Literature* (Oxford University Press, 2018), 594–96.

22. For that reading, see "Elena Shvarts v muzee Akhmatovoi, 2008, Chast' vtoraia," March 25, 2008, video, 39:48, posted by Maria Levchenko on January 29, 2016, https://www .youtube.com/watch?v=VsxMrYU6s6k; "Zver'-tsvetok" at 38:23.

23. Elena Shvarts, *'Paradise'*, trans. Michael Molnar (Bloodaxe, 1993), 105. Translation amended to include the epigraph. Shvarts usually wrote her own epigraphs, and this one is telling. The blossoms are lilac colored, but the plant is a strange graft; Shvarts puns on the name of the Judas tree (iudino derevo), yet she must have in mind the redbud tree (*Cercis siliquastrum*)—it blooms profusely on its branches, and even the trunk can be covered with vivid purple-pink blossoms.

24. Elena Shvarts, *Sochineniia*, 5 vols. (Pushkinskii fond, 2002–2013), 1:96.

25. Elena Shvarts, *Birdsong on the Seabed*, trans. Sasha Dugdale (Bloodaxe, 2008), 97.

26. Shvarts, *Sochineniia*, 1:320.

27. On poems set in cathedrals, see Martha M. F. Kelly, "*Furor liturgicus*: The Religious Concerns of Russian Poetry," in *The Oxford Handbook of Russian Religious Thought*, ed. Caryl Emerson et al. (Oxford University Press, 2020), 396–411; see esp. 404. Shvarts is discussed 405–6, including her 1974 poem "Black Easter," where the church is compared to a womb.

28. For the poem, see Shvarts, *Sochineniia*, 1:234–35. A translation, as "Kindergarten: Thirty Years On," appears in Shvarts, *'Paradise'*, 19–21. I analyze this poem in "Cultural Memory and Self-Forgetting in a Poem by Elena Shvarts," *Rereading Russian Poetry*, ed. Stephanie Sandler (Yale University Press, 1999), 256–69.

29. "Trudy i dni Lavinii, monakhini iz Ordena Obrezaniia Serdtsa (Ot Rozhdestva do Paskhi)," in Shvarts, *Sochineniia*, 2:168–221. For a partial translation, see "The Works and Days of the Nun Lavinia," in Shvarts, *'Paradise'*, 111–39.

30. For a comprehensive survey of divine images in Shvarts, see Elena Aizenshtein, "'Sokrovennoe, v slezakh, edva prosheptannoe slovo': Obrazy Boga i poeta v tvorchestve Eleny Shvarts," *Neva* 5 (2013), http://magazines.russ.ru/neva/2013/5/a13.html.

31. Dunja Popovic, "Symbolic Injury and Embodied Mysticism in Elena Shvarts's *Trudy i dni Lavinii*," *SEEJ* 51, no. 4 (2007): 753–71. For a further meditation on the mysticism of Shvarts's Lavinia, see Philip Leon Redko, "Boundary Issues in Three Twentieth-Century Russian Poets (Mandelstam, Aronzon, Shvarts)" (PhD diss., Harvard University, 2019), 228–75.

32. It "hears as sound something of the farthest sorrows that you are," as the American poet Christian Wiman has written of his own work. Cited from "An Idea of Order," in Wiman, *Ambition and Survival: Becoming a Poet* (Copper Canyon, 2007), 94–107; see 107. In that book, see also "Love Bade Me Welcome," 239–45, esp. 244, for comments based on the writings of Simone Weil.

33. See Shvarts, "Troeruchitsa v Nikol'skom sobore," *Sochineniia*, 1:345, translated in *Birdsong on the Seabed*, 107.

34. Shvarts, *Sochineniia*, 5:226.

35. Shvarts, *Sochineniia*, 2:140–46. A parenthetical subtitle declares it a true story, sending readers to "Pryzhov," which I take to mean I. G. Pryzhov, *Nishchie na sviatoi Rusi: Materialy dlia istorii obshchestvennago i narodnago byta v Rossii* (M. I. Smirnova, 1862). Pryzhov comments on the prevalence of poems and songs among holy fools about demons (36–38), perhaps a reason this theme resonates in Shvarts's poems.

36. Shvarts, *Dikopis' poslednego vremeni* (Pushkinskii fond, 2001), 28. Surprisingly, this poem is not in the impressively complete *Sochineniia*.

37. Anna Barkova, *Vechno ne ta* (Fond Sergeia Dubova, 2002), 34.

38. The comparison to Barkova was suggested to me by Omry Ronen many years ago, and I follow up his advice now with enduring gratitude. Barkova took a telling pen name in some of her earliest work, "Kalika perekhozhaia," and a marker of her own ways of channeling Russian "spiritual verses" (dukhovnye stikhi).

39. Ol'ga Sedakova, "Anna Barkova: Svidetel' epokhi"; Martha M. F. Kelly's translation of this essay will appear in *The Oxford Handbook of Russian Poetry* in 2025. See also Sedakova's 2006 essay, "Anna Barkova," on Sedakova's website, https://www.olgasedakova.com/Poetica/237.

40. For the poem, see Shvarts, *Sochineniia*, 5:219. The poem has a parenthetical dateline noting that it was written shortly after surgery—unusually specific for her. The poem also appears in an insightful review: Petr Kazarnovskii, "'Sineva ranimaia': Retsenziia na knigu E. Shvarts,

Sobranie sochinenii. Tom V. SPb. 2013," *NLO* 130 (no. 6, 2014): 300–305. As Kazarnovskii notes, Shvarts did not publish the poem.

41. Igor' Gulin, "Vsia poeticheskaia rat': Igor' Gulin ob Elene Shvarts," *Kommersant" Weekend* 13 (April 19, 2019), https://www.kommersant.ru/doc/3939428.

42. Transformation is also a topic taken up perceptively in Elena Aizenshtein, "Pokryvalo Salomeia: O nekotorykh chertakh poetiki Eleny Shvarts," *Neva* 9 (2014), https://magazines .gorky.media/neva/2014/9/pokryvala-salomei.html. The essay includes a long section on the topic of Shvarts and music. Shvarts is a very visual poet, but Aizenshtein persuasively writes about sound, noting, too, the exceptional rhythmic range of Shvarts's poetry.

43. Galina Rymbu, "Bormotanie nezemnoi arkhitektury," *Gork'ii*, April 30, 2019, https:// gorky.media/reviews/bormotane-nezemnoj-arhitektury/.

44. Galina Rymbu makes brilliant use of this statement in "Bormotanie." For Shvarts's own words, see Shvarts, *Sochineniia*, 5:394–95.

45. Alla Gorbunova, "Elena Shvarts: Opyt chteniia," *NLO* 165 (no. 5, 2020): 287–99.

46. On fear in Shvarts's poetry, see Sandler, "Scared into Selfhood: Lisnianskaia, Shvarts, Sedakova," *Slavic Review* 60, no. 3 (2001): 473–90.

47. The translation is by Sasha Dugdale, in Shvarts, *Birdsong on the Seabed*, 79.

48. Shvarts, *Sochineniia*, 2:145–46.

49. On the significance of this bodily organ, see Darra Goldstein, "The Heart-Felt Poetry of Elena Shvarts," in *Fruits of Her Plume*, ed. Helena Goscilo (M. E. Sharpe, 1993), 239–50.

50. Kruglov could be heard on Radio Kul'tura in 2013–14, where he hosted an interview program *Poeziia: Dvizhenie slov*. His online presence was extensive on LiveJournal, continued on Facebook and, since 2022, on Telegram.

51. Elena Fanailova, "*Zerkal'tse*: Kniga stikhov Sergeia Kruglova," *OpenSpace*, May 14, 2008, http://www.litkarta.ru/dossier/fanailova-o-kruglove-20080528094657/dossier_4278/.

52. Dashevskii, "Sofrinskie ploskie liudi," *Kommersant" Weekend*, November 21, 2008, http:// www.litkarta.ru/dossier/sofr-pl-liudi/dossier_4278/.

53. Sergei Kruglov, "Ot avtora," in *Perepischik* (NLO, 2008), 21–26; see 25–26.

54. Kruglov summarizes his reasons for stopping and then starting up again in "Ot avtora," 23–25. He tells the story in more detail and slightly differently in a 2013 interview in Goralik, *Chastnye litsa: Chast' vtoraia* (Novoe izdatel'stvo, 2017), 313–41; see 337–39.

55. Recent books include *Sinodik* (Borey, 2022), from which he read in an online event sponsored by the Moscow Pasternak Museum, March 4, 2022, video, 1:31:35, posted March 17, 2022, https://www.youtube.com/watch?v=kLyRAANeiTU. Poems from that book have appeared in some online venues, including "Sinodik," *Polutona*, December 16, 2022, https:// polutona.ru/?show=1216073021.

56. Kseniia Smirnova and Sviashchennik Sergei Kruglov, "O poezii blagochestivoi i poezii nastoiashchei," *Pravmir*, March 21, 2016, https://www.pravmir.ru/poeziya-otgolosok-rayskoy -rechi/.

57. The poet he quotes is Mikhail Kalinin. See Kruglov, "Ketchup na lavrovom liste (pometki na poliakh k razgovoram o 'dukhovnoi poezii')," *Arion* 2 (2015), https://magazines.gorky.media /arion/2015/2/ketchup-na-lavrovom-liste.html. Kruglov is also pushing back against Rodnian- skaia's "Novoe svidetel'stvo" because it tacitly separates out the poetry of Russian Orthodoxy, a categorization he does not support.

58. For a standard modern source, see G. P. Fedotov, *Stikhi dukhovnye* (*Russkaia narodnaia vera po dukhovnym stikham*) (YMCA Press, 1935), subsequently reissued. On the tradition, see Kahn et al., *History of Russian Literature*, 136–40.

59. As he said in 2013: "Generally, Christ and people, my family—that is in fact the Church, not the artifacts, cathedrals, bell towers, and not the 'public role of the Russian Orthodox Church,' as others would claim"; translated from Goralik, *Chastnye litsa: Chast' vtoraia*, 341.

60. His book *Maranafa* (Probel-2000, 2018) opens with a striking sequence dedicated to Father Alexander Mein, for example, and includes a poem to Mat' Mariia (Elizaveta Skobtseva) (see 10–15, 92). There are poems about Icarus and Ezra Pound in *Perepischik*, 144 and 155.

61. In English-language poetry, we have John Donne's Holy Sonnets (first published 1633), George Herbert's *Temple*, and Gerard Manley Hopkins's *The Habit of Perfection* (1866) as powerful expostulations of doubt and belief from the pen of a poetry-writing clergyman. Kruglov is less likely than Herbert or Hopkins, however, to denounce pleasure or to turn away from human love.

62. The poem "U poeta umer chitatel'" is dated 2005 and included in "Podsolnukh," *TextOnly* 19 (2006), http://textonly.ru/self/?issue=19&article=12915.

63. Kruglov, *Perepischik* and *Pro ottsa Filofila* (Novoe nebo, 2018). See also Kruglov, "Stikhi i risunki," *Literratura* 197 (August 2022), https://literratura.org/poetry/4728-sergey-kruglov-stihi-i-risunki.html.

64. As noted in Boris Dubin, "Rech' o Sergee Kruglove," posted January 16, 2009, http://www.litkarta.ru/dossier/gruglov-speech/dossier_4278/. Elena Fanailova concurred, finding that the sense of compassion toward the other had only intensified. See Fanailova, *"Zerkal'tse."* Compare her review of his 2003 book, which emphasizes its modernized use of familiar myths (like the work of Grigory Dashevsky), its visual metaphors, and homoerotic undercurrents: Fanailova, "O knige Sergeia Kruglova 'Sniatie Zmiia so kresta,'" *Kriticheskaia massa*, no. 2 (2004), http://www.litkarta.ru/dossier/fanailova-o-kruglove/dossier_4278/.

65. Rodnianskaia, "Novoe svidetel'stvo," the second part of the essay (see note 4).

66. Sergei Kruglov, "Banochka 'Klinskogo,'" in *Narodnye pesni* (Russkii Gulliver / Tsentr sovremenoi literatury, 2010), 85–86.

67. This quality of Kruglov's poetry was well described by Grigory Dashevsky as a source of allegory: "Everything in Kruglov's poems, whether made of concrete or cardboard, whether on film or on computer screens, including our own selves, all of this unexpectedly acquires meaning in the blinding light of allegory"; translated from Dashevskii, "Sofrinskie ploskie liudi."

68. My comments on Afanasyev owe much to suggestions from Olga Maiorova, which I gratefully acknowledge.

69. As translated by J. Kates, *Jacket* 36 (2008), http://jacketmagazine.com/36/rus-kruglov-trb-kates.shtml, very slightly amended.

70. Kruglov, *Sniatie Zmiia so kresta* (NLO, 2003), 19–20.

71. Susan Stewart, *Poetry and the Fate of the Senses* (University of Chicago Press, 2002), 1. Here is Stewart's premise: "The work of poetry is to counter the oblivion of darkness, . . . [and] to make visible, tangible, and audible the figures of persons, whether such persons are expressing the particulars of sense impressions or the abstractions of reason. . . . As metered language, language that retains and projects the force of individual sense experience and yet reaches toward intersubjective meaning, poetry sustains and transforms the threshold between individual

and social existence" (1–2). Stewart includes touch as a primary sense because it is "central to the encounter with the presence of others," along with vision and hearing (3).

72. Jean-Luc Marion, *In Excess: Studies of Saturated Phenomena*, trans. Robyn Horner and Vincent Berraud (Fordham University Press, 2002). See also Brock M. Mason, "Saturated Phenomena, the Icon and Revelation: A Critique of Marion's Account of Revelation and the 'Redoubling' of Saturation," *Aporia* 24, no. 1 (2014), http://aporia.byu.edu/pdfs/mason-saturated_phenomena.pdf.

73. For the poem, see Kruglov, *Perepischik*, 124–25.

74. Kruglov, *Zerkal'tse*, 46.

75. My thanks to Andrew Kahn for suggesting this source.

76. Pasternak's poem begins "Ia konchilsia, a ty zhiva": see Pasternak, *Stikhotvoreniia i poemy*, 2 vols. (Sovetskii pisatel', Leningradskoe otdelenie, 1990), 2:63.

77. That use of archaic and sometimes Church Slavonic diction aligns Kruglov with the trends identified in Martha M. F. Kelly, "*Furor Liturgicus*."

78. That phrase ("vera sinkopirovana") occurs in the poem "Lui Armstrong," in Kruglov, *Sniatie Zmiia so kresta*, 148. The poem could be considered productively alongside Brodsky's "In Memory of Clifford Brown," treated in chapter 4: Kruglov's poem similarly relies on the radio as a source for its music of "slow, slow love," but it presents a more fetishized, object-filled view of America.

79. For the poem, see Kruglov, *Perepischik*, 276–78, from which quotations below are taken. The fullest version of the Nathan cycle is in the book Kruglov jointly published with Khersonsky, also discussed below.

80. Compare the first poem in the cycle, "Natan edet v poezde," where God comes down from on high to Nathan, listens to him, sighs, and leaves: Kruglov, *Perepischik*, 259–60.

81. For a full translation of the poem by Vitaly Chernetsky, see *Jacket* 36 (2008), http://jacketmagazine.com/36/rus-kruglov-trb-chernetsky.shtml.

82. Kruglov, *Perepischik*, 277.

83. His work in the context of war is an ongoing research project for Amelia Glaser, with a special focus on the poetry he has been writing in Ukrainian. See Glaser, "There's No There There: Political Poetry from Eastern Europe on Facebook," *TLS*, September 4, 2020, https://www.the-tls.co.uk/articles/political-poetry-from-eastern-europe-on-facebook-essay-amelia-glaser/; and Glaser, "Re-reading Babel in Post-Maidan Odesa: Boris Khersonsky's Critical Cosmopolitanism," in *Cosmopolitan Spaces in Odesa: A Case Study of an Urban Context*, ed. Mirja Lecke and Efraim Sicher (Academic Studies Press, 2023), 273–304.

84. For other translations, see "'Every hut in our country is on the edge': Contemporary Ukrainian Poetry by Boris Khersonsky," trans. Amelia Glaser and Yuliya Ilchuk, *Lithub*, March 11, 2022, https://lithub.com/every-hut-in-our-beloved-country-is-on-the-edge-contemporary-ukrainian-poetry-by-boris-khersonsky/; translations by Olga Livshin for *Words for War*, https://www.wordsforwar.com/boris-khersonsky-bio; and the translation of "Missa in tempore belli" by Martha M. F. Kelly, in "'Bleed—My Heart—Bleed': Ukrainian Poems of War by Boris Khersonsky, Iya Kiva, and Vasyl Makhno," *Los Angeles Review of Books*, February 27, 2022, https://lareviewofbooks.org/short-takes/ukrainian-poems-of-war-khersonsky-kiva-makhno/.

85. He has published more than thirty books, nearly all poetry, since 1993.

86. See, for example, Khersonskii, *Novyi Estestvoslov* (Art Khaus Media, 2012); *Psalmy Solomona, ody Solomona* (Folio, 2009); and "Chasidskie izrecheniia," in *Ploshchadka pod zastroiku* (NLO, 2008), 154–97.

87. Some are included in Khersonskii, *Poka ne stemnelo* (NLO, 2010), 300–309; there are many more, including the wreathes of *vos'mistishiia* in *Odesskii dnevnik 2015–2016* (Folio, 2017): for the wreathes, see 126–29, 165–68, 198–201, 262–65; some three dozen individual *vos'mistishiia* are scattered across the book.

88. See the convincing reading of Babel offered in Leonid Livak, *The Jewish Persona in the European Imagination: A Case of Russian Literature* (Stanford University Press, 2010), 300–336.

89. This prayer and the one that will follow are also translated by Dale Hobson and Ruth Kreuzer, "Family Archive," Dale Hobson website, http://www.dalehobson.org/khersonsky /archive.html, as are other poems from *Family Archive*.

90. Boris Khersonskii, *Semeinyi arkhiv* (NLO, 2006), 94. I treat this poem at greater length in "Poets / Poetry in Diaspora: On Being 'Marginally Jewish,'" in *Finding Home: The Russian-Speaking Jewish Diaspora*, ed. Zvi Gitelman (Rutgers University Press, 2016), 266–85; on Khersonsky, see 268–72.

91. Khersonskii, *Semeinyi arkhiv*, 149.

92. Irina Rodnianskaia concluded that the poetry is the "fruit of a believing consciousness that is open to nonbelief." Translated from Rodnianskaia, "'Nikakoe lekarstvo ne otmeniaet bolezni' (iavlenie Borisa Khersonskogo)," in *Mysli o poezii v nulevye gody* (Russkii Gulliver, 2010), 73–87; see 87.

93. Khersonskii, *Semeinyi arkhiv*, 140.

94. Another kind of object that lives on is family photographs, the subject of many poems in the volume.

95. To take one example, which begins "Pisano v pisaniiakh: vo vremena ony": its Old Testament scene of the pharaohs and Moses in Egypt opens out onto a vista of Jesus's wanderings. It was published as "Faraony" in "Pesni vostochnykh slavian," *Polutona*, December 14, 2011, https://polutona.ru/?show=1214020741.

96. In the view of Ilya Kukulin, these two "contrastive" projections of the poetic subject, the Orthodox and the Jew, remain distinct, and "their interaction can never be fully normalized." See Kukulin, "'To Create a Person When You Aren't One Yet': Notes on Russian Poetry in the 2000s," trans. Liv Bliss, *Russian Studies in Literature* 54, nos. 1–3 (2018): 58–83, quotation on 81.

97. The comment about heresy is noted in Il'ia Kukulin, "Novye Stranstvovaniia po dusham," in Kruglov, *Natan*; Khersonskii, *V dukhe i istine* (Ailuros, 2012), 5–18.

98. The experiment also shows us how these two poets, both associated with the new epic poetry, differ: Khersonsky is more likely to foreground the story itself. Vitaly Chernetsky has observed that the Nathan poems have a cinematic and ekphrastic quality in "The Unusual Case of Fr. Sergei Kruglov: Poet, Priest, and Postmodernist in Post-Soviet Siberia," *Russian Literature* 87–89 (2017): 375–405. This essay also provides an excellent account of Kruglov's changing poetics.

99. Khersonsky's poems about Archbishop Gury appeared in *Ploshchadka pod zastroiku*, 164–94, and in *Poka ne stemnelo*, 164–95. Kruglov's Natan poems are in *Perepischik*, 259–81.

100. For the texts, see "Kinfiia," in Shvarts, *Sochineniia*, 2:6–24. Some poems from the cycle are translated in Shvarts, *'Paradise'*, 53–65. A substantial new reading of the Cynthia poems as a

"pseudotranslation" appears in the first English-language monograph on the poet: Georgia Barker, *SPQR in the USSR: Elena Shvarts's Classical Antiquity* (Legenda, 2022), 95–161.

101. He has written so much that it is entirely possible that I missed it, but I find no poem that accounts for the choice to convert, only a brief reference to his having worn a cross and presented himself to others as a Christian long before the fall of the USSR: Boris Khersonskii, *Kladez' bezumiia: Zapiski psikhiatra* (Spadshchina, 2012), 67. According to a news report, as of 2015 the poet felt far from the ROC. See Sally McGrane, "A Craftsman of Russian Verse Helps Ukraine Find Its Voice," *New York Times*, April 10, 2015, http://www.nytimes.com/2015/04/11 /world/europe/a-russian-poet-helps-ukraine-navigate-its-new-identity.html?_r=0.

102. In *Doubly Chosen: Jewish Identity, the Soviet Intelligentsia, and the Russian Orthodox Church* (University of Wisconsin Press, 2004), Judith Deutsch Kornblatt documents the experiences of Jews who converted to Orthodoxy in the Soviet period. Among her findings is a transformed attitude toward Judaism among converts, which might explain Khersonsky's intense loyalty to Jewish experience and history.

103. Kruglov, *Natan*; Khersonskii, *V dukhe i istine*, 65.

104. Sedakova called Shvarts "a powerful poet with rare gifts" and included her in the short list of contemporary poets who were her friends. See her interview with Valentina Polukhina, "Conform Not to This Age: The Poetry and Personality of Ol'ga Sedakova," in *Reconstructing the Canon: Russian Literature in the 1980s*, ed. Arnold McMillin (Harwood Academic, 2000), 33–78; see 35 and 72. Shvarts mentions Sedakova several times in her own interview with Polukhina: "Coldness and Rationality: An Interview with Elena Shvarts," in *Brodsky through the Eyes of His Contemporaries*, ed. Valentina Polukhina (St. Martin's Press, 1992), 215–36.

105. Sedakova, *Slovar' trudnykh slov iz bogosluzheniia: Tserkovnoslaviansko-russkie paronimy* (Praktika, 2021). The first edition of this volume, under a slightly different title, appeared in 2005 and has gone through several editions with expansions.

106. For the latter two, see Sedakova, *Poetika obriada* and *Mariiny slezy: K poetike liturgicheskikh pesnopenii* (Dukh i litera, 2017). Many of Sedakova's poems, translations, and essays are available in Russian on her well-curated website, https://www.olgasedakova.com. There is a page for English translations of many texts as well.

107. Her book *Perevesti Dante* (Izdatel'stvo Ivana Limbakha, 2020) was reissued in a second edition in 2021. She also published *Mudrost' nadezhdy i drugie razgovory o Dante* (Izdatel'stvo Ivana Limbakha, 2021), which includes writings on Dante that had not appeared in Russian and translations from *Vita Nuova*.

108. Alongside many other poets, Sedakova joined in the pro-democracy demonstrations that were a feature of Russian public life in the first two decades of this century, and she was active in supporting the work of Memorial. She has condemned Russia's aggression in Ukraine. See Anna Danilova, "O zhizni v temnye vremena: Poet Ol'ga Sedakova," *Pravmir*, March 29, 2022, https://www.pravmir.ru/o-zhizni-v-temnye-vremena-poet-olga-sedakova/; and "Senza cultura è la catastrofe: Intervista a Ol'ga Sedakova," *Il Regno* 12 (2022): 345–48.

109. Benjamin Paloff, "A Loving Heresy: The God Function in Joseph Brodsky and Ol'ga Sedakova," *SEEJ* 51, no. 4 (Winter 2007): 716–36; and "If This Is Not a Garden: Olga Sedakova and the Unfinished Work of Creation," in *The Poetry and Poetics of Olga Sedakova: Origins, Philosophies, Points of Contention*, ed. Stephanie Sandler et al. (University of Wisconsin Press, 2019), 17–39.

110. She emphasized in 2006 that "Creative tasks and mental tasks are truly fulfilled when they give someone freedom. And the capacity to give freedom is of course in and of itself a gift"; translated from Sedakova, *Moralia* (Universitet Dmitriia Pozharskogo, 2010), 54.

111. I write about some of these longer texts in "Constricted Freedom: On Dreams and Rhythms in the Poetry of Olga Sedakova," in *Poetry and Poetics of Olga Sedakova*, 116–38.

112. For a clarifying account of how Sedakova's poetry is not doctrinal, see Sarah Pratt, "Disruption of Disruption: The Orthodox Christian Impulse in the Works of Nikolai Zabolotsky and Olga Sedakova," in *Poetry and Poetics of Olga Sedakova*, 191–213, esp. 194–96.

113. See Olga Sedakova, Valentina Polukhina, and Robert Reid, "Collective Analysis of Olga Sedakova's 'The Wild Rose,'" *Essays in Poetics* 22 (1997): 237–57.

114. Vladimir Bibikhin, *Grammatika poezii* (Izdatel'stvo Ivana Limbakha, 2009), 271–86.

115. Sedakova recorded the cycle in 2003 in Arkhangelsk, *"Ty gori, nevidimoe plamia"* (2005). The title of the CD comes from a poem in the third notebook of "Old Songs."

116. The connection to folklore-collecting expeditions is made in N. G. Medvedeva, *"Tainye stikhi" Ol'gi Sedakovoi* (Udmurtskii universitet, 2013), 78–79.

117. For a compelling study of childhood in Sedakova's writings, see Emily Grosholz, "Childhood and Vibrant Stasis in the Poetry of Olga Sedakova," in *Poetry and Poetics of Olga Sedakova*, 64–88.

118. My English translation from Sedakova, *In Praise of Poetry*, trans. and ed. Caroline Clark, Ksenia Golubovich, and Stephanie Sandler (Open Letter, 2014), 24; Russian from Sedakova, *Stikhi* (Universitet Dmitriia Pozharskogo, 2010), 183. The volume *In Praise of Poetry* includes a translation by Caroline Clark of the title essay, 105–88.

119. "An Interview with Olga Sedakova (January 2012)," trans. Caroline Clark, in Sedakova, *In Praise of Poetry*, 191–207, quotation on 199.

120. Cited from my translation in Sedakova, *In Praise of Poetry*, 30, slightly modified.

121. Sedakova, *Stikhi*, 189.

122. Sedakova's predecessors in that choice of free verse for a large cycle of poems include Pushkin's "Songs of the Western Slavs" ("Pesni zapadnykh slavian," 1834) and Mikhail Kuzmin's "Alexandrian Songs" ("Aleksandriiskie pesni," first published 1919), both also cycles of songs. On the use of free verse in Russian poetry, see Mikhail Gronas, *Cognitive Poetics and Cultural Memory: Russian Literary Mnemonics* (Routledge, 2011), 71–96; for the mention of Sedakova, see 143n2.

123. I build this approach on the foundation of long-standing work on apostrophe, including Jonathan Culler, "Apostrophe," *Diacritics* 7, no. 4 (Winter 1977): 59–69; and Barbara Johnson, "Apostrophe, Animation, and Abortion," in *A World of Difference* (Harvard University Press, 1987), 184–99. As Johnson puts it, in apostrophe "the absent, dead, or inanimate entity addressed is thereby made present, animate, and anthropomorphic" (60).

124. See Dal', *Tolkovyi slovar'*, 2:650.

125. On the heart and its incarnations, see Milad Doueihi, *A Perverse History of the Human Heart* (Harvard University Press, 1997).

126. Sedakova, *Stikhi*, 59. Martha Kelly reminded me that this wound may also refer to Jesus's stigmata. See Sedakova, Polukhina, and Reid, "Collective Analysis," 242–45.

127. Sedakova makes this point in a 2010 conversation with Ol'ga Balla, "Poeziia—protivostoianie khaosu," in *Veshchestvo chelovechnosti: Interv'iu 1990–2018* (NLO, 2019), 293.

128. I discuss this syntactical structure with multiple other examples in "Thinking Self in the Poetry of Ol'ga Sedakova," in *Gender and Russian Literature: New Perspectives*, ed. Rosalind Marsh (Cambridge University Press, 1996), 302–25; see 309–14.

129. Sedakova, *Stikhi*, 305–8. For a splendid close reading of this poem, see Andrew Kahn, "Sedakova's Book of Hours and the Devotional Lyric: Reading 'Fifth Stanzas,'" in *Poetry and Poetics of Olga Sedakova*, 141–64.

130. Similarly, she names God's love as offering salvation from terror and slavery ("spasenie ot zapugannosti i rabstva"). See "Totus Tuus: Pamiati Papy Ioanna Pavla II," in Sedakova, *Moralia*, 826. This view, that the lack of inner freedom is a kind of bondage, was a tenet of unofficial literary culture and of the generation of the 1960s, the *shestidesiatniki*. On that generation, see Petr Vail and Aleksandr Genis, *Shestidesiatniki—mir sovetskogo cheloveka* (Ardis, 1968).

131. For her most direct statements about freedom, see "Svoboda kak eskhatologicheskaia real'nost'," in *Moralia*, 13–29. Sedakova has also associated freedom with pleasure and with beauty. In that same volume, see "Razgovor o svobode s A. I. Kyrlezhevym," 30–64, esp. 52.

132. Excellent texts for seeing this pattern in her work include "Azarovka: Siuita peizazhei" and "Gornaia oda" (in Sedakova, *Stikhi*, 119–25, 231–35), but this is such a productive structure of representation in her poetry that one could look at nearly any set of texts and find it.

133. I came upon this sentence in an essay by Eve Sedgwick on Proust, an unlikely pathway, admittedly. The sentence comes from Pierre Hadot, *Plotinus, or the Simplicity of Vision*, cited in Eve Kosofsky Sedgwick, *The Weather in Proust*, ed. Jonathan Goldberg (Duke University Press, 2011), 34. Her writing about affect theory and the external world, particularly in "The Weather in Proust" (1–41), has informed my thinking about inner and outer worlds in Sedakova.

134. Sedakova, *In Praise of Poetry*, 69, translation modified.

135. Sedakova, *Stikhi*, 218.

136. Compare Medvedeva, *"Tainye stikhi,"* which finds the central work of "Old Songs" to be about the relationship of man to God (78).

137. Sedakova, *Stikhi*, 415. The next quotation is from this poem as well, 414. There is a full translation of the poem by Emily Grosholz and Larisa Volokhonsky in Sedakova, "The Subway, Moscow and Other Poems," *Hudson Review*, special edition, Spring 2007, 2–3.

138. Sedgwick, "The Weather in Proust," 34. Sedgwick was writing about a side of Proust that reaches toward mysticism, and thus toward a set of spiritual realities that are perhaps less far from Sedakova's worldview than one might expect. Her remarks on air pressure and "air as a site of alchemical state change" (9) also resonate with some of the ways I have written about air throughout this book. Sedakova has referred multiple times to Proust, specifically to the kind of epiphanies that Sedgwick has in mind. See, for example, although the rhetoric is quite different, the remarks about Proust in "Komu my bol'she verim: Poetu ili prozaiku?" in Sedakova, *Poetica* (Universitet Dmitriia Pozharskogo, 2010), 158–65; see 164.

139. Two interviews about Russia's war in Ukraine are noted above. Sedakova has long taken stances against militarism, for example: "O politicheskoi kul'ture i sovremennom rossiiskom obshchestve" (2015 interview), in Sedakova, *Veshchestvo chelovechnosti*, 532–47; see 537–38; and, in the same volume, "Neotlichenie zla," 517–31.

140. I have in mind such major texts as *Puteshestvie s zakrytymi glazami: Pis'ma o Rembrandte* (Izdatel'stvo Ivana Limbakha, 2016), with a new and expanded edition (Art Volkhonka, 2021); *Mariiny slezy*; and *Mudrost' nadezhdy*.

141. Sedakova, "Totus Tuus," *Moralia*, 828. On Sedakova's respect for the pope, especially for his hope of uniting the church, see Liudmila Lutsevich (Ludmiła Łucewicz), *Pamiat' o psalme: Sacrum / profanum v sovrememmoi russkoi poezii* (Wydawnictwa Uniwersytetu Warszawskiego, 2009), 255–66, which includes a brief account of the three poems dedicated to the pope.

142. For a more expressive translation of this poem, see Martha M. F. Kelly's translation in *Poetry and Poetics of Olga Sedakova*, 74, which is part of Emily Grosholz's essay, "Childhood and Vibrant Stasis."

143. Sedakova, *Stikhi*, 399.

144. Similar ideas are compactly laid out in a video lecture Sedakova gave in 2019, "Poetika bogosluzhebnykh pesnopenii," video, 21:45, posted by Tserkovnoslavianskii iazyk segodnia on January 7, 2019, https://www.youtube.com/watch?v=WEawhCf-9VA. This lecture includes Sedakova's comparison of hymnography to the poetics of the Baroque, as does her introduction to *Mariiny slezy*, see 12.

145. That example is given in "Poetika bogosluzhebnykh pesnopenii" and in her introduction to *Mariiny slezy*, 11–13; the latter also includes the texts of the *tropar'* (11) and its *kondak* (14).

146. Sedakova, *Stikhotvoreniia shagi* (Art Volkhonka, 2017), 5. An earlier and different version (with a different l.5, without the line-centered format, the space after the first quatrain, and without most of the commas) was posted by Sedakova to Facebook, December 27, 2014.

147. Sedakova, *Stikhi*, 74, 84, 92–94, 98, 100, and 362–65. I call these books because Sedakova refers to them as books, but neither actually appeared separately. They are included as separate sections in the volumes Sedakova began to publish after the fall of the USSR. *Dikii shipovnik* is included, for example, in *Stikhi* (Gnozis-Carte Blanche, 1994) and in *Stikhi: Proza*, 2 vols. (En Ef K'iu/ Tu Print, 2001). *Vecherniaia pesnia* first appeared in *Stikhi* (2001), but "Vosem' vos'mistishiia" are not there. They appear in the smaller selection from *Vecherniaia pesnia* included in *Vse, i srazu* (Pushkinskii fond, 2009), 112–15.

148. For the full text of the poem, see M. Iu. Lermontov, *Sobranie sochinenii*, 4 vols. (Khudozhestvennaia literatura, 1975), 1:123.

149. For the poem, see O. Mandel'shtam, *Polnoe sobranie stikhotvorenii*, ed. A. G. Mets (Gumanitarnoe agenstvo "Akademicheskii proekt," 1995), 163. Kirill Taranovsky calls the Lermontov reference "an overt poetic polemic" on Mandelstam's part in his essay "Concert at the Railway Station: The Problem of Context and Subtext," in *Essays on Mandelstam* (Harvard University Press, 1976), 1–20; he writes that "a strong sensation of an impending cataclysm is sharply opposed to Lermontov's sense of cosmic harmony" (15).

150. In "Concert at the Railway Station," Taranovsky also mentions Mandelstam's method of composing poems silently in his head, as is well known from Nadezhda Mandelstam's memoirs; see 19.

151. Osip Mandel'shtam, *Polnoe sobranie sochinenii i pisem*, 3 vols. (Progress-Pleiada, 2010), 2:155–202; see 159.

152. Sedakova knows this essay well, mentioning it in her *Perevesti Dante*, 15, and elsewhere, for example, praising Mandelstam's capacity to describe the acoustic, imagistic, and energy-charged body of the *Divine Comedy*: see Sedakova, "Poeziia za predelami stikhotvorstva," in *Poetica*, 120–26; see 121.

153. Pratt, "Disruption of Disruption," 196.

Afterword

1. The footage is widely available, for example, in an ITV news report, "Russian Journalist Interrupts Live TV State Media Broadcast with 'No War' Protest," March 14, 2022, video, 2:22, https://www.youtube.com/watch?v=rWgV0gtUIv0.

2. Widely reported, including Isabel Van Brugen, "Russia Arrests Multiple People Holding Up Blank Signs," *Newsweek*, March 14, 2022, https://www.newsweek.com/russia-ukraine-war-invasion -protests-police-arrest-activists-holding-blank-signs-paper-1687603. The gesture has its own history: Compare Daniel Victor, "A Man in Kazakhstan Held Up a Blank Sign to See if He'd Be Arrested. He Was," *New York Times*, May 9, 2019, https://www.nytimes.com/2019/05/09/world/asia /kazakhstan-protests-blank-sign.html. Protests over COVID restrictions in China took it up late in 2022, and "Some protesters told The New York Times that the white papers took inspiration from a Soviet-era joke, in which a dissident accosted by the police for distributing leaflets in a public square reveals the fliers to be blank." See Chang Che and Amy Chang Chien, "Memes, Puns, and Blank Sheets of Paper: China's Creative Acts of Protest," *New York Times*, November 28, 2022, https://www.nytimes.com/2022/11/28/world/asia/china-protests-blank-sheets.html.

3. By OVD-Info, Twitter, February 25, 2022.

4. See *NLO* 175 (no. 3, 2022): 7–9.

5. Radio Svoboda operates its website and many podcasts; see https://www.svoboda.org. Meduza, long working out of Latvia, continues its work: https://meduza.io. The Nobel Prize–winning *Novaia gazeta*, after a hiatus of several months in which its older reporting was left frozen on its website, https://novayagazeta.ru, resumed publication under conditions of censorship until a second team created *Novaia gazeta Evropa*, https://novayagazeta.eu, which was also declared undesirable in Russia and forbidden. It continues to appear. TV-Rain (Dozhd') was transmitting from Latvia until it lost its license, but it persisted on YouTube: https://www .youtube.com/c/tvrain. For all these sites, transmission in Russia is blocked but accessible to those with VPN, and Telegram channels continue to operate.

6. Nikitin was known and admired as a founder of the Telegram channel Metazhurnal, @ metajournal. It has continued full force with a large staff of moderators, and Nikitin posts on the channel Negromkie stikhi, @quite_poetry, which he moderates with Andrei Cherkasov.

7. Dmitrii Kuz'min, Facebook, March 5, 2022.

8. Ol'ga Sedakova, Facebook, August 13, 2022.

9. See Charlotte Higgins, "For Ukrainians, Poetry Isn't a Luxury, It's a Necessity during War," *Guardian*, December 9, 2022, https://www.theguardian.com/commentisfree/2022/dec/09/for -ukrainians-poetry-isnt-a-luxury-its-a-necessity-during-war, for a strong account of the quantity and nature of current work.

10. A particularly interesting example is "Animal bodies" by the Ukrainian poet Nikita Ryzhikh, a text he presented in English, then in Russian translation, posted to the Metazhurnal Telegram channel by Evgenia Ul'ianka, December 21, 2022, with her insightful commentary.

11. "Kul'tura vo vremia voennykh operatsii," *Colta*, March 3, 2022, https://www.colta.ru /articles/specials/27777-opros-kultura-i-krizis.

12. Elena Fanailova interviewed Lavut and Evgeny Gindilis for Svoboda news, and the poem is included in their conversation. See "My davno govorim 'voina,'" Radio Svoboda, March 25, 2022, https://www.svoboda.org/a/my-davno-govorim-voyna-o-sposobah-soprotivleniya-vlasti

/31767174.html, for a recording and transcript. The conversation includes a description by Lavut of an antiwar concert and reading she had organized that was canceled at the last minute, as speaking out was increasingly being criminalized. The poem is also included in Iurii Leving, ed., *Poeziia poslednego vremeni* (Izdatel'stvo Ivana Limbakha, 2022), 111–15.

13. Ilya Kukulin, "Writing within the Pain: Russian-Language Anti-War Poetry on Either Side of the Frontline," *Slavic Review* 82, no. 3 (2023): 657–67. I take this opportunity to thank him for sharing this essay in advance of its publication, and for sharing PDFs of the anthologies discussed in this afterword. His observations about the need for recovering a sense of agency were also articulated in an online discussion of several antiwar anthologies hosted by the Telegram channel Metazhurnal, "Antivoennye antologii 'byskazybanie' vs 'postupok,'" December 22, 2022, video, 1:33:12, https://www.youtube.com/watch?v=IsAskTtn18E.

14. For *ROAR* 4, see https://roar-review.com/ROAR-00c2004b06604db2a4b9a-2da4d338c26; this issue has the journal's original name, *Russian Oppositional Arts Review*. In March 2023, in her editor's note for *ROAR* 6, Goralik announced a name change to reflect the site's role as a platform for not just Russians: *Resistance and Opposition Arts Review*. See https://roar-review.com/ROAR-ad4362991ffd42b3ac5b3e17fc608f02.

15. They include *'Eto smert' podletaet ko mne: Poety i poetessy Rossii i Ukrainy protiv voini*, ed. Kseniia Kalaidzidu, which appeared in Greece (2022); *poniatye i svideteli 2*, which came out in Israel (Babel, 2022); *Disbelief: 100 Russian War Poems*, ed. Julia Nemirovskaya (Smokestack, 2015), published in the UK and including translations into English; and *Voina: Stikhotvoreniia 24.02.2022–24.5.2022*, ed. Liubov' Machina (Software und Verlag FR, 2022). Compare the emergence of a single albeit excellent anthology during the Chechen wars: *Vremia "CH": Stikhi o Chechne i ne tol'ko*, ed. N. Vinnik (NLO, 2001).

16. The volume produced a furious scandal on Facebook because it included a poem by Ivan Bobyrev. A good snapshot of the controversy can be gained from the response of Nikita Sungatov, Facebook, October 28, 2022. It was a welcome reassertion of poets' capacity to argue with each other in public, but emotions ran very high.

17. It is not the total picture, nor does it mean to be: Leving excludes the kind of work hastily assembled in *PoZyVnoi—Pobeda! Antologiia sovremennoi patrioticheskoi poezii* (Veche, 2022). Other such commissioned pro-Russian volumes are forthcoming (see Kukulin, "Writing within the Pain").

18. Leving, *Poeziia poslednego vremeni*, 13.

19. Leving, *Poeziia poslednego vremeni*, 316.

20. Cited from the Telegram channel Orden Kromeshnykh Poetov, @kromeshnie, December 5, 2022, and Kotova posted it to Facebook, November 7, 2022.

21. Her medical knowledge is keenly felt in her book *Anatomicheskii teatr* (kntxt, 2019). It made Kotova a dreadfully apt poet for the pandemic; her next book of poems, *#temperaturazemli* (NLO, 2021), was in the diploma list of the Moskovskii Schet Prize in 2022: see https://mospoetry.ru for the full list.

22. Skidan wrote other shorter poems in the first months after February 24, some of which were also quickly reposted. See the posts on the Telegram channels Orden Kromeshnykh Poetov and Metazhurnal; the latter also reposted his "prezentatsiia," May 24, 2022.

23. Translation by Kevin Platt, concluded within hours of the original post, and published by Olga Zilberbourg on her blog, *Punctured Lines*, April 5, 2022, https://puncturedlines

.wordpress.com/2022/04/05/new-world-new-plane-a-letter-by-ivan-sokolov/; subsequently published in *World Literature Today*, March 2023, https://www.worldliteraturetoday.org/2023/march/two-russian-poems-saint-petersburg-and-tbilisi-alexander-skidan, from which I quote, with the formatting changed to match the Russian.

24. See Aleksandr Skidan, Facebook, March 1, 2022, for the original post; I use that post's format here. Also published in *Poeziia poslednego vremeni*, 50–52, where there are useful notes by the editor; and in *poniatye i svideteli*, 98–100.

25. Skidan posts them regularly, and many from the late 2010s are collected in *Kontaminatsiia* (Poriadok slov, 2020).

26. The poem is Kira Freger, "vse my, kak by my ni khoteli," posted by Olia Skorlupkina to the Metazhurnal Telegram channel, December 18, 2022; that channel is distinguished by its multiple hosts and by hosts' normally posting notes about their chosen poem. In this case, Skorlupkina's commentary is unusually detailed, and she describes the rhetorical challenge of the poem's *we*. Skorlupkina is also the regular moderator on another important Telegram channel, Orden Kromeshnykh Poetov.

27. Stepanova shared the poem in a closed post on Facebook, July 9, 2022; it was published in the anthology *poniatye i svideteli*, 9, and translated by Ainsley Morse: Stepanova, "Two Russian Poems from Berlin," *World Literature Today*, March 2023, https://www.worldliteraturetoday.org/2023/march/two-russian-poems-berlin-maria-stepanova.

28. Cited from *Disbelief*, 39; a different English translation by Andrei Burago is also there (38).

29. For a memorable short poem that travels that route by quite different means, see Gali-Dana Zinger, "zakony voennogo vremeni," posted to the Telegram channel Orden Kromeshnykh Poetov, March 14, 2022.

30. For the poems see Daria Serenko, "The Bridegrooms," trans. Eugene Ostashevsky, *New York Review of Books*, November 3, 2022, https://www.nybooks.com/articles/2022/11/03/the-bridegrooms-daria-serenko/—The Russian original was posted by Serenko to Facebook, September 29, 2022; and see Ostashevsky, "Two Hearts," Facebook, December 18, 2022.

INDEX

A NOTE ON THE TYPE

This book has been composed in Arno, an Old-style serif typeface in the
classic Venetian tradition, designed by Robert Slimbach at Adobe.

Printed in the USA
CPSIA information can be obtained
at www.ICGtesting.com
JSHW021743181124
73834JS00007B/64